The Millionaires' Unit

The **Millionaires'** *Unit*

THE ARISTOCRATIC FLYBOYS
WHO FOUGHT THE GREAT WAR
AND INVENTED AMERICAN AIRPOWER

MARC WORTMAN

PublicAffairs

New York

Duxbury Free Library

For my mother and father, Doris and Bernard Wortman

Contents

SECTION III: FIRE

SECTION IV: HOME

And generations unfulfilled,
The heirs of all we struggled for,
Shall here recall the mythic war,
And marvel how we stabbed and killed,
And name us savage, brave, austere—
And none shall think how very young we were.

—From Archibald MacLeish,
"On a Memorial Stone"

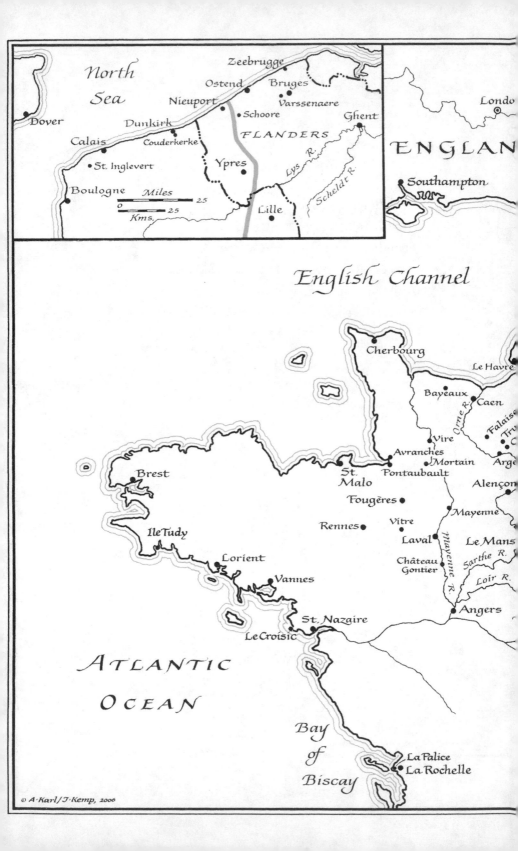

Western Front as of March 20, 1918

Europe and America, 1916

How Very Young We Were

IN 1916, TWO YEARS INTO THE BLOODIEST WAR THE WORLD HAD YET SEEN, nearly half of the 9 million soldiers, sailors, and airmen and 5 million civilians who would be killed in the First World War already lay dead. Still, from the skies over London to the depths of the North Sea, and from the snowy steppes of Russia to the deserts of Mesopotamia, and all along the 450-mile Western Front, the cataclysmic attrition of the forces of Germany, the Austro-Hungarian Empire and their allies—the Central Powers—and of the Allied armies of France, Great Britain, Russia and Italy would not abate. The world's first truly global conflict had sucked nation after nation down into its murderous vortex. Some 65 million men were at arms, more than all previous wars combined. The front lines convulsed with bloody clashes that massacred 5,000 men on average every single day—but the opposing forces barely advanced.

Only one great power remained aloof, regarding the dreadful slaughter from afar: America. The 3,000-mile barrier of the Atlantic Ocean kept the horrors of the war far removed from the lives of most Americans. The occasional sinking of ships near American ports increasingly poisoned U.S.-German relations, but not even the infamous torpedoing of the British passenger liner the *Lusitania* as it steamed from New York to Liverpool could rouse a distracted people to war or shift the government from its policy of strict neutrality.

The United States had not fought a large-scale war of massed armies since the Civil War a half century earlier. With its nineteenth-century-style standing army smaller than the Great War combatants lost in a typical month's fighting, a sparse navy charged with defending the nation's thousands of miles of coastline and an air force smaller than Bulgaria's or the Belgian forces that had escaped German occupation, the United States was ill-prepared to fight even a small-scale war.

Instead, other matters occupied the mind of a fast-changing, swift-moving nation. America was building. With its own internal frontiers awaiting conquest, the nation was racing ahead with a commercial exuberance that spread across a vast, largely untapped landscape. Wall Street financiers drove a blinding pace of consolidation and expansion, and business and industry boomed like never before. New factories opened and then expanded. Locomotives carried passengers and goods coast-to-coast at record speeds. Drivers ventured out along a growing network of paved roads. Shoppers with money to spend enjoyed an ever-expanding array of goods at glittery new retail emporiums. Motion picture-goers delighted at the exploits of Charlie Chaplin's *Little Tramp*. And sports fans marveled at the hitting prowess shown by a young Boston Red Sox pitching star named Babe Ruth. A veritable tidal wave of European immigrants, many fleeing war and oppression in their former homelands, was further flooding the New World's already teeming urban neighborhoods. The new Americans came looking for opportunity, with a drive to succeed in a land of freedom from oppressive ancient regimes. The result was the creation of unprecedented wealth and a people preoccupied with the business of the day.

Why should America mix itself up in a brutal war between the Old World's royal powers?

A few outward-looking Americans, though, believed that sooner or later their nation would be drawn into the fight. At the dawn of the modern age, no country remained an island. Oceans that had once seemed insurmountable barriers could now be crossed in a matter of days. America's growing wealth depended on the free movement of goods to trading partners worldwide. The foreign war would soon strangle world commerce, which was the lifeblood of American growth. Already an industrial giant, America was racing toward what many recognized would prove to be a decisive, hemispheric shift in global affairs. A few loud voices predicted the United States would have no choice but to fight.

Although their warnings went largely unheeded in government circles, a group of determined eighteen-, nineteen-, and twenty-year-old boys decided they would try to do something about the situation. Mostly college students from Yale University, they were the sons of America's early twentieth-century aristocracy— one a Rockefeller, one whose father headed the Union Pacific railroad empire, another J. P. Morgan's partner. Others traced their roots to the Mayflower, several counted friends and relatives among presidents and statesmen, and some were famed collegiate athletes. All were fabulously wealthy. Leading members of the group included Bob Lovett, Trubee Davison, "Di" Gates, "Crock" Ingalls, Kenney MacLeish, and Al Sturtevant. Despite their youth, they had grown up in a time when their elite position brought with it special responsibilities that may seem distant to us today. They were schooled in heroism, made ready as schoolboys for leadership and sacrifice, even before their nation called upon them.

Fascinated by the new sport of motorized flight, and dimly aware of its growing military importance, they decided to create their own flying militia. In total, twenty-eight young men would pioneer military aviation, on their own initiative and with their families' immense private resources forming the First Yale Unit—what began as a college "aero" club became the originating squadron of the U.S. Naval Air Reserve. From there, many of these boys emerged as war heroes, and all served as leaders in America's entry into a new dimension. Their every move caught the attention of a nation and inspired other young men across the country to follow their lead.

For a military ill-prepared to fight in the air, the "Millionaires' Unit," as a fascinated press dubbed the squadron, provided the nucleus of the burgeoning navy air corps. Although some were still just teens, all would become officers— in some instances with thousands of men under their command. Most faced death daily in the battle for Europe. One planned the nation's first strategic bomber force and headed its first night bomber wing. Another became the navy's only Air Ace of the war. A few would never return. When America finally went to war, Admiral William Sims, commander of the U.S. Navy in Europe during the First World War, credited them as "twentieth-century Paul Reveres." Following the Armistice, a grateful nation commended their foresight and courage. The rest of the world marveled: one of the finest and largest air services had grown out of what amounted to little more than a summer camp hosted by a group of college sophomores.

Those who returned home lost neither their love of flying nor their belief in its crucial role in any future military conflict. Members of the unit continued to lead in the dawning years of civilian aviation and throughout the interwar years of waning military aerial power. Their heroism and initiative during the First World War was not forgotten. Later, when America entered into World War II, President Franklin Delano Roosevelt recalled nearly all of the former flyers to service. He was tapping old friends and comrades. He had come to know them well even before the First World War when he was a young assistant secretary of the Navy. After nearly twenty-five years on an isolationist, peacetime military footing, they again faced the complex and daunting task of creating a modern air force capable of knocking down a far better-prepared foe.

Their numbers during the Second World War included the undersecretaries who ran the army and navy air corps and the military commanders of the Pacific Air Transport, the vital Pearl Harbor Naval Air Station, carrier groups and numerous other crucial aviation facilities. Before the war's end, the boys who had fought just to fly for their country in 1916 came to rule the world's skies. In post-war years, one of them became a thoughtful, respected Cold War-era secretary of defense, convinced of the importance of aerial power for national security. That conviction was based on experience. As a twenty-one-year-old, he had witnessed that power, in 1918, becoming the first man in American uniform to fly in bombing raids over the Western Front. What he learned on those early missions stamped U.S. military policy from the massive bombing raids over Europe today.

In war and out, the men of the First Yale Unit carried forward the life of service, personal sacrifice, and leadership for which they had been groomed. That life did not result by accident. Today, relatively few young Americans from comparable backgrounds would consider military service—or self-sacrificing service of any kind—as an obligation that comes with the privileges that define their lives. That marks a major change in the nature of America's elite and its national leadership. In their day, the members of the First Yale Unit were prepared to make the greatest sacrifice and were envied for their opportunity to serve and lead the way into battle.

Those privileged to lead emerged from an increasingly deep-rooted national establishment composed of church, private preparatory schools and colleges, clubs, business and family networks, mountain and seaside vacation resorts, and country estates. At one level it was extremely undemocratic: its doors were closed to women—except as wives and mothers—and it fenced out nearly all Jews, Catholics, and recent immigrants, as well as all Asian-, Native-, and African-Americans. Unlike the Old World aristocracies, within those sweeping restrictions, lack of blue-blooded family heritage did not necessarily block an otherwise exceptional young man's rise within that system, nor did a plutocratic father's name assure an unremarkable son's success. Absence of wealth, however, was an absolute barrier.

Membership in the elite was not for the faint of heart in any case. It demanded conformity to unwritten rules. Much of a young man's education was devoted to learning those rules. Their enforcement could be violent, and physically and emotionally bullying. As he made his way, many eyes kept close watch over his progress. And the upper-crust world in which he moved was so self-enclosed at times as to become inbred: marriages were not arranged, but they nonetheless possessed a royal element of the conjoining of bloodlines for the purposes of doing business, often in the form of heirs and heiresses. Families were quite clear about the choices that a young son or daughter should make.

For those living amid the imported ancient trappings of aristocratic Europe, especially England, which surrounded the emerging ruling class—for truly the interlocking WASP families and fortunes that came to the fore in the last years of the nineteenth century and the first years of the twentieth century formed the American ruling class—one forged-steel democratic principle governed all those who expected to take their share in that class's leadership privilege. They had to give of themselves; they had to be ready to sacrifice for their country and to deliver their expertise and money when called upon to serve America in time of war and, if needed, to ante up their lives and, far more painful, those of their own children when duty required. Before self-betterment came self-sacrifice.

In their rigorously classical prep school studies, all had read Thucydides' history of the Peloponnesian War. Thucydides wrote that Pericles told the Athenian Assembly during his funeral oration that the greatest courage in war is shown by those men who act with the most to lose—"who would feel the change most if trouble befell them."[1] These Abrahams of the New World did not hesitate to sacrifice their own Isaacs for what they believed was their divinely sanctioned mission to lead their growing nation.

This amalgam of selective institutions and a close-knit world of privileged families that inculcated in their sons a sense of sacrificial mission crafted an increasingly stable leadership coterie that could sustain its elected rule and the legitimacy of its power over a roiling, fast-changing nation in a dangerous world. In twentieth-century America, the group of men who eventually came to be known as the Liberal, or Foreign Policy, Establishment, or just "the Establishment," succeeded despite the immense chasm between their privileged lives and the daily toil of most Americans. It was this stability and legitimacy that enabled the nation's leadership-elite to forge the world's most powerful nation and build the American century.

This book tells the story, in part, of how that leadership ideal emerged in the early lives of the men who would one day lead a nation. The members of the Millionaires' Unit were decidedly representative men of their class, heirs to all their world had to give. They were the youthful beginnings of the next generation of the Establishment, determined, sometimes in defiance of their own government, to fulfill their roles with the chance to serve that the dawn of flight and the coming of the Great War gave them.

America has changed as has its ruling class, but the nation that today straddles the globe with its power would be impossible to conceive without these young men and their determination to serve.

Their efforts and inspiration carried America into the sky, helped to bring the Great War to a swift end, and set the nation on its path to world power. But before then, they were boys.

Couderkerque, Belgium, October 14, 1918

The Handkerchief

"CONTACT!"

The British mechanic in oil-blackened canvas coveralls pushed up a blade of the wooden prop to prime the cylinders and then drove it down as if pounding a stake into the ground. Still warm from the morning's patrol, the valves in the Sopwith Camel's big rotary engine popped in rapid succession and then the pistons began to bite. With a great jet of blue exhaust and a spit of pungent castor oil, the engine exploded into an earsplitting roar that drowned out all other sounds from the fifteen Camels lined up in front of the row of canvas Bessoneau hangars. The maelstrom of the slipstream blew dust back fifty yards behind the tail and lifted the mechanic clinging to the fuselage off his feet.

Settled into the wicker seat of the biwing Sopwith Camel, Kenneth MacLeish listened intently as the engine fired. Even though the American navy lieutenant had turned twenty-two less than a month ago, his friends in the British Royal Air Force Number 213 squadron thought he had aged years in the last few months. A bout of the Spanish flu in the epidemic that had killed so many of his comrades over the past month had subtracted fifteen pounds from his already slender frame. The stress from flying high into combat so often had also taken its toll.

Still, Kenney was a fortunate man. He was alive; he had braved dogfights, low-level bombing runs, anti-aircraft fire, and nightlong bombardments. Moreover, he had a fiancée he was crazy about who was waiting for him back home in the States. And now he was back doing the one thing he truly loved: flying a scout.

Arriving late the night before in the officers' mess, he had left the crowd of Yank and Limey flyboys in stitches with self-mocking stories of the penny-pinching ways of his Scots cousins. Having just rejoined No. 213, he revived friendships with the surviving members, shared memories of those who had "gone West," and retold the bawdy jokes he remembered from college at Yale.

Checks complete, he nodded and waved his hand side-to-side to the members of the crew holding onto the struts and wing tips. Another crewman pulled the chocks away from the wheels. When his flight commander, Canadian Captain John Edmund Greene, signaled the "all clear," MacLeish chopped his hand forward and the crewmen gave him the thumbs up and released the wings and tail. He flipped the blip switch off and on; the propeller alternately windmilling and grabbing, the Camel rolled and bounded ahead onto the cinder runway. The way clear, he throttled all the way up. In just a few yards MacLeish leaped into the sky.[1]

It was two o'clock in the afternoon of October 14, 1918, and after four years of war—a year and a half since America had entered the fight—the Central Powers were finally on the run. All hands had been thrown into the air to rain hell down on the Germans still holding their positions in Belgium and France and turn their orderly retreat into a terrifying rout.

MacLeish could not wait to get back into the air. Rumors were shooting about that the war might soon end. He was worried that peace would come before he got a final chance to make his mark. He came back to the front intent on making "one last try at really doing something."[2] Nothing in his life compared to that hope. Flying in combat for the first time with No. 213 six months earlier—then the Royal Navy Air Service, No. 13 squadron—he had written to his family back home in Glencoe, outside Chicago, about his good luck in being sent out on fighting patrols with the British, after nearly a year of training with a squadron of his Yale College mates in the United States and then in France and Britain. "I'm so happy," he gushed, "I can't see straight."[3]

His fighting days had not lasted long enough for him. He had been sent for more training and then to help build up the U.S. Navy's bomber force. After an extended stint at a receiving base in England assembling and testing the first American-made aircraft to arrive in Europe and then a week in bed with the flu, he had finally gotten the chance to return to the front. He came back with bloody vengeance in mind.

A week and a half before, his closest and oldest friend, Di Gates, had been shot down while flying with a French squadron during a dogfight over enemy territory. No word had been heard of him since. MacLeish was distraught. Kenney and Di had gone to the same small boarding school in the Connecticut countryside where the two homesick Midwesterners had bonded among the clubby Easterners. They had continued on to Yale together, and Di had brought Kenney into the Yale Aero Club, the beginnings of his flying career. In the intervening months, MacLeish had seen so many men fall with that unforgettable crunch of an airplane striking the earth. Like all men at the front, witnessing death had become a commonplace experience for him. But "Di was different." He had been brought up with him. "He's one of two men that I actually love," he wrote home. His brother Archie, now back in the States after a tour in the artillery fighting on the Marne, in France, was the other.

"I'll get even with somebody!" he swore.[4]

MacLeish had enjoyed his first taste of revenge just that morning. He began his flying day as he always did, dressing in layer upon layer of silk, wool, canvas, and fur, including the now fraying wool sweater his fiancée back home, Priscilla Murdock, had knitted for him just before he shipped out. A bullet hole through it reminded him of what he faced. Last, he sniffed the lingering perfume on the silk handkerchief Priscilla had given to him before tucking it away into the pocket of his flying suit.

After a fifteen-minute early-morning test flight, he flew his first patrol in the bright sunshine. The squadron of nineteen planes went off on a bombing run against columns of retreating German troops on the roads behind the front near Ardoye, Belgium. After dropping his four twenty-five-pound Cooper bombs on the terror-stricken men and horses, he swooped down low over the road, joining a chattering strafing line that left men, wagons, and horses in blasted bloody heaps. His heart leaped at the sight of the fallen and fleeing enemy. He thrilled to the full-out chase close enough to earth to witness the terror in the Germans' eyes as they looked up at him bearing down on them, dual guns blazing.

Soaring back up several thousand feet, he spotted a squadron of German Fokker biplanes. His flight of five Camels pounced. The results for the Anglo-American squadron were bloody. In the ensuing dogfight, the Germans shot down three of the Allies. Before making their escape, though, MacLeish and Greene converged on an enemy fighter. They machine gunned the German flyer until he went spinning down in flames and disappeared among the remnants of the village of Theurout.

For the Air Ace Greene, that kill marked his fifteenth victory. It was MacLeish's first, his first taste of enemy blood.

MacLeish returned to the aerodrome and wolfed down lunch. His orders for the afternoon called for the squadron to be back in the air patrolling for targets behind the German lines, deep in Belgium.

He flew up into formation within the fifteen-machine Camel circus—in a three-bird flight with Greene and an English airman, Lieutenant Allen. They flew north along the Belgian coast. In the thick shoreline cloud cover the pilots separated and lost sight of each other. After searching for a few minutes, MacLeish, Greene, and Allen gave up on finding the others and decided to continue patroling alone. Seeing no enemy targets, they turned eastward and flew inland several miles behind the German lines to where the cloud cover lifted. Two miles north of the blasted ruins of the town of Dixmude, they spotted two German aircraft flying a few thousand feet below them.

MacLeish scanned the clouds, staring intently into the sun until he had to avert his eyes. Seeing no enemy aircraft, he waggled his wings for his flight mates to follow him down. They banked over and dove at nearly two hundred miles an hour, guy wires screaming in the wind. Tracers streamed out of both barrels as they came in range of the two unsuspecting aircraft.

Entranced by the target in his gunsight, MacLeish did not notice the counterattack until the white sparks of tracers zipped past and he caught the whiff of burning cordite and heard the snap of the bullets. Plunging out of a hiding place in the sun or the clouds, seven German Fokker biplanes were on top of the three Americans. A melee followed. The Camels were quickly separated in the dogfight, leaving them unable to defend each other. Allen's plane burst into flames and spun downward. Greene followed quickly, a German scout firing into the great dogfighter as he fell slowly, along with his plane, an unfurling spiral of smoke to his death.

MacLeish knew how to stunt his jumpy bird, up and down, snapping turns, desperate to dodge the German bullets and snake away from their less-agile but faster machines. The hard-charging German fighters clung to his Camel's tail and pressed their lethal intent home. Everywhere he looked he could see enemy aircraft running in on him. Strings of pockmarks popped through the fabric of his wings and up the fuselage. Rather than keep running, he jumped up and swooped around to face the nearest enemy.

SECTION I

Earth

CHAPTER 1

New Haven, June 3, 1916
Sand

As Frederick Trubee Davison's sophomore year drew to a close, he had begun to bask in the sunshine of Yale. No light shone brighter, before or since, than on the young men at Yale, Harvard, and Princeton at the dawn of what was to become the American Century. Those glorious rays did little to warm the twenty-year-old Trubee, as everyone knew him, while he sat in the balcony within the soaring heights of Yale's Battell Chapel. The nor'easter-blasted spring air brought shivers to the sleepy young men packed together in the pews. The temperature barely clung to fifty degrees that Saturday morning, June 3, the closing month in the 1915–1916 academic calendar. The day had dawned with gray, low-hanging clouds, slanting rain, and frigid winds lashing the southern New England coast. It was just the latest in a month's worth of raw, wet, and gloomy days—the worst spring in years, complained Long Island Sound resort owners who worried their summer season would be ruined before it began.

As he did shortly after eight o'clock each morning, Trubee sat with his 420 fellow sophomores in their designated hard-backed pews of the underclassmen's gallery in Battell. They chanted their daily prayers together with the rest of the Yale College "cousinhood" at mandatory chapel. The university's Congregationalist religious seat, as big as a train station, was a mushroom-color, Victorian stone fortress shoehorned into a gap in the corner of the Old Campus quadrangle. Yale made up for the slight by overdoing the church's interior to the point of giddiness. The walls, ceiling, and floors were a polychromatic carnival of gilding, bright stenciling, and mosaic tile art, embroidered with colorfully painted and intricately carved woodwork. In the sunless morning's gloom, the stained glass windows seemed painted into their niches in the walls. The hulking confection commemorated the 140 Yale men fallen during the Civil War—for both the Union and Confederate armies. Memorial bronze wall plaques and inscribed quotations from famous Yale men stared out at Trubee and his fellow students.

That kaleidoscopic color and ancestral glory helped keep some of the bleary-eyed students awake under the scanning eyes of proctors assigned to mark down any absentees. Each morning within Battell's confines, Yale College took a quick, cleansing dunk in the purifying waters of Christian spirituality and heard a few lines from the King James Bible before the onrush of the day's earthly demands. Mandatory Morning Prayer was a reminder of Yale's beginnings by Puritan clergymen in 1701—seventy-five years before the United States was born—for the purpose of "perpetuating the Christian Protestant Religion, by a succession of Learned and Orthodox men." Like nearly all his classmates, Trubee was neither particularly learned nor pious, though he dutifully recited the prayers with the eleven hundred other young men and professors on hand. He glanced down impatiently at President Arthur Twining Hadley, who stood in the pulpit with a young faculty member at his side leading the assembled college in prayer. That was followed quickly by the professor's breathlessly short homily based on the day's reading, reminding them to do their duty, as the college's de facto motto told them, "For God, for country and for Yale."[1]

Shifting uncomfortably in their hard seats, Trubee and his classmates looked as if the same tailor had uniformed them from the same bolts of black or brown wool. In their stiff coats or tweed sack suits and starched white shirts, they tugged at the pinching, stiff high collars or fiddled with their gold watch fobs slung across their vest front or their shiny black ties and bowties. Most wore black felt bowlers or herringbone ivy caps that for the moment rested in their laps. Only the seniors sitting on the floor below had "earned" the right to go hatless on campus. Many of the seniors wore black academic robes and mortarboards, which was the clerical garb of the scholar since medieval times. Fashion, like most things at Yale, changed at a glacial pace. Their student predecessors over the half-century since the end of the Civil War would quickly recognize them as brethren. In fact, many of the students in chapel were sons of Yale fathers and grandfathers and even great-grandfathers, the latest in the generational lines of Yale men who had traveled the roads and railroads to New Haven before them.

Through their fathers' accomplishments, above all the money they donated to fill Yale's coffers, and their devotion to Yale and all it represented, the university had grown and now enjoyed its stature as the place a father sent a son for whom he held bullish visions. Trubee and his classmates knew that the world was watching them, wondering who among them would rise to the top in the hierarchy of social advancement at Yale and beyond. They were, observed the New York papers, not just any young men off to college for four years of fun, games, drinking, and gentlemen's Cs before getting along with the real business of life. They exemplified something larger, hungrier, something peculiarly American, swelling with the romance and vast promise of the American landscape. Each class carried on the celebrated "Yale Spirit," an amalgam of ruthless competition and fair play, boyishness and elegance, brashness and tradition that an entire nation looked up to and honored. "Nothing," commented the popular philosopher and Harvard professor George Santayana after a visit to Yale, "could be more American—not to say Amurrcan—than Yale College."[2]

The boys in chapel had a name of their own for that representative American quality found in their best Yale classmates in 1916. They called it "sand," after the sand spread beneath the wheels of locomotives to make them grab the track as they spun. A student needed sand, needed to prove his Yale Spirit on the campus tracks. Sand was the public demonstration of character. A boy who had sand was going places. To show his sand during his time in New Haven, though, he had to prove his measure by doing something for his college. The Yale men with sand hit the line hard in football games against Harvard, and toured the nation singing in white tie and tails with those increasingly famed "gentleman songsters," the Whiffenpoofs, gained election to the editorial board of the *Yale Daily News*, recited the class oration at commencement and, in recognition of their sand, won the most esteemed honor of all: election at the end of junior year to one of the three exclusive secret senior societies, especially Skull & Bones. They regularly found their names and photographs in the papers. America was watching.

America knew that in Battell Chapel, each morning, sat many of its future leaders.

Trubee Davison stood out—not, however, by his physical presence. He dressed in his Yale dark suit "uniform" and parted his straight, pomaded auburn hair down the middle, little different from all the boys around him. Not quite handsome, the features of his face carried on an argument with each other. His broad forehead, crease over the bridge of his thick nose, square jaw, and pugnaciously protruding lower lip evidenced his hardnosed days running over boys at football while prepping at Groton School outside Boston before coming to Yale. That bulldoggish look smacked up against a pronounced Cupid's bow on his upper lip that could make his brightening face look downright angelic.

Although he had a towel-snapping sense of humor and loved to tell a good story, he did not turn heads when he walked into a room. With Trubee, what you saw was what you got. Sitting near him in Battell, his friend and classmate John Farrar—who would later establish the publishing house today known as Farrar, Straus and Giroux—found Trubee's nature so "straightforward" that he practically defied description. "Clear and without picturesqueness," according to Farrar, Trubee was not given to lingering too long over what needed to be done. He just went and did it.[3]

Much of his time was spent with friends. The pleasure Trubee took in them was clear. Until he returned to his dorm room bed, he was almost never alone. At the end of his second year on campus he was already known to have plenty of sand. Not surprisingly, he enjoyed big gatherings and kept things lively at Psi Upsilon, his fraternity. He regularly organized classmates on campus, whether to cheer on a Yale team taking the field or to raise money for the American Ambulance Service with which he had volunteered the previous summer carrying the wounded off the trains returning from the Western Front into Paris. His room was now a clearinghouse for his effort to finance and staff a new ambulance service he planned to set up that summer where the German and French lines met in the Vosges Mountains, in northern Europe.

Most of his extracurricular hours, though, were spent at the crew team boat-house on the New Haven Harbor. At five feet eight inches tall when he stretched out and barely 150 pounds and only a middling prep school athlete, he was never in contention to row in the eight. But Trubee had devoted himself to convincing his classmates that he had the makings of a strong crew team manager. That was no small matter. Yale sporting events brought the entire college and thousands upon thousands of other fans out to cheer the Elis' on-field heroics and created national stars of Yale's top athletes. Professional collegiate coaching and sports team management were still in their infancy; so team managers functioned as the brains behind the brawn, often overseeing operations and finances, arranging schedules, booking travel, ensuring upkeep of equipment, even hiring coaches and support staff, and sometimes coaching the team themselves.

Athletics provided the one sure infusing energy unifying the otherwise un-gainly and centrifugal Yale campus into a spirited, fast-paced college full of likeminded brethren. It brought out "heelers," which was the campus term for competitors, such as Trubee, who were in the race for leadership posts, and made heroes of stellar athletes, including some of his closest friends. Cheering on the football team on a blustery fall day at the immense Yale Bowl bound together classes, professors, and alumni "with hoops of steel," according to

Wilbur Cross, a Yale graduate, popular English professor of the day and future four-term Connecticut governor.[4]

As such, athletes and team managers were the campus royalty, standing out as the biggest of the big men. And among intercollegiate sports at Yale, rowing was the crown jewel. Crew was a major American sport in the period—regularly making front-page news in the leading daily papers—and, since the first Yale-Harvard boat race in 1852, nine years before the first shot of the Civil War was fired, it was the oldest intercollegiate sport. Even the nation's most closely followed athletic team, the Yale football team, ceded place-of-honor to crew. More students tried out for seats on the crew team—close to two hundred in a typical year—than any other sport, and alumni support kept the team in high admiralty style. Election as captain or manager of the crew team was, according to one alumnus of the period, "the very grandest honor at Yale."[5]

Trubee Davison toiled hours each day for the entire year in hopes of winning the election to become manager. To get the nod meant taking on tasks that were largely menial: making sure the oarsmen had their gear and beer, clean clothes, dry towels, salve for their sore muscles and bottoms that had been rubbed raw from the daily hours rowing over the harbor—whatever the crew needed to keep its focus on winning, and doing so with good cheer and enthusiasm. With the crew team set to leave that afternoon for three weeks of training camp in preparation for the final and all-important race of the year—The Race—the Harvard-Yale Boat Race, Trubee had trouble keeping his mind on Morning Prayer. He had much work to do before the team's scheduled departure at 4:30 that afternoon.

Near him in Battell sat his classmate Robert Abercrombie Lovett. Two boys could not be more different than Trubee and his Long Island Gold Coast neighbor. If Trubee was foursquare to a point, his fraternity mate was a closed circle. Bob exuded a standoffishness and hauteur that stood out even at Yale, bringing him classmates' respect, though not winning him the popularity Trubee enjoyed. Observant, serious, brooding at times, and always impeccably tailored in clothing and manner, he revealed little of himself even to those who thought they knew him well. His long face, hooded eyes, beaked nose, and rare half smile could seem off-puttingly patrician, even priestly, to some of his classmates. Everybody knew that he was usually the smartest man in the classroom, often even smarter than the professor. He was, however, invariably courteous and self-possessed. In freshman chemistry lab, classmate Wilmarth Sheldon Lewis accidentally sprayed sulfuric acid on him, leaving Bob's fine white pongee silk shirt a tattered rag. Lewis recalled how, "instead of emptying the test tube of his wrath in retaliation," his gentlemanly classmate shrugged off the matter, went back to his room to change, and never again mentioned the incident.[6]

Trubee and Bob were an odd pairing in many respects. If Trubee loved to play court to Yale's vaunted sporting world, Bob loathed anything resembling exercise. Instead, he spent his time with the campus wits, singing in the Glee Club as a freshman, and heeling for manager of the Yale Dramat—the student theater company—and sometimes acting in its productions. However, Bob and Trubee did share a few things in common. Trubee's father had come from small-town roots to soar to the heights of Wall Street where he was now, as the managing partner of J. P. Morgan & Company, one of the most powerful bankers in the financial world. Unlike so many of his classmates, though, Trubee came to New Haven without deep family roots at Yale or an old family fortune. Bob's father also had a Horatio Alger story to tell of a phenomenally swift climb to astounding wealth and power built upon the crest of the enormous wave of industrialization, frontier growth, and financial consolidation that had swept the land over the past three decades.

Robert Scott Lovett was a former small-town Texas lawyer and, briefly, a judge, who, though possessing only a high school diploma, had emerged as one of the top railroad attorneys in the state. He represented the Southern Pacific system when Edward Harriman had come to Houston to see him. The "Little Giant" of the railroads had combined the vast Union Pacific and the Southern Pacific lines into the Harriman System, the planet's largest transportation network that stretched from one corner of the continent to the other. Harriman eventually persuaded Judge Lovett, as he was known, to move to New York City and serve as Harriman's general counsel. Following Harriman's death in 1909, the elder Lovett had succeeded him as chairman of the executive committee and president overseeing the vast Harriman System.

After moving from Texas as a child, the younger Bob Lovett had grown up alongside the Harriman brothers, Averell—a future banker, New York Governor, international diplomat, and confidante of presidents—and his younger brother Roland—also a future banker and Red Cross president. Despite his own disinterest in rugged pursuits, the young Lovett could occasionally be coaxed onto horseback together with the outdoors-loving Harriman boys on visits to Arden, their baronial thirty-square-mile estate with its ninety-five-room mansion above the Hudson River, a little north of New York City. The two families also shared vast ranch holdings in Idaho.

Bob did not see much value in riding through the wide-open spaces, but he thoroughly enjoyed the cultured pleasures society offered its privileged members. Just the past summer of 1915, in the course of a carefree month of travel through neutral Europe, he and Roland Harriman had gone racing through the mountain passes and villages of Switzerland by auto and motorbike, stopping to sample fine wines and cuisine, ignoring the grisly war raging on the other side of the border. After another stellar year at Yale including election to Phi Beta Kappa, Bob looked forward to a summer of swimming and boating on the Long Island Sound. He also planned to renew his courtship of the family's young and beautiful Long Island neighbor, Adele Quartley Brown, the lively daughter of James Brown, senior partner in his family-banking firm of Brown Brothers & Company, one of the oldest and most powerful banks on Wall Street. Like the union of heirs to thrones in the Old World, theirs held the promise of a good match, uniting two of the leading financial and industrial families of America.

Sitting nearby, Bob's classmate Artemus Gates did not see much he liked in the brainy, silver-tongued New Yorker. He bristled at his haughtiness and often missed the humor in his biting wit, yet Di, as Gates was known, practically worshipped Trubee Davison. Trubee knew how to make the big quiet boy from small-town Iowa feel at home among the wealthy, urbane Easterners. All three were fraternity brothers. If Trubee thought Bob was the right sort of pal, then Di Gates was prepared to trust him, too. Di lacked Bob's polish and incisive mind and Trubee's backslapping warmth, but his outsized physical presence overwhelmed their social gifts. In fact, he was the true star among the trio. Wherever he went, his lineman's size and the bone-crunching power of the muscles rippling beneath his suit stood out in any crowd off the football field. Matinee-idol handsome, his full black hair, thick nose, heavy lips, and broad brow, along with his occasional long silences, led some friends to call him "the Indian." He sometimes found the attention embarrassing, but the shy two hundred-pounder had grown used to people on the street pointing him out as he passed, even in New York City.

As a starting tackle on the Yale football team the past fall season, his first year of varsity eligibility, Di had won sports columnists' praise for his aggressiveness and heads-up play while running the field nonstop for the full sixty minutes—offense and defense, kick offs, and points-after, without substitution, as was then the norm. Playing football for Yale put a young man in the spotlight that, in the early days of media-stoked celebrity and before the rise of most professional sports leagues, shined otherwise only on the likes of boxing champs, campaigning politicians, robber barons, and the emerging stars of the nickelodeon like Charlie Chaplin, Mary Pickford, and Rudolph Valentino. No other sports team in America could boast a comparable following. The demand for tickets to see Yale play football had brought a flood of alumni donations to build an engineering marvel, the Yale Bowl, the largest stadium since the Roman Colosseum. Five Sundays in autumn crowds larger than the population of some entire states filled the 71,000-seat Bowl beyond capacity.[7]

Yale fans had not had much to cheer about of late. The team had shown little fight during the past season. After a string of disappointing campaigns, reporters pointed to Gates as one of the returning standouts around whom Yale hoped to rebuild next year.

All that attention and the bright lights of New Haven and the jostling sidewalks of cities in the East were a long way from home for him. He came from a dusty stockyard town: Clinton, Iowa, on the banks of the Mississippi River. That was where the railhead met the end of the northern cattle drive and carried the herds the remaining 140 miles west to Chicago's vast slaughterhouses. His father had run an insurance company in town until his death a decade earlier, leaving his mother to raise her son alone. Although times got tough as they often moved between small towns, his grandparents had made enough money from a riverboat company, including the paddle wheeler called the *Artemus L. Gates*, to send the young Di east for a few years of preparation at Hotchkiss, a Connecticut prep school, before entering Yale.[8]

Never entirely at home among the big city prep school boys, Di stuck close to his easygoing friend, Kenneth MacLeish. His closest pal other than Trubee, Kenney was from Glencoe, Illinois, a suburb on the shores of Lake Michigan, north of Chicago. Like Di, he had been sent off by his parents to prep for Yale at Hotchkiss. There the two Midwesterners had become inseparable, like brothers. Like brothers, they went on to college together.

Kenney had introduced Di to the right places in New Haven. Although Kenney had grown up nearly a thousand miles away, Yale was in some senses his own backyard. He had only to follow the bright path blazed for him by his older brother Archibald. Voted "most brilliant" by his classmates, Archie had taken just about every prize Yale had to give by the time he graduated in June 1915. Now he was gaining professors' applause at Harvard Law School. Faculty and administrators seeing Kenney's name would ask him if he was related to Archie, who had been the very definition of the campus Renaissance man— football player, captain of the water polo team, brilliant in his academics, and popular and respected by classmates. If that were not enough, Archie had made a name for himself as a promising young poet, editing the prestigious campus literary magazine, the *Lit*, and reciting his verse as the official class poet at graduation.

All of Archie's Yale achievements were crowned by his election to Skull & Bones, the most elite of the secret senior societies. The ultra-exclusive student clubs met in their mysterious, members-only, padlocked clubhouses—windowless "tombs" scattered about campus that were scenes of rumored but unknown initiation rituals and cabalistic preparation for success in life beyond campus. Through the societies' annual selection of fifteen new members each, they served as the ultimate arbiter of a student's sand, the crown of his triumphant progress throughout his Yale career. Any Yale student who could dream aspired to a "tap," selection to a senior society at the end of his junior year.

Kenney dreamed of the day he, too, would step into one of the tombs, but he had struggled just to get into Yale, and now sometimes felt he disappeared within the long shadow of his brother's example. But whatever Kenney's shortcomings, he made friends easily. Handsome, lighthearted, and funny, he had a flirtatious twinkle in his eye, a jaunty set to his chin, a winning smile, and more than a dram of his Scottish immigrant father's romance in his heart. "Kidded ever since I can remember," he said, by the other boys about the supposed skinflint ways of the Scots, their jokes may have caused him to ignore price tags; he always chose the most expensive items on the menu and had his suits made up by tailors selecting the finest British tweeds and woolens. Still, he took genuine pride in his ancestral heritage, dressing in kilts and playing the bagpipes with Archie at family gatherings. "Scotch," as some friends called him, could put on an impeccable brogue in a pinch. Women flocked to him.[9]

From the balcony in Battell Chapel, Kenney and the rest of the underclassmen made a point of studying the seniors on the floor below. After four years at Yale, the big men among them exuded an air of wellbeing; even their walk was confident. In the battle for status within the rigid Yale social hierarchy, they had prevailed. Life was good to them; greater fortune yet beckoned beyond campus. Few classmates had made more enviable lives for themselves at Yale than Albert Sturtevant. Al, said one of his professors, represented "the finest type of college man." A mechanical engineering student at Yale's Sheffield Scientific School—Sheff as it was called—he was all set to attend Harvard Law School in the fall. He was also a standout oarsman on the famed Yale crew. A walk across campus with him was rarely swift as friends and classmates stopped him constantly to get his take on the eight's chances in the coming weekend's regatta.[10]

At six feet two inches, sharply tailored, blond-haired, blue-eyed, and baby-faced, he towered over most of his classmates, and not just in height. When he strolled into the afternoon tea dances at the nearby Taft Hotel, hearts fluttered.

Al's classmates had already voted him among the "handsomest" and "best dressed" members of their class. At Yale, he stood with the most glorified of the big men. Like Di Gates, Al could count on being recognized wherever he went in his creamy white "Y" letter sweater. As a sophomore in 1914, he had been moved up at the last moment from the varsity's second crew to the first boat's eight during preparations for the all-important Harvard race. Yale had won that race by a nose in the closest finish in the storied regatta's long history. The sprint to victory had brought him and the team national glory. Last year, his fame had peaked when he stepped into the captaincy of the team after the previous captain left school. Al led his team to a sweep of every regatta, crushing Harvard in the final, decisive race of the year.

His good looks, warm smile, academic prowess, and polished bearing could be deceiving. Pressing his team on, he could swear or joke like a drunken sailor. After long muscle-searing, bottom-grinding days on the water, tempers often flared, especially in the elbows-out competition for prized spots in the varsity boats. More than once, he had stepped between fighting teammates. "If the sparks flew," recalled a friend, "that winsomely boyish manner of his was enough to cool them."[11]

This year, though, had put Al through a trial that was tougher in its way than a four-mile race. Although he had completed his three-year program at Sheff, he had decided to stay on at Yale for an extra year to captain a team some prognosticators had believed would be one of the greatest ever. That glory was not to be. The team had struggled and midway through the season, Coach Guy Nickalls had pulled him aside and asked that he relinquish leadership of the team he had helped build. Nickalls turned, instead, to Seth Low, a fellow veteran rower. Al stamped about afterward for hours, cursing and declaring his intention to resign, but the next day he held his tongue and his place in the boat.

With the school year rushing to its end, Al Sturtevant had shown his sand on behalf of Yale. Trubee, Bob, Di, and Kenney had done what was required of them to make their way toward the top at Yale, to climb the steep, demanding ladder to reach for the campus prizes. All of them looked forward to the freedoms of summer vacation, but their efforts at Yale were not yet finished for the year. For Al and Trubee, the next three weeks would be the most important days of their Yale lives. What none of them knew as they listened to the morning's homily was that their lives and the lives of all their friends around them would soon change radically. They rolled their tired eyes to the brightly painted Battell Chapel ceiling, waiting for Morning Prayer to end.

CHAPTER 2

Gales Ferry, June 3–18, 1916

Preparation

Two hundred miles north of New Haven, David Sinton Ingalls scoured the sports pages daily where he followed the exploits of Sturtevant, Gates, and other Yale athletes with a youngster's fevered interest. Recently turned seventeen, he was about to graduate from Saint Paul's School, a church preparatory school in Concord, New Hampshire. He could barely wait for the three months of summer vacation to pass so he could get to New Haven. During the long snowy winters of New Hampshire, "Crock" Ingalls's slick stick handling at St. Paul's brought comparisons with the man considered by some to be the greatest American collegiate hockey player ever to play the game, Hobey Baker, who had gone on from St. Paul's to Princeton and national athletic fame six years earlier.[1]

Although most of Crock's classmates would stay closer to Cambridge for college, he looked forward to easy skating from prep school into the Yale Blue. The path to New Haven had already been smoothed for him. Crock Ingalls came from Ohio's royal family and one of Yale's as well. Back home in Cleveland, his father, Albert Ingalls, was a vice president for the New York Central Railroad and a successful businessman. His mother, though, counted for even more: She was a Taft. In Ohio, the Taft name rang clear like a bell from Cleveland to Cincinnati. Its influence extended far beyond the state borders. By 1916, the Taft family already stood out as one of the most distinguished political families in the nation's history, right there with the Adams family a century earlier and the Kennedy and Bush clans later in the twentieth century. Mrs. Ingalls was the daughter of Charles Phelps Taft, a former Ohio Congressman and powerful Cincinnati newspaper editor and publisher.

He had gone to Yale. In so doing, he had followed in the footsteps of one of the college's most influential men, his father, Alphonso Taft. As a student in 1832, Alphonso Taft had co-founded Skull & Bones. Establishing the family tradition of public service, he became President Ulysses S. Grant's Secretary of War and Attorney General. All his sons had attended Yale and then gone on to build stellar reputations of their own. Charles's brother Horace had founded the respected Taft School, a Connecticut prep school. His half-brother, William Howard Taft, had reached the loftiest heights of national power in public service, winning election in 1908 as the nation's twenty-seventh president.

Since leaving the White House following his defeat in 1912, the former president had moved his famously portly girth, jarringly loud cough of a laugh, and his family to a big house on Prospect Street in New Haven, where he taught law at Yale and played as much golf as he could. From his office across Chapel Street from Old Campus in the elegant Taft Hotel, which his brother Horace had built, he made a point of attending every campus sporting event his busy speaking schedule permitted.

Like all Taft men, Crock Ingalls pinned a Yale banner to his wall and readied himself for the day when he would get his chance to spend four years there. With his great uncle's high-pitched laugh that wheezed out like a dying motor, he was recognizably a Taft. His athleticism, squinty smile, shock of dark hair, and gift for making friends added to his appeal. Taft men made a point of outdoing each other in their Yale careers. Crock looked ahead to the fall when he could begin to make his mark on the Yale campus.[2]

Crock and his friends in prep school and the boys in Battell Chapel were among the young strivers in the nation's elite colleges and prep schools who had studied the occult lessons of social advancement to be learned from each other, from upperclassmen like Al Sturtevant and older brothers like Archie MacLeish. There was one other source they also consulted: a juvenile novel about an idealistic football hero's career negotiating the social boot camp at Yale. *Stover at Yale*, declared F. Scott Fitzgerald, Class of 1917 at Princeton— until the liquor bottle he tossed through a window of the university president's house got him thrown out—was the "textbook" for his generation of Ivy Leaguers. Written by Owen Johnson of the Yale Class of 1901, the 1912 best-seller follows John Humperdink "Dink" Stover's emotionally fraught journey up the campus social ladder among young men with strong chins, plenty of money, a passion for success, a love of fellowship, and a few dark secrets.

The novel opens with Stover's arrival at Yale from prep school, ready for "the happy, carefree years that everyone proclaimed." A vaunted football prospect, Dink came in expectation that at Yale he would enjoy "four glorious years, good times, good fellows, and a free and open fight to be among the leaders and leave a name on the roll of fame. Only four years, and then the world with its perplexities and grinding trials." However, he is quickly disabused of his naivete. The perplexities and grinding trials have already begun. He has barely set foot on campus when an upperclassman pulls him aside to explain the "system" to him, its unwritten yet ironclad regulations. To succeed at Yale he would have to conform to fashion, work for his class and make a leader of himself while acting judiciously at all times and choosing his associates accordingly. Breaking the rules spelled an end to any hope for leaving a name at Yale, and certainly of winning a tap for a senior society.

"Remember," his first Yale mentor concludes ominously, "you're going to be watched from now on." Dink realizes that college life "was not all so simple—no, not at all simple. It wasn't as he had thought. It was complex, a little disturbing."

Although *Stover* stirred up a tempest among Yale alumni who protested its dark vision of the underside of the hard-bitten Yale democracy, the reality of campus life was anything but carefree for undergraduates such as Trubee and his classmates who entertained hopes for success at Yale. In fact, they had to fight for what they wanted and conform to the unwritten code of behavior. Until banned by the faculty, campus life literally began with a beating—a run through the gauntlet of fists and kicks from upper classmen during freshman rush. Later that year came the Cane Rush in which sophomores armed with bamboo poles held the College Fence running along the inner roadway of Old Campus against the attacks of howling, tackling, and punching freshmen. Classmates immediately suspected the courage and fighting spirit of any student who came away from the battle royal without a broken nose, cuts or blackened eyes, and his clothes in tatters. Did he, those watching wondered, lack sand?

From there, freshmen ran the race to prove their worth by doing "something for Yale." The campus burst with their energy, the drive of ambitious young men scrambling to show their sand. "Everything but scholarship," Henry Seidel Canby, a Yale graduate and professor at the time, observed, "was . . . an 'activity,' and called 'doing something for the college.'"[3] Left to their own devices, the students built their own self-contained, restless community of like-minded, uniformly attired, ambitious young men, "a limited Utopia," thought Canby.[4]

Heelers founded and joined club after club: prep school alumni, fraternal, religious, and charitable associations; theatrical, madrigal, and dancing groups; clubs for sporting events of all kinds, from shooting and fishing to gambling and drinking; and organizations devoted to advancing political action, book and stamp collecting, mandolin and banjo playing, smoking and bridge, as well as artistic and literary inclinations of all socially acceptable persuasions. There were even clubs for those too snobbish or bored to join a club.

Stephen Vincent Benét, who entered Yale in the fall of 1916 and emerged soon after graduation a well-known author, and his roommate J. F. Carter, memorialized the manic organizational energy at Yale with a ditty they penned. They advised their classmates:

> *Do you want to be successful?*
> *Form a club!*
> *Are your chances quite distressful?*
> *Form a club!*[5]

Building, guiding, cheering, playing, cajoling, organizing, selling, keeping company, heeling—above all doing something for Yale—filled most students' every waking hour.

The bruises and cuts from campus savagery were not the only medals a student strived to collect during his four years. Various emblems such as varsity letters— the blue "Y" that athletes and managers got to wear on their sweaters—or gold trinkets dangled from the watch fobs of less-athletic students, were awarded for their contributions to campus organizations and publicly symbolized a student's accomplishments for Yale. They also served as chits he would one day cash in for advancement in the campus social hierarchy.

And what of academics? At Yale, "scholarship," as classroom learning was called, seemed a wasted pursuit. What bookish knowledge Trubee and other Yale men were ever likely to acquire had already been absorbed during the long, cloistered years of classical studies in an adolescence spent at boarding school before arriving in New Haven. Anybody who thought he had come to study at Yale was soon relieved of that quaint and laughable notion. "Learning," sniffed Trubee's classmate Wilmarth Lewis, "was not fashionable."[6]

Success in academics brought mockery, or worse. Nothing ruined a man's reputation more than the label of "greasy grind." Although Bob Lovett had slid easily into Phi Beta Kappa, he made it seem so effortless that nobody could hold it against him. Al Sturtevant balanced his engineering brilliance with an athleticism that made him immune to derision. Envious of student devotion to everything except study, President Hadley avowed "half-humorously" to a gathering of alumni in 1915, "We need to elevate study to the level of an extra-curriculum activity."[7]

Yale was, of course, not all blood and sweat for the strivers and tears for the outcasts. Social graces were also tested. Popular dance orchestras set the rhythm of the campus social year at formal teas and balls in the fraternity clubhouses, faculty and administrators' homes, the Taft Hotel, and New York's finer ballrooms. Beyond their regular gatherings, each winter and spring the fraternities went to New York for their "germans"—named for the formal waltzes the students danced. The white-tie cotillions were weighted with the protocol of ancient European royal courts and introduced Yale men to New York society debutantes. Any lingering hint of interest in academics vanished from campus in an explosion of gaiety each February when the junior class tried to outdo the previous year's Junior Promenade. The celestially grand ball, the zenith of the social year, culminated a week of fizzy events that put all those who could afford the prom's steep costs on public display—in the company of divinely proportioned young women, or so their dates assured them in seductive tones as they spun through the ballroom until sunrise.

The sophomore classmates shared a rarely whispered but gnawing worry about what lay ahead after the summer break. A great, final triumph or crushing blow would come to them the following year. The moment of ultimate recognition would arrive at five o'clock on the second Tuesday in May, Tap Day, when the selection of the new members of the college's three secret, closed-door, senior societies—Wolf's Head, Scroll & Key, and, looming above all others, Skull & Bones—would be announced.[7]

Their locked and impenetrable tombs stood like cryptic sentries opening not to the underworld but to something greater, a place within Yale's Valhalla, side-by-side with the select few glorified for their true sand.

After lengthy and secret debate over qualifications of the juniors under consideration, the fifteen departing seniors in each society chose their own successors. Qualifications included family heritage and personal characteristics, but principally admittance was determined by who had done the most for Yale. The students who had managed any of the most important campus organizations, the *Yale Daily News* or the *Lit*, the Junior Prom, the Glee Club, the Dramat, or the four major varsity sports teams—baseball, crew, football, and track—or who had captained or otherwise starred on one of those teams, were virtually assured election. Other athletes, talented performers, and the occasional "high stand" man who combined scholarship with clear evidence of more rounded qualities also merited consideration.

Nothing quite like this all-embracing social system existed on any other American college campus of the age. Entry into Porcellian and Harvard's other exclusive final clubs and Ivy, Cottage, and the rest of Princeton's elite eating clubs was predetermined, granted primarily to those with the right family standing and club ties. "But to get into Bones," said proud Bonesman and future Cold War statesman Averell Harriman, "you had to do something for Yale."[8]

The opportunity to enter into these Olympian strongholds underlay the years of hard work for Yale. A significant segment of the undergraduates in each class dedicated themselves completely to the quest for entry. Should scholarship or a more leisurely enjoyment of the liquid fruits of a father's wealth seem better ways for a student to spend his college years, Harvard, Princeton, or some other worthy college beckoned. "Yale took pride," Wilmarth Lewis remembered, "in the story of the visiting English don who asked at Cambridge, Mass., how far Yale was from Harvard and was told, 'As far as Sparta from Athens.'"[9]

President Hadley was a specialist in railway economics and Yale's first president drawn from outside the clergy. Unlike the academic reformers and intellectuals who presided over Harvard, though, he was a practical man with little ambition to send philosophers and scholars into the world. His Yale would remain dedicated to readying young strivers to take the reins of American power through their willingness to win a place in command of the Yale system. The social capital they managed and accumulated in moving upward within the campus hierarchy confirmed a widely held belief in their moral destiny to lead. Captains of football, chairmen of the *Daily News*, and presidents of fraternities would one day become chairmen of banks, captains of industry, and presidents of governments.

Even God's affairs were not to distract a young man for too long. Whatever Yale's heavenly aims, its founding charter also called for students to be "fitted for Publick employment both in Church & Civil State." There was real business to take care of. President Hadley had once advised a visiting minister to keep his preaching brief: "We have a feeling here at Yale," he said, "that no souls are saved after the first twenty minutes."[10]

Closing with a racing benediction, he scurried down the central aisle past the nodding heads of the seniors who hurried out after him. Yale College raced out into the streaming rain and whipping winds of Old Campus quadrangle and on to the business of the day: the departure of the Yale Crew for three weeks of preparation, far from the distractions of campus, ahead of The Race.

Trubee, the other heelers, and of course the oarsmen and their coaches and supporters would be traveling together to New London, Connecticut, a small port town on the Thames River, midway between Harvard and Yale. The Harvard-Yale Boat Race had become such an institution that it was now held in June each year on the neutral waters of the Thames, where both teams maintained large training compounds. It had come to mark a special moment in the

Yale and Harvard academic calendars as the boisterous final event of the school year and the beginning of the summer vacation season. No day was grander. It arrived at the end of Commencement Week on both campuses. Thousands of alumni and families had already traveled from around the country to New Haven or Cambridge for several raucous, well-oiled days of reunion festivities, speeches, and graduation ceremonies. From there, most on hand continued on to Race Day in New London. Tens of thousands of other sports fans and revelers also witnessed The Race, which had come to mark the beginning of the summer season for shore resorts.

By mid-afternoon, nearly the entire Yale student body had gathered on Old Campus to send the crew team on its way. A brass band with a great bass drum played Yale fight songs including "Mother of Men, Old Yale" followed by "Bulldog, Bulldog Bow-Wow-Wow!" "Bingo, Eli Yale," one of the many Yale fight songs penned by Cole Porter from the Yale Class of 1913, drew a roar from the crowd:

> *Fight! Fight! Fight with all your might!*
> *For Bingo, Bingo, Eli Yale!*

Behind the band and the cheerleaders, Trubee and the rest of the thousands of parading students began marching out through Phelps Gate from Old Campus to the Adee Boathouse on the New Haven Harbor. Two motorized schooner yachts rested at anchor in the harbor's quiet Morris Cove, ready to welcome team members. As she had each June since her eldest son Averell came to Yale seven years earlier, Mary Harriman made her 187-foot, topsail steam schooner *Sultana* available to the Yale crew for the duration of its race preparations. On a blue flag, large enough to drape a small house, white lettering spelled out "YALE." The flag fluttered from the rear mast and a Yale pennant flew from the foremast. Stroke on this year's varsity crew, the Harrimans' youngest boy, Roland, planned to take a group of his Yale friends aboard the *Sultana* after The Race for a six-week cruise through the Caribbean and the Panama Canal, which had opened to traffic two summers earlier, and from there up the coast of Mexico and on to San Francisco.[11]

He, Al Sturtevant, the rest of the varsity A crew, along with Trubee Davison and the other heelers, would travel aboard the *Sultana* to New London.

An ardent yachtsman, Colonel C. L. F. Robinson, president of Hartford's massive Colt Firearms and a Yale Class of 1895 graduate, dispatched his sumptuous two-masted, 114-foot auxiliary schooner, the *Savarona*, from its mooring near his Newport cottage for the varsity B crew's use each spring.

According to newspaper reports, both ships boasted galleys capable of serving up gourmet meals for the hungry boys, plentiful staterooms, salons "more like the drawing room of a gentleman's house than that of a yacht," and crew enough to meet all their shipboard needs.[12]

Although the weather was not promising, the two yachts planned a slow cruise up the Long Island Sound through the night and the next day, dropping anchor seventy-five miles north of New Haven in the New London Harbor the following evening. From there launches would ferry the crews some four miles up the Thames River to Yale's Gales Ferry compound, the crew team's sprawling training quarters. At the same time, less than a mile downriver, the Harvard navy took up residence at its own training quarters, a whitewashed multibuilding compound called Red Top. Through the nation's newspapers and newsreels, sports fans could follow the two teams' every stroke, as well as their coaches' and prognosticators' reflections on their chances for The Race.

Yale coach Guy Nickalls, a famous Oxford University rower and the highest paid coach in any college sport, had raised expectations as high as possible before the season. "We have," he projected, "a foundation for the best crew that has ever rowed in America, England or anywhere."[13]

Yale had crushed Harvard the previous year and had several returning oarsmen besides Al Sturtevant. The Elis' fans had every reason to expect greatness. One hundred seventy-five candidates, "the physical flower of Yale," had fought for spots on the team. With such a turnout, *The New York Evening Post*'s crew reporter could see "no good reason for doubting the prospects of another successful season."[14]

So far, however, the predictions had proven wrong. Yale had yet to win a race. A victory over Harvard, however, would make fans forget the previous losses.

By 4:30, the *Sultana* and the *Savarona* had weighed anchor and were steaming out of the New Haven Harbor. The boys had set their gear in the cabins and returned topside. As the yachts sailed out past Lighthouse Point into the Sound's open waters, they studied the looming gray hull of the U.S. Navy's super dreadnought, the *Utah*.[15]

The previous year, she had joined the festivities in New London, serving as Secretary of the Navy Josephus Daniels's personal yacht while he attended The Race. She would not return there this year. With German U-boats marauding shipping between the United States and Europe, and American and Mexican forces skirmishing along the southern border, a dormant nation had begun to stir and looked toward bolstering its porous national defenses. The possibility of open warfare loomed large. The military hoped to inspire voluntary efforts by citizens and encourage support for greater national preparedness. The *Utah* had anchored at New Haven so that hundreds of her crew and officers could march in a preparedness parade set for the next day in Hartford.

The shoreline disappeared quickly as the yachts steamed out under leaden skies. Across the Sound, New York's Long Island, less than twelve miles distant, never came into sight through the low, thick clouds. Frothy green spray from the choppy sea swept over the bows. It was not only the bounding ship that made the young men on board feel queasy. With increasing talk of war, many worried that The Race might not be held at all.

The two massive pleasure yachts anchored in New London Harbor the next evening, the *Sultana* close to the railroad bridge over the Thames River, and the *Savarona* further out near the mouth of the harbor. (They would remain on hand until race day, taking the crew team cruising on rest days. Harvard's crew also kept two yachts, the *Gypsy* and the *Needle*, at their disposal in New London.) From the anchorage, the three Yale team launches, *Elihu Yale*, *Bingo*, and *Bulldog*, ferried the crew team and their accompanying support upriver over the course they would race three weeks hence, and on to Gales Ferry on the northern bank. Trubee had traveled back and forth the previous week readying the camps for their arrival. The heelers had set out the floating docks, given the boathouse a new whitewash, rigged shells, and hauled in ice, beer, and food. In their whites and blue blazers, the boys stepped onto the dock and climbed the grassy slope to the houses.

Although already dark out, Trubee raced ahead to begin setting up with the other waiters and heelers. He was ready for three weeks of grunt work. As the days went along, he would track almost every detail of the team's onshore life. The two varsity and one freshman boat practiced on the Thames in the company of coach Nickalls and his assistants in the launches. A tail of alumni and press trailed after them in other boats. They also kept a watchful eye on the Harvard crews practicing a mile downriver at Red Top. At Gales Ferry, the Old Blue, as alumni were known, gathered throughout the three weeks of training to inspect the crew team, in the boat and out, assessing their qualities, the clarity of their eye, the sturdiness of a handshake, their willingness to endure pain, like a breeder his thoroughbreds. One crew alumnus expressed the common sentiment "that in the boat and on the campus a fellow showed of what stuff he was made, that it marked him for future failure or success."[16]

Tended by the heelers, the crew athletes sat before the fire in the oak paneled Varsity House salon soaking in the atmosphere that, after more than thirty years of rowing on the Thames and half a century of The Race, was just beginning to feel ancient. Pictures of varsity crews extending back nearly to the first Harvard-Yale regatta lined the walls. A wall relief with a bust of George St. John Sheffield, a longtime supporter of Yale rowing from the Class of 1863, kept watch over the timeless scene. The brothers Harry and Payne Whitney would frequently join the boys and talk about the great teams and men of years gone by. The Whitney brothers, wealthy sportsmen and avid Yale supporters, spent so much time assisting the crew that they had built the handsome Coach's House next door to have a place where they could keep a steady watch over the team—and Nickalls—in comfort. (Each man also kept his own luxurious yacht, as well as their father's *Aphrodite*—which at 330 feet was then the world's longest steam yacht—moored at strategic viewing points along the river race course.) In the pre-Prohibition days, beer flowed freely. Trubee and the other heelers scurried to make sure the crew team, the coaches, and the Old Blue never went thirsty.[17]

With occasional breaks for cruises on the yachts, practice continued with daily pulls over the four-mile course. Yale's team that had struggled all year seemed to be at its peak. In the final days before The Race, the long string of poor weather finally broke. The clouds fled the sky; the sun shone down and glinted off the diamond-water river against the perspiration-drenched bodies of the straining oarsmen. Observers clocked both teams rowing near-record times in their course-length practice runs. "Given conditions anywhere nearly as favorable as the record-holding crew of 1888 had," predicted one newspaper, "either the Yale or Harvard crew of this season would easily clip the record."[18]

Trubee watched excitedly from shore as his friends Al Sturtevant, Cord Meyer, Seth Low, Bill Rockefeller, George Lawrence, Jr., and the president's son Morris Hadley—all of whom he knew from his prep school days at Groton— and the rest of the crew tuned up their boats to a peak that had eluded them all year. Rowing fans prepared for an epic contest.

Then, as feared, the regatta itself ran into the shoals.

CHAPTER 3

Gales Ferry, June 18–23, 1916

The Race

THE LOUDEST CRY RINGING OUT OVER THE THAMES RIVER WAS NO longer "Stroke!" but "War!" The wave of outrage felt in nearly every corner of America washed over the quiet reaches of the Thames. For the first time since the War of 1812, a foreign invader had attacked American soil and, for the first time in two decades, the United States faced the possibility of a major military conflict.

Hoping to stir up rebellion in Mexico, Doroteo Arango, a Mexican sharecropper's son known widely as Francisco "Pancho" Villa, headed a peasant army battling the Mexican government in the northern part of the country. Outraged by the United States' support for the shaky government of dictatorial President Venustiano Carranza and the American embargo of arms to his army of "Villistas," Villa began attacking Americans in Mexico in hopes of provoking a U.S. military intervention that would inflame his own popular support. On the morning of March 9, 1916, he and five hundred of his men attacked the 13th U.S. Cavalry in its sleep at Camp Furlong near Columbus, New Mexico. During the Villistas' retreat, they stopped to plunder the town, setting it afire. When the raiders finally rode off, fourteen American soldiers and ten civilians lay dead, and the town of Columbus smoldered in ruin.

Villa succeeded in stirring up the "gringos." American newspapers cried for his head. President Wilson appointed Brigadier General John J. "Black Jack" Pershing to lead a 4,800-man horseback brigade, supported by aircraft and motor vehicles (the first time either was used in U.S. land warfare) on the so-called "Punitive Expedition" into Mexico to capture Villa. The man for whom the description "ramrod erect" seemed to have been coined, Pershing was a decorated veteran of every post–Civil War military campaign. He had yet to experience frustration on the battlefield. Villa's brilliant guerilla tactics would change that.

Responding to an informant's tip in early June, Pershing's troops had assaulted the small village of Carrizal, thinking they would capture Villa there. Instead Villa had duped them. They found themselves battling Mexican national troops, not Villa's army. Villa was reported to have watched in delight as his two baffled enemies battled one another. Scores of Mexican soldiers were killed or wounded. The American attack provoked angry Mexican denunciations. Carranza threatened war and mobilized his forces. The situation led President Wilson to call up 75,000 National Guardsmen into federal service to police the U.S.-Mexico border. He also ordered sixteen warships to sail for Vera Cruz.[1]

With the Harvard-Yale race scheduled for the following Friday, the June 18 banner headline in the *New Haven Sunday Register* declared, "War with Mexico Seems Inevitable." Responding to President Wilson's request, the following day the Connecticut State National Guard ordered all members to report for duty immediately. Massachusetts also called up its guardsmen. That sent prospects for the Harvard-Yale race sinking.

At least one member of Harvard's crew and four members of the Yale crew packed their bags and prepared to leave training camp to report. Among those called up from Yale were team captain Low, Lawrence, and Hadley, all from the varsity A boat. Without them, Yale would be lost. With less than a week to go until Friday's race day, preparations for the regatta were put on hold.

Both the Yale camp at Gales Ferry and Harvard's at Red Top were in an uproar. Coach Nickalls at Yale and Harvard's Coach Robert Herrick had worked their crews to a pitch of readiness for Friday's races. New London merchants and hoteliers despaired. With every bed in town reserved, special trains scheduled, observation trains sold out, thousands of ship passages booked, yachts chartered, and tens of thousands of people, automobiles, and boats beginning to surge toward New London from around the nation, team representatives met to discuss what to do. They considered the possibility of starting the race that very day without spectators on hand. In the crisis, some suggested The Race should be cancelled altogether.

War was now on the horizon, not just on the southern border but across the globe, and many Americans were eager for a fight. That was true especially among college boys. For many, their champion was former President Theodore Roosevelt, who had been beating the drum for U.S. entry into the war in Europe and who lashed out at President Wilson, whom he called the "yellow" president. The previous spring, Colonel Roosevelt—as he was known since his Rough Rider days—had published a book arguing for American condemnation of the lawless German occupation of Belgium. He also warned that, without adequate preparation for the nation's defense, "New York and San Francisco would be seized and probably each would be destroyed," as had occurred in Belgium's most important cities. Nearing sixty, he assured his audiences that he and his four sons "would go to the front" in the event of war.[2]

As on most other college campuses, when it came to a fight Yale students found themselves at odds with the American majority. Most Yale students shared their parents' disdain for Roosevelt's economic populism, but they loved his proudly proclaimed patriotism, hearty manliness, and belligerently moralistic stance. In May, primarily on the strength of his bellicose pronouncements, Roosevelt won by a large margin over the leading presidential candidates, including Wilson, in a straw poll of students. After the vote, the *Yale Daily News* editorialized, "It is . . . gratifying that an overwhelming majority of these voters have declared themselves for the one candidate who stands preeminently for 'straight Americanism,' genuine military and civic preparedness and for restoring the United States to a position of honor and respect among the nations of the world."[3]

Some students like Trubee Davison had immediately taken a hardened position upon the outbreak of war in August 1914; a few students had even left campus to join the armies of one side or the other. A larger number enlisted in the New Haven regiment of the Connecticut National Guard and pushed to establish a militia force right on campus.

For most students, though, the war was an excuse for jawboning, arguing for or against one side or the other, for or against American participation. Stephen Vincent Benét, from the Class of 1919, found that most students supported the Central Powers or the Allies "not from reason but more from the fun of taking sides, a fun comparable to that of backing the Cubs against the Giants." The outcome of the war meant little more to them than did a baseball game. Their grandfathers were the last Americans to take up arms in large numbers for a major conflagration—the Civil War a half century ago. That was a time more distant to them than were the days when students arrived in New Haven by horse and buggy and memorized their Latin texts by gas lamplight.[4]

The first stirrings of preparedness were already being felt around the nation and on campuses, though. In the summer of 1915, the nation took tentative steps toward creation of a national reserve corps of officers with voluntary summer training camps in Burlington, Vermont; Plattsburgh, New York; and

Gettysburg and Tobyhanna, Pennsylvania. The men, including many college students, attending these so-called "millionaires' camps" paid their own way and bought their own uniforms, with the army providing tents, horses, guns, and officers to instruct the men in cavalry and artillery drills.

Returning to campus in fall 1915, few students, including those who had attended the millionaires' camps, bothered to concern themselves with the real war across the ocean. One freshman at the time recalled, "How comparatively small the war . . . appeared on our mental horizons."[5]

Most went on with their campus lives, oblivious, wrote Benét, "that each casual step taken was on earthquake-ground."[6]

A few prescient students did look ahead. Editors of the *Yale Daily News* had pushed throughout the past school year for students to ready themselves to enter the military should the need arise. One student found, with "the public opinion of the whole country . . . focused, as the rays from a converging mirror here at Yale," preparedness for country became another form of heeling for Yale.[7]

Yale President Hadley had been leading the call for student participation in the military. "There are two ways for a nation to become involved in an international controversy," he had told an alumni gathering during spring 1915. "One is to be too much prepared for war; the other is to be too little prepared. I believe we are in the latter boat."[8]

At Harvard, President A. Lawrence Lowell, too, admonished the nation that the British experience proved the need for many more officers "than our regular army and the militia can possibly supply."[9]

They decided their colleges should lead the way.

With no national reserve training force, Yale and Harvard established their own state National Guard regiments—affiliated militias to begin training students. Harvard students swelled the ranks of the 8th Regiment of the Massachusetts National Guard in Cambridge. Students at Yale brought the same parade-ground fervor to preparedness that they did to rooting for sports teams. With President Hadley's encouragement, a first announcement went out in the fall of 1915 for students to join the newly forming Yale Battery of the Connecticut National Guard. The State hoped to muster at least 135 members. *Nine hundred fifty* heelers showed up the first day. The state limited each company to just under five hundred men, so those on the waiting list drilled with broomsticks and lumber alongside their enrolled schoolmates several times each week, and practiced artillery on the Yale athletic fields. They also performed calisthenics on Old Campus, attended classes in military theory, battlefield tactics, and weaponry, and paraded proudly through the streets of New Haven. A New

Haven newspaper reported, "Not since 1898 when President McKinley called for volunteers has such a martial spirit prevailed in New Haven."[10]

The army and navy pressed for Yale recruits for its summer camps. On June 1, Major-General Leonard Wood, the army's most highly decorated officer and its former Chief of Staff under President Taft, had spoken to 2,500 students at a preparedness rally held in the campus' Woolsey Hall. The students revered Wood. A physician by training, he had received the Medal of Honor for his service during the Indian Wars of the 1880s. During the Spanish-American War he served as commander of the famed Rough Riders, the First Volunteer Cavalry, with Colonel Roosevelt as his second-in-command. "At the present time," he warned, "the country is woefully unprepared to resist a great power." He appealed to the students' sense of democracy and duty. "The obligation to defend the country rests on everyone. The foundation stone of this democracy is equality of opportunity and privilege, and this equality enjoins also equality of obligation." One obligation was preparing for "sacrifice" in time of war.

He brought the crowd roaring to its feet. "Have you nothing to defend!" he shouted. "Surely those who believe in the defense of liberty, so dearly bought by our forefathers, in defense of religion, of principles and of family, cannot have any but one opinion on the subject." Students came from the class "that the country looks to produce the officers necessary to make any body of troops efficient." That nation was now calling on them to ready themselves for leadership.

At the end of the rousing meeting, Professor Hiram Bingham III, an 1898 graduate of the college who had led the Yale- and National Geographic Society–sponsored expedition five years earlier that had "discovered" the "lost city of the Incas"—Machu Picchu—jumped up on stage. He shouted out to the wildly cheering students that he would personally give an engraved silver loving cup, "valued at one hundred dollars," to the class enrolling the most members in military training.[11]

When Wilson called the nation's militias to arms in response to the Mexican crisis two-and-a-half weeks later, students traded their woolen suits and spats for khakis and puttees. The *New York Tribune* reported that Yale's campus was "an armed camp," and observed, "The spirit of 1860 stalked on the Yale campus today." An entire alumni class returned to campus for their reunion dressed in military uniform and set up a military-style encampment on the Yale athletic fields for the duration of the reunions.[12] Large numbers of students planned to pick up their diplomas and head straight into the military.

At the June 21 graduation ceremony, the pomp and circumstance that, as usual, marked a Yale commencement stood out from previous years. The 216th commencement, reported the *Tribune*, was "rendered strange" by the presence of so many young men in uniform. Not since the Civil War had Yale graduates appeared uniformed in the commencement procession.[13] If war came to the U.S. border, Yale and other college men were ready to lead the charge.

While students on campus readied for the possibility of war, the oarsmen and their supporters at Gales Ferry were marooned on the verdant riverside croquet lawn and floating docks and in boats skimming over the Thames tidal flow. The outside world provided few distractions until word of possible war reached even the sequestered oarsmen. They may have rowed hard while on the water, but from the training table to the docks, the talk was of war. "It could never be said that the race with Harvard was forgotten," Trubee Davison recalled, "but it did lose magnitude as the prospect of war with Mexico loomed larger."[14]

Trubee pulled some of the heelers and crew team members aside. He knew about war firsthand. Although he was still just a sophomore and not even an oarsman, they listened to what the popular heeler had to say. Like many Ivy Leaguers and other well-off young men, he had spent the previous summer as a uniformed volunteer on an ambulance crew in Paris. He helped in carrying the endless stream of wounded men off the long trains from the front and then driving them in the open-frame "birdcage" ambulances to the American hospital outside Paris. He was among the few Americans who had witnessed the war's terrible toll in ruined men coming off the trains. "While my firing line in front was Paris and nothing else," Trubee said of his previous summer's service, "I at least saw enough of the fellows over there who were actually in the service."[15]

He cared deeply about the Allies' cause. After his return to Yale the previous fall, Colonel Roosevelt had sent him a personal note praising him for "showing that Americans are really willing to do something practical to help those who are battling bravely for their homes and for high ideals."[16]

Trubee felt he had not done nearly enough. He planned to return to France. This time he intended to be where the action was. "Possessed," said his friends, "of a courage that was almost reckless," he had been raising money and organizing volunteers for his own ambulance service he planned to set up in the Vosges region of the Western Front.[17] There he would be in the real line of fire. His dormitory room had served as the campus headquarters for the ambulance program. His younger brother, Harry, near completion of his final year at Groton School, would be coming as well.

While the sophomore Trubee served up the crew team their beer at Gales Ferry, even the seniors on the team wanted to know what he had seen over in France. The boys gathered around him in the Crew House salon to listen to his tales. They were especially keen to learn about the most exotic new form of war-making that had been gaining so much attention: aviation. Trubee had much news to share.

During the previous summer's ocean crossing, Trubee had traveled in the company of Robert Bacon, a Harvard classmate of Colonel Roosevelt, former Morgan partner and past ambassador to France. Bacon had come out early in support of the Allies. In Paris, he helped organize the American Ambulance Field Service for which Trubee and other college boys volunteered. That 1915 summer in Paris, two younger Harvard graduates—Norman Prince, a student pilot who came to Paris for the express purpose of forming a volunteer aviation squadron composed of Americans, and Victor Chapman, a graduate student in Paris when the war broke out—along with William Thaw, a Yale student from a wealthy Pittsburgh railroading family, had approached Bacon and other wealthy Americans in Paris. They had volunteered in the French Foreign Legion, but their idea now was to form an all-American aerial squadron. They sought Bacon's help organizing and underwriting it. Their *Escadrille Americaine* had finally materialized in April 1916. After German complaints about the violation of U.S. neutral status, the squadron was renamed the Lafayette Escadrille. Their exploits quickly became celebrated throughout the United States. Over the ocean, a nation was swept up with the romance of these "knights of the air."[18] Trubee shared the common passion for the miraculous new world of motorized flight.[19]

Flyers in the war typically came from the aristocratic families of Europe and, unlike the trenches below where men by the thousands simply disappeared each day, the "knights of the air" fought in single combat, jousting in the sky before vast audiences on the ground. Moreover, as the industrial world continued to mechanize warfare, the future of flight was virtually limitless.

"That put the bug in my bonnet," said Trubee. "If we ever got into the war, where I personally wanted to be was in the air service." Back at Yale the previous fall, Trubee had shared the notion of going into aviation with Bob Lovett. Neither knew anything at all about the reality of flying, but both agreed that, if called to fight, the sky was the place for young men like them to enter the fray.[20]

Bob Lovett seemed in many ways an improbable comrade-at-arms for such a warrior enterprise. Along with his disdain for exercise, the rail-thin Lovett was already suffering stomach problems that would plague him throughout his life. Unlike the boisterous Trubee, he cloaked himself in a mantle of gentlemanly reserve around all but his closest friends. Lovett was also regarded as a genius on a campus where brawn counted for more than brains. Shy and rarely caught smiling, some took him for a patrician snob. A quick study with a cautious, analytic mind and photographic memory, Lovett eased past classmates' questions about his campus status through his social grace and gallant ways. Born in the malarial railroad town of Houston before the discovery of oil set off its explosive growth, the young Bob was the pride of his ambitious parents who carefully nurtured their only child's many gifts.

His genteel, Alabama-born mother, Lavinia Abercrombie, counted Confederate military leaders among her relatives and maintained an antebellum courtliness in her home that found favor in New York high society. Along with their East Side apartment, the Lovetts built one of Long Island's most elegant Gold Coast estates, Woodfold, a short drive from the Davison place at Peacock Point. Lovett's mother expected her child growing up in the Yankee city to sustain his family's heritage in which personal honor, civility, and love of country were as closely intertwined as the ivy clinging to the brick and stone walls of their Long Island mansion. Young Bob's mother, college-educated and a former school teacher, encouraged her son to read widely, especially books that recounted the glories of the days of chivalry.

In later years, Lovett credited his father with doing more to shape his outlook on life and intellect than any formal schooling. Even when his son was a mere schoolboy, Judge Lovett had focused on developing his mental acuity. He began training his memory early on by asking for detailed reports about the things the young Bob had observed during his daily bicycle rides home from Hamilton Military Institute, his New York City grade school military academy. Father would trail son home in a carriage and then ply him with questions. The carts hauling steel girders for construction of the new midtown Manhattan buildings were favorite quiz topics. "How many horses were pulling the cart?" he asked. "How many steel girders were in the cart?" As his son grew, the observation game intensified. "How were the horses hitched to the cart?" A correct description earned him a quarter while a slip cost him the same. As an adult, Lovett's total-recall capacity became legendary. His father had abandoned his fundamentalist upbringing—and his son, too, had no interest in formal religion—but expected that Bob would follow a religiously inspired sense of duty and character and comport himself, even in his thoughts, as a "Christian gentleman."21

At Yale, the judge's son won many admirers among classmates and faculty members. Yale academics, however, rarely tested him. As a freshman, after his Latin instructor became ill during Christmas break, Bob taught the class for the rest of the year. Like most Yale students, he found more reward in heeling. He competed for election as manager of the Dramat, the student acting company. His Shakespearean wit, on stage and off, also won him a following among the campus literary set and an invitation to join them for afternoon tea and the smoking of clay pipes at the Elizabethan Club. The recently founded "Lizzie"

was a campus clubhouse in an eccentric colonial building that boasted posses-
sion of a collection of priceless First Folios of the works of Shakespeare and first
editions by other English authors, portraits of British royals on the walls, and
other anglophile adornments throughout. There, young men and professors de-
bated the merits of the great authors and the latest offerings in the *Lit* and the
Yale Review.

Yale's beloved Shakespeare professor William Lyon Phelps wrote in the Class
of 1918's *History* that among his chief regrets, as the four hundred-plus members of the class departed campus, was never having gotten to know this brilliant student personally. Few ever did. Still, before leaving campus, Lovett
would win classmates' votes for the "hardest working," "most thorough gentleman," and "most brilliant" member of their Yale class.[22]

Despite his aversion to exercise, Lovett was physically coordinated—a gym-
nast during his prep school days—and showed a flinty and even daredevil side
from time to time. Although he wore tailored silk shirts, he still loved pulling
apart all kinds of engines and speeding in his own rattletrap Hudson over the
back roads of Long Island. He enjoyed any machine that could move fast. He
went racing on a rented motorcycle through the mountain passes of Switzerland the past summer of 1915, until he had skidded to the ground on fresh tar
outside St. Moritz. The encounter with the pavement left him "a terrible
mess," recalled his friend since boyhood, Roland Harriman, his companion for
the trip.[23]

That rare combination of a gentlemanly exterior, brilliant and dexterous
mind, and hidden risk-taking toughness made Lovett the right man for Trubee
to share his air-warrior dreams with after his 1915 summer in Europe: "I picked
out Bob Lovett and poured it into his ear." The nineteen-year-olds made "a sort
of compact" that if war came they would somehow find a way to go into aviation. "That was the life." Neither really knew what that might entail, "because
. . . there really wasn't any [air service in the United States] that amounted to a
row of beans," but both knew that above, and not inside, the trenches was the
place they wanted to fight in Europe.[24]

They were not alone. Several Yale crew team members had already found
their way into the new sport of flying. Some on hand could recall the excitement of the crowds witnessing the first flight over the Thames River course
made five years earlier by pioneer aviator H. N. Atwood. Team leader Cord
Meyer had soloed even before coming to Yale at an aviation school in Mineola,
Long Island. "Altogether there was an aviation atmosphere at camp," said Allan "Alphie" Ames, another crew team heeler on hand at Gales Ferry who listened in as Trubee talked about the air service in Europe.[25]

As little as they knew about military aviation, they understood that the United States was woefully ill prepared to enter any battlefield in which aircraft flew overhead. The Army Signal Corps Aviation Service only possessed a few crude aircraft. Assigned to support Pershing during the Mexican "Punitive" campaign, the First Aero Squadron was equipped with six Curtiss JN–2 "Jennies." Pershing, who was never reported to have set foot in an airplane in his life, knew nearly nothing about aircraft operations and maintenance. He charged forth into the desert with his air support and after barely a month had lost all six of his planes to mechanical failure and crashes.

Several of the heelers and oarsmen on hand at Gales Ferry thought a summer spent learning to fly would be a bold stroke for national preparedness—not to mention good fun and sport. Several ideas for ways to go about it popped up. Pleased to support the boys' interest in aviation, Harry Whitney offered to put up a few of them at his estate on Long Island that summer while they learned to fly land machines. The three leaders of the crew team, Sturtevant, Low, and Meyer, took him up on his offer.

Trubee and the others weighed their own options, including joining the Yale Battery for the Mexican border war call-up. Trubee's focus was on the war in Europe. The Mexican outbreak had brought the country to a boil, but seemed minor in comparison. The U.S. military could handle a border war with its weakly governed and impoverished southern neighbor. A far better equipped potential enemy loomed. With the government unable or unwilling to recognize the growing importance of aviation, that was a battlefield where Trubee might contribute. It was an era in which state militias dominated military preparedness and privately funded and armed battalions still mustered when called as they had since colonial days. Although he was barely out of his teen years, when it came to aviation he could pick up the slack. It was a brazen move for a college sophomore, but he could see no better way to fulfill the clarion call of "for God, for country and for Yale" than by taking on the task of building an American air force. The United States had few machines and fewer aviators. In any crisis the nation would not be prepared in aviation. Far-seeing men recognized that aviation would become a determinative force on the battlefield. "Here," said his classmate John Vorys, "was a place where he could help."[26]

Aviation also offered the last open frontier in the latest chapter of America's self-proclaimed manifest destiny to explore and conquer. The planet's surface had been sailed, trekked, explored, mapped, and settled, from pole to pole and deep into its remotest reaches. The opening of America itself was now complete. Thanks to the work of the boys' own fathers and others in their generation, the continental frontier had been pushed to its limit. The American empire now straddled the Caribbean and the Pacific, reached Alaska in the far north, and possessed a passage from sea to sea through Panama. With American railroads crisscrossing the land, auto roads extending farther and farther out into the wilds, and ships plying the seas, the sky was the last place left for a young man to look to fulfill his dreams of conquest. Trubee thought he could serve his country best by gathering his friends into a private aerial militia. Together they would extend the age of exploration into a new, still largely uncharted dimension. For an aristocratic young man of the age, aviation offered a last chance to lead, to serve, and to explore where few before him had dared. Trubee's friends shared his excitement. His Long Island neighbors Alphie Ames and Erl Gould, heelers at Gales Ferry, were ready to sign up for Trubee's aerial summer camp.

Instead of returning to France to form the new ambulance service or joining the river of Yalies flooding into the Yale Battery or one of the growing numbers of the official army and navy summer training camps, Trubee put his pact with Bob Lovett into action. He telephoned Bob, who had already returned home for the summer, and asked him to drive to Mineola, where the New York National Guard maintained an aerial militia service. Pioneering aircraft builder Glenn Curtiss and others had turned the airfield into the country's leading center for aeronautics. What he found should have indicated the woeful state of affairs they were facing. In Europe, the age of the fast scout and the huge, multi-engine bomber had already begun. America's foremost aviation facilities were rudimentary, with only two primitive working airplanes. One was an original Wright-type, open box kite with warping wings and bamboo spars. Chains drove its two pusher propellers from one motor. The elevators sat in front of the exposed seats of the pilot and passenger. A glaring opportunity to do more presented itself. "I don't know what Bob did over there except look at things," Trubee would later laugh at their boyish pretensions, "but he looked and he was always pretty good at that." With Lovett's report in hand, Trubee began to formulate his plan in earnest.[27]

He called his mother, Kate Trubee Davison, the family's strong-willed matriarch. Aghast at the thought of her son taking to the air, she raced over to New London to nip the idea in the bud. "Flying," she scolded, "was but one step removed from death." Trubee argued that rather than enter the Yale Battery and head to the Mexican border or return to France, he could make a greater contribution to national defense by leading the way toward the creation of a civilian aerial reserve force in anticipation of the nation's likely needs should it enter the war in Europe. His mother was more than skeptical. She did not need to lose her boy to what she believed to be "spectacular suicide" in "the most dangerous avocation on earth."[28]

Trubee argued back. His persistence began to wear her down. After a long talk, she returned to the family house at Peacock Point on Long Island ready to consider the summer's possibilities for her son and his friends. First she would need to consult with her husband. Trubee's father knew much more about the reality of flying and war. At the moment, he was in Labrador, Canada, salmon fishing. When his wife's telegram reached him, he cabled back bluntly: "Have you all gone crazy?" Keep the boys away from all aircraft, he commanded, and await his return before doing anything.[29]

Before then, there was a race to be rowed—or not. The departure of the National Guard members of the Yale and Harvard crews was imminent. The teams decided to face off on the morning of June 20, with no crowds but the few score heelers and alumni boosters on hand. Presidents Hadley and Lowell appealed to their respective state governors for a delay in the call up of their crew team members. Before the starting gun fired, the governors' offices called: the team members were granted leaves of absence through Race Day.[30]

The traditional afternoon starts for the freshman and varsity B races would be moved up to the morning to ensure that the varsity A race would have plenty of time to be run in the afternoon, if river conditions were questionable. With just three days remaining until Race Day, the Harvard and Yale crew teams began their final, feverish preparations.

For the Yale crew team, the tallies of two important votes had first to be announced. The members gathered in the Varsity House and emerged shortly to inform Cord Meyer that he would captain the team the following year. They then turned to Trubee. He had won election as next year's assistant manager, automatic steppingstone to managing the team his senior year. In the customary initiation, team members picked the fully clothed Trubee up and carried him by the arms and legs down the lawn to the float from which they heaved him into the river.[31]

An elated Trubee climbed back up, drenched, onto the dock amid his cheering team. He had proven his sand. His place in the Yale hierarchy was secure.

With just hours remaining until the starting gun fired, all attention turned to The Race. Alumni streamed into the camps and urged on their young brethren. New London townspeople hung crimson and blue bunting and Harvard and Yale flags in their store windows and homes. On the eve of the regatta, desperate late arrivals crowded the hotel desks hoping for any available room while hotel proprietors ransacked their storage closets for cots to set up in the halls and revised prices on the menu cards upward.[32]

"Overnight indications," the *New York Tribune* reported, "are that many visitors will sleep picturesquely but uncomfortably around the docks. The hotels reserved even the last billiard tables many days ago."[33] Once again the town would overflow with race fans and the thousands of others out to enjoy the gala day's festive bedlam.

The night before Race Day, at Gales Ferry and Red Top the boys, coaches, and alumni—more than one hundred men in each compound—gathered to make speeches, toast their teams, and urge them to give it their all for their schools and for each other. Al Sturtevant went around to his teammates. He had never lost a race against Harvard and told them he had stayed at Yale an extra year to win it one more time.

Downstream in New London, a glittery and colorful scene unfolded. More than two thousand cheering and singing Yale rooters poured out onto the town docks from each of the rusty steamers, the *Chapin* and the *Richard Peck*, wheezing up the Sound from New Haven. In record numbers, private yachts sailed into the harbor, stretching for several miles at anchor and presenting, in the sweet first night of summer, wrote the *New York Times*, "a magnificent spectacle, the anchor lights sparkling and reflecting on the water's surface in every direction." Among the line of boats was Jack Morgan's "big ebony-hued floating palace," the 302-foot-long *Corsair II* with its seventy-man crew. As he did each year, the Harvard graduate brought a large, festive party from New York with him.

Before dawn, another fifty yachts had already passed through the railroad drawbridge to drop anchor at choice spots along the course.[34]

A line of tenders ran in and out from the docks like taxis at a train station shuttling people from the yachts into town where, according to news reports, "yachtsmen in natty uniforms, with rich dressed women, soldiers in khaki garb, sailors from the sub base, and highly decorated college students mingled with the more sedate and conservative pedestrians throughout the city." With many students set to report for military duty, those in uniform found "great favor with the hosts of pretty girls and matrons."[35]

A hot sun rose over New London on Race Day beneath crystal clear skies. "A finer day for a boat race could not be imagined," the *Times* reported. Crowds continued to pour into town by special train, automobile, and excursion boat throughout the day. An estimated fifty thousand people were on hand by the afternoon. Special duty police officers from New York, Boston, Providence, and New Haven struggled to keep the crowds under control. Detectives stationed about the city collared "suspicious characters," putting them in the city jail to wait out the day, although none was ever actually charged. Boosters from both sides with faces painted in school colors paraded through the streets, many marching under the banner of their graduating classes. With the town "jammed as it has never been before," it was nearly impossible to cross State Street, the main thoroughfare out to the racecourse. Police tried in vain to handle the massive traffic jam. It did not help that "pretty girls, resplendent in summer finery, were everywhere."[36]

The day's races would be rowed downstream, starting two miles upriver from the navy's submarine base and finishing one hundred yards short of the closed railroad drawbridge at New London. Harvard gave notice quickly that it came prepared to win. In the morning, the Crimson squeaked out narrow victories in the first two races, the two-mile freshmen race by just one-third of a boat-length and the three-mile second varsity race by a length. Bolstered by the morning's results, Harvard fans went running through the streets singing, "Oh, who's going to bet on Yale?" Goaded by the Harvard rooters, many Yale supporters responded, and soon "every odd dollar in the town was put up in wagers."[37]

The last of the largest flotilla of pleasure craft yet to witness a Harvard-Yale Boat Race—crimson or blue flags flying from their masts, colorful pennants suspended from their rigging—steamed under the raised drawbridge in the late afternoon. With so many boats lining the course, spectators standing on the shoreline would barely be able to catch a glimpse of the two shells' progress between the walls of yachts. Speculators scalped tickets at double their six-dollar face value for the two sold-out observation trains. Each pulled more than a quarter-mile of flatbed railway cars with covered four-tier grandstands set up on top, and ran along the opposing banks of the river for the length of the four-mile course. Black minstrels played ragtime music on banjos and mandolins at trackside, while a quartet dressed in blue and yellow costumes "did a land office business" playing for the crowds scurrying to find their seats among the seventy-six cars of the two observation trains. Tens of thousands of people who had not secured a place on the observation trains or on one of the boats lining the course squeezed in along the riverbanks next to the bridge or walked onto the abutments of a new auto bridge being built over the Thames. From there they would have a clear view of the finish line.

With the solstice sun still high in the sky, at five o'clock Jack Morgan descended from a tender, with a dozen striking young women and men who were staying with him on the *Corsair*, to board the observation train on the east bank of the river. He delayed the train's scheduled departure as his entourage stopped to shake hands reaching out to them from the other observation cars. Both trains were loaded to capacity as they finally chugged out to the starting flag at Bartlett's Cove near Red Top. The two schools' rooters kept up a steady competitive cheering as the trains crawled along.

On the river, conditions were ripe for a fast race. The water's surface was mirror smooth, the tide running out with a steady downstream breeze. Those sitting on the east bank train shaded their eyes against the glare of the hot sun in the west.

The crowds cheered each stroke as the Harvard crew left its float at Red Top and slowly paddled over to the starting flag. A roar went up as the Yale eight came down to the mark from Gales Ferry. The rippling muscles worked within the oarsmen's broad bronzed backs and shoulders as they bent forward and slid back in steady unison. Yale's blue and white- and Harvard's crimson and white-tipped oars rose and fell like synchronized pistons, slicing into the glassy river with a sun-flecked splash. The shells' wakes unfolded behind them in a spreading crease as they slid to the starting mark. The *New York Times* reporter exulted, "There has probably never been a more picturesque regatta in America than the one which afforded today's spectacle."

An official spoke briefly to the crews; the crowds along the banks grew silent. Steam-release hissed out of the locomotive pistons. At 5:51, the starter's gun cracked, the train engineers pulled their whistle cords and blasted out a full-throated roar audible four miles away at the finish line. The two shells shot to life. Cheers exploded from the spectators.

Coach Nickalls had hoped to capture a quick lead that would force the Harvard eight to exhaust itself early trying to catch up. Yale flew out ahead. The onlookers marveled as the braids of muscle and flesh tightened and loosened in unison up and down the backbones of the oarsmen. They swayed and rocked over the glassy water in perfect reciprocal motion. The Eli lead did not last long. At an eighth of a mile, Harvard drew even and then steadily advanced. More telling for those counting strokes, Harvard had taken the lead despite rowing a slower stroke pace.[38]

At the mile mark, Harvard, maintaining its clockwork stroke, had moved three-quarters of a length ahead. The Yale crowd in the trains that crawled along with the advance of the shells shouted, "Hold 'em, Yale!" but, wrote the *New York Times*, "Yale couldn't hold 'em."

After the mile flag, Yale coxswain Thomas Lasher ordered his eight oarsmen to pick up their already muscle-searing pace. Yale cut into Harvard's lead, bringing Yale partisans in the trains jumping back to their feet. The prow of Yale's boat drew nearly even with Harvard's, but the effort proved too much. The Eli boat began to tail off its rival until a gap of nearly four lengths opened. The race became a procession down the widening river, with neither side giving way, but Yale unable to pull back into the race. As they entered the lane of boats lining the last mile of the course, every yacht on the river pulled its whistle, "and such a tooting and screeching resounded as has never before marked the last mile of a race here." As each shell swept through the bedlam, successive, shore-shaking cannons boomed from its supporters' boats. Race fans' clashing cheers echoed back and forth across the broad river and mixed in with the caterwauling horns and sirens. The cacophony of noise kept rising to a crescendo as the shells swept into the crowds packing the shores and bridge abutments near the finish line.

The end in sight, a desperate Lasher called out above the howling noise to the taut red faces in front of him to lift their already sinew-snapping stroke count still higher. Ahead Harvard continued to row machinelike, driving forward at the same unvarying, pendular pace. Flashing across the line, the Crimson eight seemed fresh enough to row another four miles. Fifteen seconds later, three boat lengths back, the Yale eight shot past the finish line.

A timer called out twenty minutes and two seconds as the Harvard time. The disbelieving crowd let out a scream. Grown men hugged and danced. The Harvard oarsmen cheered and slapped each other on the back when they realized that they had smashed Yale's seemingly unbreakable, twenty-eight-year-old course record by eight seconds. In losing, Yale had rowed the third-fastest time in the history of the New London race. No matter. Exhausted, despondent, the Eli oarsmen let their oars fall, dropped their heads, and slumped back as the shell, oar blades dragging, disappeared under the arches of the drawbridge. Spent, Sturtevant fell over his oar unconscious. Teammates splashed water on his face to revive him. A continuous roar from thousands of delirious Harvard fans, along with the crowing steam whistles, blatting air horns, blasting cannons, and blaring sirens on the yachts, resonated in the air.

Harvard owned New London. "Thames Is Dyed Red," a New Haven newspaper's front-page headline declared the next morning.[39]

After fifty meetings, the historic series stood tied at twenty-five victories apiece. Dejected Yale fans shuffled back to their waiting ships, trains, automobiles, and yachts. Harvard rooters stayed on, snake dancing through the city. "Gray-haired, dignified old Harvard graduates," proclaimed the *New York Times*, "tonight are parading the streets locked arm-in-arm. Cambridge students are chanting the triumph of Harvard to the skies."[40]

For the Harvard and Yale crew team members who had to report for National Guard duty early the next morning, there was little time to reflect on the day's events, to savor victory or mourn defeat. While they hurried to depart for possible deployment along the southern border, almost at the same moment an ocean away, the British military fired the first shell of a week's continuous bombardment of the German lines in preparation for the launch of its planned massive breakout-assault along the River Somme in northern France. At dawn on the morning of July 1, an hour-long barrage sent nearly a quarter-million high explosives into the German positions—a shelling so intense that the faint flow of thunder could be heard in London 100 miles away. After the barrage lifted, 120,000 Allied troops went over the top of their trenches along a 25-mile front. By mid-day, mostly in the first few minutes of the attack, nearly 20,000 British troops and 1,000 officers lay dead in No Man's Land, along with more than 35,000 seriously wounded. Most were mown down like meadow grass by the raking fire of German machine guns that had remained protected from the hellacious British shelling within their armored emplacements. The attack continued. By the end of the big push five months later, together the French, British, and Germans had tallied some 1.3 million casualties. Their lines had barely shifted.[41]

The battle marked Britain's first sustained, coordinated aerial support for an attack. The results were dismaying. The Royal Flying Corps (RFC) started the battle with 410 airplanes and 426 pilots. By the end of the five months of carnage, 782 British planes had been lost and 499 aviators killed. With an attrition rate more than 100 percent, the average pilot at the front lasted around three weeks.[42]

After The Race, Trubee Davison had much on his mind. He returned to Gales Ferry and helped close up the compound in anticipation of the crew team's return next year. Little did he realize that he had witnessed the last time The Race would be rowed for three years. Several of those on hand that day would never return.

CHAPTER 4

Peacock Point, July 1916

Converted

AFTER THE SCHOOL YEAR AND CREW SEASON CONCLUDED, TRUBEE Davison returned to Long Island where he and Bob Lovett put together a list of their friends who they thought might prove right for their summer flying adventure. Trubee's mother was still convinced that flying was about the fastest way for a brave young fool to die, but she never completely discounted her son's ideas. She turned to an expert and invited family friend John Hayes Hammond, Jr., to meet with her at Peacock Point, the Davisons' fifty-seven-acre estate, with its sprawling Georgian mansion overlooking the Sound. The 1910 Yale engineering graduate had won fame—and boosted his family's already considerable fortune—with his inventions for radio and wireless remote-control devices, including pilotless ships and torpedoes. An amateur pilot, he hoped to see his wireless telegraphy systems carried aloft in airplanes. As a governor of the Aero Club of America, a group of wealthy sportsmen who had banded together to promote flight and license pilots, Hammond was pushing the United States to beef up military aviation preparedness.

Mrs. Davison sat with Hammond and the boys in the great room overlooking the Sound. Hammond expressed his wholehearted support for the boys' flying ambitions. He described the advanced state of modern aviation and its backward status in the land of its invention. Since the outbreak of war, European air forces had surged ahead of America in industrial output and training, numbers of pilots and aircraft, aviation and weaponry technology, and development of flying tactics.[1]

Turning its back on aviation except for experimental purposes, American military forces operated almost entirely in two-dimensional space, barely aware of the dawning of warfare from above. One high-level review by the navy declared that at this point, "the aeroplane was a toy."[2]

The army was no better off. Including the American pilots from the Lafayette Escadrille, the army could count on a grand total of twenty-six qualified aviators. The National Advisory Committee for Aeronautics reported that the army's Air Service Section of the Signal Corps—the army air force—possessed a rickety fleet of fifty-five training aircraft of which "fifty-one were obsolete and the other four obsolescent"; most were grounded in any case for lack of flying funds.[3]

The government, Trubee told his mother, was "asleep at the switch."[4]

Hammond concurred. Enthusiast groups like the Aero Club had stepped into the breach where they could. The Aero Club had solicited private donations for a fund to train civilian pilots and acquire reserve airplanes for the navy and army. When the Aero Club announced creation of the fund, Hammond and the other governors issued a statement laying out the present primitive conditions of American military aviation, saying, "The U.S. Army and Navy have, together, less than twenty aeroplanes available. Only half a dozen of the licensed aviators of the United States have made flights of more than fifty miles, and none know even the rudiments of military aeronautical requirements. Our army, navy, national guard, and naval militia have had no experience in handling aircraft operating with them."

They sounded an alarm: "If England with 3,000 aeroplanes and aviators and the output of 18,000 men cannot supply sufficient aeroplanes for its forces—what could Uncle Sam—who has less than a score of aeroplanes—do in case of immediate need?"[5]

Federal law, however, forbade the military from accepting private funds, so the Secretary of the Navy, Josephus Daniels, urged the club to focus on building up state militias.

If little ready to accept aircraft as a part of a modern military, the navy seemed more farsighted—at least in its public statements. Already in 1914, Daniels had announced that "aircraft must form a large part of our naval force for offensive and defensive operations."[6]

However, he refused to put his department's money where his mouth was; the navy had yet to spend more than $10,000 in a year on aviation, barely the price of a single military aircraft with nothing left over for operation or training. Without private efforts to bolster aviation preparedness like the one Trubee and Bob contemplated, Hammond told Mrs. Davison that Uncle Sam would be lost.

The Aero Club had a plan. With Germany threatening U.S. shipping, Henry Woodhouse, also a governor of the Aero Club, and the navy rear admiral and famed North Pole explorer Robert E. Peary had discussed ways of protecting America's weakly defended Eastern seaboard and its vital shipping lanes. Slow-moving navy patrols could easily miss even large enemy warships slipping into the thousands of miles of coastline, let alone submersibles. In theory airborne patrols offered a means of spotting enemy vessels over far greater distances than ships. However, few people within the U.S. military establishment could testify to the benefits of aircraft from practical experience. In fact, in view of the perceived danger of flying, Congress in its Naval Appropriations Act of 1914 stipulated that no high-ranking officer was even permitted to fly.[7]

Admiral Peary headed the National Aerial Coast Patrol Commission, a group including Hammond that promoted the idea of establishing a string of air stations to monitor the nation's meagerly defended coastline. The commission called for bases set about one hundred miles apart, closer together at strategic points, to consist of four seaplanes, with crew. The patrol stations would be interspersed with larger squadrons of as many as two hundred airplanes kept in ready to attack an encroaching enemy ship or fleet. Hammond's wireless telegraphs would be installed in the patrolling aircraft from which signals could be relayed to the ground and then telephoned on to the larger bases when enemy activity was sighted.

Peary campaigned around the country for the aerial picket line concept. He dramatically called for "such a fleet of aeroplanes as could in an emergency rise from our shores literally like a flock of seagulls to defend and ensure our national integrity."[8]

His vision extended beyond an active coastal defensive cordon to the creation of a reserve cadre of trained pilots ready to step forward in a crisis and, eventually, a Cabinet-level air defense department fully equal to the U.S. Navy and Army. He declared, "We need a broad plan for the formation and development of air service and system for the country, and we need, just as rapidly as it can be formed, an aviator class throughout the country similar to our present chauffeur class."[9]

Peary's hopes for aviation seemed ambitious beyond imagining to most regular military men. At the time, the entire navy aviation fleet consisted of six airplanes, two assigned to the battleship USS *North Carolina* and four to the Naval Aeronautic Station in Pensacola, Florida, the navy's sole aircraft base. The navy had less than forty pilots it considered qualified and even fewer mechanics who knew how to keep the bulky aircraft aloft.

Mrs. Davison invited the Aero Club's Woodhouse out to Peacock Point. He, too, was elated to learn about Trubee's plan for a summer flying school. The boys' brimming desire to fly in preparation for possible military need fit neatly into the club's own coast patrol program. The boys could serve as a vanguard militia squadron and as a model for the creation of a naval air reserve corps, then being considered in Congress. Woodhouse, Trubee recalled, "gave us an earful," describing the limitless horizon for the young men. For the wide-eyed boys, Woodhouse's linkage of their half-baked scheme cooked up among themselves at Gales Ferry to a national aerial defense cordon and, beyond that, to a congressional-level military preparedness project seemed wildly exciting, big and bold. They "were the great experimenters," proclaimed Woodhouse. They had "heard the call."

Just as important as their specific work, they would serve as an example that, Woodhouse insisted, "Every young man throughout the country would follow." Flying would become the most desirable service.[10]

Woodhouse was not above inflating the truth. He claimed to have government backing at the highest level for his plan. "All we had to do was to say we were for it, and the government would gobble us up like wildfire," said Trubee. Woodhouse, he muttered, "had a lot of fantastic dreams."[11] The boys were in for much disappointment.

Woodhouse's glorious vision of an aerial fleet defending against all invaders swept up the boys. They were ready to do their part. But flying remained a dangerous sport and most levelheaded adults had the good sense to keep both feet firmly on the ground. Hammond and Woodhouse set out to convince a still-skeptical Mrs. Davison that flying was as safe as driving "when properly done." Their patriotic plan for building up the aerial coastal patrol and promoting the boys as role models for an entire nation finally, in Trubee's words, "converted" her. If her husband agreed, she proclaimed herself "willing to aid as much as possible in preparing my son to serve his country as an aviator."[12] Getting Henry Davison to go along was another challenge altogether.

Trubee's mother's crucial backing won, the boys now sought out a way to learn to fly. That was not a simple matter. Few qualified instructors or airworthy flying machines were available anywhere in the country, but the boys were in luck. Just thirteen miles below Peacock Point in Port Washington, the Trans-Oceanic Company maintained a ramshackle flying boat station and school. Trans-Oceanic was the plaything of Lewis Rodman Wanamaker, the heir to a department store fortune, who, in aviation's earliest days, had hoped to sponsor the first trans-Atlantic flight, despite Orville Wright's contention that it would be "impracticable and foolhardy" to attempt. He had pioneering aircraft builder Glenn Curtiss construct an enormous flying boat, the *America*, to attempt the crossing. The outbreak of the Great War made it impossible, and, its ambitions much reduced, Trans-Oceanic now kept just one flying instructor on payroll at Port Washington: David McCulloch.

McCulloch was of that peculiar breed attracted to machines that could do more than seemed possible. Gruff and colorful, the itinerant pilot was still in his early twenties and completely devoted to flying. He was also utterly indifferent to the demands of whatever outfit he happened to sign up with. But he knew flying machines inside and out. He had already flown for six years, including service instructing pilots for the Brazilian government and in combat for the Italian Royal Air Force in the war. He agreed he would teach the boys flying from the ground up. Literally. That, he said, would include stripping down engines and maintaining bracing and cables. He scoffed at the wealthy Yalies' glorious ambitions and promised them only "a greasy, dirty, backbreaking job."[13] They were game.

Wanamaker offered the boys the complete run of the Trans-Oceanic station as well as flying instructions for the summer with McCulloch in the *Mary Ann*, a pusher F-boat, at the princely rate of one dollar per minute—in five minutes more money than the typical factory worker earned in a day! McCulloch assured Mrs. Davison that he would keep her boys safe. "A dead aviator is of no use to anyone," he deadpanned.[14]

Trubee's mother called Hammond and Wanamaker and came away reassured. They convinced her that within his ungovernable exterior lay a superb pilot and "very competent instructor" who did "not believe in taking risks or doing stunts."[15] They agreed to his terms. However, he never promised them just when their flying lessons would get underway.

With the table set, the only thing remaining was to convince Trubee's father. Having already expected his son to face sufficient danger in the ambulance corps in France, he cut short his salmon fishing vacation in Labrador. Rushing home by train, Henry Davison was intent on keeping his sometimes reckless son from doing anything unreasonably dangerous. However, he knew that only those who dare, who demanded more of themselves than others believed possible, could make great things happen. His own life was testimony to that.

His life almost ended before its promise could be fulfilled. In 1891, a twenty-four-year-old paying teller at the Astor Place Bank in New York, Henry Pomeroy Davison, "Harry" to his friends, glanced up from his counting through the teller cage into the business end of a revolver barrel. Hands shaking, a crazed-looking man presented a check for one thousand dollars drawn to the order of "The Almighty." Harry called out, "One thousand dollars for the Almighty! How will you have it?" With the twitching gun pointed at his head, he coolly began counting out the money in small bills, all the while repeating the charge to pay "One thousand dollars for the Almighty." Finally a guard overheard the transaction and pounced on the insane bandit. Newspapers made much of the story and the young teller's aplomb.

A year later, the recently formed Liberty National Bank needed a new assistant cashier. The bank's president recalled the incident, Harry's composure, and his quick thinking. Harry got the job. The new position put him within the orbit of some of the leading lights of the Wall Street banking world. Most importantly he came within the purview of George F. Baker, Jr., the powerful head of the First National Bank and a director of the smaller, affiliated Liberty National. With his mutton chop sideburns, gold watch fob, and aversion to public statements of any kind, Baker was the epitome of the conservative Victorian banker. He quickly saw Harry's "preeminent gifts as a banker, his caution and yet his courage, his uncanny gift for handling men," according to his biographer, Thomas Lamont, himself a future leader of J. P. Morgan & Company.

Harry apprenticed himself to Baker and studied his success closely, and, in less than seven years, at age thirty-two, he rose to the bank's presidency. He was one of the youngest bank presidents in the country, by far the youngest on Wall Street.[16]

That marked an extraordinary ascent. Harry had grown up in the small, hardscrabble north central Pennsylvania hill town of Troy. His mother, from a local banking family, had died when he was seven. His itinerant farm-tools salesman father had split apart his four children and left them, the poor relations in the homes of aunts and uncles. Harry showed early promise, but with no money for college, he went to work in his uncle's bank in town. Dreaming of Wall Street, he soon found his way to the entry-level post at the Astor Place Bank in New York City.

Once he became president of the Liberty National he quickly proved a banking innovator. Davison conceived the idea of a trust depository for national bank money and formed the Bankers Trust Company, which for many years served as a central bank to a large group of Wall Street bankers. Though much younger than his banking peers, Davison found himself moving in the highest circles of American finance. During the Panic of 1907 and the subsequent run on the banks, Davison worked constantly with leading fellow bankers, quickly bringing in substantial infusions of funds from a trio of New York's most powerful and wealthiest men: Baker, J. Pierpont Morgan, and James Stillman of the National City Bank (today's Citibank). That halted the run on the banks and staved off a general national collapse.[17]

The steely J. P. Morgan was deeply impressed by the young man's ingenuity, calm, and directness in dealing with much more senior men during the Panic.

He also observed the confidence they placed in him. Davison had already made a reputation for international banking, participating in banking partnerships with governments from China to Europe. His ability to bring fellow bankers and government officials into mutually beneficial relationships won him broad respect. Years younger than other banking titans, other bankers nonetheless looked to him to lead because, beyond his financial acumen, he made his agenda clear, enjoyed a reputation for reliable honesty, and hid nothing from those under his command. The following year the man muckraking journalist Lincoln Steffans called "the boss of the United States" invited "H. P." to become the eleventh of his partners.

At age forty-one, the small town orphan who had never attended college sat at his desk at 23 Wall Street alongside Jupiter in the Olympus of world finance. His banking peers marveled at his unmatched ascent. In the world of Wall Street, Lamont exclaimed, Davison "was not simply a leader. He was a king, an idol, if you please."[18]

Although he hid the warmth prized by intimates behind a steely countenance, Davison's accessibility and public-spiritedness contrasted markedly with Morgan's fortress outlook, eyes glaring like bright headlights on a midnight road, fist-pounding temper, and acid taciturnity that dug a moat between him and all who dared approach him, except his mistress. In an era when bankers readied themselves for their counterparts' backstabbing and stock manipulation by doing it first, Davison dealt with his rivals openly, encouraging greater transparency and cooperation throughout the banking community.[19]

"Men enjoyed following him," explained his renowned competitor and sometime collaborator Paul Warburg of the Kuhn, Loeb Investment House.[20]

Davison, in turn, enjoyed keeping the bright young men of Wall Street around him. Vigorous and manly, he took his sons and his young banking colleagues on regular hunting and fishing excursions and kept a plantation in Georgia in part as a private hunting preserve. Taking visitors on tours of his Long Island estate or his in-town mansion on Park Avenue, the senior Davison would point out the rhino and elephant heads among the various big game trophies mounted on his study walls, telling how he had faced down the charging beasts during his safari up the White Nile.[21]

His sociability was legendary. Rarely did he sit down to the family's regular Sunday suppers with fewer than twenty at the table.

Davison's value to the Morgan bank continued to soar. Trying to bring stability to the boom-and-bust cycles that plagued the American economy, he worked closely and in secret with other bankers and members of Congress developing a model for what later became the Federal Reserve System that still reigns today. As the aging and frequently ill Morgan began to withdraw more and more from his bank's daily operations, he worried about its future leadership. He lacked confidence that his son Jack possessed the flinty toughness, piercing human insight, and volcanic energy he deemed essential to guiding a vast banking empire through the piratical world of modern finance. Both Morgan father and son trusted Davison, who was utterly loyal to the Morgan name, and they recognized his unmatched operational skills, his talent for motivating men, and his overriding self-confidence. J. P. Morgan began turning over more and more control to Davison. "The greatest banker America has ever known found in Henry P. Davison the greatest partner he ever had," gushed B. C. Forbes, founder of *Forbes* magazine, in a glowing 1917 portrait of the young banking star.[22]

With Morgan's death in 1913, Davison, still in his mid-forties, effectively took over leadership of the world's dominant private bank. With more leverage over capital than even U.S. presidents had at the time, he was counted among the country's few most powerful men, courted by industrialists, prime ministers, and kings. He was a lord of the American financial aristocracy, an equal to the princes and dukes of the Old World's aristocratic nobilities. But their worldly power was on the wane. His was growing.

The banker's influence extended far beyond his nation's borders. With affiliated firms in London and Paris, Morgan & Company maintained close ties to the allied governments. Truly bicultural, Jack Morgan lived half of each year in London. That made the leading U.S. bank an ideal partner to European governments. The Morgan bank came to serve as fiscal agent for the Allies, negotiating the enormous American loans that financed their war. A first loan of $500 million in 1915—only about twenty percent less than the entire U.S. federal budget at the time—was followed by hundreds of millions more, with Davison leading the negotiations for all of them. Morgan & Company could not afford to see the Allies lose the war. (In later years, some saw conspiracy and accused Davison of engineering the sinking of the *Lusitania* in a bid to draw the United States into the war to ensure repayment of the loans.)[23]

Fearing a backlash from the pro-neutrality public, with as little notice as possible, Davison also organized the Allied Purchasing Commission, the Morgan-operated instrument through which the Allies acquired $3 billion in munitions from U.S. manufacturers. The bank's special team of more than 150 men purchased an average of $10 million in war materiel every day, making Morgan the single largest consumer in history. With Allied cannons frequently firing 200,000 shells in a single day, the Morgan men drove American munitions makers to build new factories virtually overnight to meet the war's insatiable demands. The company received a one percent commission on each purchase contract.[24] For Davison, winning the Great War in Europe meant business.

Unknown to Trubee, his father was already deeply immersed in the growing preparedness movement, even its still-tentative aviation branch. In fact, earlier that spring he had donated a flying machine to Captain Raynal C. Bolling, a prominent New York City attorney who had organized the National Guard's first true aviation unit, the Aviation Detachment, 1st Battalion, Signal Corps, of the New York National Guard, based at Mineola Field. And unlike the entire U.S. military leadership, he had actually flown over the lines, inspecting the European battlefield.[25]

When the senior Davison arrived from Canada by train in Greenwich, across the Sound in Connecticut, an anxious Trubee motored over in a launch to bring him home. "Half scared to death," Trubee did not even bring up the subject foremost on his mind. He had a trick planned to convince his father that there was little difference between sailing over the water or through the air. As father and son pulled up to the dock at Peacock Point, McCulloch flew into the cove in the *Mary Ann* and landed on the water alongside the launch, sliding up to the beach "just like a motor boat."

Trubee Davison's father "knew a lot more about [aviation] than he let on."[26] He was not so easily impressed. With barely a glance over at the *Mary Ann*, he stepped to the dock and strode quickly up to the house.

Trubee had not played all his cards. Woodhouse and Hammond were waiting inside, and then Harry Payne Whitney arrived. Seth Low, Al Sturtevant, and Cord Meyer from the crew team, as well as Charles Wiman, a 1915 Sheffield graduate who served as the team's assistant coach, planned to begin training at Mineola while staying at the Whitney place nearby. The Davison family gathered together to listen to their perspective on Trubee's plans. Afterward Henry Davison announced, "I am very much opposed" to the whole idea. Trubee was crushed. Then his father added, "I have an open mind and will investigate." He promised the gathering he would mull it over and consult with some other experts.[27]

Early the next morning, Henry Davison took Woodhouse and Hammond with him aboard his yacht, the *Skipaki*, for the commute into Manhattan. At the last moment, unable to wait for an answer, Trubee raced out to the boat and jumped on board.

A few hours later, an excited Trubee telephoned his mother, "Father is converted."[28]

CHAPTER 5

Peacock Point,
July–September 1916
A New Life

Now TRUBEE HAD TO ROUND UP HIS FRIENDS. ALTHOUGH A NUMBER OF the potential members of the proposed squadron lived nearby, many other candidates Trubee and Bob had in mind were scattered in distant parts of the country. Telegrams and telephone calls went chasing after them. Trubee sent messages to John Vorys in Columbus, Ohio; Di Gates in Clinton, Iowa; John Farwell III in Chicago; Curtis Seaman Read at home with his family north of New York City; and Malcolm Baldridge (like Vorys a future U.S. Congressman), who was moving between Omaha and Wyoming. All were football players or other varsity sports stars or team managerial heelers in their Yale class and members of their fraternity. Flying, though, was the last thing on their minds, and how their learning to fly might benefit the country proved hard for them to fathom. They knew one thing: it was dangerous. Trubee and Bob had an "awful job to make the thing clear." Whatever they were planning for the summer, they were being asked to "give up their very lives" for a scheme that made little sense to them. The telegrams explained that Trubee's family would finance the group, which would be working with the Aero Club of America, and through that private group for the government. Although no enlistment would be necessary, after learning to fly they would form a squadron providing coastal protection for the nation. And they would remain college students. Trubee's plans seemed vague at best, very likely ill-conceived, and unsafe to boot.

Baldridge's parents said flat out, "No." Read's family kept him away and hoped that a state organization would eventually develop that he could join. A leery Gates returned east not to join the outfit "but to be convinced." Trubee soon persuaded him.

A telegram reached Vorys in the hospital where he was still groggy from having his tonsils removed. He tossed the "long and rather incoherent" message aside before, he said, he "turned over and went to sleep." A few days later, Trubee telephoned him at home. Vorys recalled Trubee's feverish explanation that "we were not to fly very high and that because we flew over water we wouldn't get hurt if we did fall occasionally." Vorys wanted to do his part for preparedness, but after his surgery he was too weak for the rigors of a summer military encampment. A summer spent at a Long Island shoreline estate occasionally soaring over the water sounded about right. Even more ignorant about the dangers of flying than Trubee, he packed a carpet bag and proceeded to Peacock Point, "knowing little . . . of what I was getting into."[1]

A group for the summer began to coalesce. Along with Trubee and his younger brother, Harry, following his return from France later that summer, a roster of ten boys from Yale emerged—Trubee and Bob, together with crew heeler Alphie Ames; Gates and Vorys, both from the football team; star high hurdler Farwell; hockey player and crew heeler Erl Gould; as well as Sturtevant and Wiman. The latter two had already committed to spending the first part of the summer flying at Mineola and then at Governor's Island in New York Harbor with the State National Guard, but intended to join Trubee's squadron afterward. Locust Valley neighbors, Wellesley Laud Brown and Albert Ditman, Jr., two junior associates at Morgan & Company, rounded out the initial group of twelve.

All on hand would live in a large room, known as the "Dormitory," upstairs at the Davison house. They would drive over to Trans-Oceanic each morning for lessons with McCulloch. Whatever adventures, great or small, awaited them, Trubee mustered his friends together on the lawn at Peacock Point and saluted the newly formed Yale Aerial Coast Patrol, Unit No. 1.

As the boys began to arrive, Trubee wanted to formalize in some manner the nascent unit's relationship with the navy. Woodhouse sent Trubee to Washington with a letter of introduction to Secretary of the Navy Josephus Daniels, describing Trubee as "one of twelve well-to-do young men who wish to prepare themselves to be of service to their country in case of trouble, and are learning to fly." Woodhouse reminded Daniels of his past support for the Aerial Coast Patrol plan and asked that the navy recognize this initial unit "in the nature of a reserve in the near future."[2]

Trubee met with Daniels, who welcomed his interest in aviation. The avuncular Daniels was a powerful former North Carolina newspaper editor who had never served in the military. To date he had paid little more than lip ser-vice to the promise of aviation. He quickly tossed cold water on the idea of a stupendous aerial navy Woodhouse had fed Trubee, or even a navy air reserve corps in the near future. "There is no provision," Daniels informed the boy, "whereby the Navy Department can give official recognition to the Aerial Coast Patrol." Trubee had at least hoped for some sort of navy seal of approval, but Daniels insisted "that the department cannot give official recognition to persons or organizations over which it has no official control." Funding for the boy's summer enterprise was out of the question. Showing Trubee out of his office, he gave him a warm pat on the back and applauded the members of the new unit for their "patriotic desire . . . to organize themselves to assist in time of danger in the protection of their country."[3]

Back home, Trubee told the other boys what had happened. They were, said Brown, "pretty disgusted" at the navy's refusal to take them in.[4] While at the Navy Department, Trubee wandered over to meet with Franklin Delano Roo-sevelt, Daniels's aristocratic young assistant secretary. Fourteen years Trubee's senior and a fellow Groton graduate, Roosevelt seemed to understand better the young man's burning desire to serve his country. He was far more receptive to the idea of a private militia of naval aviators. He could not give official recognition to Trubee's group, but a few days later wrote to the commander in charge of the navy's New York District, "Please inform the gentlemen who are interested in this patriotic movement that the Department will assist them in every way practicable."[5] He would not forget the members of the unit.

Rear Admiral Peary also assured the Davison family that he would "do everything in his power to make this project a success."[6] For Trubee, the vari-ous words of support and assurances regarding the possibility of future recog-nition did not amount to much, but were all that was immediately available. It meant that his father would need to fund the entire summer's operations, and his mother would need to house and feed ten boys—and their adventure might never amount to more than a summer's game.

By the second week of July, though the unit was flying.

For the first day's training, McCulloch told the boys to meet him at the hangar at 5:30 in the morning. All of them, convinced, as Wells Brown said, that "fly-ing . . . [would be] distinctly a thrill," leaped from their beds in the dormitory.[7]

Before the sun had risen, they gulped down breakfast and made the twenty-five-minute dash along the winding lanes past the privet hedges, high stone walls, and wrought iron gates to the neighboring Gold Coast estates with a pepped-up, heavy-footed Lovett at the wheel of the Davisons' careening Dodge—"by all odds the most dangerous thing we did that summer," thought Brown. They arrived at the Trans-Oceanic hangar in Port Washington just as the sun began to burn off the night fog. They could see the *Mary Ann* brooding in the gloom behind the floating hangar's doors. They looked around. There was no sign of life except for the ducks quacking on the lapping water. They waited impatiently outside for McCulloch to show. And waited. Finally, at seven, they tromped over to the nearby house where he lived. He was sound asleep. They pulled him out of bed and soon hauled out the *Mary Ann*.[8]

McCulloch may have been a skilled aviator, but he enjoyed lying around even more. That drove the Yale boys crazy. Most days, the story was the same: McCulloch always swore that he would be ready for them at 5:30 A.M., but they were lucky if they could get him underway an hour later. Trubee complained that the "independent . . . and lazy" instructor "refused to be moved by anybody."[9] The ritual was the same each morning. Keen to get in a hop before the sea winds started blowing down the Sound—and Brown and Ditman had to catch the morning train into the city for work—the boys would jump at the first dawning twilight to the window and look out over the water. If they could make out the ghostly outline of the Connecticut shoreline, everything was alright for flying. They threw on greasy overalls over their swimsuits and raced over to Port Washington, where they dragged the protesting McCulloch from his bed.

Whatever his faults, McCulloch knew flying and he knew that the boys— cocky and eager as they could be—were ripe for trouble. He did not want any of them hurt on his watch—or under the close scrutiny of the newspapers that thought the idea of rich college kids playing in dangerous flying contraptions was worthy of many lines of newsprint. One by one, he took each boy up in the two-seater, dual-control *Mary Ann*. He was intent on instilling a respect for the tricks of a flying machine.

Lacquered to a gleaming black above the waterline with a white stripe down the center and along the waterline, the *Mary Ann*'s raked and sleekly stepped hydrofoil hull looked like a handsome wood runabout with biwings and a rear-facing pusher propeller. Her builder, Glenn Curtiss, intended his F-boat for the wealthy sportsman-pilot. He advertised it as the "most luxurious vehicle to ever mount the air." The flying boat would, the company catalogue proclaimed, "skim over the water like a flying fish, or soar into the clouds like a gull. . . ." Each cost $7,750 at the factory in nearby Hammondsport, New York, and weighed 1,760 pounds empty. Two people could sit side-by-side on the wicker seats within the laminated mahogany, four-and-a-half-foot-wide cockpit. Generating enough lift to get a ton or more aloft required the *Mary Ann* to skim at 45 miles per hour over the water. Once airborne, she cruised at a maximum speed of 65 miles per hour, with a range of a little over two hours. Twenty-eight feet from nose to rudder with 45 feet of wing on the upper plane and 35 feet on the lower, the total wingspan was only 13 feet less than today's 150-passenger Boeing 737. With all that wing, she got into the air easily enough, but her buzzing 90-horsepower motor still needed fully 10 minutes to lift all that weight to 1,500 feet. And a loss of power could quickly send her falling.

She was a good bird for learning the rudiments of flying, though. On the dock, the boys could easily take her apart and replace parts. The F-boat had enough space, nearly six feet, between the wings for a man to stand erect while he worked on the rear-facing engine or the wire bracing and struts. The wing struts were of steel and ash, with doped unbleached linen stretched like a drum over the frame and strapped together with piano wire.[10]

Although the boys were athletic and coordinated enough to learn to operate the yoke controls, foot-controlled rudder bar, throttle, and gas-and-air mixture simultaneously, and possessed above all that most essential characteristic of a good pilot-to-be, "keenness for flying," not one of them had a realistic grasp of the basics of flight.[11] Even on Long Island, the center of American aviation at the time, airplanes remained an uncommon sight. "Nobody seemed to know much about it," Brown acknowledged. "Nobody had done much flying."[12] Getting and keeping a motorboat aloft on cloth, steel, and wooden wings seemed to defy the laws of nature. They had much to learn—and unlearn.

Just as the first automobile drivers had to rid themselves of the ingrained notion that a motorized vehicle would slow by shouting "whoa!" and pulling back on the wheel as they might have done with a horse and its reins, the boys had to dispense with the idea that the *Mary Ann* was a sort of winged automobile or boat. They had to learn that an airplane turned by banking, that once free of the earth, its rudder served only to correct sideslipping. Aloft, her velocity—and more importantly speed through the air—could not be judged by the passing points of reference on the ground. And unlike the curves, hills, and bumps in the road, the winds, turbulence, and air currents that impinged directly on an aircraft's progress through the air remained completely invisible and came from all directions.

The *Mary Ann* offered only the most primitive instrumentation, just a tachometer, oil and gas gauges. As such, McCulloch needed to teach the boys not just how to control the *Mary Ann*, but something not always learnable: flying instinct—that artful ability to judge and react to the fast-changing unseen forces continuously acting on an aircraft. He needed to teach his students to fly literally by the seat of their pants. They had to learn to feel the pressure of their body against the seat, and the resistance or ease of the controls in changing the plane's altitude and direction. McCulloch sought to tune them in to the sounds of strain and roughness in the engine and, when possible above the engine's roar and finally when gliding into a landing, like a sailor trimming his sail, even the noise wind made in the fabric, guy wires, and struts, to judge the aircraft's relative speed, how much lift her wings had, and how close she was to stalling.

With the pusher engine suspended overhead between the wings, the flyers sat virtually inside it. The engine's roar forced all on board and those nearby on the ground to stuff their ears with cotton. That proximity did connect the pilot that much closer to the engine's running condition, which could be a lifesaver. When landing or taking off, the *Mary Ann,* like most early aircraft, could become skittish. Failing to correct the fuel mixture led to frequent engine conk-outs and, in the wrong situation, could result in a stall and crash, or just as dangerous, sudden increases in thrust with an obstacle dead ahead.

With its open cockpit, heavy drag, and quirks, piloting a flying boat took nerve. But unchecked bravado was no way to fly for long. A pilot needed a rational check on his gut instincts for self-preservation. For instance, when the *Mary Ann* stalled, and she was prone like most early flying machines to stall easily, it took courage not to pull back on the stick in terror, and instead point her nose at the ground as the machine fluttered downward. The sardonic Mc-Culloch told the gung-ho boys that courage without skill—a lack of respect for the art of flying—would soon break their necks. While Trubee may have believed briefly that the water would protect him and his friends in a crash, it took only one hard, kidney-bouncing slap by the hull on landing to convince them otherwise.[13]

McCulloch let the boys feel the controls as he piloted. Not that McCulloch could do much more than signal by gestures once the *Mary Ann* reached take-off speed. The engine's roar blotted out all but a shout directly into the ear. Even that was a challenge. With no windscreen, opening his mouth resulted in a painful grimace, except when the *Mary Ann* remained pointed up enough to keep the wind away from the cockpit. But with its nose up, those on board could not see forward over the prow except by sticking their heads over the side of the hull.[14]

To see during take off and landing, the pilot ruddered side-to-side to look ahead. Even if no other aircraft were likely to be around, boats and birds were plentiful. With so much wing, the aircraft got buffeted about constantly on the winds and air currents, but typically self-corrected and remained remarkably stable. Still, the pilot had to check his course tracking continuously and, without hydraulics, the cable controls took real strength and dexterity to keep a machine on course. By the end of a flight, a pilot landed exhausted, limbs and guts still shaky from the exertion, noise, and vibration.

McCulloch was in no rush to let the boys take the controls. He even had to teach them such fundamentals as tying down anything loose and securing everything else deep in their pockets. Loose keys, clothing, change, or tools could get sucked back into the rear-mounted wooden propeller with catastrophic consequences. McCulloch did not always take his own advice. Pulled from bed one morning, he carried his breakfast aloft with John Farwell. Soon both men and the aircraft were splattered with egg and milk.[15]

Mrs. Davison approved that McCulloch "started the boys at the bottom," learning the work of mechanics. Given that the Trans-Oceanic school had only the one machine, a single engine and no spare parts, he had no choice. They spent their days crawling over the *Mary Ann* and got to know her inside and out. "Everyone in the Unit had a soft spot in his heart for this machine," Ames said.[16] They learned how to remove a motor, pull it apart, and reinstall it. All that exposure to the mechanical underpinnings of their flying boat might serve them one day in lifesaving ways they could not predict.

With only the one aircraft at their disposal, they spent their days at the Trans-Oceanic hangar flying one by one with McCulloch, loafing, tinkering with the spare equipment, swimming, and reading airplane books and magazines. "That early flying was terribly sketchy," recalled Trubee. Sketchy but "a lot of fun," added Brown. All of them enjoyed the thrill of flying up over the Sound and back inland over the village of Port Washington. At night, the boys would return to Peacock Point "hot, tired, and dirty, and more enthusiastic than ever," said Mrs. Davison with obvious delight. Over dinner there was only one topic of conversation: flying.[17]

Through the summer, they brought in leading lights from the aviation world—including Thomas Morgan, future president of Sperry Gyroscope Company—who spoke to them about emerging instruments like the compass and drift indicators, as well as pilots from Europe who talked about the ongoing war in the air.

The cold spring had now reversed into one of the hottest summers on record. When not on "flying duty," the boys played golf and tennis, swam in the sound, rode horses on the beach and through the woods, or played polo, motored about the Long Island countryside, and attended North Shore dances and teas. The local "young belles" would "heave a . . . sigh" over the handsome, eligible young men flying overhead, according to *Time* magazine.[18] Trubee's pretty younger sisters, Alice and Francis, along with their neighbor Adele Brown, and other local girls including Evelyn Preston and Priscilla Murdock, spent the summer studying nursing at Peacock Point. They also bore the brunt of the boys' hijinks. Several times they ended up dumped in the garden fountain. Bob Lovett grew increasingly close to Adele while Di Gates and Alice Davison were seen walking together along the beach. Trubee's sweetheart, Dorothy Peabody, visited Peacock Point several times.

The boys were exhilarated by their shared adventure pursuing a dangerous, still-primitive sport—and doing it with a purpose, an ideal underscoring their efforts. A vast world almost without limits had opened to them. "It was a new life," explained Ames. The idyllic days at Peacock Point made the summer stand out for them as one of almost indescribable joy and romance. "I had," recalled Ames in later years, "the happiest days of my life there."[19]

Despite their charmed life, Trubee and Bob never lost sight of their goals. "We went into this thing [with] a sort of missionary spirit," Trubee said. As a result, "we were all intense." Woodhouse and the Aero Club expected them to serve as role models for other young men to follow them into the air service. To that end, he had alerted the newspapers. Although his parents paid the bills, Trubee insisted that any public discussion of the group focus on the entire unit. When a photographer came around, he asked Trubee if he could take his picture. He refused. "We didn't want any individual pictures taken," he explained. It was "the group; the work, not the individual," that counted.[20]

Not all the publicity was positive. With the nation still maintaining its neutrality in the European war, the formation of the unit did not go unnoticed by those who wanted the country to stay out of the fight. In a world at war, their boyish adventures set off serious repercussions. Bernard H. Ridder, writing in his family's pro-German newspaper, noted that Germany had been attempting to sustain commerce with the United States during wartime by sending merchantman U-boats to haul freight home from American ports. The U-boats could more easily run the British blockade than surface ships. Ridder suspected the boys' project was part of a wider conspiracy in which "Great Britain will . . . use every measure, fair or foul, legal or illegal, to delay or destroy the use of the submarine as a merchantman. It follows, of course, that the pro-British party in this country, led by Morgan & Co., will devote their resources to the furtherance of this British object. It might be entirely coincidental that at the very moment when German submarines are entering and leaving our ports, that the son of one of the partners of Morgan & Co., should be reported to be establishing a unit of seaplanes to patrol our coast."[21]

Ignoring such opposition, the Davisons did all they could to encourage others to follow their example. Setting gossip columnists atwitter, Mrs. Davison, wearing an ankle-length day dress, flew with McCulloch, inviting reporters to watch. "Aviation is infectious," she told the smiling reporters, pulling off her goggles and flying helmet. "With very little urging," she insisted, "I went up for a flight." The society matron proclaimed for all the nation's mothers to hear that she thoroughly "enjoyed it." Her goal, she told the *New York Times*, was "to show mothers that flying is sane, safe, wise, and constructive work for their sons to take up in connection with preparedness for our national defense."[22] She was in regular contact with the mothers of the other boys. The unit, said Ames, "became her baby. She gave her two sons, her home and her prayers" to it.[23] She admitted she felt a "great responsibility" in bringing other mothers' sons to Peacock Point to learn to fly, "but they know that I would not allow my own sons to fly if I thought it was foolishly dangerous."[24] Her husband flew twice with the group as well.[25]

Among the least athletic of the boys on hand, Bob and Trubee were nonetheless gifted pilots and leaders. They moved ahead rapidly. The others learned more slowly. Although "not very quick at first," according to Trubee, Gates soon was flying. Vorys, thought Trubee, "was too clumsy," and took longer than the others to learn. Ames and Ditman both had trouble landing without bouncing the *Mary Ann* across the water's surface like a skipping stone. Ditman could testify from experience that the mahogany hull of the *Mary Ann* "was impregnable, it could not be broken."[26]

In August, the Davison family purchased a second F-boat for the group from the Curtiss factory. Trubee's uncle Daniel Pomeroy stopped in to watch the boys at work. At first, he thought they were taking foolish risks. After spending the day with them, though, he said, "I think you can accomplish something," and bought them a third airplane.[27]

As the long hot days of August began to pass, Trubee worried that the boys were progressing too slowly. McCulloch would not let them solo. The slow pace "looked bad to me," complained Trubee. He asked McCulloch to push them along faster so they could get their licenses before the summer ended and they had to return to Yale. McCulloch looked Trubee and the others up and down and told them "to keep our shirts on." He knew what he was doing. Trubee was not so sure, but kept his own counsel, "because I didn't know anything." In late August, McCulloch let Trubee taxi out alone, but told him not to take off. Trubee pushed the throttle open and brought the flying boat up on to a hydroplane. "Somehow or other," Brown recalled, "Trubee let it slip." He was flying.[28]

After Trubee's solo, Bob soon followed. With the summer drawing to a close, the football players in the group needed to report back to New Haven for practice. Gates managed to solo. The remaining members of what Vorys called "the boob flyer class" would have to wait.[29] Trubee fumed at McCulloch's "scandalous" failure to complete their training in that first summer.

Those who could fly got a quick chance to test out their skills. In early September, the navy ran a weeklong series of war games to conclude its summer training cruise for volunteers. As a first exercise, the navy sent a mosquito fleet to search for dummy mines scattered in eighteen feet of water in Gravesend Bay in Lower New York Bay off Sandy Hook, New Jersey. As an afterthought, the navy invited the unit to participate, to see if they could provide observation assistance. The navy expected little but trouble for the effort. In a heavy fog, McCulloch, with Farwell as his observer, flew in low through New York City, making headlines for their "daring exploit" of flying under the five bridges and shooting around the boats on the East River to feel their way through the fog out to the bay.[30] In the fog, the fleet could not locate any of the mines. Within fifteen minutes of arriving over Gravesend Bay, McCulloch and Farwell had picked out all of them. They landed amid the mosquito fleet, alerted the men on board, and then flew overhead to guide them along until each mine had been recovered. The day was, said Trubee, "a revelation" to the navy. Aircraft could succeed where ships failed.

Aircraft, though, had drawbacks of their own. Planning to join in the mine-spotting exercises, Trubee and Bob followed shortly after McCulloch and Farwell from Port Washington. It was only the third time soloing for either of them. With Trubee at the controls at one thousand feet directly over the Queensboro Bridge, the motor started to misfire. Trubee shut off the engine and glided down, landing fast between two bridges just as a ferry passed by. The flying boat hit the ferry's wake and bounced high into the air before splashing down. Thousands on shore, boats, and bridges witnessed the rough sleigh ride of a landing. Docked nearby, the *Viking*, a yacht belonging to his father's banking mentor and Peacock Point neighbor George Baker, Jr., towed them to the 23rd Street landing. There they ate a leisurely lunch on Trubee's father's *Skipaki* while having minor engine repairs completed.

The tabloids had a field day, mocking the emergency landing by the wealthy young man, "whose mother, Mrs. H. P. Davison, started an aviation school to demonstrate to other mothers what a safe sport flying was." According to the report, Trubee "came near being killed." They were right, though, in noting that the boys "missed death" only because they flew high enough to glide into a landing.[31] Trubee would not always be so fortunate.

Similarly, Charles Wiman, who along with Al Sturtevant planned to join the unit after their summer training with the National Guard, fell in a spin from the sky over Governor's Island. He was not so lucky. Although he survived the crash, he had several broken bones. His flying days were over.

As part of the naval exercises, the day after the mine-spotting triumph the navy sent out two destroyers, the *Flusser* and the *Warrington*, off Fire Island along the South Shore of Long Island, to cruise in toward New York City to test the fleet's strength in surveillance and defense of the harbor against enemy attack. In the late afternoon, with McCulloch piloting and Trubee observing, they flew out to spot the ships. Flying at 3,200 feet over the ocean, they quickly located the ships and started to head in to alert the fleet in New York. Ahead they saw a strangely yellow sky. The swirling clouds came on fast and soon they began to bounce about inside a fierce storm pocket. Suddenly their airplane quivered and then plummeted precipitously into a spinning nosedive as if it had dropped through a hole in the sky. The two men slammed headfirst into the instrument panel, knocking both out. By luck, each had jammed on the left rudder. The aircraft righted itself. Regaining consciousness, they flew down, "scared stiff." They found a sheltered landing spot off Oak Island in the Great South Bay.

They had all but forgotten about the fleet, but wanted to let the others know they were fine. Finding a life-saving station with a telephone link, they called the Atlantic Yacht Club where the fleet admiral had his headquarters. Bob Lovett stood by as planned to relay any report if they found the ships. Trubee asked him to let his family know they were safe. "By the way," he mentioned, "we located the 'attacking fleet' off Fire Island!" That was all Bob needed to hear. He dropped the telephone and ran to the admiral. Recollecting his elementary school days in a military academy, he saluted and snapped his heels together and reported that the invading fleet had been found about twelve miles south of Fire Island Light. He made another salute and marched out.

The unit's success proved a national sensation. Alan R. Hawley, president of the Aero Club of America, sent a letter on behalf of the club's executive committee praising the unit's spotting of the "raiding squadron." He could barely contain himself. "Such a thing could have happened under war conditions and this achievement would have saved New York from being bombarded."[32]

The following month *Flying* magazine declared the success in locating the *Flusser* and the *Warrington* "most remarkable and convincing." The exercise "revised the opinion of naval men regarding the possibilities of employing aircraft for naval purposes."[33] It took less than an hour's flight "in the teeth of one of the most severe storms that had visited the coast this summer," proclaimed *Aerial Age Weekly*, for a new age of naval defense to dawn.[34] Nobody bothered to mention that the two flyers had barely avoided coming to grief and should not have been flying at all in such weather. All they cared about was that, for the first time, the efficiency of aviation spotting in naval warfare had been successfully demonstrated in America.

The unit's reconnaissance work stunned the navy. They could not ignore the possibilities aviation offered and the opportunity the unit presented. Secretary Daniels would still not officially recognize the unit nor help to defray the costs to their families, but with the boys' heading back to New Haven, operational officers wanted to explore further just what the unit and its flying boats could do. They asked Trubee to base two of his aircraft at the submarine station in Groton, Connecticut, fittingly back on the Thames River, the very spot where the seeds of the idea for the squadron had been planted at the start of the summer. Trubee was thrilled when the base's commanding officer, Commander Yates Stirling, Jr., asked him to "let me know at any time what he would like to have done. . . . All of our officers are greatly interested in this work and would be very glad to do all they can."[35] The Aerial Coast Patrol had begun to prove its worth.

CHAPTER 6

New Haven, Fall 1916
The Yale Aero Club

WHEN IT CAME TO STORIES OF HOW THE YALE UNDERGRADUATES HAD spent their summer vacations, the returning members of the unit stood out. A student publication proclaimed that among the activities associated with the Yale name during the past summer, "perhaps none deserves more praise and encouragement than the First Aerial Coast Patrol."[1] Trubee refused to allow individual names to be used, "like true seamen . . . preferring to have the achievement credited to the Unit," noted the campus *Daily News*.[2] In a long letter to the paper, Rear Admiral Peary called theirs "the work of the pioneer. Instead of being dismayed to find that neither the army nor the navy could supply them with textbooks and information to guide them in their work they set to work to experiment and find out for themselves. . . ."[3]

They did not rest with the opening of the school year.

That fall, unit members traveled to New London most Sundays getting, according to Trubee, "hours and hours [of flying] in." Much of it was joyriding, but the hours in the cockpit added up. They also cooperated with Groton sub base commander Stirling, who several times sent out vessels into the Sound and then invited the flyers to track them down. Although the subs were invisible beneath the murky green water, the flyers consistently managed to spot them. This was another revelation to the navy. The periscopes left a boiling wake trail on the surface and, after they dove, a chalky streak remained visible. The Yale flyers sailed out in the submarines themselves to witness their operation, and they took navy men aloft to understand their vessels' vulnerability when aircraft tracked them overhead.

Even if the navy had suspected beforehand that aircraft might change the strategic equation at sea, they had had no prior opportunity to investigate.

Duxbury Free Library

The service branch's small air corps was based almost entirely in Pensacola, Florida, far from the navy's sole submarine base. "Those fellows [in the submarine corps]," commented navy aviator Edward McDonnell later, "were all wondering, Can we do this thing or that thing? And there was no way of proving it. There was no station where they could call up and say we want a plane for maneuvers. The navy did not have anything of that kind, and it was a godsend for them to be able to call on [the Yale students] to help them in their experiments."[4]

The combined efforts also further cemented the unit's ties to the regular navy and boosted the students' own sense of professionalism. "They saw," said Trubee, "we had no selfish motives. We were out for service." Trubee and Bob worked closely with Stirling to formulate plans for a naval air service. The commander sent letters to Washington in support of the boys and their efforts. "As usual," grumbled Trubee, "you never get very far with that sort of stuff." The navy administration believed aircraft remained an experimental force. If any use for flight were to be found, it would likely primarily be in land-based reconnaissance. Congress decided not to appropriate funds in support of the Aero Club's proposal for setting up an aerial coastal patrol defense line. The Navy Department, said Trubee, continued to be "terribly asleep on this."[5]

The Yale Unit members would continue to fly on their own and wait for the government to wake up to the impending crisis.

In early October 1916, six months after the German Reichstag had voted for unrestricted warfare at sea, the U-boat war surfaced in American waters. The fully armed U-53 steamed across the Atlantic and rose unannounced in the Newport, Rhode Island, harbor. The sub's commander, Kapitänleutnant Hans Rose, presented himself to the navy base, proudly welcoming his U.S. counterparts on board the U-53 for an inspection tour. After leaving port, he was careful to observe American neutrality. He sailed just beyond the three-mile limit and then attacked. Lurking within sight of the Nantucket lightship during the second week in October, the U-53 torpedoed three British, one Dutch, and one Norwegian merchantman. Americans were in an uproar. A few days later, though, President Wilson still insisted to the American Ambassador to Germany, James W. Gerard, that he wanted "both to keep and to make peace." Wilson still cherished hopes for stitching together a peaceful resolution. Two weeks later, though, on October 28, another German U-boat sunk the U.S. liner *Lanao* off Portugal. The Kaiser, under pressure, then called off open sea warfare. Despite the United States' declared intention to stay out of the war, though, it was inexorably being drawn in. Two days before the *Lanao* went down, Wilson admitted to the Cincinnati Chamber of Commerce, "I believe that the business of neutrality is over. The nature of modern war leaves no state untouched."

A week later, campaigning as the president who "kept us out of war," Wilson won election to a second term in office.[6]

With increasing notoriety attaching to his flying, Trubee decided the time was ripe to visit the dean of the college, Frederick Jones. With his stony demeanor, Jones could be an intimidating presence. Without looking up from his work when Trubee walked into his office, the dean asked, "Was that you flying around here on Sunday?" While he kept on writing, Trubee spent the next half hour describing his flying project.

Dean Jones finally set down his pen and looked at the worried boy. "Trubee," he said, "I think that's fine. I think that's great. What can I do for you?"

A relieved Trubee laughed. He asked only for his "moral support, encouragement and everything." Jones was ready to do what he could. He was so taken with the excitement of aviation that he offered to fly with Trubee and to invite the press to "show the whole world I am in back of you." Before that could happen, though, his wife vetoed what she thought was a fool notion. Jones did set aside a room in Wright Hall, Trubee's dormitory building on the Old Campus, for the Yale Aero Club, a new campus organization for the study and promotion of flying. With Trubee as the club's president, crew team captain Cord Meyer as vice-president, and Graham Brush, an engineering student and already an experienced pilot, as club secretary, they began to solicit interest from select students around campus.[7]

Those students were not just joining another campus club to puff up their chances for a senior society tap. Although relations with the navy remained tenuous, Trubee intended to enlarge the unit the following summer. The navy would, he believed, take up the unit as a regular reserve corps at that point. Congress had begun to debate a bill to establish military reserve forces, including an air corps. With Dean Jones's blessing, Trubee and his classmates organized the Yale Aero Club as a theoretical training ground for its members before entering the Navy Reserve. "There is undeniably a great future development to be expected in aviation," proclaimed the *Yale Daily News* in support of the Aero Club's ambitious program, "and it would be a very creditable thing for a Yale extra-curriculum activity to prepare men to take part in any such development."[8]

The Club was besieged with candidates. Most of the students Trubee considered as likely flyers were athletes or heelers for the teams. At Yale, they already stood out. They possessed, said Trubee, "a spirit of adventure—of cold risk taking." But there was more than simple adventurism. Those who joined had to share his own "sense of Christian mission which transcended the bounds of patriotism." They saw themselves as part of a titanic "struggle for freedom, justice and democracy for all mankind."[9]

Along with the eight on campus from the previous summer, those joining included several members of the crew team, among them William A. Rockefeller—whose relatives, most famously his Robber Baron great uncle John D. Rockefeller, had founded Standard Oil and the National City Bank, now run by his father—Reginald Coombe, who was also big enough to play football, and George F. Lawrence, Jr. All three had attended Groton with Trubee. Trubee's younger brother Harry Davison brought his fellow freshman and closest friend, David "Crock" Ingalls, to the meetings. At 17, Crock was still too young to enlist should they be called to serve, but he declared he "loved aviation," and insisted on joining anyway.[10] The manager of the varsity hockey team, Henry Landon, was one of just a handful of seniors to join. Another senior who signed on, Samuel Sloan Walker, had been in the ambulance service in France with Trubee.

Erl Gould's roommate, Curt Read, a pint-sized, sweet-natured baseball player and manager of the football team whose mother had kept him out the summer before, now joined the club as did his freshman brother, Russell, whom all called Bart. Never one to miss a chance to socialize with his well-heeled friends, Archibald "Chip" McIlwaine, the University's golf champion and a witty harmonizer with the Whiffenpoofs singers, signed up along with his roommate Freddie Beach. John Vorys and Di Gates convinced a few other football teammates to join, including Kenneth Smith. It did not take much to get Di's fellow-Midwesterner and closest friend from their prep days at Hotchkiss School, Kenney MacLeish, to come along. The lighthearted pole-vaulter had always wanted to find new ways to leap high into the air. Flying sounded like an even better way to get off the ground to him.

Al Sturtevant, now a student at Harvard Law School, kept in touch with Trubee and would occasionally travel to New Haven for club meetings. Another addition to the club, William Payne Thompson, Jr., nephew of Lewis Thompson, a Davison family friend, and scion of the Payne family of millionaire sportsmen, had been bitten by the flying bug while in England three years earlier, but his terrified parents had made him swear he "would never even glance at another aeroplane." They relented and he returned to the air the previous summer, getting his pilot's license from the Curtiss flying school in Newport News, Virginia.[11]

Soon there were close to fifty students—a few licensed pilots, but mostly undergraduates who had never set foot in an airplane and some who rarely had even seen one—attending the weekly Aero Club meetings.

Several aviation authorities met with the group, including Glenn Curtiss himself, the great aircraft engineer and builder, and Lawrence Sperry, the brilliant industrialist and navigational equipment inventor. The Yale boys were especially enthralled when Yale dropout and Lafayette Escadrille cofounder

William Thaw flew to campus by flying boat to meet with them. Already a decorated combat pilot, the dashing veteran with a turned-up mustache and a fondness for strong drink was on a tour of the country to drum up American support for the Allies. Thaw had first fought in the trenches with the French Foreign Legion before helping to form the Lafayette Escadrille. His dispatches from the frontlines in France had appeared regularly in the *Yale Alumni Weekly*. He sought now to spread the romantic image of the pursuit pilot, the single-seater combat flyer rising up to fight gloriously in the sky, a media-stoked concoction just beginning to penetrate American public consciousness.

The Yale Aero Club members lapped up his tales of war above the trenches. They even envied him the wounds he had received in the titanic battle for Verdun that had left his arm permanently crooked.[12] He encouraged their fighting dreams with both fists. He urged them to leap at the chance to do what no one had done before. They had, he said, "an opportunity here now which will never be duplicated for this generation." Here was a chance to lead, to soar literally to new heights. He listened to Trubee's plans for his unit and shared his "hope that within the next few months the Yale aviators will have formed a standing unit, cooperating with the Government."

He knew aerial combat, though, and warned them not to take flying lightly. Flyers were an elite breed. "Not every man can be an aviator," he said, "and mighty few can command aviation." In any case, he noted, cost would keep most of them grounded. If not, there was a bigger price to pay. "This game," he warned them, "costs money, but if you fail to get the very best of everything, you will come to grief sooner or later."[13] That made the game all the more enticing for the eager students.

A few months later Admiral Peary joined the parade of campus visitors to fire up interest in aviation. He told the eager students "naval aviators would become the eyes of the fleet." That was all they needed to hear.[14] They wanted to fly.

But without enough aircraft or equipment to train additional flyers, Trubee was reluctant to announce an expanded membership in the Coastal Patrol Unit. Nonetheless, other students clamored for spots as talk increased of the possibility of the unit departing campus to become part of the regular navy. A second group of students, mostly from the sophomore class, formed a unit of their own under the leadership of sophomore Ganson Goodyear Depew. Handsome, tall, and charming, Gans Depew was the son of a Buffalo business baron and nephew of Chauncey M. Depew, president of the New York Central as well as a former U.S. senator from New York. Among the new group's members was First Unit member Ken Smith's diminutive younger brother, Edward "Shorty" Smith. A third unit formed later that year, but a change in navy policy prevented it from completing its training as a unit. Before its breakup, members included freshman Juan Trippe, who would go on to found Pan American Airways after the war.[15]

In consultation with his father and the Aero Club—and the navy as it showed interest—Trubee began to think about the coming summer and to make plans for the club members' training.

Flying and military preparedness were not the first things on every club member's mind. As a star tackle on the Yale football team, Di Gates, as well as teammates Alphie Ames, Ken Smith, John Vorys, Reg Coombe, and heeler Curt Read, attended the Aero Club meetings in the evenings, but could not make the trips to Groton for the work with the sub base. The eyes of Yale and the nation were on them for they still had more traditional games to play for a few months yet.

With few other sports teams—professional or amateur—to root for, football at Yale stood at the pinnacle of American college sports popularity. Through the influence of coach Walter Camp, one of the pioneers of the game, Yale reigned as the great powerhouse of the early decades of the sport. In 1890, Yale defeated Princeton, 32–0, to start a winning streak of 37 consecutive games over the next three years. Thirty-six of those victories were shutouts, including 35 in a row. During the streak, the Elis outscored opponents 1,268 to 6.

Despite recent ragged performances, Yale football remained the most closely followed athletic team in the country, drawing tens of thousands of spectators to games. Throngs of spectators even lined the practice field daily. Above all, fans cared about the Harvard-Yale contest, since 1875 the final and singularly important match of the season—The Game.

This year Yale played host and on a sunny, crisp autumn day, New Haven went "football mad."[16] Fans by the tens of thousands flooded into the city "from every quarter and by every means of conveyance from the now little known horse to the vibrating, soaring aeroplane," according to the *New York Times*.[17] David McCulloch reportedly planned to fly Trans-Oceanic's giant flying boat, *America*, to New Haven for the day. Necks craned when Cord Meyer, together with his Saint Paul School friend and former Princeton hockey star, Hobey Baker, flew into New Haven. A smaller airplane, later reported to be piloted by William Thaw's brother, circled over the city and the Bowl.[18] The number of fur coats in the stands was "so large," according to the *Times*, "as to suggest the jungles must have been scoured."[19] Bursting the stadium's confines, attendance swelled to more than eighty thousand, possibly the largest ticketed crowd ever to witness a sporting event in the nation's history up to that point, more than the population of the entire state of Nevada and one fifteenth of the total population of Connecticut at the time. It would take a crowd of more than 225,000 to equal that attendance today.

The two teams faced off with seven victories apiece against just one loss. But Harvard, the dominant team for the past decade, was a strong favorite. Yale had not won The Game in nine years, not even managing to push the ball over the goal line in the past seven. Oddsmakers favored the Crimson to win once again. "Yale," contended the *New York Times*, "will have to accomplish almost the superhuman if Harvard is to be defeated."[20]

If the echoing roar and cheering in the stadium were not enough, in the locker room before kickoff, Yale coach T. A. D. Jones tried to inspire his eleven. A decade later he would famously tell a Yale team, "Gentlemen, you are about to play Harvard in football. Never again in your whole life will you do anything so important." Today, he presaged Knute Rockne's "win one for the Gipper" pregame speech. Jones knew that even if they had not been able to win for his coaching predecessor and dear friend Tom Shevlin, who had died suddenly after the previous season, they had loved their late coach. Jones walked among his team. "If any of you boys believe in the hereafter," he told them, "you will know that Tom Shevlin is pacing up and down across the river, smoking that big black cigar and asking you, boys, to go out there and do it once again for papa."[21]

The two teams charged out onto the field where they were greeted by a deafening roar. Cheerleaders, including Prescott Bush, a senior who would later father a political dynasty, shouted through megaphones at the base of the rings of benches, while tens of thousands of Yale and Harvard fans facing each other from opposite sides of the field yelled their practiced cheers and sang their fight songs back and forth. "No spectacle of the kind, perhaps, has ever rivaled [the crowd] for enthusiasm and grandeur," observed the *Times* reporter.[22]

At first it appeared that Yale once again lacked the punch to take down Harvard. The Crimson jumped out to an early lead on a field goal. Then Yale buckled down. The two teams responded with the closest defensive contest in memory.

With Harvard holding tightly to its 3–0 lead, in the middle of the second quarter a fortunate break bounced Yale's way into Di Gates's waiting arms. He picked up a teammate's forward fumble on Harvard's forty-yard line. The muscular, hard-charging lineman rumbled down the field knocking over several would-be tacklers before being forced out of bounds at the twelve-yard line. A few plays later, Yale's long scoring drought ended with a touchdown. The roar from the jubilant Yale crowd could be heard across the city. After the point-after attempt failed, the teams moved the ball up and down the field, but neither squad managed to push it over the line for another score. Yale substituted only once the entire game. As the final gun sounded sealing the Yale victory, 6–3, Eli fans spilled from the stands and mobbed the team on the field. Roman candles and fireworks fired off across the Bowl. Thousands of students and alumni snake-danced back downtown and then through the city. Celebrations went on all night.

Joe Vila, sportswriter for the *New York Evening World*, hailed Gates as "the great individual star" of the game.[23] Gates's run with the fumble, the *Yale Daily News* wrote, had "won [him] lasting fame."[24] His performance also helped him win election the following week as captain of the 1917 squad, putting his photograph into newspapers across the country. Many columnists predicted that the coming year's Yale team could take its place among the greatest Yale ever fielded. A jubilant Curt Read won election as its manager.

The team would never play a down. A headline in the *New Haven Register* on the day following The Game read, "Sub Boat Scare Becomes General." Of the thirty-three Yale players in uniform the day before, thirty were in military uniform a year later.

The school year continued, but for Trubee the Aero Club had become all-consuming. His father left to spend the winter on the Georgia plantation of his friend Colonel Lewis S. Thompson. Over Christmas break, Trubee joined them in Georgia where they laid plans, in the event of a declaration of war, for the unit to leave college. Rodman Wanamaker's Trans-Oceanic Company and David McCulloch had taken up winter quarters near Palm Beach, Florida. Trubee called the company's business manager and set up a deal for the Yale Unit to take over the entire Palm Beach facility on short notice if the group decided to leave school.

He returned to Yale and began to look for aircraft for training an enlarged squadron of the Aero Club at Yale. Its eventual final size would be determined by available machines. Money was no issue, but acquiring enough aircraft was. Very few could be found. The government, Trubee discovered, had "practically none at all." In any case, the navy made it clear that, were a reserve flying corps established, it would, a navy commander wrote Trubee, be "gotten up, of course, with the idea that the officers and men own their own machines."[25] Trubee purchased one flying boat he found at an air show in New York and located two others in private hands. Along with the three existing Curtiss F-boats, that gave him only enough machines to think of enlarging the unit to around thirty men. "When you have very little equipment," he explained, "you have to build on that and on nothing else."[26]

He did at least receive clear indications from the navy that the unit members would join as reservists, with ensign rank, and, should war break out, would be taken up by the regular navy. With the navy now offering to associate itself formally with the unit, which was to be known as the First Yale Unit, Trubee established a more official organization for the group. The members of the group had to get permission from their families, and also agree that they would follow orders, including being ready to pack up and leave Yale on short notice if called up by the military. Even if the navy never called them to service, Trubee expected the unit members to carry themselves like military men and to obey the chain of command, regardless of the fact that the boys remained classmates and friends.

When Di Gates's friend Kenney MacLeish decided to join the Aero Club, he understood the commitment he was making—at least to his friends. His parents were not so naïve. Their son sometimes leaped before he looked. He wanted to win his friends' respect and the campus honor that being part of the Yale flying fraternity would bring him. His parents wanted to keep their favorite son alive. Then the commitment to abandon college, possibly in midterm, to train for war with a private militia seemed unnecessary when the nation was doing all it could to stay out of the war.

Education mattered deeply in the MacLeish household. His mother, the former Martha Hillard, traced her roots back to William Brewster, the dissident lay leader responsible for bringing the Pilgrims to America on the Mayflower in 1620. A long line of ministers and educators had descended from him. After graduating from Vassar College, she had served as a school principal and then, following her marriage, had applied the progressive educational principles of the social philosopher John Dewey to the tutoring of her own children. A member of the Illinois Child Study Society, she read systematically and daily to her children from the Bible, Shakespeare, and ancient classics, as well as tales of heroic adventure such as *Ivanhoe* and others among Sir Walter Scott's novels and Scots legends and ballads of conquering warriors.[27]

The family's commitments were not only to education. Both parents were devout churchgoers, public minded, and committed to social causes—sensibilities they made sure their children acquired. Kenney's mother served on the boards of several educational, religious, and civic organizations, and volunteered in Chicago's famed Hull House settlement, founded by Jane Addams, the first alumna of Rockford College, which had grown out of the school Martha had headed before marriage. Kenney's father, Andrew, had helped to found the University of Chicago and served as a leading layman at his church. At Yale, Kenney kept up the family commitments to social causes, joining the Yale Hope Mission, a campus Christian group aiding the poor in New Haven.

There was, however, another side to the family, newer and driven for success in the booming world of American commerce. In contrast to his mother's lofty, intellectual, and aristocratic New England roots, his father had journeyed as a teen to America from his native Glasgow, Scotland, with romance in his heart and dreams of making his fortune. In 1856, at age eighteen, a shopkeeper's apprentice with little more than his ship's passage to his name, he left for America to seek the hand of his Scottish love, Lilias Young, who had immigrated earlier with her family to the frontier town of Chicago. They married and had two daughters. Then tragedy struck. Lilias died in 1878. In the meantime, he had risen to partner in the wholesale dry goods merchant Carson, Pirie, Scott & Company. He founded and managed the company's flagship Chicago retail store. In 1888, at the age of fifty, Andrew married Martha, eighteen years his junior. While the taciturn Scot rarely smiled or showed much interest in his lively children's activities, the gregarious Martha devoted herself to raising their four children at their rambling lakeside home, Craigie Lea, named after a romantic Scots ballad.[28]

Kenney's father's had a headstrong and romantic past, but he was adamant that his son should be more sensible and finish Yale before considering entry into the military. Kenney appealed to his parents' notions of public service, their desire to help the downtrodden, and their sense of Christian mission. British propaganda and the Allies' American supporters had spread inflammatory reports from Belgium, some true, some never confirmed, of German atrocities, of soldiers crucifying British soldiers, lopping off the hands of young boys and the breasts of Belgian women. The nations of Europe under the heels of Germany required rescue. The violation of U.S. dignity by the Central Powers demanded vengeance. The Hillard family counted as ancestors Yale men, who had served in the Revolution, War of 1812, and Civil War. Tales of the brave warriors of ancient Scotland defending the honor of their land and homes had been a large part of Kenney's childhood. Like his fighting forebears, the inspired boy would step forth to meet the call.

"Do you think for a minute," he wrote home in a letter pleading for permission to join the club, "that if Christ had been alone on the Mount with Mary, and [a] desperate man had entered with criminal intent, He would have turned away when a crime against Mary was perpetrated? Never! He would have fought with all the God-given strength he had." Like all of the boys, he insisted to them, "I could never stay at home if there was fighting of a real nature. I could never be content at home if the life and honor of anyone dear to me was in danger."

Kenney spoke in a language his parents understood when he proclaimed, "Religion embraces the sword as well as the dove of peace."[29] Honor and duty called him to do his part in the coming crusade. His father reluctantly gave in. Kenney's mother and father, along with the other parents, agreed to let their son take to the air and, if called, enlist in the navy.

CHAPTER 7

New Haven,
January–March 1917
We're Off!

On January 9, the Kaiser unleashed his admirals once and for all. Beginning February 1, "All sea traffic will be stopped with every available weapon and without further notice," announced a blunt German memorandum.[1] U-boat commanders were free to attack any ship sailing under any nation's flag, without warning, whatever cargo or passenger load it carried, whether armed or not. The Kaiser acknowledged that this would inevitably mean war with the United States.

His advisors assured him that the new policy would drive the Allies to a speedy collapse. Their calculations were persuasive. As they planned for the renewed submarine offensive, their fleet was already lethally effective. That January, the month prior to the new open-warfare policy, the Kaiser's present 100-plus U-boat fleet at sea (some 40 more were docked for repairs or refueling) had sunk 180 Allied ships, six every single day on average, a total of more than 300,000 tons—the equivalent of nearly ten *Lusitanias*. One out of every four ships sailing into or out of British ports was being sunk by the U-boat and mine cordon. With American ships now in their sights, the admirals expected to double that rate. At a projected pace of 600,000 tons of shipping each month, they would cinch the knot so tight about the island nation's throat that, its food supply choked off, its people would soon stand at the brink of starvation. The blockade would also deprive the French and Italian allies of the British coal they depended on to power their economies. (The German Admiralty underestimated its fleet: in April, U-boats sunk 373 ships, more than ten a day, weighing a total of 873,754 tons—well over a month's worth of food and munitions for England and its army, and faster than replacement ships could be built.) The Allies, claimed the German admirals, could not hold out more than five months with their supply lines bottled up, and America would never be able to mobilize in time to rescue its allies. And of course, any American troop ships that dared to cross the ocean would become fair game. "I give Your Majesty my word as an officer," Admiral Holtzendorf, Germany's Chief of the Naval Staff, promised the Kaiser, "that not one American will land on the Continent."[2]

President Wilson's hopes for a negotiated peace and the general American reluctance to enter the war could not forestall the crisis that began to unfold. Germany prepared itself for the expected hostile reaction from the United States to its new unrestricted submarine warfare policy by seeking to open an entirely new front—this time inside America itself. On January 19, German foreign minister Alfred Zimmermann sent a coded telegram to the German minister in Mexico City. He was to offer the Mexican government "generous financial support" if it would launch a war against the United States to "reconquer" the Texas, New Mexico, and Arizona territories Mexico had lost seventy years earlier. The Zimmermann telegram invited the U.S. neighbor, fuming over Pershing's Punitive Expedition force that still wandered through the northern Mexican desert in search of Villa, to "make war together, make peace together." British intelligence intercepted and deciphered the message, and of course turned it over to their American counterparts. Wilson read the infamous telegram in late February and then released it to an angry public outcry. Outraged war backers rallied throughout the nation. The tide of opinion started to turn.

Attacks began on American ships. On February 3, the same U–53, whose commander, Kapitänleutnant Rose, had guided U.S. Navy officers on a cordial tour through his submarine in Newport less than four months earlier, torpedoed the *Housatonic*, an American cargo ship loaded with grain off the Scilly Islands. Wilson had to acknowledge the emergency his nation faced. His efforts at finding a way to a peaceful solution were at an end. That day he broke off diplomatic relations with Germany. He began to coax the nation toward open conflict, although not quite war. He advocated something he called "armed neutrality." He called back "Black Jack" Pershing and his army from the heat and dust of Mexico. They had not succeeded in capturing Villa or defeating his army. Now Pershing had to prepare a small, antiquated force for war against a vastly larger, more modern and war-hardened enemy.

On February 26, two days after reading the Zimmermann telegram, Wilson asked Congress for permission to arm merchant ships. The House of Representatives approved the measure, but a Senate filibuster killed it.

The strongly hawkish majority of Yale students took to the streets, calling for war. On returning from their Christmas break, their campus-based preparations for war took on greater seriousness. In the middle of January, the college held a straw poll, voting by an overwhelming margin, 1112–288, for some form of universal military service.[3] As part of the National Defense Act passed by Congress the previous June, the newly established Reserve Officers Training Corps (ROTC) took over the enlarged Yale Battery's nearly nine hundred officers the opening of the second academic term. Military preparedness became part of the regular curriculum for almost all students. The student-officers drilled in the new Yale Armory constructed on athletic fields near the Yale Bowl and studied military matters in campus classrooms. Most understood that they were likely to be called up if—or what now appeared to be when—war was declared. They followed intently the unfolding war of words and then arms between the United States and Germany.

Little else was on student minds but war. A declaration of war was coming, but when? Would they finish out the school year? If they were called up, where would they train? Young men who spouted brave words secretly wondered whether they were capable of deeds to match.

While war fever gripped the campus, college life continued. After more than two hundred years, Yale could not abandon its most cherished traditions. An indispensable occasion in Yale life was Junior Promenade Week, the "Greatest Social Event of Year," declared a *Yale Daily News* headline.

The "brilliant junior promenade," as the *New York Times* celebrated it, marked the apex of the Yale high society calendar, the apotheosis of campus fashion, glamour, charm, and gaiety. That made the sixty-fifth annual prom, set for February 6, the perfect stage for Bob Lovett, Yale's ultimate socialite. He could exercise all his behind-the-scenes organizational and theatrical skills and stage charm on behalf of Yale's grandest carnival of the high life. That glittery all-night ball culminated a weeklong extravaganza of concerts, parties, fraternity and social club cotillions, and teas in hotels and private salons. The chaperoned gatherings, like the rest of the extra-curriculum, were organized by student managers who had heeled for election to the prom committee and then spent months planning for the big week. Bob won election to the committee and headed its music subcommittee. The prom committee anointed him as the prestigious floor manager for the prom itself. The floor manager stood out at Yale as the junior class's social leader.

The Junior Promenade—a misnomer because men from all classes were welcome and even some townspeople purchased tickets—required careful forethought. The young men planning to attend invited their prom dates months in advance. The women were expected to stay the entire week in New

Haven—under chaperone at all times, of course. They faced an exhausting weeklong social minuet with many partners, not just a *pas de deux*. In advance of prom night, the Yale men would pass their dates' dance cards out among friends, lining up an entire night of dancing for the women. Scores of stags also bought tickets and arranged dances with their friends' dates for the night. While in New Haven, the women would attend a series of teas and fraternity "germans" before the ball, where they would be introduced to the many men with whom they would dance through the prom night. Not that they could remember all of them: a woman might easily dance fifty numbers or more during the night. For the young men and women, otherwise kept separate throughout the academic year, this was a rare opportunity to meet members of the opposite sex. They had no time to spare, no dance number to sit out.

With women entirely absent from campus in all but service settings, Yale boys fell back on rumors, movies, and their sisters and older brothers to learn about these mysterious, alluring, and costly creatures who danced into their lives and then whirled back out. "The Yale Prom Girl," wrote the Sheff Class of 1916 historian, "is without exception the cutest, choicest, daintiest, loveliest little thing imaginable; she appears each year in the latest creations; she captures our hearts and then returns from whence she came, leaving us low in spirit and lower in pocketbook."[4]

Women were exquisite, cultivated flowers who blossomed in the campus hothouse just this one week a year. Although many women longed to meet a Yale man, sexual relations were virtually out of the question—for her reputation and his. Sophomore Hugh Le Baron advised Dink Stover upon arriving on campus, "No fooling around with women; that isn't done here." Yale's unwritten code of conduct forbade it; chaperones and parietal rules enforced it. As a result, Wilmarth Lewis could recall that as prom night approached, not one in ten of his 1918 classmates had had any sexual experience. They plowed any frustration they may have felt into doing something for Yale. "Sex," he wrote of campus life, "was sublimated in the furious extracurricular activity."[5]

For some, that extracurricular life undoubtedly had homoerotic aspects. With no women in the college, the plays staged by the Yale Dramat under Lovett's management required men to perform in drag for the female parts. Nobody seemed disturbed or even found it unnerving or more than passingly funny to see their classmates take the stage in dresses, wigs, fake breasts, and lipstick and rouge. There were very likely furtive campus homosexual encounters, but they remained deeply hidden. Even the flamboyant Cole Porter wrote hundreds of songs and musicals while at Yale—many performed at his Delta Kappa Epsilon fraternity—offering zany tribute to the general superiority and heterosexual prowess of the Yale male. His many, well-documented homosexual liaisons, often in the company of old friends from Yale, seemed to commence shortly after leaving New Haven. The frothy merriment he served up for his classmates provided one more extracurricular distraction, another form of sublimation amid the largely chaste reality.[6]

Junior Promenade Week may have rarely brought a Yale man more than a fantasy of sexual possibility, but the week with his date did relieve him of a small fortune. The glittery week was not for the faint of wallet. From the price of tailoring and rental of a vehicle for ferrying his companion and her chaperone from event to event, to the auction for coveted boxes at the prom itself, total expenses for the week could easily top $300—nearly double the college's tuition for the year! The auction price for the most desirable tables alone could add $100 to the basic $20 ticket price.

Bob Lovett, Roland Harriman, and their circle could easily afford it. For some, the astronomical cost proved too much. At the approach of Junior Promenade the year before, one broke father and alumnus feared the outlay would split Yale along economic lines, perhaps harming the class's beloved fellowship. Calling the week a "gross extravagance," he complained "it creates feelings of envy in the minds of the young men not able to meet this financial strain, and becomes not a class dance, but an aristocratic rich man's inner-circle affair, in no way representative of Yale or the class." His sentiments fell on deaf ears. That year, some seven hundred couples attended, more "this year than last," according to the *Yale Alumni Weekly*.[7] For the 1917 gala ball, seven hundred more couples visited the finest tailors and most fashionable boutiques in New York and New Haven to furnish their wardrobes for the week.

As the long-anticipated night of February 6 finally arrived, the campus lights twinkled festively against the piles of snow. The grim, Victorian visage of Yale, further darkened by the gathering clouds of war, gave way to the chatty excitement and earnest self-inspection of young men and women making themselves ready like actors on opening night. Exemplifying the spirit of the day, that morning the *Yale Daily News* ran a ditty on its front page:

> *A top hat for a student's cap,*
> *A dress suit for a gown!*
> *Immune from worry and mishap*
> *We'll dance the planets down.*

The stars were in alignment as the clocks struck nine and the big doors to Woolsey Hall were flung open. Dapper young men in white ties, tails, and top hats drove from their dormitories and apartments in gleaming Packards, Hudsons, Mercers, and Stutzes to escort their dates and their chaperones from their hotels to the prom. The lovely "little things" stepped out beneath fur coats, corseted and layered within long low-cut silk ball gowns of unearthly hues with fur trim. Their hair was piled high with plumes, ornaments, and false tresses in fat sausage curls.

The line of autos pulled up to the sweeping curve of the grand colonnaded entrance to Woolsey Hall's rotunda lobby. Like stars and starlets at a film premier, photographers snapped the elegant arrivals stepping to the carpeted curb. Blue and white bunting, imported palm trees, and tropical flowers filled the lobby and ballrooms. In the vast Commons, where the dancing was to take place, the most coveted boxes sat on platforms surrounding the dance floor. The two dance orchestras Lovett had engaged for the night, Markel of New York City and Danz from New Haven, had set up in the balconies at either end of the hall. Markel would play the dances; Danz provided musical background during intermissions. Soon the white linen-covered tables lining the dance floor were filled. Corks popped for the champagne service at each table. At 9:30 P.M., Lovett, master of ceremonies for the all-important dancing, stepped out in his white tie and tails and signaled to band director Markel, who struck up the first number of the evening. The elegant junior and his regal New York neighbor, Adele Brown, his date for the week, stepped smartly to the center of the floor. They danced a graceful, lively waltz to the first few bars alone and then the other members of the prom committee and their dates followed after them. Lovett signaled and all seven hundred couples stepped to the floor for the "Grand March." Markel's strings danced them in a stately promenade through the ballroom. At the tables, stags, chaperones, and their hostesses applauded the elegant and fashionable parade passing at a measured pace.

With a nod from Lovett, the orchestra broke into a fast dance number and, like a crazed solar system, couples whirled away in their planetary orbits across the floor. Some of the chaperones tut-tutted as waltzes gave way to the herky-jerky steps of the popular ragtime and Tin Pan Alley dances like the Turkey Trot, Fox Trot, Bunny Hug, and Grizzly Bear. As the numbers changed, new partners stepped out onto the floor. The women danced and danced. After more than an hour of dancing, Lovett again gestured up to Markel who sounded the chimes for supper. The crowd moved through the lobby to Woolsey Hall where a floor had been laid and candlelit tables set over the orchestra seating.[8]

After supper, the dancing resumed and never stopped. Few acknowledged the breaks; dancing couples crowded the floor all night, even swinging on during intermission. Women consulted their cards and moved from partner to partner. All through the night, the music, dancing, drinking, and merriment continued. At 5:30 the next morning, Lovett invited the remaining partiers—very few had retired for the night—to applaud Markel and Danz. A raspy-throated hurrah went up for Lovett and the promenade committee. The exhausted couples and their chaperones returned to their waiting cars and carriages. "With a lassitude that forgets the crumpled gown or the disarranged coiffure," Walter Camp wrote of the Yale Prom, "happy girls and their equally exhausted chaperones thr[e]w on their wraps . . . and [were] whisked back to the hotels, where they [were] soon dreaming over again the events of the week."9

As they returned to their rooms, some glanced at the front page of the previous day's *Yale Daily News*. Its chilling headline read: "Berlin Not to Change Policy; Washington Continues War Plans."

Trubee Davison did not attend the prom. Outsized events that would soon overtake all American lives were already in command of his. After learning Wilson had broken off diplomatic ties with Berlin, he and his brother Harry had hopped the first train to the nation's capital to meet again with Secretary of the Navy Josephus Daniels. The moment he had anticipated for so long had finally arrived. War could break out at any moment. The navy needed them now. They had to take the boys in. The Aero Club was ready to move into the navy's official orbit. All the members of the unit had secured their parents' permission. President Hadley and Dean Jones had given them permission to leave if called. They had aircraft and a southern base. They were ready to enlist and leave Yale at a moment's notice.

The brothers took a taxi straight from Union Station past the White House to the State-War-Navy Building, today's Eisenhower Executive Office Building. Racing to the Navy Wing, they were again greeted by the gracious Daniels in the secretary's ornate office overlooking the White House's West Wing. Waiting in the office, Admiral William S. Benson, Chief of Naval Operations, and Rear Admiral Robert Peary stood to greet them. Trubee barely waited for Daniels to sit down behind his massive carved oak desk before launching into his description of the Yale Aero Club. He reminded the men about the impressive achievements of the Aerial Coast Patrol, Unit Number 1, during September's fleet exercises in Gravesend Bay and that fall in their work with the navy sub base in New London. They wanted to do more. They wanted to be ready to serve when the inevitable war call came. Before then, they would need to earn their navy aviator's Wings and learn to fly under military conditions. The time had come, Trubee explained, for the expanded organization to leave college and to prepare itself for war. The navy would need to do little more than recognize them. Nearly thirty young men were ready to join the navy.

He explained the standing arrangements with Wanamaker's Trans-Oceanic Company's flying school in Palm Beach. Without exaggeration, the Yale Unit possessed an air force larger than the U.S. Navy. Their parents and other wealthy men were ready to do more yet. Training pilots took months. With war almost certain to break out any day, it was already past time to begin. Otherwise the navy would face months of delay before it possessed even a minimal number of pilots within its ranks who were ready to contribute to the fight. The two decorated admirals nodded intently as Trubee spoke. After he finished, Daniels smiled benevolently at the two young men. He was impressed. "You fellows are a great crowd," he finally said in his thick North Carolina drawl, "and it's wonderful" to have such a patriotic offer. "We don't need you."[10]

As a consolation prize of sorts, Daniels sent them to see his assistant secretary, Franklin Roosevelt, who invited Trubee to join the Committee on Aeronautics he was forming to review aviation preparedness. For Trubee, more talk and no action would be worse than just returning to heeling for the crew team.

The Davison boys were crestfallen. They went back to the train station. Throughout the trip Trubee fumed. His anger about the navy's lack of foresight and the nation's continued unwillingness to fight boiled over. "The United States has been subjected to the most revolting humiliations time and again," he fulminated in a letter to the *Yale Daily News* when he got back to campus, "and still we hesitate to take steps which alone can prove that America pledges herself to join the champions of international morality and to establish beyond dispute a precedent which will well nigh render impossible a repetition of the German self-outlawry." Daniels had scoffed at a college boy's dream of a great navy air corps. Trubee, though, knew better. College students may be young, but their "sentiments," he insisted, "on the subject of war or peace must bear more weight than the experience of its members would seem to permit." Without adequate national military preparedness, they were the ones who would bear the brunt of the burden if, as appeared likely, there came a sudden need for large numbers of men to take up arms. Poorly trained young men like them would be thrown into the military and called on to pay a high price for the government's wanton failure to prepare for war. The nation's leaders were blind to what all on campus could see. "Yale sentiment is to all intents and purposes unified in the conviction that we should forthwith take arms against Germany."[11]

Trubee turned to his father. If Daniels could not see the value of the Aero Club for the time being, he soon would, insisted Trubee. Why wait for the government to come to its senses? "We ought to go," he told his father, "regardless of the secretary."

"You are wrong," his father answered. Flying was a dangerous game. The boys would face serious risks that the wider public would not understand without government backing. They had all seen the articles about Trubee's forced landing in New York City. Should anyone come to harm without the government on board, it could derail the entire enterprise. The senior Davison had not built his fame and fortune as a banker through reckless risk taking. His son proposed the equivalent of the Morgan bank floating an unsecured note. He knew where that could lead. "You fellows won't gain anything by acting against the secretary's wishes," he said. The government could offer training resources that the boys did not otherwise have access to. If they did not wait for the navy to call them up, he warned his son, "if anything happened, as is liable to happen, you could never forgive yourselves. Let it simmer a little longer."[12]

The senior Davison did not believe they would wait long in any case. He had no doubt that the navy's view of the unit's offer of service would alter shortly. With American factory orders and finances bottled up by the German blockade, "damming up a wall of commerce," he wrote, the need to respond would come quickly—"much like the stopping of some arteries in the leg; either the blood must be forced through and the circulation restored or the leg amputated." He was certain that "events will follow each other so rapidly that it can be but a short time before they will be requested to go." When that moment came, he asked his old friend, Colonel Thompson, to be ready to move south with the unit, to act "as the Grand Master," an older, wiser head to watch over the sometimes reckless boys.

Trubee's father cautioned his eldest son against "hasty action," and forbade both boys from enlisting without his consent. His word was final: "There is nothing to do . . . unless a hurry call comes from the government."[13]

Trubee feared the call might never come without his prodding of the naval establishment. Although he had returned to campus, he continued in his attempts to bring the issue to a head. By this time, Trubee knew the small world of naval aviation well. He learned that Lieutenant John H. Towers was visiting New York. Towers was already a legendary figure in flying circles. In 1911, he had become just the third pilot to earn his navy Wings. A year later he established the world's flight endurance record, flying over the Chesapeake Bay for more than six hours and ten minutes. He began a small, informal navy air corps training program two years after that, setting up the first training station in an abandoned navy yard at Pensacola, Florida. Later that year, he commanded a detachment of U.S. navy flyers in Mexico's Tampico Bay, spotting snipers during the occupation of Vera Cruz in 1914, and thus became one of the very first U.S. pilots in combat operations.

During the first two years of the war in Europe, Towers had been posted to the U.S. Embassy in London as assistant naval attaché. While there he had observed the Allied forces and came to understand just how far the United States had fallen behind the warring nations in the development of military aviation.

He had returned to Washington in September and now directed the navy's small experimental aviation program. No man in the navy was more apt to appreciate Trubee's overweening desire to serve in the air, nor more likely to recognize the value of the Yale boys' offer.[14] Trubee tracked him down in New York City.

"What can you fellows do?" asked Towers. Trubee explained the situation to him and assured him that the unit was "ready to move at a minute's notice."

Towers did not hesitate. "You fellows ought to go," he said. Trubee could not believe his ears. Towers asked Trubee to send a letter to Secretary Daniels telling him about their meeting. Trubee wrote and waited to hear back. No response came. Trubee telegraphed Towers: "We still stand ready to move on your orders."

Finally Trubee returned to Washington, this time accompanied by Colonel Thompson, to meet Towers in his Navy Department office. Towers was again sympathetic and asked, "How do you fellows feel about leaving college?"

Trubee had of course been ready for months. "We are perfectly sure we will have to go sooner or later," he responded. "We think we ought to leave," he added, "but we cannot unless the Navy Department wants us to leave."

"If this is the case," repeated Towers, "you ought to go." Towers suggested that the Aero Club members enlist promptly in the Navy Reserve and then follow their plans to train in Palm Beach. Towers made the final arrangements with Daniels.

Trubee feared they might still change their minds. He and Thompson rushed out of the State-War-Navy Building to catch a train home. Trubee could not wait. Before leaving, he wired Bob Lovett back at campus: "We're off!"[15]

By the end of the following morning, Thompson had raised $200,000, plenty to support the unit in the months to come. Morgan & Company provided half, Thompson put in $25,000 of his own money, and Harry and Payne Whitney and George Baker contributed $25,000 a piece. Other donors later added thousands more. Thompson arranged initial housing for the entire unit at the Breakers, a palatial Gilded Age resort-hotel on the beach in luxurious Palm Beach, and began shopping for everything from tobacco to hats and handguns for his squadron. He brought Foster Rockwell on board as his assistant. Rockwell, a 1904 Yale graduate, had won fame as an All-American quarterback on the football team and as coach of the 1906 national championship team. He had since moved to Phoenix, Arizona, where he owned a large hotel, but set off to meet the group in Florida. A physician, Kenneth McAlpin, joined on at the recommendation of Walter B. James, a leading New York physician and father of Oliver James, a crew team and Aero Club member. The senior James purchased a flying boat for the group, as did the father of

James's crew teammate Bill Rockefeller. Other aircraft, some barely flyable, were located in Florida. "We bought every one we could," Trubee said, "picking them up all over the place." With so few available, the unit was "not too proud to grab old flying boats in various stages of decrepitude."[16] Thompson arranged for a private train to move the boys and all their equipment south.

At Yale, Bob raced around spreading the news that the unit members had just five days to enlist, close up their rooms, pack for hot weather, and say their goodbyes. "The final news was so sudden that it made you dizzy," recalled John Vorys. He was at Harvard debating the establishment of a league of nations when he was handed a telegram from Lovett telling him the news and calling him back to New Haven. He was stunned as the significance of what he read dawned on him. In a flash he went from being a college junior to joining the navy. "Talk about the great moments in a young man's life!" he exclaimed.[17]

On campus, the members of the unit went about their remaining student hours in a daze, unsure what lay in store for them. Until this moment, none of it had seemed real. Reality still had not set in. Leaving behind Yale for this unknown future, felt, Bart Read said, like "a sort of pipedream." The university agreed to credit the unit members for their service while in Palm Beach as part of the work toward their degrees. That made the prospect of leaving Yale even more enticing. "It was like being told you would have to go on a vacation instead of taking mid-years," he said.[18]

The campus was abuzz with the news on the evening of Friday, March 23, that the unit would enlist in the Naval Air Reserve Corps in New London the next day and leave campus the following Wednesday to begin formal training. Hundreds of chanting students pulled those among the twenty-nine members of the unit on campus out of their rooms and then paraded them through campus and out into the streets of the city. The torchlight parade sang Yale and patriotic songs until the mob reached the big house of President Hadley. The unit members stood around his front steps as Hadley stepped out to address the rowdy throng that jammed the streets before him. In his high-pitched voice, he praised the boys' recognized leadership in the national preparedness movement. He called for their classmates to ready themselves to make similar sacrifices—"for God, for country and for Yale." The road ahead promised to be long, difficult, and dangerous. Show the spirit of the bulldog, the Yale mascot, Hadley told them. "Brag," he shouted out, "is a good dog, but holdfast is better."[19] The crowd roared and then sang out,

Fight! Fight! Fight with all your might!
For Bingo, Bingo, Eli Yale!

The next morning, the Aero Club traveled to the sub base in New London where Commander Stirling enlisted them into the navy as the service branch's first air reserve squadron, the First Yale Unit. Trubee was given the rank of lieutenant, junior grade. The others who had already soloed—Alphie Ames, Al Ditman, Wells Brown, Harry Davison, Jr., Di Gates, Erl Gould, and Bob Lovett—received the rank of ensign, while those who had yet to fly were made petty officers, electricians, or engineers. Al Sturtevant arrived from Harvard law school as promised to join the group. Cord Meyer decided to stay on campus to continue as captain of the crew team, but expected to join the squadron that summer. Ditman and Brown left work in New York to enlist.

Freshman Crock Ingalls, still too young, could not join the others in enlisting, but insisted on going with them to Florida. Hadley could not refuse and permitted him to withdraw with the others.

For the students on campus, their classmates' impending departure was sobering news. The idle college debate over the war and choosing of sides had now become very real. The unit was the vanguard. Many others would soon follow. "Things are beginning to look like business," commented the *Yale Daily News.* "It may not be long before . . . all the undergraduates of twenty-one or over at Yale will be summoned to protect the flag."[20]

The following week, on March 28, gear packed and their Palm Beach base made ready for their arrival, the unit reported for duty—to Sherry's, one of New York City's finest and most exclusive restaurants. Henry Davison threw a festive going-away luncheon for the entire squadron. "That," admitted Trubee, "was not a bit warlike."[21] Then the boys marched to Pennsylvania Station where they boarded their waiting train and, with families waving, began their journey.

As the unit left, newspapers around the country reported that the "Millionaires' Unit," as some reporters had taken to calling them, had departed campus to begin training as navy pilots.[22] They were the first boys called out of any of the nation's colleges for formal military training. For a nation just beginning to understand that nearly all her sons would soon go marching off to war, they were leading the way. Life would soon change for all of America. A new age was being born.

As the members of the Millionaires' Unit packed their bags and marched away, students still on campus recognized that this was no ordinary band of brothers heading off to war. "Many a man when he saw them leave," observed a classmate, "began to doubt Sherman's famous sentence concerning war. We could but envy them."[23]

SECTION II

Air

CHAPTER 8

Palm Beach, April–May 1917
The Wags

"I⟩⟩T was a long way from France," remarked a gleeful but earnest Trubee Davison. The brightly lit string of cheerful green Pullmans sped southward through the night. As the high-spirited boys bounced and jostled along, they studied the semaphore alphabet, practiced radio telegraphy, and read aviation magazines in the parlor car. From time to time they leaped to their feet in mocking salute of their officer-ranked friends when they passed—typically followed by a playful jab to the ribs.[1]

Still, they understood they were embarking on a serious and potentially perilous journey. And not just because of the physical dangers they might face. John Vorys buttonholed Trubee in the corridor to press him about their "anomalous position." He pointed out that several of the boys were worried about the unit's place within the military. They had followed Trubee almost blindly, abandoning college and its certainties for an ill-defined future. The unit remained suspended in a sort of military netherworld. Although Trubee had secured an official navy stamp of approval for their training project, the government was still not contributing a penny in direct funds to their efforts. They did not have anything except their enlistment papers in support of their mission. Unlike the Yale Battery, the First Yale Unit of the Navy Air Reserve—now their official name—did not even have a home base of its own. They were not even sure how long the navy would permit them to continue their training, or that the government would call for their service once they had completed it.[2]

Moreover, the unit was flying blind when it came to navy life. Nobody knew much more than they had learned on civilian ships about naval organization, rules, and procedures. Unsure how to proceed, Trubee created what he admitted was "a queer kind of organization." Avoiding military designations, which nobody quite knew how to apply, he became the unit's "First Officer," Bob Lovett "Second Officer," and Curt Read "Business Manager."

According to Wells Brown, the young banker on leave, the unit was more gang or school club out on a field trip than military squadron. "We knew nothing about rank or discipline and could care less," he admitted.[3] The result was not quite chaos, but, said Trubee, "There was no discipline, other than what you can imagine from a bunch of fellows getting together."[4]

In hopes of aligning their efforts as much as possible with regular naval aviation training, Trubee had sent Al Ditman ahead to the navy air station in Pensacola, Florida, to learn what he could about how the real navy operated. What he saw shocked him. Naval aviation in Pensacola was a lifeless swamp. The air training station was a forgotten backwater, even within the navy base itself, grown indolent from Washington's indifference to its fate. The student pilots rarely got airborne, lacking enough money to pay for gas and spare parts. Things were no better on land. The navy made no effort to train them in gunnery, bombing, combat tactics, or any other branch of modern military aviation. Ditman found the sum total of the base's munitions in a moldy armory: two antiquated American and French machine guns and a German bombsight "on exhibition as curiosities and not used." When he told the Pensacola sailors in the aviation service about the unit and its big plans, the navy men were dumbstruck. They could not understand why anyone would bother. As far as they could tell, the United States had no plans to enter the war and, should war sneak up on the nation, aviation would be the last to fight. Ditman told his fellow unit members that the navy had paid so little attention to aerial warfare that they had nothing to learn there.[5]

While the train stopped over in Washington, D.C., Trubee and Colonel Thompson met with Lieutenant Towers. They explained their concerns about their paper-thin ties to the navy. Towers agreed to supply a commanding officer, as well as navy signalmen and mechanics, to assist while the unit trained in Florida. They would have real navy men on board. As the train rolled on, the boys felt better. The unit would not exactly be in the navy, but more and more they were truly of it.

The Northeast's bare trees, slushy snow, and cold gave way gradually to greener landscapes. Finally, at 4:30 in the morning, they tumbled from their berths and out of the sleepers into the humid perfume of the subtropical South Florida night. In the night mists, the shimmering lights of the Royal Poinciana Hotel, a massive white structure rising next to the tracks on the shores of Lake Worth, looked like a ghostly ship bearing down on them. The first glimmers of dawn edged the ocean horizon as the boys shambled bleary eyed across a bridge toward the site of the Trans-Oceanic air station in West Palm Beach. To their shock, Dave McCulloch, dressed in evening wear, white tie undone, came tearing toward them over the bridge in a "Red Bug," a sputtering gas-powered wooden cart. He shouted out a drunken welcome to the Yalies. Those who knew him from the previous summer were not surprised that he had stayed out all night carousing with friends before racing out to greet them. The new members of the group murmured among themselves questions about the quality of instruction that awaited.

As the dawning sunlight spread an orange hue over the still water, they walked the half mile to the Trans-Oceanic facilities on Lake Worth. What they saw was not much for the eye. McCulloch showed them a shed with space for a small machine shop. Five plank runways along the curving sand beach trailed off into the lake. The wreckage of old dinghies and storm debris littered the shore above the tideline. Thompson could not believe his eyes. "The Wanamaker hangars? There aren't any," he complained in a letter to Henry Davison.[6] Costly frail aircraft sat perched on stands open to the weather like big awkward pelicans drawn up for the night.

After completing their inspection, they hired cars to carry them and their luggage the three miles to Palm Beach, where they soon settled into their rooms at the storied Breakers on the oceanfront. They immediately began pushing each other through the halls and over the sweeping porch decks in the wheeled chairs kept there for invalid guests come for the sea cure.

Thompson soon decided that keeping his raucous young charges at the refined Breakers might not be wise. He hired out the entire fifty-room Hotel Salt Air closer to the Trans-Oceanic site in West Palm Beach, for $75 a day. He also took over a nearby building for administration and lectures and as a place for support staff to bunk. If the Salt Air was not quite up to the Breakers' standards, each boy would still have a private room and shared bath. To make up for the less-splendid accommodations, Thompson hired the man who managed both the Breakers and the Royal Poinciana to oversee the unit's living quarters. At Thompson's urging, he engaged the most renowned chef in Palm Beach to prepare their meals.

Their arrival had not gone unremarked. The following day, more than a thousand people turned out in the main public park of West Palm Beach for a patriotic salute to the unit. The local militia paraded and a brass band played military songs, followed by windy speeches from local dignitaries as well as Thompson. A Palm Beach newspaper reported about the "boys born with a gold spoon in their mouth . . . who are working harder than many born on the other side of the track." Their commitment to national service represented "a new kind of patriotism."[7] The boys became local celebrities and, as often comes with celebrity, quickly met several of Palm Beach's eligible young women. Yale's unofficial codes of conduct around the opposite sex no longer held. They made arrangements to spend their few free evenings and Sundays together at the local movie houses and hotel dances and teas. "War," Alphie Ames joked, "was hell."[8]

At the crack of dawn the following morning, the whole aspect of the situation changed.

McCulloch was of course nowhere to be found when the boys arrived at the air station. Trubee did not wait. He divided the unit into seven groups and assigned each a machine and an instructor from among the boys who had already soloed. He instituted the same maintain-it/fly-it protocol of the previous summer. The groups were responsible for keeping their own machine airworthy. Their schedule called for roll call mornings at six, flying until noon, lectures from two to three, then more flying and mechanical work until six. Trubee made one gesture toward regimented discipline: failure to get out of bed in time for roll call resulted in a beaching for the day. That was enough to get even the heaviest sleeper up before the first hint of light.

The boys immediately set to work assembling the crated aircraft with Fred Golder, the head mechanic. Golder proved to be, said Trubee, "the best man around planes I have ever seen." He could "smell something wrong" with a machine. A number of times during the next two months, Trubee saw him walk past a machine as somebody made ready to fly. Golder would stop, climb in with the pilot, and show him, to his amazement and relief at the discovery, "that the machine was," Trubee recalled, "about to fall to pieces in a very vital place."[9]

Flight instruction began once McCulloch ambled in to give those who had already soloed a refresher course. Their teams were soon competing for who could get the most flying time out of their machines. Nearly always, somebody worked late into the night on a flying boat, hoping to be the first one out in the morning, or to increase his flying time the next day. The finicky motors were changed at least once, and sometimes twice daily, as were many wires and cables. If a flying boat broke down, that group did not fly.

Still they remained amateurs. Colonel Thompson invited unit backer Harry Payne Whitney to come "see the old man as he lashes these young ducks into line."[10] His boys' intentions may have been noble enough, as he wrote Henry Davison, to make "the old man's eye gleam and his breast heave," but that would never bring them through to military proficiency.[11] More professional help was needed. It soon arrived.

First Caleb Bragg strolled into camp, an experienced amateur aviator, but an amateur with a professional racecar driver's cool bravado. Already well-known to the boys, at least by reputation, the son of a wealthy Cincinnati publisher, and a 1908 Yale grad, he had garnered international fame on the booming race-car circuits around the country. The boys found his style irresistible. Handsome, always attired in sharply tailored suits and soft leather gloves, Bragg was nicknamed the "Chesterfield of the racing crowd." He had earned his swagger. When fresh out of Yale, he had challenged the famous barnstorming auto racer Barney Oldfield on a California track. Nobody gave him a chance to beat the man some still consider the greatest driver of all time. Bragg was so sure of himself that he put up $2,000 of his own money for the winner. He kept his money, beating Oldfield in two straight heats on a wooden oval track.

He went on to win many Grand Prix trophies in this country and abroad. He entered the inaugural Indianapolis 500 in 1911, only to lose his car shortly before the start when another driver went out of control and plowed into it on the sidelines. The following year, he set a world speed record for five miles, covering the distance in a blazing three minutes and eleven-and-three-quarter seconds. He went on to win the Fourth International Grand Prix automobile road race at Milwaukee to take the Vanderbilt Cup as the world's leading driver for the year.

A lover of speed and motor sports of any kind, Bragg was a natural for aviation. He moved to Paris in 1914, where he was serving as an attaché at the United States Embassy when the war broke out. The following year, he returned to America where he learned to fly. He soon sought out the maker of the country's highest performance aircraft, the Glenn L. Martin Company. He purchased Martin's fastest machine and then acquired a partial ownership of the company that he helped to merge into the Wright-Martin Company in 1916. In later years, he would set numerous altitude records before turning to championship motorboat racing.

Wintering in Palm Beach, Bragg stepped away from the Palm Beach social circuit to pitch in as a flying instructor. Although he had made his fame as a daredevil, he refused to let his flight crew race ahead. He soon found his white Palm Beach linens covered in grease, as he required his charges learn aircraft maintenance as a first step to safe flying.

The boys could not compete with Bragg in the fashion category. Covered in grease and reeking of gas and oil, even Bob Lovett rarely changed out of his filthy uniform of overalls or khaki pants and shirts, white linen hat, and sneakers. Still, each flight team quickly developed a style of its own. Leader of the Razz Crew, crew team stalwart Al Sturtevant organized an "Anvil Chorus" to count out in unison the number of bounces a machine took in a rough landing. He led the chorus until he took such a bone-crunching bounce of his own that he was beached.

Lovett's group, nicknamed the Wag Crew, aped his style. Its members soon gained the reputation for having the most dashing and haughty attitude. Taking their cue from their witty leader, they harmonized to popular songs as they worked and took special pride in their cockiness. They made sure those on land knew just who it was darting about overhead, and painted an insignia of their own design—a top hat and cane—on the bottom of their flying boat. That way, said Sam Walker, one of the Wags, "Not only did the unit itself gaze up at the Wag crew with the most profound admiration as it soared above them in the air, but the people of the Palm Beach colony would sigh wistfully as the plane passed by. It personified their ambition to be able to fly like that, but they could never hope to achieve it. Only a few men, five of us in fact, possessed the requisite qualities."

Even a Wag could run into rough patches. When Walker soloed for the first time, his air pump blew off as he banked into a turn over the north end of the lake. The pump flew back into the spinning propeller, shattering it. The entire aircraft shook, screeched, and hammered. "My one idea," Walker recalled, "was to get down before I fell down." He laughed it off with a rakish shrug afterward. "Being a Wag and therefore a superman, I managed to get down all right." Back on the water he found his engine destroyed and one blade of the propeller completely gone. The other blade had sliced into his aircraft's tail, badly damaging the hull. The other men marveled at his ability to land in such a wreck. "If this had happened to some other crew," he boasted, "imagine the consequences! But why knock?"[12]

Eddie McDonnell finally arrived to bring a semblance of military order to the unit. As Lieutenant Towers had promised, he sent a regular navy man to serve as the unit's C.O. and to supervise its training. McDonnell soon made it clear that he expected the unit to become more than a preening gang of rich kids on a Palm Beach vacation. Faced with authentic military authority, the boys snapped to.

Lieutenant Edward Orrick McDonnell had graduated from the Naval Academy in 1912. Although only twenty-five, his naval experiences dazzled even the Wags. He had won fame during the 1914 Vera Cruz engagement, a prior skirmish with Mexico. Landing as part of the three thousand-man invasion force, he set up a forward signal station on the tower roof of the Terminal Hotel while troops battled their way into the city. He provided the sole communication link between them and the ships in the harbor. Continually under fire on the exposed rooftop, he never stopped raising the signal flags to direct the naval bombardment, even as one man was killed and three others fell wounded at his side during two straight days of fighting. Afterward Congress awarded him the medal of honor. With a taste for risk, later that year he entered the aviation service.

Standing tall in his brocaded uniform with his shoulders held back and his chin tucked in, he was the epitome of a military officer. With his dark, deep-set eyes, he looked over his new squadron mustered haphazardly on the runway. Several of the boys tried not to smirk. Others snapped off their best imitation of a navy salute. He had his work cut out for him. He quickly put into place a navy-style training program. He also attempted to teach the boys to salute superior officers and otherwise follow naval regulations. Those efforts at military decorum largely failed. As soon as he turned his back, according to Trubee, the boys showed "no respect to anybody" except their new commanding officer.

Despite McDonnell's spit and polish background, he was not rigid. He adjusted quickly to the unit's quirky organization and even looser style. They were living separate from the orderly world of the military bases he knew. He understood the ordinary channels and rules of the navy did not apply to this special unit. What he cared about was getting things done. They had to learn not just to fly, but to fly on targets, drop bombs, carry out reconnaissance, chart and navigate flights, and fire a machine gun. Along with their daily flying and gunnery lessons, McDonnell lectured the unit each afternoon on bomb sighting, communications, navigation, naval discipline, and fighting tactics. Above all he emphasized the value of practical experience in the air. "You've got to do it with your own hands," he told them.[13]

McDonnell's arrival seemed to signal bigger events in the world. He came to the squadron in Palm Beach at the same time the United States declared war on Germany. With the final lifting of restrictions on submarine warfare, the German Admiralty's U-boats were now openly attacking American shipping, sinking three U.S. merchantmen on a single March day. President Wilson could no longer sustain any vestige of American neutrality. The national clamor for war overwhelmed the remaining voices of resistance. On the evening of April 2, a somber Woodrow Wilson traveled past cheering throngs lining Pennsylvania Avenue all the way to Capitol Hill. Before a special session of Congress, he reviewed the developments in the German U-boat campaign, declaring it a "war against all nations." He asked America to "accept the status of belligerent which has thus been thrust upon it. . . . The world," he concluded, "must be made safe for democracy." The gathered legislators, Cabinet members, Supreme Court justices and military leaders rose to their feet, wildly cheering.

Returning to the White House that night, Wilson wandered into the Cabinet Room. His personal secretary Joseph Tumulty found him sitting at the table staring into space. "Think what it was they were applauding," the despondent president finally murmured. "My message today was a message of death for our young men." He put his head down and sobbed. On April 6, Congress approved the president's call to arms, and with that America was at war.[14]

As the navy made ready for war it could call on just thirty-eight fully qualified flying officers in its regular ranks.

The declaration of war proved that Trubee had been right all along. His efforts to build even a token reserve now seemed brilliantly foresighted.

Since the unit's arrival, Trubee's life was a blur of activity. He awoke well before dawn and finalized the day's schedule with Lieutenant McDonnell and Colonel Thompson and then, working with Foster Rockwell, sorted through requests for badly needed aircraft and engine parts, radio equipment, gas, oil, and other supplies. At six each morning, he gathered the unit on the beach where he called roll and issued any special orders before sending the boys on their way. During the day, he instructed his own flight group and then attended lectures and learned military tactics with the others. His aviation skills continued to improve. Thompson wrote to Trubee's father that his son "flies like a buzzard."[15] Each evening, he met again with McDonnell, Thompson, Rockwell, McAlpin, Bragg, and McCulloch, along with his "officers," as well as Golder, to review the day's work, check on the progress of the student pilots, make sure all equipment remained airworthy, plan for the coming day's flying and instruction, and deal with any problems. "He was always on the job," said Vorys. The demands of running the operation could be overwhelming. The others watched and "often wondered where he had the tremendous strength and vitality to bear up under it."

Despite the pressures and long hours, Trubee never varied, said Vorys, from his typical "sympathetic, cheerful and jovial and friendly" outlook. He never drew rank on the others—except for the rare times when someone overslept—and still managed to remain close friends with the entire unit.[16] That was even true when Charlie Stewart who, despite being a member of the Wag crew, proved unfit for flying and left the unit in May. "Nervous and high strung," according to Ken Smith, Stewart "was never meant to be an aviator."[17]

For the others, though, flying was a dream come true. "We were willing to do any amount of work to get it," said Trubee's younger brother Harry. The rivalry for airborne skill and, above all, flying time became fierce. As engines broke down and spare parts grew scarce, crews began to pilfer from each other. "As burglars we were good," said Dave Ingalls, who enlisted when his eighteenth birthday arrived. What mattered was time in the air. If it meant working on an engine all night, so be it. "The more we did the more we flew, and that was the mark we were shooting at."[18] Anything to fly. For nearly all of them, flying was proving the most exhilarating experience of their remarkable young lives.

Kenneth MacLeish found that learning to fly was changing him in ways he could not have imagined when he had convinced his family to let him sign up for the Yale Aero Club. From the moment he left the earth, he knew he was born to fly. "This flying," he gushed to his parents, "simply fascinates me, and I fairly dream about it."[19] At first, unable to "get over the fact that I am not in an auto," he skidded about through the air. But soon he found flying came naturally to him. He wrote to his sister proudly that he had advanced faster than anyone else in the group of those who had joined the unit during the winter at Yale and even raced ahead of some of the boys who had spent the previous summer learning to fly at Peacock Point.[20]

That marked a turn in fortune for the twenty-year-old college junior. He had struggled to find his place at home and on campus. To his fretting parents in Glencoe, Illinois, he bemoaned their mistrust of his ability to take care of himself. "I wish," he complained, "you could both have the same confidence in me that I have in myself."

Winning their confidence was not easy. There was more to their worries than flying. Their fun-loving boy had been slow to respond to their large ambitions for all of their children. His mother found Kenney "never deeply thoughtful." He was instead the sort who "took events as they came and found cause for joy in all."[21] He had followed his big brother Archie in preparing for Yale at Hotchkiss, but required further study at a Tennessee tutoring school to pass the Yale entrance examination. A good enough athlete to win his "Y" as a pole vaulter on the track team and to play water polo, he lacked his brother's size and could not win a spot on the famed football team.

Once in the air, though, he discovered that flying was a path he could make all his own.

Like the other members of the unit who were gaining experience in the air, Kenney had never before experienced such a sense of freedom—and sheer terror—as he did when, a little more than a month after arriving in Palm Beach, Lieutenant McDonnell walked up to him on the runway late one afternoon in early May. He ordered MacLeish up alone for the first time. He had been aloft a total of only eleven hours, an hour less than the standard instruction time before soloing. "I quaked in my boots," MacLeish admitted. "I was so new at the game that I had very little confidence." McDonnell, however, had seen something special in MacLeish. The lieutenant told the clearly nervous MacLeish to fly as he knew he could, with care and confidence, "very quick and yet not nervous . . . perfectly cool all the time. . . ." Alone in the F-boat cockpit, he went through his checklist as his mates floated him away from the runway and out onto the glassy surface of the lake. He taxied out to the open water, opened up the throttle, looked back at the rooster-tail of spray, felt the hull jump up onto the step that indicated she was ready to take off, "sort of shut my eyes and 'let 'er go.'"[22] And then he was free of the earth, alone, charging up into the sky shining clear and blue as a china plate above him.

Sitting in the open cockpit of the gleaming mahogany hull, MacLeish held the yoke back and kept the gas-air mixture rich and the throttle wide open. With so much wing and nearly a ton of blunt-nosed weight dragging through the air, the flying boat seemed to crawl its way up.

Leveling off at two thousand feet, he held tight to the yoke as he banked over the broad expanse of the lake's blue-green waters. He could see through the Palm Beach Inlet out to the Atlantic Ocean to the east. He circled back above the ramshackle white wooden shop and the weathered plank runways of the squadron's base and looked down on the tops of emerald green palm fronds, freshly watered lawns twinkling in the late afternoon sun, and the burnt-red clay tile roofs of the small hotels, lake houses, and the sprawling Royal Poinciana resort. Once his anxious absorption in getting off the lake was past, he discovered something completely unexpected and thrilling: He was free to "fly the old machine just as I darned pleased." In the air, he had to contend only with the continuous thunder of the engine and the wind rushing by. No instructor sat next to him ready to bawl him out for climbing too slowly or banking too abruptly. He was on his own above the earth.

All his previous nervousness dissolved. The fear he felt flying had been anxiety about making a mistake when the instructor was with him. He had shaken off the last adult hold over his life. For the first time, he felt completely at ease.

Alone at the controls with nobody telling him what to do was like nothing he had ever known before. He was master of his machine, of space, of time, and, looking down at the small creatures scuttling across the land below, even of life itself. He was flying, and he loved it. He found himself grinning from ear to ear and trying to whistle, though the wind blew his lips flat and the roar of the motor and propeller behind him bleached out all other sounds. Deliriously happy, he flew eight miles up the coast.

Then came his first landing, "a thing I will never forget in all my life." He spiraled down toward a lagoon. His throat tightened as he leveled off above the water. He suddenly realized how much he had depended on the instructor before this. He had reached a moment of truth. "Here's where you show yourself that you can fly," he thought, "or here's where you bust something." He cut his engine and floated down. The hull sliced into the limpid water with a splash, a patter, a whispered shush, and then silence. The boat gently rocked on the lagoon's surface, water quietly licking against the hull. He let out a deep breath he had not known he was holding. He clapped once, listened to the echo over the still water and smiled at what he thought was "the most perfect landing ever made."

He cranked the engine and was soon climbing to begin the flight back to the base. Once back at cruising altitude, all the joy drained out of him. He watched as the "fool sun" dropped like a shot into the light-tipped sawgrass and palms of the Everglades. In his excitement, he had failed to notice the time. Up a couple thousand feet, the reddening rays of the sun boiling down into the horizon still reached him. The earth below was already shrouded in thick dusk, with only darkness visible below the treetops. Alone in the air for the first time, he had to find his way home as the last of the glowing ridge of light disappeared along the horizon. He flew south along the coast until he recognized the cut of the Palm Beach Inlet into the blank darkness of Lake Worth. Boats rested at anchor near the shore. A few bare light bulbs cast shadows beneath the trees and in doorways. He circled overhead several times. He could not stay in the air forever.

Finally he swept down toward the black void below. Unable to see the water's surface, he used the silhouettes of the masts of the faintly visible boats as reference points to keep his wings level during his descent. He felt the warm, wet air exhaling off the water and shut his engine off. Striking the surface, he bounced into a "fair landing." The unit shined a beam off a launch to guide him into the flyway.

A first solo flight complete, a first airborne crisis overcome, his confidence soared. He soon felt "absolutely sure that I could get out of anything that could happen to me." A few more solos and he was ready to declare himself "perfectly at home" in an airplane.

That newfound love of reaching high into the sky was a rediscovery of sorts. In the summer of 1910, his family had traveled to his father Andrew MacLeish's ancestral home: Scotland. They traveled to the Isle of Arran, a rustic and hilly island off the southwest coast. Looking up from their village inn, the young Kenney had been fascinated by Goatfell, the island's highest peak. Its heather-covered and granite boulder-strewn flanks rose up sharply from the sea to a bald cloud-dappled crown nearly three thousand feet high. Kenney pleaded for permission from his parents to climb to the top, but they had no interest in hiking up the steep, rocky trail. Finally, out for a walk on the hillside with the family one day, he ignored his parents' wishes and continued ahead while the others stopped for a rest. He disappeared around a bend in the trail. His mother and sister tried to follow, but, their long skirts soaked by the heather, they were forced to retreat back down the trail. His worried mother recalled, "I had to trust Kenneth's salvation to his own native sense."[23]

He raced up the steep incline. For the young, headstrong boy, the moment when he reached the summit left an indelible impression. He was stirred as he stood out on a narrow ledge of rock watching the sunlight stipple the village and seeing the white caps on the sea and green hills stretching into the distance and feeling the cold wind on his cheeks. Then the moving clouds, rolling like glowing sea foam toward him, gradually spread out beneath him and then billowed up around him. "Thrilled" to be so high above everyone else, he found himself "in perfect ecstasies of joy" in his cloud aerie. "The thought of being in the clouds," he later reflected, "was the very last word in altitude, as far as my own comprehension was concerned."[24] Now he could fly over the clouds.

His parents still worried. He tried to reassure them that the flying boats he flew were "as safe as a church." For himself, he knew now he had, at last, found his place high above the earth. "In an airplane I have lots of faith, and I'm not worried in the least." Here was the place he had felt so compelled to reach on that climb up Goatfell. The weeks in Florida were changing him. "I feel perfectly confident in myself for the first time in my life."[25]

CHAPTER 9

Palm Beach, April 19, 1917
The Tap

THE APRIL 6 DECLARATION OF WAR CAME WHILE STUDENTS AROUND THE country were away from college for Easter vacation. Many students old enough to enlist without parental permission—twenty-one at the time—withdrew from school immediately to join the military. "Most everyone else," a Yale student reported, "wished to or was trying hard to leave."[1] The already swollen rolls of the Yale Battery of the ROTC swelled further, and nearly all students on campus took part at least in informal artillery training. Previously carried on in haste, Morning Prayer was shortened to a blur so that students had extra time to spread out together across the Old Campus each morning for physical exercises. Even faculty members drilled.

Within a month after the declaration of war, some seven hundred students from the college and the Sheffield Scientific School—nearly one in five undergraduates—had left campus to join the army or navy. ROTC drills required some twenty hours a week from students.[2] From the classroom to the playing fields, the campus looked less and less like the Yale of old. "Yale," quipped another student, "was no longer a college—it had become a military camp."[3] The same situation held true at other colleges across the country.

The sudden, startling changes on the Yale campus forced students to alter, if not abandon, most normal extracurricular activities. Even intercollegiate sports fell by the side or were drastically scaled back. Once war was declared, Yale, Harvard, and Princeton decided to cancel their remaining contests, as did many other colleges. The next year looked like more of the same. Football coach T. A. D. Jones warned that only students in ROTC or otherwise engaged in military service would be considered eligible to play for Yale the next fall.

A student "has got to be a soldier or he cannot be a football man at Yale," he announced.[4] With so many students departing campus in military uniform, there would be few left to wear the Yale uniform in any case.

Some felt that in a time of war Yale should attempt to retain some appearance of normalcy. A large group of alumni came forward to oppose abandoning competitions against Harvard, calling upon their alma mater to "do everything in our power to make athletics take on as natural appearance as possible" despite the wartime conditions. Students on campus disagreed. The spirit of The Game had been transferred from the Bowl to the Western Front, they responded. "The glamour of the old régime," wrote the *Yale Daily News*, "has been sacrificed to allow preparation for a greater game. . . . Yale is training men who will leave, some within a few months, to join a team whose numbers are in the hundreds of thousands and whose game is war."[5]

With the student body in such flux, other campus activities also faced unprecedented wartime alterations. The senior societies decided to move up Tap Day by nearly a month from its traditional date, the second Tuesday in May. The annual campus ceremony notified juniors of their selection as members for the coming year by the otherwise secret clubs. The three major societies— Scroll & Key, Wolf's Head, and Skull & Bones—also announced another startling change. Fifteen leading members of the junior class were now completing their school year in Palm Beach. The societies would send representatives there for a separate Tap Day.

Since the late 1870s, Tap Day had been the seminal Yale experience, even for those who knew they were not in the race for election (before that, the juniors selected were notified privately). "One of the most picturesque features of Yale undergraduate life" according to the *New York Times*, Tap Day combined the solemn, arcane rites of a clerical ordination and the rowdiness, politics, and pain of boys' picking sides for a football game.[6] The "peculiar custom," as one Yale history called it, served up "the most impressive and the most ludicrous exhibition." It was either "consistent with the best traditions" of Yale or "undignified and inhuman," depending upon a student's disposition—and his personal stake and success in the outcome.[7]

Even those who had no hope of a tap wanted to know who among the possible worthies would receive one and who would be overlooked. Campus handicappers had a field day. Just how the three societies sorted out the most desirable candidates among themselves also gave rise to wide speculation and jockeying for position. In some cases, a sufficiently hubristic man might refuse one society's tap in expectation of gaining that of another club he desired more (in a few cases, to his horror, leaving him out in the cold). The experience could play havoc with young men's febrile emotions, because, as a 1905 student remarked, Tap Day provided the spectators and the participants alike with "a show, an open drama of the primeval passions—fear and jealousy; a drama in which we are the puppets of the play."[8]

Begun at the stroke of five in the afternoon, the regular ceremony occurred beneath the Tap Day Oak, a century-old tree spreading over the Old Campus in the shadow of Battell Chapel. Three years earlier, the Hadley administration had banned all but members of the junior and senior classes and select alumni and faculty from the event. Before its closing to the public, the ceremony had regularly attracted thousands of spectators, hanging from trees, standing on steps, and sitting in the windowsills of the surrounding buildings. Hadley had responded following complaints that expectant juniors who had failed to win a tap faced unbearable public humiliation while others enjoyed the crowd's undivided adulation.[9] Even after the public's exclusion, more than one thousand people filled Old Campus to witness the choices for the forty-five available slots. Newspapers nationwide reported the results and detailed the worthies' accomplishments—and sometimes also reported on surprises among campus leaders who had been overlooked.

The high tension, public exultation, or humiliation could overwhelm the young men at the culmination of their drive for success at Yale. No honor at Yale counted for more than the stamp of approval from Bones or the other societies.

As the clock struck five on April 19, Prescott Bush, a senior class member of Skull & Bones, moved into the pitching, expectant junior class crowd. He reached Newell Garfield, his baseball teammate, a basketball star, and a president's grandson. A roar of approval went up. Bush clapped him firmly between the shoulders—the tap. Then with the command, "Go to your room!" Garfield marched off, proud and relieved, to await further ritualistic orders that would begin his initiation into the society. One by one, thirty-two other students were tapped before the cheering crowd greeted the tap of football and basketball star, champion debater, and academic standout, Charles P. Taft II, son of the former president, the last man tapped on campus for Skull & Bones.

At about the same moment, Tap Day was underway at the Salt Air Hotel in West Palm Beach.

The powerful emotions tied to the senior societies at Yale—and their equivalents at other leading colleges of the day—seem quaintly removed from today's more diverse, less-hierarchical versions of college life. In 1917, the society system and all it signified at Yale embodied the democratic meritocracy and its hypocrisies among young American elites. This great stepping-stone to a future place of leadership in American society formed and informed their outlook and, in turn, created a leadership class that guided America into the twentieth century. For nearly the entirety of each Yale College class before the great changes following the Second World War, the society system provided a sense of purpose, a goal to aspire toward and, in those who won a tap, demigods to admire, envy, emulate, compete against, and despair over. Yale valued the society system as the ultimate, most exclusive reward that powered the character of each college class and drove the real education—the one outside the recitation halls and labs—students acquired during their years in New Haven.

According to President Hadley, proudly a Bonesman, the societies were "a characteristic product of Yale life." That life, at its core, he defined by "its intensity of effort, its high valuation of college judgments and college successes, and its constant tension, which will allow no one to rest within himself, but makes him a part of the community in which he dwells."[10] As Yale understood it, the society system set the wheels of campus industry into motion, spurring driven and able young men, recipients of the longed-for tap or not, to achieve at Yale and beyond.

By the time Tap Day rolled around, comparatively few students in each class, by virtue of their hard work, talent, social grace, family name, and fortune, could be considered candidates for election. Yet nearly all students accepted the dominance of the society system over their lives. Most believed wholeheartedly in its value, even for those who never hoped to bask so fully in Yale's brightest sunshine. "On the eighteenth of May," the *Yale Courant*, a campus monthly, noted after the previous year's Tap Day, "eighty men at most were vitally worried as to whether they were to have the fateful 'Go to your room!' Yet the event was a class affair, the most important in its history. Forty-five men were made happy; painfully bitter was the disappointment of a few; and the rest? Were they witnesses merely? No, it was a great thing in the lives of all; it was good discipline even for the least; it was better for most than if they had been tapped. For who was there that did not feel the least thrill and experience the smallest introspection, who did not leave the campus with a smile on his face, but 'I'll show them sometime!' in his heart."[11] Whether they won a tap or not, the society system built their character and continued to inform their pursuits later in life no matter where they went.

Once anointed by a tap, pledges entered into a special network, never spoken of in public yet widely acknowledged. An air of mystery, legend, gossip, and, well, skullduggery hung about the societies. Their closed meetings in sepulchral clubhouses and retreats at the Canadian woodland camps the societies owned, communication using club code words and inner-circle nicknames, and mumbo jumbo signs and totems combined to lend the societies a compelling, even awe-inspiring, status in Yale's, and frequently the world's, eyes.

For those tapped, they had a place to call their own, a club in which their rigorously maintained campus leadership persona could be set aside among fellows and friends. Rumors abounded of Bones pledges unburdening themselves of their darkest secrets and sexual history as part of their initiation rites and even masturbating while lying in a coffin surrounded by other Bonesmen. Nobody other than Bonesmen ever knew. What went on in the tomb stayed in the tomb. The tap created a closed circle of friends who cemented their bonds through the societies' secret and elaborate rituals. Those bonds forged a reliable coterie whose members could call upon one another in the years to come for access to the highest levels of society. Just as the iron doors to the mystery of the tombs had finally opened to the select few, so did the gilded doors to worldly success beyond Yale. The prestigious culmination of a successful college career—reported widely by the press—established connection and preferment in entry to coveted positions in banking, industry, and government.

That former U.S. President William Howard Taft had been tapped by Skull & Bones was not lost on present students. Undergraduates recognized that valuable ties of society membership endured throughout life. President Taft had named two fellow Bonesmen, including Secretary of War Henry Lewis Stimson, to his nine-man Cabinet. In the same post under Franklin D. Roosevelt, Stimson would in turn call upon several other Bonesmen to fill the upper echelons of the military's civilian hierarchy during World War II. A number of the men on Wall Street who had supported Taft in his fight for Republican Party control in 1912 with his former mentor, President Theodore Roosevelt, had been tapped while at Yale. (Roosevelt could in trust call upon his own loyalties from Harvard's ultimate senior society, the Porcellian Club.)

As Bonesmen and other society members gained high government, judiciary, media, and finance posts, the senior society system also provided a compelling sourcebook for conspiracy-buffs to sort through. Indeed, the list of twentieth century members of the secret societies includes an outsized proportion of American leaders in many fields, particularly finance and government. Society members were especially active in the creation of American national security agencies during World War II and the Central Intelligence Agency afterward, further fanning the belief that a hidden cabal of Ivy League elites had extended their power through the government's clandestine operations.[12]

On Tap Day in 1917, a significant segment of the junior class had come to Yale determined to prove their sand. Winning a tap mattered deeply to them. For those who succeeded, the moment was never to be forgotten. The absolute

sway the class society system held over Yale could, however, prove terribly destructive for some. For those who once had hoped but failed to win a tap, the
irreversible blow could be devastating. Even into the 1950s, rumors circulated
of suicides among those who failed to gain a tap.[13] The society system built the
class that built modern Yale and, with it, the American Century. Witnessing
the 2004 race for President of the United States between George W. Bush and
John F. Kerry—two out of some eight hundred living members of Skull &
Bones—the struggle for the first prize offered by Yale still underlies the moti-
vation for a vital quarter of America's elite.

The unit members gathered at noon in the lobby of the Salt Air Hotel. Even
more than among the class of 1918 as a whole, a tap had been every unit
member's dream. At prep school, selection on Tap Day—often anticipated
through junior versions of secret societies—was something to dream over. For
some on hand it was practically a birthright; for all, it represented an indelible
confirmation of success at Yale. Former football manager and Yale senior Albert Olsen had traveled to Palm Beach to represent Skull & Bones for the Tap.
Unit member Samuel Sloan Walker, a senior, stood in for his secret society,
Scroll & Key. Alternating turns, Olsen and Walker clapped the backs of the
chosen among the fifteen members of the junior class on hand and sent them
off to their rooms. Each was cheered as he stumbled away up the stairs.[14]

Kenney MacLeish watched his classmates leave one by one for the next step
in their journey. He awaited his tap. He tried to suppress his nervous excitement. Archie MacLeish was a member of Skull & Bones. Kenney had not
stood out like his extraordinary brother, but he was popular, a letterman in
track, active in the campus religious mission, a fraternity brother, closely tied
to his class's leaders, and a member of a family with the deepest American and
Yale roots. Now he had taken his place within the elite First Unit. A tap
seemed a certainty.

It was not to be.

As was widely reported the following day, Albert Olsen sent Trubee Davison, Bob Lovett, Di Gates, John Vorys, and Alphie Ames upstairs to their
rooms to receive their instructions for pledging Skull & Bones. Walker tapped
Chip McIlwaine, Reg Coombe, George Lawrence, Erl Gould, John Farwell,
and Curt Read for Scroll & Key. Oliver James and Bill Rockefeller turned
down Wolf's Head. The few seniors on hand were already society members,
the underclassmen would be tapped when their turns came.[15]

Almost alone among his junior classmates, MacLeish had been blackballed.
At Yale, social conventions counted. He understood the expectations. He had

failed to live up to them. "I know why I didn't [get tapped]," he said, without specifying what his fatal misstep had been. Something, or someone, had sealed his fate. It could have been as trivial as smoking the wrong brand of cigarette, forgetting to wear a hat on campus, not holding his liquor well after a night of hard drinking, studying too much, or passing an evening in the company of the wrong kind of woman.

Nearly six months later, the wound from missing out on a tap still bled. Even those closest to him could never understand, he told his girlfriend, "how terribly disappointed I was in not making a senior society." The pain from the blow, he admitted to her, "almost kills me."

After cheering on his friends, he wandered off down the beach by himself to find a secluded spot where he could let the tears fill his eyes. Half a year later, as he prepared to ship off to Europe and the war, he recognized the failed bid for a tap had confirmed the "many chances I've missed to make something of myself." Flying and fighting for his nation would give him a new opportunity to prove himself changed, show himself worthy in a way he had not been able to at Yale. He vowed to "get to France and forget the whole thing and start over again." There, he could regain his honor.[16]

CHAPTER 10

Huntington, June–July 1917

Flights of Romance

As word about the unit's work in Palm Beach and rumors of an expansion of its program spread, letters from across the country poured into Trubee and Harry Davison's father's office at J. P. Morgan & Company, more than two hundred from Yale undergraduates alone. Henry Davison cabled to Lieutenant Towers at the navy department that he was "being deluged" with applications for admission.[1] But the unit had no plans to expand, and the navy itself was struggling to get its own training program up and running.

Besides, flying was expensive. Colonel Thompson looked at his ledger books and began to worry. Although the unit's backers had nearly bottomless pockets, the money poured out as fast as the costly castor oil burned in their engines. Telegrams went out to unit backers asking for new infusions of cash. He had a sixty-man staff from night watchmen and maintenance crew to chefs and waiters. Skilled mechanics earned $15 to $35 a week, while master planeman Golder pocketed a princely $75. Keeping the cranky aircraft flying required not only constant upkeep, but frequent purchases of difficult-to-obtain motor parts, spares, and radio equipment. Thompson calculated the unit's training costs at about $57 per hour of flying—less than the government's own rate, but still a breath-taking sum for the period. Once the aviators had qualified, though, Thompson expected the government to "pay back to us a certain amount for each man's training." Although Secretary Daniels had suggested he would remunerate the unit's backers, he never put that commitment in writing. He happily consented to the unit's continued training through to their aviator qualifying tests, with private donors footing the bill.[2]

Almost as soon as the unit arrived in Palm Beach, Thompson began to plan for its return north before Florida's progressively steamier and stormier days and dive-bombing mosquitoes drove his charges indoors. He investigated several sites on Long Island's North Shore, including a large property owned by Bragg, before settling on the Castledge estate, seventy-five acres with a rambling shingle-sided mansion overlooking a quarter mile of shoreline on Huntington Bay. The property was less than half an hour's drive from Peacock Point. Thompson engaged builders to construct hangars, runways, a machine shop, radio shed, and docks, and set Trubee and Harry Davison's mother to oversee the work.

The boys flew until the very last moment on the last Friday afternoon in May. That evening, the mechanics labeled every engine, spare part, and piece of machine shop equipment. Each of the aircraft was broken down and crated and stowed aboard the private train. Before midnight, the Yale Unit Special left Florida. In just three Pullman and six express cars, the lion's share of the U.S. Naval Air Reserve headed north.

As they chugged along toward their first home, tanned and happy, several lamented the end of their Palm Beach days. Sitting in the parlor car, they looked out at the dark landscape. Ken Smith sighed and spoke aloud the general sentiment: "I certainly don't ever remember having quite such a good time."[3] "We worked like dogs," remarked Trubee. But he was proud of "the most extraordinary spirit of good fun and kidding that you can possibly imagine."[4]

Their instructional work complete, McCulloch and Bragg remained behind. The irrepressible Bragg continued to reach for the limits of whatever machine he was in. That summer, he set American altitude records twice within a few days, first by exceeding 20,000 feet for the first time in the country, then by reaching 21,000 feet. After enlisting, he became an army captain and test pilot at McCook Field, Dayton, Ohio, where he later directed flight activities. In 1918 he flew from Dayton to Washington, D.C., in two hours and fifty minutes, then a speed record. The next year he established an altitude mark for a seaplane by flying to a height of 20,000 feet. McCulloch joined the navy and served as an experimental test pilot for the new equipment American factories began to turn out.

On the train ride north, the unit members had their first reminder that a state of war existed. Their train was routed onto a siding through Philadelphia, instead of making a scheduled stop, after rumors reached them that foreign agents were plotting to blow it up. Family members waited in vain at New York's Pennsylvania Station as the unit remained locked on board all the way through to the new base.

Once they reached the Castledge estate on Sunday evening, they moved quickly to set up their equipment. Walking among the extensive new installations along the beach, they felt for the first time like they were on something resembling a real military base, apart from the civilian world. Armed guards and a sign at the gate warned away outsiders from the "U.S.N.R.F.C." base. The arrival of the khaki navy aviator uniforms Thompson had ordered also bolstered their increasingly professionalized approach as did the addition of more navy enlisted men to the staff.

Although they continued to be members of the Gold Coast branch of the navy—most of the unit quartered in the paneled luxury of the mansion, with maids to clean up after them and a private chef to prepare their meals—the work was real enough. The first airplane was back in the air the day after they arrived in Huntington, and within a week they had reassembled and tested out their full flying boat fleet. Along with their new Navy Reserve Air Station, their flying became more and more professional and systematic. The navy supplied two new seaplanes, including a Curtiss-designed N–9, the navy's standard trainer. A larger-wing, pontoon version of the army's JN–9 "Jenny," the N–9 was more like the types of modern machines being flown overseas. The pilot sat alone in the cockpit behind the engine and propeller of the tractor-motor-powered aircraft. An observer/gunner or instructor in the rear cockpit could communicate with him via a voice tube and used a harness to guide or override the student-pilot at the controls. Harry Payne Whitney provided another, quirkier machine, a cockpit-less, swept-wing Burgess-Dunne that looked like a box-kite version of today's Stealth Bomber. The pilot and crew literally sat atop the pusher's wood fuselage with the canvas wings sweeping out in a raked V behind them. The unit continued to work in five-man teams, but now had enough aircraft that all the flyers could spend at least some time in the air daily. Their hours aloft mounted quickly. One by one, all of the boys soloed.

As the boys flew, Colonel Thompson and his friends spent the day watching them from the deck of the *Whileaway*, Whitney's massive pleasure yacht that he had put at the unit's disposal. Henry Davison also loaned his ninety-five-foot motor yacht, *Shuttle*, to the unit.

Davison had no need of his commuter boat now. With the open outbreak of armed conflict, the oft-reviled, frequently subpoenaed by Congressional committees leader of Morgan & Company now found himself most welcome in Washington. A truce was declared in the ongoing war of words between the national government and the "Money Trusts." Less than a month after the declaration of war, Henry Davison's former adversary Woodrow Wilson came calling. The president asked the banker to tackle the "unlimited opportunities of broad humanitarian service" that the war presented by chairing the new Red Cross War Council.[5] Forsaking his million-dollar-a-year salary "as easily as he would lay aside a winter hat for a summer one" according to the *New York Times*, he took a leave from Morgan & Company and moved to Washington.[6] Wilson charged the council with raising vast sums of money from the public and organizing the resources needed for field and civilian relief in the war zones and at U.S. bases.

Appointed major general by Wilson, Davison threw himself into the task with his usual energetic confidence. He immediately pulled together a coterie of leading young Wall Street bankers whom he dispatched throughout the war zones to assess the need for Red Cross services. They reported back on continent-wide devastation nearly beyond imagining. Davison set to work raising money for the Red Cross. His War Council colleagues listened in disbelief when he announced his plans to launch a $100-million fundraising drive, an unheard of goal for charitable contributions, many-fold greater than any previous level of giving in history. They were left speechless when he told them the campaign would take just seven days to complete.

He succeeded beyond all expectations. "Kick the Kaiser" Red Cross charity events became as common a part of the Great War homefront as "Victory Gardens" were a generation later. Davison's drives were so successful that nearly one in three Americans became either a contributing Red Cross member or served as a volunteer. Before the war ended, 20 million adults—8 million active volunteers—and 11 million youths claimed membership in the American Red Cross. In less than 18 months, the Red Cross under Davison had succeeded in raising more than $400 million. His pay: one dollar a year.[7]

The Red Cross used the money to recruit 20,000 registered nurses to staff the jammed military and civilian hospitals in the United States and overseas. Red Cross volunteers served hundreds of thousands of doughboys hot food and coffee at scores of frontline canteens. Aid reached thousands of POWs behind the lines. Millions of refugees from the war zones received relief services.

Many other financiers and industrialists answered the call to join the war effort. President Wilson also knocked on the door of Bob Lovett's father, Robert S. Lovett. Leaving his Union Pacific chairmanship, Judge Lovett formed the powerful Council of National Defense along with famed stock speculator Bernard Baruch and Robert S. Brookings, a prosperous St. Louis woodenware manufacturer and distributor—later founder of what became the Brookings Institution, still a prominent Washington, D.C., think tank. The trio oversaw a purchasing commission assigned to boost national productivity and guide an expected annual federal outlay of nearly $10 billion for war goods. Each took charge of a business category: Judge Lovett set priorities, while Baruch oversaw the purchase of raw materials, and Brookings finished products. If the government's own push for aviation was not sufficient, Lovett's son would make sure he understood the importance of directing the economy toward building up the lagging American aviation industry.

Although American factories had already been churning out munitions for the Allies, the previous peacetime economy still required radical realignment. The three men had to relocate and in some cases establish entire industries, guide raw materials and agricultural products away from civilian uses to military needs, and straighten out convoluted transportation networks to serve the training, transport, arming, and supply of a new multimillion-man army and navy. The new industries demanded an unprecedented industrial workforce. Millions of men and women migrated from the countryside into the new industries. No country had ever attempted such a rapid, wholesale economic transformation and industrial build-up. With the full support of the federal government, its military and the courts—and the $15 billion in Liberty Bonds purchased by the public—Lovett, Baruch, and Brookings converted the barely regulated American economy into a tightly controlled command economy. Largely rural before the war, workers migrating to the new factories quickly generated the world's most productive industrial economy. America would never be the same.

While titanic forces began to move the national population, the unit flew on. Before the end of June, the entire squadron had soloed. At that point, they began their final preparations toward the navy's pilot's license test scheduled for the end of July. Besides completing a written exam, they also needed to pass a flight test in which the pilot spiraled down from 6,000 feet, cut his engine and leveled off at 3,000 feet before bringing the aircraft in for a landing within 200 feet of a designated mark on the water. They also practiced flying with machine guns and shooting at kites. Firing on a target—or dropping a bomb—from a moving airplane required an eye able to calculate and correct for the relative difference in motion of the aircraft and, when moving, the target. Many pilots never learned deflection firing. Reg Coombe had his doubts when he noted that "Somebody always managed to find a hole in that kite when they got back. I don't know whether it was there when they started or not."[8]

Their flight training included landing approaches to bring them tight on a mark. One of the duties of a navy chief petty officer assigned to the unit was to sit in a rowboat that served as a marker for the planes when they splashed down. The pilots tried to land and bring the plane up as close as possible to the boat. John Farwell, whose steadily weakening eyesight eventually grounded him, hit the water fast and ran up so close to the terrorized officer that, in full uniform, he dove off the boat into the water. The aircraft came to rest just short of the mark.[9]

With their mounting solo hours, their confidence at the stick grew. As the young aviators became better navigators, they began taking off on long flights using only their compasses and charts to bring them home. Soon, they were flying out in search of fog banks to get lost in and then find their way back out. As they mastered the controls, they became more aggressive. While visitors were kept away from the base, unit members made sure those living around them knew what they were up to. They flew along the beaches and sent the bathers in their knee-length swimsuits and straw hats ducking and scampering out of the way. They skimmed up the lawns of neighboring estates and buzzed over the local towns. The booming engines of the aircraft starting up at dawn each morning were hard to miss in any case. The owner of a neighboring estate complained about the early morning noise pounding over the still waters and echoing through the coves, waking him and his dogs. The neighbor asked the unit to push off its flying time to a more civilized hour. Their jingoistic C.O., Lieutenant McDonnell, wrote back incensed "that any man who pretends to be an American could make a proposal [like that] . . . when everybody is bending every effort to defeat Germany in the war." He threatened instead to move the start of their flying time back from five to four in the morning.[10]

The press also kept up with the unit's exploits. With the nation now at war and pushing to recruit other young men into the military, the unit members were lionized, turned into the first of the brave, veritable young deities who had literally soared off the Yale campus and into war. The *Saturday Evening Post* ran a photograph of the unit mustering on the docks at Huntington to accompany a story about "The Aviator's Sixth Sense." "The aviation service," the author wrote, "attracts the very finest of our young men, and offers them everything they crave in the way of romance, adventure and action." He explained the scientific process the aviation services had begun to employ to select only the most promising candidates and warned would-be pilots that getting into the aviation service "is impossible for one who does not possess the sixth sense of a hawk."[11]

The *Washington Post* sent a photographer to the Huntington base to shoot the unit as it went about its business. The resulting full page of pictures appeared in the newspaper's Sunday "Rotogravure Section" under a headline that proclaimed, "Yale May Justly Be Proud of its Aerial Station on Long Island." The photographs showed various members—some looking busy, others striking heroic poses, a few lounging about in the grass studying aviation texts, all very dashing. The identifying captions noted their athletic or managerial accomplishments at Yale and their well-known fathers' names.[12]

For David Ingalls, the attention was everything he had imagined for himself in coming to Yale, and much more. Flying was more of a thrill than a fast hockey game. He quickly became one of the unit's most agile pilots, as well as the most fearless. Taking risks suited him just right. At home in Cleveland, he had already smashed up more than his fair share of the family autos. His father would shrug it off each time, telling his son as he walked away from another smoldering wreck, "It is a good thing so long as nobody is hurt, as you have the experience."[13]

The "Baby Daredevil," as the others took to calling him, seemed destined to get plenty of such experiences in an airplane. He would regularly fly over the base upside down. Just for fun, he would zoom up in the largest machine on hand, a big, slow-moving two-engine boat, and then deliberately drop it into a tailspin. Even smaller, more maneuverable aircraft can be hard to pull out of a tailspin, the most dangerous of all stalls. Sickened by the rotation of the machine and often panic-stricken, few pilots knew how to halt a spin to the earth. The heavy centrifugal forces on the corkscrewing aircraft could also tear it apart. People on the shore and in boats watched anxiously as he spun down closer and closer to the water before he managed to slip his tail sideways, catch lift on a wing, and bring his nose up. In a final flourish, he would swoop down onto the landing mark. Motoring in to the runway, he whooped with glee at each new acrobatic triumph. Others in the unit tut-tutted at what Henry Landon called Crock's taking of "fool chances."[14]

Kenney MacLeish aimed to prove his parents wrong by flying far more cautiously than the underclassman. Increasingly confident as his hours alone in the cockpit mounted, Kenney would, nonetheless, "stop and say to myself that I won't do it" each time before he leaped off the next precipice of flying skill. He assured his worried mother that he took "absolutely no chances." He practiced the required climb and spiraling, steeply banked power turns, long powerless glides, controlled landings, and learned to recognize and recover from a stall. With so much wing and load, the aircraft he flew wanted to remain level and hold a straight course. The ailerons resisted the cable controls and pushed back against the stick. He had to wrestle the flying boats into maneuvers. Each time he succeeded he understood more about flying. He also recognized something new in himself. He was maturing, and not just as a pilot. "I really think I am getting some intelligence after years of fruitless effort!" he joked.[15]

The navy also recognized Kenney's flying ability and caution. After less than three months of training, he and other unit members were already among the most skilled pilots the navy had to call on. The New York Naval Militia's Bay Shore Air Station, then in development on Long Island's South Shore, had students but lacked practically everything else to teach them to fly. A few students each day traveled to Huntington for instruction. McDonnell ordered Kenney to take the Bay Shore students up each time a group arrived. Kenney accepted his duty, but feared he would be stuck instructing for the duration of the war.

He despaired at the thought. "I'm just scared to death that they'll make me stay around here and instruct when I've finished my training," he wrote his mother. He wanted to get overseas to face the test of the real fight. The idea of spending the war teaching other pilots who would then get the chance to join the battle while he was stuck at a training base was "a regular nightmare."[16]

With Peacock Point and the village of Huntington so close by, each day at noon the boys hopped into their Mercers, Fords, and Overlands and raced out in a cloud of dust and exhaust to spend their lunch hour with the Davison family or at local luncheonettes. Many members hoped to convince the seven pretty young women on their base to join them for lunch. The girls, all from the Long Island North Shore area, were learning wireless telegraphy together. Following the declaration of war, Mrs. Davison had brought together a group of her daughter Alice's friends to form the Girls' Radio Unit. The young women, including Bob Lovett's sweetheart Adele Brown, received instruction in sending and receiving code and radio equipment assembly. The unit's own radio instructor, Charles Stewart, called "Radio" to distinguish him from the washed-out unit member of the same name, spent each morning in the base's radio shed with the women. When lunchtime rolled around, the boys fought over who would drive the "fine bunch of lizzies," as Reg Coombe called them, off the base. If any flying boats were free in the afternoon, the boys would take willing girls up for a thrilling hop over the Sound and the neighboring countryside.[17]

One of the few members of the unit with no family nearby, the homesick Kenney MacLeish complained that sometimes he was left alone on the base while everyone else went off. Soon though, he struck up a friendship with the family of one of the radio girls, Priscilla Murdock. Her father, a New York City building contractor, kept a rambling shingle cottage on Peacock Point next to the Davison place. A few years Kenney's junior, his daughter Priscilla attended Westover School, a girl's boarding academy in Connecticut where Kenney's aunt, Mary Hillard, was headmistress and his younger sister, Ishbel, a student. He recalled the doe-eyed Priscilla as a shy teen when she and Ishbel had visited him during his freshman year at Yale. Priscilla had grown into a demure, round-faced young woman, gently pretty with warm, wide-set eyes. Her fashionably voluptuous figure brought her the nickname Chubby and the attentions of many in the unit.

She enjoyed the attention, Kenney's most of all. He became a regular guest at the Murdock house. He would stop in to see Priscilla in the radio shed during free moments and picnic at lunch with her on the lawn. He took her up for a flight over Peacock Point. Soon they were spending nearly all their free

time together. As the warm breezy days of summer accumulated along the
shore, they walked hand in hand down the beach. They talked about seeing
more of each other after the war ended.

The war had become the Davison family business. Along with managing support for the aviator's base and the Girl's Radio Unit, Red Cross Major General
Davison's wife also threw herself into volunteer activities in support of the war
effort. As new munitions factories and entire military cities sprung up
overnight, women migrated into jobs and places they had never been before.
Provisions were being made by the government and the Red Cross to provide
housing, aid, and comfort for the millions of young men in the military. No
similar effort existed for the many tens of thousands of young civilian women
who served as secretaries, cooks, nurses, factory laborers, and farm workers in
those same bases and towns. "What are you going to do for our girls?" mothers
from around the nation asked Mrs. Davison.

After a marathon five-day meeting in New York City of high society women
from across the country, Mrs. Davison helped to organize and became treas-
urer of the War Work Council of the National Board of the Young Women's
Christian Association. "War," she told the *New York Tribune*, "is woman's
problem as well as man's, and they must be taught to meet it adequately." Girls
were being "taken out of their homes" and needed "to find boarding places and
recreation and safeguarding." Along with Bob Lovett's, Erl Gould's, and Wells
Brown's mothers, she campaigned to raise more than $1 million for the
YWCA to build scores of clubhouses, recreation centers, camps, and cottages
for women from coast to coast. The War Work Council also dispatched workers to provide similar assistance for women in England, France, and Russia.[18]

Mrs. Davison supported her husband's Red Cross work as well. She founded
and chaired the local chapter of the Red Cross and brought many of her wealthy
neighbors in on the efforts to raise funds. Flyers from the army base in Mineola
had challenged the Yale Unit to a baseball game. As a Red Cross fund-raiser, on
Bastille Day, July 14, the two teams met on a diamond laid out on the polo field
at Peacock Point. Several hundred New York and Long Island socialites filled the
grandstand. They oohed and ahhed when more than a dozen army aircraft and
nearly as many unit flyers circled over Peacock Point and then put on an aerial
circus, looping, spinning, and rolling overhead. The army pilots landed on the
grounds and the unit flyers—including McDonnell, Lovett, Sturtevant, and
Ingalls—pulled up on the beach. The spectators cheered as the dashing young
men in their flying uniforms stepped into the stands for the game.

The day marked a happy reunion for many on hand. Meeting unit members'
parents and supporters, Henry Woodhouse went about boasting how he and

the other governors of the Aero Club had put Trubee onto the idea of forming the Aerial Coast Patrol, Unit Number 1, in the first place. Several French army officers sent by their embassy charmed the local socialites with tales of daring from the war. Former President Teddy Roosevelt's son, Quentin, who had been a year behind Trubee at Groton, had left Harvard to join the army's newly formed Signal Corps First Reserve Air Squadron and was training in Mineola. He sat in the stands with the Davison family to watch the game.[19]

The warm days of flying continued. For the boys, those balmy summer days were nothing less than a "terrific game," as unit member Chip McIlwaine described it. "We did have a lot of *esprit de corps* and a lot of fun and a great time together. It was pretty de luxe."[20]

But for some the game could turn dangerous. In a low-level turn, Curt Read side-slipped into the shore, smashing the aircraft. He crawled out of the wreckage unhurt, but worried that the next time he might not be so lucky. Similarly, Harry Davison, Jr., came down hard, destroying his seaplane. Shaken and bruised, he decided nonetheless to get back into the air the next day. A navy seaman on the base was not so lucky. While cranking a propeller, the engine backfired and the wheeling end of the prop caught him on the arm, knocking him headfirst into the spinning blade. He died that night.

CHAPTER 11

Huntington, July 28, 1917

Broken Wings

SATURDAY, JULY 28, DAWNED CLEAR AND WARM. A SOFT, STEADY BREEZE blew down the Sound and the tide ran high beneath the wind-ruffled surface. Perfect flying conditions. After a gala luncheon for unit members' parents and supporters beneath a tent set up on the grounds of the Castledge estate, Lieutenant Commander Albert C. Read, C.O. of the Bay Shore Naval Air Station; Lieutenant Commander Earle F. Johnson, superintendent of aeronautics at the Pensacola Naval Air Station; and Lieutenant McDonnell boarded the *Shuttle* together with Colonel Thompson, his aide-de-camp Foster Rockwell, and unit surgeon Doctor Kenneth McAlpin. Motoring out to Huntington Bay, they stood together on the rear deck, the navy officers' brass buttons glinting in the sun, discussing the afternoon's program. Nearby, the *Whileaway* swung at anchor. Onboard, Trubee's father and mother, along with several of their friends, the parents of many unit members, and the yacht's owner Harry Payne Whitney and his brother Payne, sat protected from the sun on the covered deck. Dozens of smaller yachts and other watercraft cruised back and forth over the Sound.[1]

At the base, three F-boats warmed in the shallows off the runways. More than one hundred people gathered on the decks and shore, where they watched the pilots and mechanics readying the aircraft. Their white navy hats and bonnets fluttered in the propeller wash. In the cockpits, Trubee Davison, Bob Lovett, and Di Gates could not hear the cheers over the roar of the engines, but twisted about to see the smiling faces, and waving arms and fists pumping proudly. The three pilots checked their controls. Trubee being the chief officer of the unit would take to the air first, followed by the next two most senior members.

All twenty-eight members of the unit had passed their written examinations. Now came the flying test for their navy Wings. It was the most important day in the short history of the unit, Trubee's unit, a day for honors and celebration. Trubee fidgeted with his controls and nodded over at Bob and Di. Di eyed him uncertainly. Trubee had complained to him earlier about his lack of recent experience in an F-boat. He had spent virtually all his time aloft since coming to Huntington instructing others, and nearly all of that in the N–9 seaplane. After flying with a stick control for the past two months, the F-boat's yoke controls felt strange to him. He worried about getting the aircraft down close enough to the mark. And he still felt queasy and lightheaded. Under the hot sun the day before, the exhaustion from the long days of work and the stress of running the unit had finally caught up with him. He had fainted on the dock. Reviving quickly, he had insisted he felt fine, but now he was not so sure.

During the lunch earlier on the grounds, he had sat quietly amid the buoyant crowd. At one point, he turned to Foster Rockwell and remarked that he just was not sure he had what it took to pass the flight test. Rockwell was baffled. He reminded Trubee of his long and distinguished solo record. He had spent more time in the air than any man in the unit, hundreds of hours already. The test requirements—flying up some 6,000 feet and then spiraling down before cutting the engine at 3,000 feet and gliding the rest of the way into a landing within 200 feet of the mark—would barely tax his flying skills.

His engine warm, Trubee turned back to see Fred Golder. The ingenious mechanic stood in waders holding his tailplane. He gave Trubee the thumbs up. His aircraft was a healthy bird. She was ready to soar.

Trubee bounced across the water's corrugations and rose up over the Sound. As he flew away, Di and Bob taxied out and soon were chasing up after him. After nearly half-an-hour's climb, Trubee reached the required ceiling. On the boats and shore below, the examining committee and spectators shaded their eyes against the sun as he spiraled downward in tight gyres. Banking through his turns, Trubee kept his eyes on the *Shuttle*. He cut his engine at three thousand feet and began to glide downward in widening spirals, swooping over the cheering crowd at the hangar and then back out over the Sound. As he descended and slid over the base in what was to be his final turn, Trubee realized he would need to extend his glide in order to reach the required distance from the landing mark. He flattened the aircraft out. At two hundred feet above the water, he stared down at the men on the stern of the *Shuttle*. His F-boat remained flat while he ruddered stiffly through the final turn. Rockwell muttered aloud, "He's flying like he's never been in a machine before." A puff of wind from Trubee's left buffeted the slow-moving aircraft. Overreacting he threw over his controls in response. The aircraft suddenly banked heavily to the left, lost all airspeed, and then fell over the leading wing as if it had rolled off a table. Trubee had no time to react as he corkscrewed a half turn and hit the water nose first.

Those in the boats and on shore gasped when the aircraft hit. The sound of the mahogany hull crunching and splintering could be heard across the Sound. The sharp impact snapped it in two and knocked the engine from its bracing. The broken and splayed wings floated upward over the partially submerged, severed hull. The *Shuttle* raced over to the crashed machine. The tangle of wire and wood poking through torn canvas was unrecognizable as a flying boat. Trubee lay stunned within the shattered cockpit, pinned by twisted wire, crushed bracing, and shattered planks. He struggled to free himself, but was trapped within the swamped wreckage that was sinking and pulling him under with it. The splayed wings, floating wood, and his upturned face were all that remained above the surface. Lieutenant McDonnell, the Medal of Honor recipient, dove off the boat in his uniform and swam to Trubee. Unable to lift him out of the debris, he dove under the water into the submerged cockpit to unlace the tangle of wires and broken planks around Trubee's legs. Those watching worried that he, too, would become ensnared in the wreckage. He resurfaced, dragging Trubee free as the remains of the F-boat sank into the Sound. The men waiting on the *Shuttle* lifted him onto the deck. Nobody even noticed as Di and Bob splashed down nearby.

Otherwise one of the most competent and experienced pilots in the unit, Trubee experienced what today would be recognized as a panic attack. "Aviation," Chip McIlwaine observed, "depended on the coordination of your nerves."[2] Exhausted, nervous, anxious to succeed, worried about his ability to perform, inadequately prepared, Trubee lost his nerve. In response to minor turbulence, he made fundamental errors that sent his aircraft into a stall and final, calamitous dive to earth.

The *Shuttle* sped him to the New York Yacht Club Landing on the East River. As Trubee lay on the deck in pain, he whispered to Rockwell, "I had no business flying today." Bob Lovett and Dave Ingalls raced in Curt Read's speedy Marmor roadster to New York. A policeman on a motorcycle about to pull them over heard their shouts about the accident. He escorted them across the Queensborough Bridge. They found the family's doctor and brought him to meet the yacht at the landing. An ambulance transported Trubee from there to Saint Luke's Hospital.

As Curt Read watched the *Shuttle* carry the unit's fallen leader away, he turned to his mother, Caroline. "If it had been any of us but Trubee!" he cried. "You never can know what he means to us!"[3]

CHAPTER 12

France, August–September, 1917

We Are So Green

Trubee's horrifying crash left the other unit members feeling fragile and badly shaken. Still, they managed to pass their examinations and qualify for their Naval Aviator ranking. The twenty-seven flyers counted among the first hundred men ever to win their navy Wings. By the Armistice on November 11, 1918, the navy had 6,716 flying officers, including 1,650 with their Wings.[1] Since then, tens of thousands more have won that distinction, but the unit could forever boast of being among the first one hundred. Di Gates took pride of place, qualifying first in the unit, and was designated Navy Aviator Number 65; Bob Lovett came next at 66; Henry Landon was the last from the unit to earn his Wings, and received Aviator Number 93.[2]

The unit quickly saw action—of a bumbling sort. In the first days of August a German submarine was reported prowling off the South Shore of Long Island. On August third, the navy ordered the Huntington Station to send out an armed patrol. With Trubee's brother Harry as observer, Curt Read took off in the N–9 seaplane with a ring-mounted recoilless Davis Gun. They flew across the island and then searched offshore for the phantom U-boat. After patrolling for two hours, sighting nothing more than schools of feeding blue fish, they flew back to Huntington Bay. Floating on the water, Harry decided to test fire his gun. He let off a burst that succeeded in shooting the propeller blade to bits. The first wartime aerial combat mission flown from the United States ended with a tow to shore.[3]

That Keystone Cops' beginning was in keeping with the general state of aviation affairs as America went to war. The enormity of the task facing the country was finally starting to dawn on the military. The nation's institutions of war were new, its leaders inexperienced, their equipment nonexistent. In no military branch was the United States further behind than aviation. When war was visible on the horizon, America had "remained . . . inert in demanding at least a nucleus of an air force," observed Lieutenant Commander W. Atlee Edwards, Aide for Aviation to Rear Admiral William Snowden Sims, the Commander of U.S. Naval Forces in Foreign Waters. The navy fielded a collection of obsolete aircraft and ill-trained men that could barely be labeled an air force. The day war was declared, the nation's most technologically advanced and best-funded service branch could call on just 22 operable seaplanes, 38 qualified pilots, and 163 enlisted men for aviation duty.[4]

America was launching itself into a war of unimaginable ferocity against a hardened, modern, well-equipped foe. Germany was producing as many as one thousand airplanes a month in 1917. In its entire history, the American aviation industry had built fewer than 1,000 airplanes in total. More importantly, the German air service, though smaller than the French and British, held a technological edge. German pilots enjoyed a distinct advantage in combat.[5] America did not even know how far it lagged behind the British and the French—let alone the Germans. Its military was flying blind into the air war.

What the United States lacked in experience and equipment, though, it was determined to make up for with financial brawn, industrial genius, and an indomitable will to win. Aroused from its torpor, a government that had formerly sniffed disdainfully at aviation suddenly came to worship this new winged god of war. In July, Congress earmarked $640 million toward building up an air force—only $53 million less than the previous year's entire federal budget and the largest single appropriation in U.S. history.

The results bordered on a fiasco.

With effectively unlimited funds, a sudden, unconstrained enthusiasm was unleashed for a military field that nobody in power understood in the least. "We were dealing with a miracle," gushed Secretary of War Newton D. Baker. Like all religious awakenings, rationality could not be allowed to impede the vision of its converts. "The airplane itself was too wonderful and too new, too positive a denial of previous experience, to brook the application of any prudential restraints which wise people know how to apply to ordinary industrial and military developments."[6]

Indeed, no restraint or wisdom stood in the way. The results were monumental, mostly in their waste. "We were not only unprepared, but we had very little idea of how to prepare for aerial warfare," admitted Edwards in his postwar report to Admiral Sims. Never, contend some military historians, did so much spending bring so little in return.[7]

The British and French expected a great deal from their new ally. The United States did not fail in making promises. Even a simple review of industrial conditions would have made clear the promised goals could never be met. France asked for 12,000 fighting planes, 5,000 trainers, 24,000 engines, 50,000 mechanics, and 6,200 trained pilots in the field by July 1, 1918. The United States did not demur. The proclamations bordered on the ludicrous. General George Squier, chief of the Army Signal Corps, the air service branch, called on his country to "put the Yankee punch in the war by building an army in the air, regiments and brigades of winged cavalry on gas-driven flying horses."[8]

There was not even a remote chance of such a vast and wondrous force reaching Europe in the short term. Even a nation with America's immense financial and material resources could not swell its miniscule design and production capacity and nonexistent training facilities at such an astronomical pace. American industry and military required complete retooling and the acquisition of nonexistent skill sets on a heroic scale. (The impossibility of the United States achieving anything like those levels eventually convinced Pershing to contract with France, England, and Italy to supply aircraft and to train his men until the United States could gear up sufficiently to develop its own flying force. As the war continued and more realism—if not prudence—entered Allied reckoning, that was no longer considered possible until spring 1919. In the end, France supplied eighty percent of U.S. combat aircraft, England and Italy most of the rest.)[9]

Pershing eventually agreed that "in no other service was unpreparedness so evident and so difficult to overcome."[10] His appointments rarely helped. In 1918, he named his West Point classmate, Major General Mason M. Patrick, an army engineer, to head the AEF Air Service. When notified of his new command, the baffled Patrick sputtered, "I have never before seen an airplane except maybe casually. . . ."[11] Hiram Bingham, Yale's brash explorer of Machu Picchu, trained briefly with the unit and then, after completing his flight lessons privately, joined the army, where he directed the new training schools being set up around the country. Wherever he traveled he found "splendid courage accompanied by a high degree of disorder." The nation lacked experienced men, officers who knew the first thing about aviation and airplanes fit for war service. "America expected to win the war in the air," he observed, "and was utterly unprepared to do so."[12]

The European allies quickly learned just how backward their New World ally was when the Yanks began asking questions. Secretary Daniels cabled Sims requesting that he inquire among his British counterparts, "What style of aircraft is most used and what is most successful over the water? What is the method of launching at sea when carrier vessel is under way? For coastal patrol and submarine searching what are the types of aircraft used?"[13]

Although thrashing about wildly, the long-dormant nation began to assemble its forces. From the single Pensacola training station—with a capacity for just sixty-four pilots—the navy set out to establish the foundations of a training program. A new ground school at MIT took in its first recruits in September. Other even larger ground schools eventually opened at the University of Washington in Seattle and at the Dunwoody Institute in Minneapolis. The navy developed flight schools and patrol and experimental stations up and down the two coasts, including massive new installations at Hampton Roads in Virginia, Miami, Key West, and San Diego, and expanded the Bay Shore and Pensacola air stations for advanced ground and flight training. The fantastic vision of a chain of aerial coastal defense stations promoted by Admiral Peary, Henry Woodhouse, and the Aero Club was finally becoming a reality, with new patrol stations popping up from the Panama Canal Zone to Nova Scotia.

The navy also geared up for production of its own aircraft. With no limit on funds, speed counted above all else. Just 228 days after breaking ground, the navy test-flew the first flying boat produced in a newly constructed 900,000-square-foot aircraft manufacturing and assembly plant in Philadelphia. The choice of aircraft design flip-flopped several times, but before the war ended, the vast factory was turning out Curtiss H–16 twin-engine, long-range flying boats in large numbers. Many entered service at navy air stations in England, Ireland, and France. Despite much fumbling, appalling waste, and suspected fraud, in the nineteen months from the declaration of war to the armistice, the navy had much to boast of, including creation from virtually nothing of thirty-nine naval air stations, twenty-seven of them overseas. Navy and marine aviation eventually comprised nearly forty thousand men, two-thirds more than the entire navy's personnel when the United States declared war and a nearly four hundred-fold increase in aviation alone.

Ironically, the most backward military branch, aviation, was the first to plant the American flag "over there." Despite being unable to staff even a single air station on a war-footing when the United States declared war, a contingent of seven naval aviation officers and 122 enlisted men arrived in Paris on June 5, preceding by three weeks General Pershing's own far more ballyhooed entry into Paris with the first of his expeditionary force. Under the leadership of Lieutenant Kenneth Whiting, the First Naval Aeronautical Detachment rented a house and set up American Naval Aviation Headquarters in Paris, the first official American military post in Europe.

Disorganization and miscommunication continued to be the order of the day. Whiting ventured into the war zone without instructions of any type except to make contact with the French Admiralty. A former commander of the Pensacola training station, he may not have been the most judicious choice for the first American military officer to deal directly with the French. The submariner-turned-pioneering aviator (Naval Aviator Number 16) was an impulsive dare-devil who had once had himself shot out of the torpedo tube of a sub and otherwise found ways to take part in every risky naval enterprise he could.[14] He reviewed the situation in France. Without waiting word from Washington, he committed the United States to the creation or takeover of a chain of naval air stations along the French seaboard, including one, at Dunkirk, the Allies themselves considered largely indefensible.

The confusion reigning within the navy chain of command became increasingly clear to all. At a meeting of the Board of Admiralties in London, Admiral Sims, who had sailed over in mufti shortly after the declaration of war, was asked why the United States had chosen to concentrate such a large aerial force in France when the enemy submarine campaign had turned the bottleneck passages right off the English and Irish coasts into a graveyard of hulls. The white-bearded, thoughtful, and strikingly handsome former president of the Naval War College had no answer. He did not even know Whiting had been dispatched to France. Sims eventually thought it better not to undercut Whiting's initiative and supported his plan. However, he soon recalled Whiting and put his own man, Captain Hutch I. Cone, who had previously overseen the modernization of the navy fleet to steam, in charge of naval aviation overseas.[15]

Sims, though, was in for another shock. Admiral Sir John Jellicoe, the Admiralty's First Sea Lord, revealed that shipping losses had placed his country "within measurable distance of strangulation." He confessed to Sims: "The Germans will win unless we can stop these losses—and stop them soon."[16] Britain, by his staff estimates, could hold out only until November. What was the solution to the U-boat encirclement, asked Sims? An ashen Jellico replied: "Absolutely none that we can see now."[17] The United States still faced months of preparation before any force large enough to influence the war's outcome would be available; by then, American rescue for the beleaguered Allies might prove too late.

The navy that once snubbed the unit now desperately needed its help. The newly licensed pilots increased the navy's total by more than half and—especially with Whiting's detachment overseas—provided almost the entire nucleus of flying officers around which to build an air force. The navy turned to them first. Nothing could have been more disappointing for the gung-ho unit members. Their ambition was to get to the front. They wanted to fly and fight.

As their orders began to arrive, several members were sent to set up new training stations and bases in the United States. Many despaired over the instructional and organizational tasks being assigned to them. Kenney MacLeish's nightmare of training others to chase the glory he hoped to win for himself seemed to be coming true. Gloom began to spread through the unit base. To sustain morale, Lieutenant McDonnell asked the navy to send his two most senior officers, Di Gates and Bob Lovett, to France. "It . . . would show that exceptional ability and industry will be rewarded." The navy consented.[18]

After a send-off celebration in Huntington, on August 15, the two twenty-one-year-old ensigns, both soon to be promoted to lieutenant, boarded the *St. Paul*, an armed merchantman out of New York bound for England. At long last, more than a year after its founding as Aerial Coast Patrol, Unit Number 1, the first contingent of Yale Unit pilots, was heading off to war. The others looked on enviously. "I wish," wrote Alphie Ames, who had been posted across Long Island to Bay Shore, "we were all going on the same boat."[19]

Any romantic ideas about war Di and Bob may have harbored slipped away with the last sight of the New York skyline. Intent on sapping American morale by bagging as many U.S. vessels as possible, the Germans had redoubled their U-boat campaign. A North Atlantic gale raged as all eyes aboard the tossing *St. Paul* scoured the horizon. As they entered the most dangerous zone of passage, they stood watch for four hours on and four hours off, seventy-two hours straight. Their eyes ached from the wind-propelled slap of salt water spray and rain sweeping over the deck. Life within the stuffy, bouncing ship was even worse. Total black-out conditions prevailed. Even smoking was forbidden except deep amidships. Lovett felt seasick the entire crossing.

The harsh realities of war intruded before they reached port. In the middle of the night the ship steamed into the Irish Sea, the most active German hunting ground. The watch spotted five distress signals fired off from several different points on the horizon. Three hours earlier a ship had been sunk nearby. The day before three ships in a convoy had gone down. Ships sailed under orders not to stop to pick up survivors to keep from becoming the next victim of lurking U-boats. In some cases, cunning German submariners fired off distress signals themselves to attract ships away from their protective convoys. The *St. Paul*'s captain maintained his zigzag course toward England. "It was awful!" Lovett wrote from onboard about the inevitable fate of the men floating about in open boats in the storm. "Ye gods, this is a cruel game!"[20]

Finally, he and Di arrived in Liverpool and took a train to London. For Gates, it marked his first visit overseas. With the more widely traveled Lovett as guide, the two made the rounds of well-known tea shops and attended the theater. They bought canes and gloves, customary for British officers, and enjoyed the recognition they received on the streets that teemed with soldiers and sailors from around the world. The relatively uncommon sight of American officers still elicited comment. Everywhere they encountered signs of shortage. The strapping Gates complained that he could not get enough bread at meals, while the pastry shops were bare and sugar rationed. They soon came to know the rotating schedule of "heatless," "meatless," and "wheatless" days forced by the U-boat cordon. Many cold days lay ahead.

When venturing out at night, they wandered through an eerily dark and silent city, windows shuttered and street lights darkened, while overhead patrols droned and searchlights darted about scouring the sky for Zeppelins coming over the Channel. The occasional air raid sent Londoners scurrying into cellars and tube stations. All over Europe people lived underground in cold, wet darkness. Since the lamps went out over Europe in 1914, its once great civilizations had descended into a new dark age. Bob and Di were a long way from the gaily lit world of home.

On August 30 they crossed the Channel and reported to Lieutenant Whiting at Naval Aviation Headquarters in Paris. What they found was dispiriting. Nearly all of the original detachment had been dispersed. Beyond Whiting, the complete naval aviation staff in Europe now consisted of a paymaster, an assistant paymaster, and a yeoman as office boy. Even more downcast were the French themselves. The war had almost crushed the once-proud nation. Bob complained that the people he encountered were "fatalistic and degenerate." The French were "fed up with war and its suffering—they would never have been able to face the future if we had not brought hope just in time." The Americans heard stories of mutiny, of desperate men in the trenches shooting their officers or deliberately wounding themselves—"anything rather than another winter in the hell of the Front."[21]

They also learned to their dismay that, Bob reported, "the Germans are masters in the air."[22] The Germans had aerial weapons the Allies could not match. Their Rumpler photographic machines flew at ceilings beyond the reach of the Allies' chase planes, making them virtually invulnerable on their reconnaissance missions. By flying at night, the big Gotha bombers could penetrate dense aerial cordons on their raids over Paris and London, terrorizing millions of civilians. The enemy's Fokkers were more agile and faster than the current generation of

Sopwiths, SPADs, and other scouts the Allies sent into battle. The Allies were growing desperate.

Whiting dispatched both Lovett and Gates to a French flight school in Saint Raphael on the French Riviera. Expecting war, Di found himself instead at another glamorous coastal resort. After his past spring of basking in the sun and luxury at Palm Beach, and then summer along the Long Island Gold Coast, he feared, "When the real thing does come, I probably won't know how to act."[23] He would find out soon enough.

Although the front was hundreds of miles distant, the impact of war was shockingly clear to Gates. Men were wasted at appalling rates. Flyers died fast, whether in battle or in training. Half of all pilots in the war would be killed or wounded; fully half of those casualties came in training accidents before the aviators ever reached the front.[24] The call for fresh flyers was just too pressing to give them the months of real preparation required to ready a pilot for aerial combat. Men were sent into battle with only ten to fifteen hours of flying time. There was little time for such niceties as caution in the French flight school curriculum. Despite the high cost of training pilots and building aircraft, aviators were expected to fly with reckless abandon from the start. Di witnessed ten smash-ups on landing in a single day. An aircraft's tautly stretched canvas over tensioned wood and wire made a unique, unforgettable crunch in a crash and often left the bodies of those on board horrifically mangled or blackened to a crisp, yet noted Di, "no one thinks anything of it."

The French expected successful pilots to live at the edge of their equipment's power and reliability. Di and Bob soon came to fly like their French tutors, all-out at low altitudes over long distances, relying on their engines to preserve their lives. After a long flight at altitudes where any mechanical failure would have hung him up in the tree tops, Di found the training "so strange and hard to get use to after the conservative training in the States."[25] Most often pilots and observers in training walked away from their hard landings with cuts and bruises and were quickly sent back in the air. Soon, though, he witnessed the terrible price the French approach could exact. After watching an aircraft plummet to the ground as he flew nearby, Di landed in time to see ground crews extract the dead pilot and grievously injured observer from the tangled wreckage. His first sight of shattered bodies in a wreck unnerved him. "I expect I shall get quite hardened to such a thing after awhile," he reflected, "but it doesn't seem possible."[26]

Ever the driven competitor, as his aviation combat skills sharpened, he grew impatient with training. He was ready for "my share of danger and excitement." He could not wait to find out how he would react when he did finally face war.[27] He wanted to be sent to the most dangerous and exciting place of all: Dunkirk.

Site of the virtually miraculous overnight evacuation of the trapped British Expeditionary Force in the next Great War, Dunkirk had already won fame as "Tragic Dunkirk," holding out in the face of relentless bombing and air raids. The small industrial port city sat at the furthest northwestern corner of France, a precarious thirteen miles below the point where the Western Front dropped off into the sea. North of the major ports of Calais and Boulogne, its strategic deepwater harbor provided the closest link between the Continent and the British Isles. Ships and aircraft made the swift traverse between the two by crossing the English Channel where it constricted to the narrow Straits of Dover before opening back out into the North Sea.

Opposing British, French, and German bases, ports, and air installations dotted the landscape around the strategic region. Southeast of Dunkirk, the notorious Ypres Salient in Flanders had already seen some of the most epic and vicious campaigns of the war. Following the devastation of floods and millions of artillery shells, all that remained was a desolate wasteland through which the facing trenches ran. The steady pounding of artillery fire echoed throughout the region. Flashes from explosions lit up the nighttime sky across much of the horizon. Bombs from air raids, ship guns, and artillery shells rained down on the streets of the ruined city day and night. Few outposts of civilization sat closer to the clashing armies.

The U.S. Navy had decided that its first contribution to aerial support of shipping should come at the hottest spot on the French coast. Affirming his predecessor's commitments, Captain Cone agreed to man a French-built station among the Dunkirk docks. As soon as Di heard about the plans for Dunkirk, he knew this was where he wanted to go, "because there one comes in constant contact with the Huns." He would do whatever he could to get there.

His chance came when, walking through Bordeaux, he stumbled upon Lieutenant Godfrey deC. Chevalier, Naval Aviator Number 7. Di practically fell to his knees, begging the man the navy had already designated the C.O. of the new Dunkirk base to bring him along. Chevalier could promise nothing but would not forget him.

Bob Lovett found himself shoved quickly forward into a position of responsibility. The navy at war was far removed from staging campus theater performances or managing the Junior Prom floor at Yale. But leading other young men in the fast build-up of naval aviation would require a man who could master details and not get lost in them, remain resolutely focused on his goals while the world swirled violently about him, and keep his composure when all eyes were on him. Navy brass soon recognized his leadership gifts.

As Di's classmate's standing rose, he feared he might be overlooked. After months together with the tall, slender Gold Coast patrician, the brawny small-town Midwesterner at times found himself at odds and in competition with Lovett. Sometimes he envied his unit mate's rising stature and grumbled that Cone and other superior officers "can see no one else when he is around."[28]

For his part, Bob found his newfound status a mixed blessing. The small store of aviation knowledge he possessed was already more than all but a few Americans could offer the navy. Despite his outward show of confidence, he felt little equipped to tackle the increasingly large tasks handed him. The navy gave him responsibilities and an authority that he found "alarming" and "loosely granted." Others within the regular navy should have been better prepared for the task of building an overseas air corps. But the price of not having prepared for war was not only in equipment, but in experienced officers. He was concerned about his nation's reliance on untested leadership. "We are so green," he worried in private.[29]

His flight training complete, Lovett went to the first of the new American Naval Air Stations, at Moutchic on Lake Lacanau, four miles inland from the Atlantic, thirty miles from Bordeaux, and five miles from a French sister flight school at Hourtin. He drove down a rutted sandy road through unbroken pine forest covering miles of sand dunes to reach an uncleared lakefront site. There was nothing there except a handful of men, their tents, and trucks. Made second in command of the station, he threw himself into carving out of that wilderness what would become the navy's principal overseas flying, bombing, and gunnery school. Every American flying boat pilot would pass through there to gain his final fighting skills before moving to his assigned station.

Bob's days of luxury were over. All the skills he had acquired over the previous year came into play as he began to build the foundations of a large military base in the former wilderness. He chopped trees and built hangars. For now, the aristocratic Ivy Leaguer and the gathering stream of enlisted men arriving from the United States roughed it together like woodsmen, sleeping in shacks constructed from canvas-draped airplane crates, cooking food over open fires, and washing in the lake. Soon temporary roads were cut into the forest, wells dug, and three Bessonneau hangars erected. Eventually an entire military city would be built from this nucleus.

Lovett personally assembled the first of the crated French FBA flying boats trucked in to the base. On September 27, he made the new base's inaugural flight, the first flight ever by a naval aviator at an American overseas base.[30]

CHAPTER 13

America, September 1917
Building an Air Force

ONE BY ONE, THE REMAINDER OF THE UNIT RECEIVED THEIR ORDERS AND steadily dispersed from the Huntington base to the new installations popping up like weeds on existing navy bases or at completely new sites around the United States. The navy understood the value of their knowledge of aviation and recent experience of aviation instruction and put them to work building a brand new air force. The largest new base in the works was at Hampton Roads, an air station, flight training, and experimentation base built up over a few weeks on a five thousand-acre site in Jamestown across from the massive Norfolk navy yard. A group of student aviators, mostly from Harvard, who had spent the summer learning to fly at a former Curtiss school nearby in Newport News moved up the James River to Hampton Roads. They formed the student nucleus of the new training program.

At one time or another most of the members of the unit passed through the burgeoning Hampton Roads base. Even the *Mary Ann*, the unit's beloved original F-boat from the first summer arrived there before, with much sadness on the part of those who knew her history; she had to be scrapped when her hull and bracing finally became too waterlogged to salvage.

Kenneth MacLeish received his orders to report to Hampton Roads to help in organizing the base. Intent on doing well, he nonetheless protested his assignment. "I still feel I would be able to do more in France."[1] He did not try to hide his ambitions. The unit surgeon, Kenneth McAlpin, now a lieutenant commander at Hampton Roads, remarked that of the squadron men on hand, only MacLeish seemed truly unhappy. "Ken," McAlpin wrote Colonel Thompson, "is still hoping to get orders to go over."[2] He would not be kept waiting long.

"The place isn't much now," Kenney found upon arriving, but the navy was building fast. His hopes for Hampton Roads rose when Lieutenant McDonnell was placed in charge. Curt Read and his younger brother Bart were also posted there. They had two other brothers, Curt's twin William and another brother Duncan, who had also joined the navy as aviators and passed through the base as well. Harry Davison, Jr., became the officer in charge of enlisted men and then experimental flight commander, testing out new aircraft and bombs, radio equipment, and guns. The unit reunion seemed nearly complete when their gruff former instructor from Palm Beach, Dave McCulloch, showed up to head the experimentation program.

With so few experienced pilots available to instruct, the navy exhausted the few resources it had. Among the most fatigued, MacLeish spent as many as seven hours a day aloft on "nerve-wracking" flights teaching first-time flyers. Many students washed out within a few flights. More than once he needed to strike terrified students to get them to release their death grip on the controls. Figuring out which novice pilots would make decent flyers was far more art than science.

By the late fall, a new group of cadets began arriving every Saturday after completing their technical and theoretical courses at the new MIT ground school. The evening they arrived, local mothers invited them to a dance at a country club where their daughters could meet the newcomers. MacLeish's unit mate R. Livingston Ireland, who had also been on the track team at Yale, was also instructing in Hampton Roads. He made a point of attending the dances. Although Ireland loved to dance, he spent most of his time observing the new men twirl across the dance floor, trying not to make them feel uncomfortable under his gaze. He believed a man who danced gracefully and had a good sense of rhythm would make a good pilot. On the following day, he would ask for the ten best dancers as his students.[3]

Other unit members put their own theories into practice. The myopic John Farwell, who had nearly landed on top of a navy officer while learning to fly, found his eyesight had weakened so much that he would have been of little use at the front. Instead he was assigned to take charge of the Second Yale Unit, now training at the Curtiss factory in Buffalo. He was then transferred to instruct at Pensacola. When he arrived there, he noticed something inexplicable. Many trainee pilots were missing their two front teeth. Moreover, many of the trainees had yet to solo even after twelve hours of flight training or more. He soon figured out that the trainees with the missing teeth were the same ones who had failed to solo. They had knocked out their teeth cracking up their flying boats in rough landings.

Farwell laid down the rule that those who could not solo after ten hours were washed out, a rule the navy enforced for decades to come. "If they had become flyers," he said, "they most certainly would have killed themselves in the service of their country. But as it was, they merely lost two front teeth."4

Kenney MacLeish's confidence in his flying skills grew; so did his willingness to take risks. He slipped away afternoons when he could to the army's neighboring Langley Field. He went up in a Curtiss Jenny with Eddie Stinson, an aviation pioneer and flight record-holder. Kenney considered him "the greatest American flyer." Fortunately for MacLeish, the acrobatic flyer did not have "the faintest idea what fear is." He handed the young pilot the controls and let him try out acrobatics for the first time. He dropped the Jenny's nose down and, after picking up speed, brought the aircraft zooming back up. Then he wheeled up and over and dove back down. He had looped an airplane for the first time. He carved steep vertical bank turns—"until I thought I would get seasick." Finally, over Stinson's objections, he dropped in a series of dizzying right and left tailspins. Nothing is more dangerous in an airplane. "You never know whether you will come out of them or not," he admitted. Finally he ended the session by coming down in successive stalls like a paper airplane fluttering to earth. "Talk about a circus," he exulted, jumping out of the cockpit. The radiant young man still had a beaming child inside. He could not contain himself from reporting home that "everybody clapped" when he got back on the ground. "Am I happy!"5

Part of his happiness was the thought that his love was blossoming for Priscilla Murdock, the young woman he had grown so fond of during the past summer. Before departing for Hampton Roads, he had managed to get a leave. After a quick trip home, he returned to New York to visit with her. She and the other members of the Girl's Radio Unit had moved in together at the Davison family's Park Avenue mansion. They had taken full-time jobs as radio inspectors at military contractor factories. They were, reported a New York newspaper, "among the first American women of wealthy and socially prominent families to accept manual labor so that they may release fighting men." Earning $20 for her six-day work week, Alice Davison proclaimed, "I wouldn't be doing anything else for anything."6

During his leave, Kenney and Priscilla spent parts of four straight days together, walking from the Davison house through Central Park and dining in New York restaurants. When he left her to take the train to Virginia, he wrote her, "I read, or thought I read, something in your eyes that simply made me walk on air."7

Many other members of the unit were sent off from Huntington to instruct as well. Joining Alphie Ames across Long Island at the Bay Shore station were

Al Ditman, Erl Gould, Wells Brown—all from the first summer's roster at Peacock Point—plus Bill Rockefeller. Teaching students to fly was no simple matter when there was no equipment on hand. Soon, though, Colonel Thompson turned over the unit's own private aircraft to the navy, sending most of them to the Bay Shore station. (Despite a verbal agreement with Secretary Daniels, the navy never reimbursed the donors for the $200,000 cost of training the First Yale Unit.) That did not help much when the still-under-construction station took in eight hundred raw recruits. "We could scarcely take care of the regular station personnel," Ames lamented, "and this new crowd was dumped on us." They had to train the new men from scratch. The navy was short on uniforms and the recruits were ignorant of navy dress codes, so many went about in outfits combining sailor's clothing with civilian dress. Ames burst into laughter when an enlisted man walked past wearing white sailor pants and shirt, a derby, high collar, red tie, and grey spats.[8] The motley vaudeville get-ups and madcap incidents were all part of the navy's growing pains.

"We were absolutely up against it all along the line," Colonel Thompson's nephew Bill said. He, too, was training new aviatiors. "There was no equipment and practically no organization of any kind, and no ideas of any kind." For the first few months, navy aviation truly amounted to little more than "a few machines and some men who wanted to learn to fly and one or two men who tried to teach them."[9]

Al Ditman eventually transferred to the Bureau of Ordnance where he had charge of weapons experiments. American manufacturers and inventors, eager to win weaponry contracts, submitted every kind of idea and apparatus for inspection. Anything remotely practical had to be prototyped and tested. Ditman tried out virtually every weapon before it went into production, from machine guns to bombs. He did not have much help in his dangerous task. As he went around to the various bases, he found that the typical ordnance officer had no experience with explosives and generally knew only that TNT was likely to go off if dropped. As a result, inexperienced ordnance officers wanted nothing to do with explosives and foolishly believed they would be safer to "leave the stuff entirely alone rather than to keep it in operation." That made for doubly hazardous conditions. Exposed to corrosive salt air at naval air stations, bombs and ammunition were kept stored in shacks, often so close to the highly flammable hangars that any accident would have destroyed the lot.[10]

Asked by the navy to figure out why an experimental bomb refused to explode when it struck the water, Ditman traveled to the Rockaway air station where he experimented with several different fuses. To test out a new trigger mechanism he had devised, he enlisted a pilot at the station to assist him in dropping a pair of fifty-pound bombs at sea. Strapping bombs to the bellies of two seaplanes, they flew out about twenty miles offshore. Before they had a chance to drop their payloads, mechanical troubles forced the pilot in the other machine to land. With the seas running high, waves started breaking over his wings. Circling overhead, Ditman realized he would not be able to get back up off the water should he land to pick up the other pilot. He turned back to shore to send out a boat to tow the stranded seaplane in. However, with night falling it was too late for a patrol boat to reach the aircraft. Ditman contacted the captain of a large transport steamer on its way into New York, who sailed about until he located the foundering machine and craned it on board.

Once on deck, the pilot informed the ship's captain that he still had a bomb strapped to his seaplane. The startled officer ordered him to take it off and toss it overboard immediately. The pilot explained that he did not know how sensitive the fuse was or how to defuse the bomb. It might go off when it hit the water, potentially rupturing the hull and sinking the ship. The alarmed mariner ordered the pilot to take charge of the bomb. Unsure what to do with it, the scared man brought it to his cabin where he gave it a comfortable berth on a bed of pillows for the remaining hours to port. Upon docking in New York, the exhausted pilot was commanded to take his bomb and leave the ship at once. Stepping onto the pier, a shore officer ordered him to get it away from the docks immediately.

He walked wide-eyed out into the busy New York City streets cradling a fifty-pound bomb in his arms, uncertain whether it might explode at any instant. Finally he hailed a taxi and persuaded the driver to take him back out to Rockaway. Even then New York taxi drivers would not turn down a large fare. The nervous pilot cradled the bomb in his lap like a sleeping child the entire way back to Rockaway, warning the driver to avoid potholes and sudden stops. Arriving at Rockaway, he handed the bomb over to Ditman and fled in tears.[11]

Erl Gould was soon ordered on from Bay Shore to the Key West Naval Air Station. On the train down, he passed through Palm Beach and fondly recalled the idyllic days when the unit had lived together there for an exalted season of flying and luxury. Life seemed very simple then in comparison. Where Palm Beach was sophisticated and, even in the off-season, ready to meet any need, he found Key West a languid, undeveloped tropical town, accessible only by rail and sea, more Caribbean than American, and "void of everything needed for normal comforts of life, except cigars."[12] The naval air facilities adjacent to a large navy base were, if anything, even less energetic than the town. He quickly changed that. In less than two months, the twenty-two-year-old was promoted to lieutenant and put in command of the entire air station—the youngest of the navy air station C.O.'s. His command was initially not much to look at: one hangar housing five planes, officers' quarters, two barracks with space for less than one hundred enlisted men, a mess hall, and a dirigible shed under construction. He oversaw its growth until two large flying beaches were in operation, with hangars housing fifty planes, two dirigibles, and four kite balloons. In less than a year, the force under his command grew to 1,000 enlisted men and nearly 100 officers, with about 250 student pilots at any time. He set in place the "fly-the-machine-you-work-on" First Unit system Trubee had employed. By the armistice, 600 pilots qualified as Naval Aviators at the station and found their way overseas.

While there, Gould worked with the already world-renowned Thomas A. Edison. Like nearly all engineering-minded Americans, the famed inventor had turned his attention to military technology. For two months Edison lived at the navy base while he attempted to develop a listening device for detecting submarines. With Gould, he also tested a novel camouflaging technique for airplanes. In a primitive version of today's Stealth technology, Edison hoped to utilize light reflection and absorption to "hide" an aircraft flying overhead. Camouflaging planes against the sky would be a great help in combat. Unlike the faster aircraft of later eras, the slow-moving machines were like clay pigeons to the anti-aircraft batteries and, at low altitudes, entirely vulnerable to small arms fire from the ground.

Edison thought that combining black and white on the wings of the plane would render them invisible. He painted the bottoms of the wings of a plane with black and white stripes of equal width on one side of the fuselage, while the stripes had twice as much white as black on the bottom of the other wing. He theorized that invisibility could be obtained only by some combination of white—the lack of color—and black—the complete colors of the spectrum. Edison's idea was clever, but the scheme never quite worked. As the plane flew over, Gould observed that one wing would be clearly visible while the other was not. And as the pilot climbed, the invisible wing would come into sight and the other went out.[13]

Given their comfort in high society, several of the unit members ended up serving dual roles as military men and diplomats in the early days of the war. The United States hoped to convince Cuba to contribute more to the fight. Flying the ninety miles to Havana on a diplomatic mission to build stronger military ties, Gould landed in the harbor. The president of Cuba and other national and U.S. dignitaries met him on the shore. Later that afternoon, the

U.S. embassy's naval attaché asked to be taken up for a hop. Few people in Cuba had ever seen an airplane. A crowd gathered swiftly along the waterfront to watch as Gould put on a flying exhibition.

By the time Gould landed, sixty thousand people had packed in along the quay. As he stepped from the aircraft, a phalanx of soldiers and police had to hold back the tumultuous, wildly cheering mob. Women and children reached their hands out to touch him as he passed by. Eventually, Gould and the naval attaché made their way through the crowd to a waiting car. The driver, police, and soldiers beat people away with sticks, but the car could not move forward through the tumult. As if easing his way out of mud, the driver put the car into gear and drove forward and then in reverse several times until he had cleared a path about twenty feet ahead of the car. Then he shot straight out through a gate into the street. Numerous people were flung aside by the mudguards as the car raced ahead.[14]

Most of the unit members soon became chief pilots or station heads, leading the scramble to build an air force almost overnight. Bill Thompson credited the unorthodox training of the unit members for their success in their scattered postings in creating largely effective organizations under such primitive conditions and time pressure. Their lack of training in standard navy ways of doing things actually made them better able to respond to the sudden emergency of building an air force where none existed before. In Palm Beach and Huntington, Thompson said, "We absolutely refused to conform to the navy regulations about minor details. I mean if we needed things and they had to go through a regular order, we would thumb our noses at the supply officer and go downtown and buy them."[15] The navy bureaucracy proved mostly a hindrance to be skirted. Relying on the organizational model under which they had learned to fly, the unit members knew how to get things done.

There was also something else unique to the First Yale Unit. Even after scattering across the country and then around the globe, they could call on one another for advice, help in securing the materials and men they needed, and provide friendly support as they kept bumping up against one wall after another. They also felt proud to be part of an elite cadre within the navy. For the sake of the unit, for the love of their friends, they hoped to show the navy—and now the world—what they could do.

CHAPTER 14

Peacock Point, 1917–1918

The Fallen Leader

His back broken and spinal chord injured, Trubee Davison lay for six weeks in St. Luke's Hospital. The unit members who were not able to stay in direct touch with his family read about his condition in the national newspapers. Reports on him even reached Gates and Lovett in English-language papers overseas. President Teddy Roosevelt visited him in his room. Roosevelt felt a special bond with the young man. At age fifty-eight, eight years out of the White House, the colonel's offer to raise and lead a militia as part of the expeditionary force had been rejected by the government. However, all four of his sons had enlisted in the army, and his youngest and favored son, Quentin—a friend of Trubee's from Groton—would soon ship over to France as an Army Air Corps pilot.

Trubee sorted through the letters that poured in from unknown admirers across the land. One contained a poem, "To F. Trubee Davison—An American Hero," that promised, "A hundred men will take your place,/ Inspired by example grand."[1]

President William Howard Taft's beloved son Charles II, a Bonesman from Trubee's class at Yale, would soon lead a battalion into battle in France. The senior Taft expressed the common feeling that "it is most disappointing to have been the pioneer as you have been in the United States in this new field of effective war making, and to see those whom you have taught and led go to France and be delayed yourself. But you must reconcile yourself with the thought that your present disability cannot be distinguished from ones secured in the air over a German submarine, or over the trenches or a hostile battleship. It was in the line of duty for your country's defense." The fellow Skull & Bones member closed his note: "Yours in the Bones."[2]

For the unit members off to war, losing Trubee forced them to reflect on their own lives and the choices they were making. Like many Anglo-Saxon patricians, Bob Lovett constitutionally abhorred open displays of feeling. In public he carefully cultivated a gracious reserve, and even with his peers he often hid behind his rapier wit. After living and working together for months, many in the unit could not claim to know the real Bob at all. However, Trubee's crash had been especially hard on him. After nearly a month living together with Di Gates in France, he tried to confide in him about its deep effect on him, "but I couldn't do it and there's an end o' it."[3] When he learned that his orders to move to the front would soon come through, he felt he had to write his thoughts down for Trubee, "since I may not have a chance to see you again."

In a long letter written late at night alone in his room, he cursed the "rotten luck" that had brought his dear friend down just as his dreams and plans were coming true. While not comparable to Trubee's physical injuries, the crash had also been devastating for Lovett. "I had hoped," he wrote, "to come over here under your leadership and inspiration." Trubee's injury had forced him ahead. He recognized that he now had to take Trubee's place as the leader of the unit in Europe. He was, he owned, "a pretty rotten substitute." He had learned much from Trubee, never ceasing "to admire the splendid manner" in which he had managed the twenty-eight pioneers. His admiration had grown for Trubee, who remained stoic in the face of this devastating injury. With great and as-yet unknown danger lying ahead in just a few days, he wrote, "I only pray I can look any misfortune in the face in the same way you have done."

When they had started the original Aerial Coast Patrol unit together that first summer at Peacock Point, Lovett had been a Yale sophomore, concerned above all with making good in his campus social life and enjoying the advantages of a high society gentleman. The thought that he had something more to contribute to others—let alone his country—had rarely entered his mind. Trubee and the Davison family had set his attention to doing something else, something beyond mere self-interest. Trubee's creation of the Millionaires' Unit had enabled all the members to make something more meaningful of their privileged lives. Thanks to Trubee's vision and hard work, they were now fully engaged in a vital effort for their country and, in a grave and dark time for freedom and democracy, for the future of the world.

He would strive to live up to his friend and leader's exemplary spirit in all he did in the days ahead. Trubee had helped him to see what he owed to his country and given him a path to follow. He understood now, "There is such a thing as sending men to fight for you and inspiring them with a desire to prove their worth and acknowledge their debt by service." Trubee had taught him a lesson that would last him a lifetime. Through Trubee's leadership, he had learned to serve.

He closed with a courtly flourish, one young gentleman to another, "I take off my hat to you."[4]

In late September, Trubee returned to Peacock Point to convalesce. His front in the war would be right where he began. In his imagination he could hear the echoes of his unit mates' voices and, for the rest of his life, could call off the entire unit roster from memory without faltering. He would walk again without assistance only with difficulty and lived the rest of his days in pain.

That did not hold him back. Although off active duty, he retained his officer's appointment. He formulated a program to set up junior aviation cadet programs in preparatory schools. From time to time, he consulted with the navy on training issues. He also went to nearby Amityville on the navy's behalf to watch the test of a "flying bomb," a primitive version of guided missile weaponry. Taking a Curtiss-built scout plane, Lawrence Sperry, the inventor of the automatic pilot and brilliant son of the industrialist Elmer Sperry, himself inventor of the navigational gyrocompass, devised a gyroscopic guidance system for an unmanned airplane.[5]

Trubee watched as a prototype "aerial torpedo," as Sperry called it, loaded with dummy bombs, took off from a moving truck. When the aircraft hit turbulence, Trubee saw it level out "as though an experienced aviator was on board." Something, however, went wrong with the diving mechanism. Instead of the engine cutting out and the aircraft nosing down on its target as programmed, it continued climbing and soon flew out of sight. No trace of it was ever found. Sperry tested several more of his aerial torpedoes before the end of the war halted the program. After witnessing that first flight, Trubee was convinced that he had seen the launch of "the deadliest weapon ever conceived." This first version of a guided missile marked, he believed, the dawning of a new age in warfare. Once again, he proved ahead of his time.

With just a few such interludes to distract him, he focused virtually all his time and attention on his comrades, now at arms. The only thing that seemed to ease his physical agony and emotional pain was keeping up his daily correspondence and, as much as possible, telephone contact with virtually every member of the First Unit. More than anything else, he hoped eventually to see the unit get together again, perhaps as a squadron reunited in Europe. "It seemed," he felt, "a dream but still a possibility."[6]

As one of the only Bonesmen still living near the campus, he also served as a focal point for efforts to sustain regular activities of the senior society while the war scattered its members. The regular visits to the New Haven tomb where the young men would normally undergo initiation rites and then meet up weekly were not possible. With the fifteen Bonesmen dispersed far and wide, their initiations took place wherever older members gathered in sufficient numbers. In several instances that meant the secret rites took place at the front. Gates and Lovett went through their intiation while posted at Dunkirk.[7]

The Skull & Bones tomb was long rumored to hold various skeletal relics of famous men taken from their graves. Members never spoke of these bones, but purportedly they were on display to be taken out for use during club initiation rites and other ceremonies. Few on campus thought ill of classmates who might plunder graves, especially those of the so-called "inferior" races. Many members of the unit shared the common strains of anti-Semitism, racism, and disdain for working class people found among wealthy Americans of the age. On campus, they turned up their noses at local scholarship boys, often Jewish and sons of immigrants and working-class parents. Only Irish maids were permitted to clean their rooms. They ate and drank in segregated New Haven eateries. When the group embarked for Palm Beach to train, nobody objected to a clause in the contract for their quarters at the Salt Air Hotel that forbade the hiring of black workers of any kind, even to wash dishes or make up beds. Once in the military, they and other white servicemen interacted with the 350,000 African-American draftees and enlisted men almost exclusively as laborers, cooks, and stewards. Trubee's comrades-at-arms reported back on battle royals they had witnessed in which, as entertainment for white troops, black servicemen were ordered to fight one another or were blindfolded and given clubs to beat each other senseless while a white audience goaded them on and bet on the outcome.

With memories of the Indian Wars of the final years of the previous century still fresh, many white Americans cared little about desecrating native graves and other sites. Artifacts from the tombs of tribal warriors were even prized as trophies. Several Bonesmen stationed together with the Yale Battery at the army's Fort Sill in Oklahoma saw their chance to add to the Skull & Bones collection. Geronimo, an Apache faction leader and iconic Native American warrior, had led Indian bands on several notorious raids against American and Mexican settlements and cavalry encampments during the Indian Wars. Pursued by American and Mexican troops through the Southwest for more than a decade, he had finally surrendered voluntarily in 1886. Eventually interned at Fort Sill, Geronimo had died there in 1909.

In a long disputed act, in May 1918, six of the Bonesmen on hand at Fort Sill, all army captains, dug open the grave. A month later, Geronimo's skull and other personal artifacts taken from the grave arrived at the Skull & Bones tomb in New Haven. "The skull of the worthy Geronimo the Terrible," confirmed Trubee's society mate Winter Mead, still a student on campus, "exhumed from its tomb at Fort Sill by your club and the K-t [Skull & Bones code for "Knight," or new member] Haffner, is now safe inside the T- [Tomb] together with his well-worn leathers, bit & saddle horn."[8] He voiced no objection to the new pieces in the Bones' collection.

Trubee Davison would remain closely associated with Skull & Bones in the decades to come. His ties to those Bonesmen who were also part of the Millionaires' Unit were as tight as family. In June 1918, less than a year after his crash, he served as best man at Erl Gould's wedding. Fighting back the terrible pain, he walked through the church to the altar, making his way without crutches or assistance for the first time.

Tap Day, circa 1901, with junior class members assembled on Old Campus and full of hope at being selected for the elite, secret societies. *Courtesy of Pictures of Student Life, Yale University, 1779–1988, Manuscripts and Archives, Yale University Library.*

he Race. Harvard against Yale on the Thames River, circa 1910. In the background is the observation train. Boats of all sizes, crammed with spectators, almost obscure the two race ews. *Courtesy of Manuscripts and Archives, Yale University Library.*

The Skull & Bones tomb in 1916. *From the photograph collection of Viola F. Barnes, Class of 1919, Yale University 1916–1919, Manuscripts and Archives, Yale University Library.*

The "Big House"—Peacock Point, the Davison home—where, in 1916, the first members of the Millionaires' Unit spent their summer learning to fly. *Courtesy of Daniel Davison.*

The original group of the First Yale Unit, in 1917, in West Palm Beach: back, left to right: John M. Vorys, Artemus L. Gates, Albert J. Ditman, Allen Ames, instructor David McCullough, F. Trubee Davison, Robert Lovett, Erl Gould; front: Wells Laud-Brown and Harry P. Davison, Jr. *Courtesy of the F. Trubee Davison Papers, Manuscripts and Archives, Yale University Library.*

Curtiss flying boat in training, West Palm Beach, 1917. *Courtesy of the F. Trubee Davison Papers, Manuscripts and Archives, Yale University Library.*

Unit members building their aircraft. *Courtesy of the F. Trubee Davison Papers, Manuscripts and Archives, Yale University Library.*

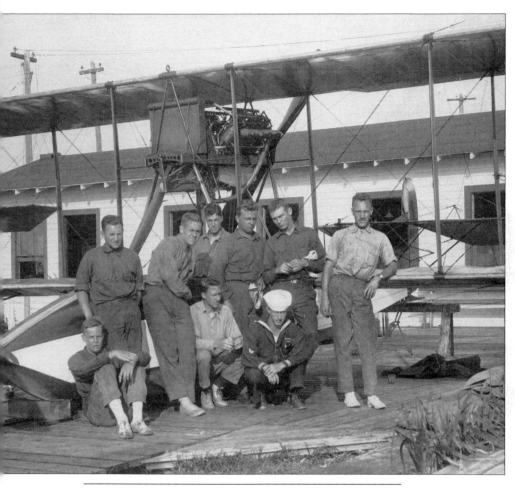

West Palm Beach. Kenney MacLeish (right), John Vorys (third from left), Erl Gould (at rear). *Courtesy of the F. Trubee Davison Papers, Manuscripts and Archives, Yale University Library.*

Erl Gould, Curtis Read, Di Gates, and John Farwell preparing to go to France. This photo was one of several taken of the unit that appeared in the *Washington Post*. *Courtesy of the F. Trubee Davison Papers, Manuscripts and Archives, Yale University Library.*

Wrecked. *Courtesy of the F. Trubee Davison Papers, Manuscripts and Archives, Yale University Library.*

The runways at Huntington, Long Island. *Courtesy of the F. Trubee Davison Papers, Manuscripts and Archives, Yale University Library.*

The wreckage of a Sopwith Camel at Couderkerque, where Crock Ingalls and Kenney MacLeish were stationed. *Courtesy of the F. Trubee Davison Papers, Manuscripts and Archives, Yale University Library.*

H-12 flying boat, as flown in the Spider Web patrols over the North Sea in search of U-boats. *Courtesy of the F. Trubee Davison Papers, Manuscripts and Archives, Yale University Library.*

The sinking of a merchantman, as seen from the deck of a
U-boat. Lifeboats visible near sinking ship. *Courtesy of the F. Trubee
Davison Papers, Manuscripts and Archives, Yale University Library.*

Zeebrugge being bombed by the Allies. *Courtesy of the F. Trubee
Davison Papers, Manuscripts and Archives, Yale University Library.*

Flying overhead in protection of a convoy below. *Courtesy of the F. Trubee Davison Papers, Manuscripts and Archives, Yale University Library.*

David "Crock" Ingalls. *Courtesy of the David S. Ingalls Collection.*

Kenneth MacLeish, 1917, as a trainee holding goggles and helmet. *Courtesy of the Adele Brown Lovett and Robert Lovett Estate.*

Robert Lovett, in dress uniform, 1917. *Courtesy of the Adele Brown Lovett and Robert Lovett Estate.*

To Trubee
from
Curtes.
1918.

Curt Read, who flew with Di Gates in Dunkirk, sent this inscribed photograph to Trubee from the front in 1918. *Courtesy of the F. Trubee Davison Papers, Manuscripts and Archives, Yale University Library.*

Albert Sturtevant. *Courtesy of the F. Trubee Davison Papers, Manuscripts and Archives, Yale University Library.*

The Millionaires' belles, left to right: Adele Brown, Priscilla Murdock, and Alice Davison. Adele Brown would marry Bob Lovett in 1919; Alice Davison, Trubee's sister, would marry Di Gates in 1922; Priscilla Murdock was Kenneth MacLeish's fiancée. *Courtesy of the Adele Brown Lovett and Robert Lovett Estate.*

The First Yale Unit of the U.S. Navy Air Reserve, West Palm Beach, Florida, 1917: Twenty-eight members plus managers and military advisors, and the mascot. Included are Trubee Davison (row 2, left, with dog); Kenney MacLeish (row 2 right, next to sailor); Di Gates (row 4, second from right); Bob Lovett (row 3, second from left). *Courtesy of the F. Trubee Davison Papers, Manuscripts and Archives, Yale University Library.*

Trubee Davison in 1966, almost fifty years later, recalling the line-up of the unit in the preceding photo. His wife, Dorothy Peabody Davison, stands behind him. *Courtesy of the F. Trubee Davison Papers, Manuscripts and Archives, Yale University Library.*

CHAPTER 15

France, Fall 1917
A Parisian Education

A MONTH AFTER GATES'S AND LOVETT'S DEPARTURE, TWO MEMBERS OF the Razz Crew headed overseas next. The handsome crew team captain Al Sturtevant and the football player and debater John Vorys crossed on the same ship that had brought Gates and Lovett over: the *St. Paul*. On watch early in the crossing, Sturtevant grew wide-eyed when he spotted phosphorescent wakelines just below the surface headed straight for the bow. With no time to sound the alarm, he braced for an explosion. Then, to his surprise, the "torpedoes" veered off sharply. A school of porpoises leaped over the bow wake.[1]

In London, they got their first taste of war. While attending a play, the performance was stopped to wait out an air raid. They stepped outside to watch the sky rockets of the anti-aircraft battery and to listen to the occasional whomp of a bomb exploding in the distance. Vorys wrote gleefully to Trubee, "Look me over! I've been under fire!" It whetted his appetite for real battle. Whether "raider" or "raidee," getting into the mix looked like "fun."[2] Once in France, Whiting quickly shipped them off for further training to Hourtin, the French flight training school near Lovett's new base at Moutchic. The French base had enough creaky FBA flying boats to practice on, but living conditions were little better than at the American base. Once a week they made their way thirty miles to Bordeaux for a hot bath. The prudish Americans had to get used to female bathhouse attendants walking in and out as they bathed. The two Americans were also surprised to see that the base's executive officers openly kept their mistresses in hotels near the base. They had "thought it was only the lower sort of officers who did it," said Vorys. They were getting a first introduction to a society transformed by war.[3]

Nine days later, seven more unit members followed on the *Philadelphia*, a merchant ship so small that Dave Ingalls at first mistook it for a tender there to carry them out to a larger liner he figured must be waiting at anchor for them in the harbor. Joining the "Baby Daredevil" on board were Chip McIlwaine, the golf-champion and Whiffenpoof, and Trubee's muscular Groton form-mate, Reg Coombe. Also making the passage were the remaining members of Lovett's Wag Crew—McIlwaine's Yale roommate, Freddie Beach; Hen Landon, the hockey team manager; Ken Smith, a football player; and Sam Walker, the senior Bonesman. During the crossing Walker regaled them with tales from his summer as a volunteer American Ambulance driver. He assured them that French women were all they had heard and more. The eighteen-year-old Ingalls could not believe the stories. He was sure the upper classman had to be exaggerating.

An eighth unit member was supposed to have joined them for the crossing. Kenneth MacLeish had finally gotten his wish and was ordered to France. However, his compulsion to test himself at war no longer seemed so pressing. The others boarded the *Philadelphia* early in the morning. The ship's captain waited for MacLeish—in vain. "Ken," observed a peeved Ingalls, "must have remembered his girl at the last minute and remembered her too long."[4] Kenney first stayed with his mother and sister, who had come to New York to see him off, and then spent his last few days on leave with Priscilla Murdock at Peacock Point. While there, she accepted his marriage proposal. Like many young men, he was shipping off to war leaving a new fiancée behind. He did not even have the money to buy her a ring. Fearful about the reactions of their parents to their precipitous engagement, they kept their marital intentions to themselves.

Kenney found leaving Priscilla unbearable. He donned a sweater she had knit for him. "It's beyond words," he exclaimed. "You will never know what [it] means to me."[5] He stuffed her perfumed handkerchief into his pocket and sprinted for the pier. The captain could hold back the *Philadelphia* no longer, and by the time Kenney reached the dock, she was already churning out to sea.

As in every crossing, the anxiety on board the *Philadelphia* became palpable when, three days out, she steamed into the war zone. "Fog was blessed and a moonlit night cursed," recalled McIlwaine.[6] An army officer on board advised the flyers to change into mufti. The Germans, he warned, would surface after torpedoing a ship and shell any lifeboat containing officers. Too proud of their hard-earned uniforms, the seven refused. Outright terror spread through the ship as twice during the eight-day crossing a U-boat surfaced between it and the rest of the convoy, but submerged without firing or, if it did send off a torpedo, missed the zigzagging ship.[7] All hands breathed easier when two U.S. destroyers arrived to escort them into Liverpool.

Walking into town, they found society transformed in ways that had just begun in the United States. Women worked in all the jobs formerly held by men, running the streetcars, sweeping streets, minding the stores, serving in restaurants, operating the mills. Lights were off at night and many foods were simply not to be found. Men in uniform filled the streets, some on leave, but large numbers dressed in a light blue uniform the newcomers did not recognize. They soon learned these men, often disfigured by ghastly wounds, were the soldiers at home convalescing. "It looked," remarked Ingalls, "as though the whole English army had been shot up."[8]

Making their way to London, they found the city at war offered a young man many pleasures. They bunked in the elegant Savoy Hotel, attended the theater, and explored private clubs where "champagne, brought in it seemed, in barrels," flowed into the early morning hours. They staggered back to their rooms with British officers and women friends they had just met, ready to continue the party. English society had said goodbye to the Victorian Age. London introduced the Yale boys to a world unleashed, knocked off its axis by the unrelenting years of violence, tragedy, and deprivation. Paris would complete their education.

While waiting for their orders for France, they visited the Felixstowe Royal Navy Air Station, less than three hours by train to the North Sea coast. "I've never been so surprised in my life," Coombe remarked about his first sight of an enormous three-engine Porte "Baby" F.5A-flying boat. As advanced as they were as flyers in America, here they were neophytes. "None of us had ever conceived of so huge a machine being possible."[9] They walked around the behemoth in awe, inspecting the wingspan as long as a basketball court and its spacious, enclosed cockpits for a six-man crew and two pilots. Carrying up to six Lewis machine guns, it could fly for six hours without refueling on reconnaissance and submarine patrols with two 230-pound depth charges slung under its wings. Although based on a Curtiss design, nothing comparable had yet been built at home.

Arriving in Paris, Crock Ingalls quickly discovered that Walker had not stretched the truth about the City of Light. He waited with the luggage while the others checked for rooms in a hotel. While he stood at the curbside smoking his pipe, a sweet-faced young woman strolled up to him. Without so much as a how-do-you-do? she asked demurely, "Will you sleep with me?" Still a teenager, like nearly all Yale men he had had precious little previous experience with women. "I had learned something in London," he reflected, "but realized I would learn more in Paris."[10]

Eventually the entire group was sent to Bordeaux. Bob Lovett met them at the train. They peppered him with questions, eager to learn what he had discovered during his few weeks overseas. The dour lieutenant took them into a private room where, in grave tones, he described the gloomy state of affairs in the war. While the lines remained stalemated, that could not continue indefinitely. The Germans were dominating the skies and choking off supply lines with their U-boat campaign, sinking ships three times faster than new ones could be launched. He also detailed the miserable lack of flying equipment his comrades would be facing and the technological edge the Germans enjoyed. Their future suddenly appeared bleak. Bob, said Landon, threw "the worst dose of cold water imaginable" on their high spirits.[11]

Without enough planes for the new men to practice on at Moutchic, they moved to the French base in Hourtin where Vorys and Sturtevant were completing their training. Even there the French rarely gave them flying time. They watched from the shore as French flyers crashed one after another. One morning a French pilot pulled up into a sharp bank just before landing, slapping his flying boat down on its tail and one wing. Somehow it did not break up or sink. Without inspecting the aircraft for structural damage, the French chief pilot ordered Landon to take it back up. He turned pale but flew as ordered. When he came down, the chief pilot sent the others up, each in succession. Somehow the machine never fell apart. Two days later, Ingalls went up again and decided to test the limits of the obsolescent French FBA trainer, looping the cranky flying boat. He did not mind being beached afterward "for doing stunts never before done in those damned machines."[12] The base commander decided he had seen enough of the Americans and pronounced them graduated.

The unit mates scattered. The navy sent Vorys and Sturtevant to Felixstowe to begin flying in the English U-boat patrols and guarding convoys crossing the North Sea. Lovett's former Wag Crew, Coombe, Landon, Smith, and Walker, were dispatched to a French coastal station, Le Croisic, in the process of being transferred to American forces. The base's patrols protected the fast-swelling river of transports starting to flow into a large U.S. disembarkation port built overnight nearby at Saint-Nazaire. McIlwaine, as chief pilot, and Beach, engineer officer, remained at Moutchic to continue the base's construction and to expand its training program as the first U.S. pilots started arriving.

Ingalls, Lovett, and Gates were ordered to report to Paris. Between minor jobs at naval aviation headquarters, they caught up with many old friends from Yale. Among them was Cord Meyer from the crew team, who was now an army aviator. He was in Paris with Hobey Baker, the famed Princeton hockey player. The pair were soon to fly in William Thaw's reformed Lafayette Escadrille, now the Army Signal Corps 103rd Pursuit Squadron. Their old friend Quentin Roosevelt, also an army pilot, joined the other young men venturing through Paris.

Much of Crock Ingalls's free time was devoted to what he called his "Parisian education." He soon discovered that his Naval Aviator's khaki tunic and wings brought him special attentions. Most people considered flying still something of a miracle and regarded pilots with awe. In a very dangerous world, their daring stood out. Besides, with its grabbing, scantily clad women, Paris in 1917 was a giant brothel. With such a fulsome curriculum offered in the cafés and street corners, he found "nothing narrow about a Parisian education."[13]

After a couple weeks, Gates and Lovett received orders to head for Dunkirk. Crock received the orders all of the men had dreamed of, the prize, the chance to train on small, fast land machines, like the single-seater Sopwith, Nieuport, and Spad scouts. He was to travel to Gosport, England, to a special acrobatic flying school. Gates had also hoped to move into scouts, but was deemed too big to fit into their tight cockpits. He grudgingly accepted the posting he had originally sought. He would fly water machines at the newly forming American air station at "the hell of a hot hole" Dunkirk. Ever the competitor, "I have one satisfaction," he observed, "and that is I will be under fire and see some excitement long before any of the others."[14] He would soon come to regret the fulfillment of his wishes.

By missing the *Philadelphia*'s sailing, Kenney MacLeish had the luxury of another full week with Priscilla Murdock before shipping out. He also got to make the trip far more comfortably aboard a large liner, the *New York*. Such creature comforts meant little once they entered the danger zone. He watched the passengers pace the decks like deer in an open field, scanning the horizon nervously for predators. But the tension and fear on board could not dampen his soaring spirits. He was in love, and, at long last he was heading "over there." The great opportunity to make something of himself, to redeem all he had failed at before, was finally within reach. He was going to make the most of this second act in his life. "Oh," he wrote to his aunt, "it's such a wonderful sensation to feel that at last I have my chance. . . . It is a fine big chance—the chance of a lifetime and of a life." This would be so much more than striving for campus status. "It's so wonderful to play a game with such tremendous odds and to have *real honor* as a reward" [his emphasis].[15] He ignored the potentially terrible price winning such honor might exact.

As the ship sailed, he wondered what his encounter with real war might do to him. His self-doubts were never far below the surface. "I'm still more or less of a boy," he acknowledged, "and I've always doubted whether I'd ever grow up." As England came into sight, he concluded, "I guess that my time has come."[16]

Once in France, he, too, would "enroll" in his introductory course in a Parisian education. "And Paris!," he wrote home enthralled. "Oh, it's far better than even the wildest tales picture it. . . . There are literally thousands of girls who say they will show you around Paris, and it's a two-fisted fight to shake them off!"[17] Amid the gaiety and licentiousness, Paris was on edge. Veterans described the outlook as "very, very grave."[18] Some thought the Allies were "licked" and would soon sue for peace.[19] The news he gathered through the censored reports and the eyewitness accounts from the front was as bleak as Lovett had told his unit mates.

Armageddon raged from the Middle East to the Irish Sea, with horrendous casualties on all sides. In the previous July on the Flanders Front while he and his colleagues were winning their wings over the Long Island Sound, the British had launched the Third Battle of Ypres, also known as Passchendaele for the pile of bricks that had once been a village on the ridge that served as a principal goal for Field Marshall Sir Douglas Haig's forces. By the time the battle ground to a halt in November after ninety-nine straight days of thrust and counterthrust for control of the heights, the British forces could boast of delivering a severe blow to the Germans—some 400,000 dead and wounded. But at a terrible cost: nearly 250,000 British casualties were expended to capture four additional miles of mud from which point the stalemated slaughter continued.

Along its portions of the front, the French army was in open mutiny and badly depleted by horrendous casualties over the past year at Verdun, and elsewhere. The poilus were effectively no longer an offensive fighting force. The pending arrival of American relief was the only boost to French morale that might keep them holding the line. Some wondered if that relief would come in time. Around the time MacLeish reached Paris, American doughboys took to the front for the first time on the afternoon of November 2. The 16th Infantry of the 2nd Battalion, the very unit Pershing had paraded through Paris upon his arrival on July 4, replaced French infantry at Barthelémont, a supposedly quiet sector. Aware of the Americans' arrival, German shock troops launched a lightning strike on a trench outpost early the next morning, killing three Americans and taking twelve prisoners—leaving the rest badly demoralized. A wave of concern went through the Allies about the Americans' preparation for the brutal reality of trench warfare. With the fall of the first Americans in battle, the local French commander, General Paul Bordeaux, wondered aloud about "the courage and ability" of the troops from overseas.[20]

If the Western Front looked precarious, elsewhere the Allies were faring much worse. Fighting over the Tirol in late October and early November in the Battle of Caporetto, Austrian and German forces took just 11 days to advance 80 miles, within striking distance of Venice, bagging 275,000 prisoners—a debacle Ernest Hemingway, an ambulance volunteer with the Italians, described in *A Farewell to Arms*. In November the Bolshevik Revolution broke out in Russia. Effectively the Eastern Front collapsed. The Germans began transferring 42 divisions, more than half a million veterans fighting men to the west. The Allies had no comparable reserves. At sea, the monthly pace of sinking had fallen off from a high of nearly a million tons a month to as few as 400,000—still equal to the destruction of about 13 *Lusitanias* each month and a pace faster than replacements could be built. Four million of the world's 30 million tons of shipping had been sunk in little over a year.[21]

The Central Powers were on the verge of triumph, "but," proclaimed MacLeish, exuding the undaunted spirit of the fresh combatant, "I absolutely refuse even to consider it."[22]

CHAPTER 16

Le Croisic, November 1917

Game to the End

THE NAVY ESTABLISHED THE FIRST OF ITS EIGHT AIR PATROL STATIONS manned by Americans on the French coast at Le Croisic. The ancient fishing village sat on a rugged point near the mouth of the Loire River on the Atlantic and about eighteen miles from Saint-Nazaire. Coombe, Landon, Smith, and Walker formed the officer corps for the rapidly growing installation—built by German prison labor—with a contingent of 330 enlisted men. The base's patrols were expected to cover out along 75 miles of coast. On November 17, Landon and Coombe left the station on a sub patrol in two French Tellier single-engine pusher flying boats. They were the first American pilots to operate officially in European waters. It was a toothless effort. They could do little more than mark the position of any enemy vessel they might have spotted. They had no weapons to carry. Eight months after the United States entered the war, increasing numbers of aviation personnel were finally starting to arrive, but their nation still could not provide them with any aircraft or ordnance. A few days later, the French installed bombs under the wings of the four French-supplied flying boats at the station.

Those aircraft were typical of the equipment provided to the Americans as they took over the coastal bases: obsolete, rickety, hazardous on the water, and reluctant to get off it and, when they did finally take to the air, likely to break down. "That was the way the whole coast went," said Smith. "With all the machines [the French] didn't want they said, 'Send them up to the Americans and let them go ahead and kill themselves if they want to, but we will use the best machines.'"[1]

As much as the mechanics were able, they kept the cranky flying boats in round-the-clock readiness to respond immediately to radioed U-boat alerts and to escort the transport convoys steaming through the treacherous U-boat hunting zone into and out of Saint-Nazaire. The station also provided a link in the relay of aerial guardians accompanying coastal convoys running to Spain and the Mediterranean. Coombe, Landon, and Walker had rowed crew at Yale. Now far from the Long Island Sound, they would fly over the Harrimans' *Sultana*, the same yacht that had carried them a year and a half ago from New Haven to New London for the Harvard Regatta in what seemed like a previous lifetime. Scores of private yachts, including Henry Davison's *Shuttle*, Jack Morgan's *Corsair* and the Whitneys' *Aphrodite*, had been loaned to the government for military duty. Lightly armed and manned by college boys from the reserves, they formed the so-called Suicide Fleet that sailed overseas to protect convoys against U-boat attacks.[2]

At Thursday, noontime, five days after Landon's and Coombe's historic first patrol, the radio shack received an alert announcing the location of a schooner under attack by a U-boat. Five minutes after the message arrived, Ken Smith scrambled in search of the sub. It was the first armed American war flight. As in too many other American aerial firsts, it would end badly.

His flying boat carried a two-man crew up with him, Frank Brady, his observer, and mechanic W. M. Wilkinson. They flew off alone—with no food, water, or signaling equipment other than a pair of homing pigeons on board. The flying boat carried about four hours of fuel. As they flew over the breakwater protecting the Le Croisic harbor, spray from big waves slapping the rocks whipped up at them. The flying boat vanished into a heavy fog bank.

As Smith piloted blind through the dense fog, he glanced down frequently at the map, which was not in a windproof case and flapped around in the cockpit. The heavy air kept bouncing the aircraft about and he continually had to right it. Neither Brady nor Wilkinson knew how to navigate by map. With no visibility, just a compass, spirit level, windspeed indicator, and altimeter for instruments, he flew as he had learned, by the seat of the pants. He charted a course for Île d'Yeu, a craggy island with a small fishing harbor about twenty-five miles out to sea near where the sub was reported to be operating. After about thirty minutes, they dropped below the fog and caught sight of the island. Smith circled it and then headed due west to pick up the course of the sailing ship. In twenty minutes they sighted the four-masted bark. They kept close to the water and flew wider and wider circles around the ship in search of the sub.

Spotting nothing, Smith flew on a due west heading for an hour and then turned back toward shore. He continued to fly low to the water and could see the white caps tossing about on its surface. The wind blew hard and the fog had begun to lift. Smith suddenly had a queer sensation. Something did not feel right. Then his motor started to sputter and miss. Too low to the water to turn to the wind and land, he kept going, trying not to lose any more height as he flew toward the coast. Then the engine died.

He glided down for a landing in the churning ocean. Suddenly the airplane shot forward. He had forgotten to turn off the switch and the motor snapped back alive full throttle. The suddenly racing plane drove hard into the crest of a swell, bouncing high into the air. Smith cut the engine. The flying boat flopped with a great splash and crunch into the sea.

The wood and canvas craft bobbed about like an unmoored float, up-and-down and side-to-side, on the twelve-foot rollers. As the biplanes crested each wave, they caught the strong wind. The flying boat lifted briefly and then pitched down into the succeeding trough. The three men in the cockpit looked at each other without speaking. They could not. Overcome by seasickness, they turned white. Each began retching. Eventually they gathered strength to crank the engine. To Smith's surprise, it started. Brady climbed over the side to defuse and drop their bombs to lighten the load. Smith tried to open the throttle, but each time the motor sputtered and nearly died. Water washed over the bow into the cockpit and splashed the engine. He shut it down.

He studied the map. Uncertain about his exact position, he jotted out a message estimating their location about twenty miles west of Île d'Yeu. "Big sea running," he noted. "Send all aid." He tied the message to the first of his two pigeons and released it. Drifting up roller and down trough, despite excruciating seasickness, they set to searching for the cause of their engine woes. Wilkinson eventually figured out that the second gas tank had a clog and was not feeding. They would need to transfer the fuel to the other tank. The late autumn sun had already started to set. The seas were now too rough to risk trying to siphon the gas in the darkness.

They began shipping seawater. Throughout the night, they alternated watches; while one man bailed the other two slept. Smith made notes in his logbook as the derelict craft pitched in the open sea. With his Yale colleagues back at the station, "We know they would do all possible things to help us," he wrote confidently, if only they could locate them. This thought alone kept their hopes up, which were otherwise, he admitted, "none too bright." Big waves rolled up and poured over the wings.

At Le Croisic, four o'clock came and went without Smith's return. A worried Coombe prepared to fly off in search of his missing friend. The others convinced him to wait for morning rather than risk losing another machine. They lit flares along the seawall to guide the lost airplane in from the sea in the dark. An alarm was sent to Saint-Nazaire, from where patrol boats were dispatched in search of the missing airplane. No word of the crew's fate arrived. Before dawn, Coombe took off and flew north. Walker and Landon in the base's other aircraft searched southward. They flew miles and miles over the churning, wintry sea. Holding their breath, they swooped down low to scrutinize the numerous collections of debris floating amid the froth. After three and a half hours of fruitless searching, all three aircraft returned to base. When they arrived, they found the homing pigeon had returned with Smith's message.

Huddled over charts, they tried to calculate how far the strong northeast wind and southerly sea currents had carried the disabled flying boat during the twenty hours since Smith had sent the pigeon off. By their reckoning, they now had to scour more than two thousand square miles of the Bay of Biscay. They refused to acknowledge the dimming chances of ever finding them.

The three rescue planes refueled and took off again. Coombe flew off toward the position Smith gave in his message. Walker and Landon ranged further south.

The wind continued to blow hard all night, clearing the skies on Friday morning. Smith sent out his last pigeon with a note about a lighthouse beacon they had seen flash in the night. "Have no food," he wrote. "We are taking in water, we are not positive of our location but are going to sea. Send help." Their hope of rescue waning, Smith and his crew decided to let the others know they had accepted their fate as part of war's chances. He wrote last words to his unit mates in the spirit they would understand, "Please tell friends that we died game to the end."

Far off in the distance, they could see a dirigible, perhaps searching for them. They had no way of signaling to it, and soon it veered away and flew out of sight.

They started to work on the motor again. Late in the morning, they got a steady fuel flow and started the engine. They tried taxiing in the direction of Île d'Yeu. But the strong seas and head wind kept pushing them back. They had to risk taking off. They powered up, but the left pontoon had filled with water. Tipping over, the wing slammed into a wave, smashing the two left planes. The men were knocked about the cockpit. As the wing tore away, it opened seams in the hull, broke the three seats loose and knocked the motor off its struts. They were stranded in the water and now completely at the mercy of the rolling waves.

They bailed steadily as the sea seeped in and slopped over the cockpit. As they bailed, taunting gulls swooped down on the castaways. Most of the oily water in the radiators had boiled off. They drank the little that remained. In the sun, their thirst grew. Swallowing became so painful that Smith's throat felt as if "I had had my tonsils removed." Salt caked on their faces and lips from the sea spray. The left wing, hanging on by the sinews of its dislodged frame, began to crack and twist apart in the pounding sea.

As night fell, the sea rose up and grew "bitter" again. Water poured into the cockpit. Each time the flying boat rolled, the wing that had broken loose swung about, scraping and pounding against the hull, grinding a hole through the planking. They alternated short watches. One slept while another lay out on the right wingtip to keep the boat from tipping down further into the waves. The third man bailed. "Growing weak," noted Smith. They were at the start of a "very long night. Our hopes . . . very low."

Following receipt of the first homing pigeon message, Coombe and his observer took off again to scour the sea. Desperate to find Smith and his crew, he flew out too far into the Bay of Biscay and did not have enough fuel left for the return flight to Le Croisic. He headed directly for the nearest station, La Pallice, a French base seventy-five miles south. However, losing his way in the dark and uncertain about the rocky coastline, he beached at the first possible safe location. Several miles from the nearest village, they stumbled upon a fisherman in a donkey cart who invited them to spend the night in his waterside stone cottage. Back at Le Croisic, his mates now feared they, too, were lost.

The next morning Coombe returned to his aircraft that had been battered by the surf. He managed to fly the fifteen remaining miles south to La Pallice. As soon as he arrived, he contacted Le Croisic. They were delighted to hear from him, but had no further word of Smith's fate. Despondent, Coombe left his damaged aircraft for repairs at the French station and took the tram to the large nearby port of La Rochelle. He went to a harborside hotel to wait for his aircraft to be made ready. The once awe-inspiring Wags looked to be anything but supermen.

Saturday morning dawned with Smith's crumpled left wing, swinging in like an unfastened boom, slamming the hull with each roller. It threatened to crush the boat and swamp them entirely. They finally cut the wing loose. In doing so, though, the right wing became an anchor and swung them immediately broadside to the swell. Water poured in faster than they could bail. They struggled to detach the remaining wing, but their wrench did not fit the nuts holding it on, and they were too weak to break it free. They sat together in the slopping seawater in the bottom of the rocking cockpit, bailing with their little remaining strength, trying to stay afloat as long as possible. After more than fifty hours without food, a few sips of radiator water, and little sleep in the bouncing sea, they "had just about given up everything." Dusk was gathering.

The remains of their bobbing vessel would not last the night. Suddenly Wilkinson gasped through his parched throat and pointed at an object he could see moving toward them from the south. They thought it was a submarine periscope. "We did not care," shrugged Smith, whether an enemy found them and, as was likely, fired on them. If it was a German vessel, "we hoped it would blow us up and end it all."

A French torpedo boat pulled up. "You can imagine our joy," said Smith. The French crew hauled the three men on board and took them below for a hot meal and drinks. The French crew tried to salvage the engine from the remains of the flying boat, but fifteen minutes after rescuing the Americans, the wreckage sank. They steamed toward La Rochelle.

Coombe had remained in his hotel in La Rochelle waiting for his flying boat to be made ready for his return flight to Le Croisic. He sat alone in the dining room staring out at the harbor. He had just about given up any remaining hope that his friend and the other members of the missing crew would be found. It suddenly occurred to him that today was his twenty-second birthday.

A waiter approached him. Another American officer wished to see him in the lobby. He walked over. He could scarcely believe his eyes. There stood Ken Smith, exhausted, disheveled, unshaven and still wearing his salt-encrusted flying suit, a birthday present Coombe would never forget.[3]

Like many aviation firsts, the first armed American patrol in European waters ended in disaster. Many men were not so lucky as Smith and his crew. As happened so often, the navy learned the hard way. But it learned. From then on, all naval aircraft in France flew in pairs, carrying a sea anchor, Véry pistol, and emergency rations of hardtack and canned tomatoes as a thirst quencher. Crews were reduced to two to lighten the underpowered flying boats' load. With aircraft frequently brought down by mechanical problems and in combat over water, the lessons from Smith's first patrol proved a lifesaver for countless other men.

Shortly after returning to Le Croisic, the navy reassigned Smith. He eventually took charge of flying at another important American naval air station, Île Tudy, near the largest American port, Brest, at the westernmost point of France in Brittany. Here was the famous "Neck of the Bottle," the sea passage taken by nearly all ships in and out of France and south- or northbound merchantmen, tens of thousands of tons steaming through daily. The ships carried cargo between ports along the French coast and on to Spain and the Mediterranean. Transports from England and the United States finished their sea cruises by passing between the French headlands and the scattered islands offshore. The

Neck was already the graveyard for hundreds of ships sunk by German subs prowling the coastal shelf. By far the largest organized transfer of humanity in history to that point, shipping traffic through the Neck was increasing daily as the transports arrived with more than one million American fighters and their supplies to France—with another two million anticipated within a year. The German admiralty, desperate to hold back the tidal wave of fresh troops, drove its submarine fleet relentlessly to increase that tally of Allied shipping losses.

Almost six months to the day after nearly being lost at sea, Smith was on patrol near Pointe de Penmarch, a rocky cape at the southwestern tip of Brittany. A notoriously predatory German sub dubbed "Penmarch Pete" often lurked in the darkness at night beneath the beacon of the Penmarch lighthouse. From there, the U-boat could spy the silhouettes of convoys passing in the night. Over the years of war, Penmarch Pete—in reality several different subs stationed in the area—had sent scores of ships and hundreds of men to watery graves.

Eight miles off shore, trailing along a couple miles behind a twenty-ship convoy, Smith and his observer, O. E. Williams, spotted a fast-moving chalky furrow on a course parallel to the ships. Small bubbles of air and oil rose to the surface within the eddy. Certain it was a sub, they dropped two depth charges ahead of the wake. The eddy disappeared and a shower of oil burst across the surface. The oil continued to bubble up over the next several days, and Penmarch Pete was not heard from again. The French government awarded Smith and his observer the Croix de Guerre with Palm, equivalent to the Medal of Honor.[4]

Smith's medal also indirectly honored the work of the unit, which in its first summer had shown an ignorant navy the value of aircraft in protecting its seagoing fleets. Prior to the arrival of the American-manned stations, the Allies lost ships at the rate of one per day along the French coast. Once the American stations became fully active, only three more ships in total were lost. Several individual American ships sailing into France were sunk, but not a single convoy vessel. The combination of convoy tactics and sea and air patrols drove the U-boats further and further into open waters where they were far less effective. Assistant Secretary of the Navy Franklin D. Roosevelt commented a few months after the war ended, "Not only was the 'Neck of the Bottle' made safe for our troops and supply ships, but the operations were extended from the defensive type to the offensive, and the very existence of enemy submarines was rendered extremely unhealthy long before the Armistice came." For that success, he credited not only the "extraordinary physical endurance" of the men at war, but those who had possessed "imagination and a genius to meet new conditions with untried weapons." The precocious work of a bunch of kids learning to fly was helping to win a war.[5]

CHAPTER 17

Felixstowe, February 1918
The Spider Web

ONE OF THE MANY CHILLING IRONIES OF THE WAR WAS THE FAMILIAL intertwining of the royal leaders who drove their nations into war. The offspring of Great Britain's Queen Victoria occupied the thrones of many countries: her grandsons wore the crowns of both her own country and of Germany. Other relations to the English crown included the monarchs in Denmark, Russia, and Greece. The Austro-Hungarian ambassador to the United Kingdom before the war was King George V's cousin. Cousins by marriage and friends before their nations' armies collided, Kaiser Wilhelm II and Russian Tsar Nicholas II had spent holidays together and addressed each other convivially in English, as "Willy" and "Nicky."[1]

One of the countless small ironies within the great, cataclysmic ironies of the war was Felixstowe. The small town on the English North Sea coast had become a chic Edwardian spa and resort after the kaiser and his family began taking regular summer holidays there starting in 1891. Across the estuary from the most important east coast navy base, in Harwich and Shotley, by 1917 the Royal Navy Air Service base in Felixstowe provided air escorts for the North Sea convoys. The base also flew intercepts against Zeppelin raiders bound for London. After completing their training at Hourtin, Al Sturtevant and John Vorys reported to Felixstowe to begin flying war patrols. They were the first American officers to serve with the British and were carefully chosen for the assignment.

After replacing Lieutenant Commander Whiting as head of U.S. Naval Aviation with Captain Cone, Admiral Sims had charged Whiting with selecting the air stations in Britain that U.S. forces would eventually take over. Soon after the two young men arrived in England, Whiting pulled them aside. "Your mission here, boys," he told them, "is diplomatic as well as a military one."[2] They were to smooth the way, through successful aerial work and personal relations, with the British navy for the tens of thousands of American sailors and flyers who were to follow. Although barely into their twenties and not career navy men, their previous experiences had fitted them well for the twin tasks.

Only twenty-one at the time, Vorys recalled, their diplomatic goal was "getting right with the British," to demonstrate they were officers and gentlemen. In the main, he acknowledged that meant "getting drunk" with their hosts. At twenty-three, older, and more experienced, Al Sturtevant was "eminently fitted" for his ambassadorial duties. Besides a hollow leg for drink, he could skewer the English officers' occasional pomposity and boast about his own country's virtues, yet did not mind when they taunted him about the one-time British colony's crude ways. The former champion oarsman could be "just crusty enough," according to Vorys, "that he would not take anything from the 'Limeys' and just smooth enough that they would take anything from him."[3]

Still, the boys were a bit awed when the English admiral in charge of naval operations in the region invited them to dine with his officers aboard his flagship, the HMS *Ganges*, an imposing 95-year-old, 84-gun, 3-masted ship-of-the-line permanently anchored in the harbor. As a long night of rich foods, claret, brandy, and cards drew to a close in the early morning hours, a tipsy Sturtevant called aside a journalist who had also been at the admiral's table. The young man was proud of finding himself in such august company. "When you go back to Washington," he asked shyly, "if you happen to meet any of my Yale friends, do you mind telling them that you met me dining with a British admiral?"[4]

The British officers generally appreciated the Yanks' presence on the base. They helped relieve not just the badly overtaxed flying officers, but also refreshed the fighting spirit of the men in tackling the grueling task they faced. "They were splendid chaps," T. D. Hallam, a Canadian squadron leader, recounted, "keen on flying, and could not be kept out of the air. They had all the fresh enthusiasm for the war which everybody that came in in 1914 and 1915 had possessed, and regarded patrolling, which the old hands looked on as a hard and exacting business, as a novel and entertaining sport."[5]

Some of that sport came after hours. Every Saturday evening after the day's flying patrol, they donned their gold-brocaded dress uniforms to attend the dinner dance held at the Felix Hotel, the very hotel in which the kaiser and kaiserin used to vacation. For the two Americans, it was a far cry from the tea dances at the Hotel Taft and the Junior Prom of the year before in New Haven. More than once, officers found themselves dashing into the hotel after the party had begun in a rush to get spots on women's dance cards before they filled all their turns. The flyers had been detained while out on patrol, caught up in battles with German seaplanes or lost in fog.

When Sturtevant and Vorys began coming to the dances, they could not take their eyes off one particularly intriguing woman, "a lady with a past but still a lady," according to Vorys, a stunning beauty known as Mrs. Dowson. What they knew of the mysterious widow was that her father was Irish, her mother Argentine. She had a hypnotic blend of ivory skin, glistening black hair, and royal blue eyes, spoke with a refined, light accent and was, the two men agreed, "very, very lovely." She also had a fiancé, a captain in the Bedford Regiment. That did not seem to stop her from enjoying the charming young Americans' enthusiastic attentions. Both the jovial, smooth-talking Vorys and the tall, handsome Sturtevant fell hard for her. "She," Vorys said with a sigh, "naturally took a shine to Al." The dashing Yale crew captain may have had the upper hand, but the rivals each managed to make plans with her to meet up in London while on leave.

One evening, the two Americans strolled into the Felix Hotel bar for a drink. The Assistant Provost Marshall for the military district sidled over and invited them to join him in the corner of the bar. "Young men," the A.P.M. hemmed, "I have a very embarrassing subject to take up with you, and that is about a certain lady here, and I hope you will not feel that I am intruding, but this young fellow," indicating Sturtevant, "is being watched very carefully by our intelligence service." Sturtevant was dumbfounded. The A.P.M. informed them that Mrs. Dowson was suspected of spying for Germany. Her fiancé, he said, "will no doubt be court-martialed."

Both of his listeners grew wide-eyed. "It would indeed be a great pity," he continued circumspectly, "if two of the first American officers to be attached with the British, or one of them would be, because of any indiscretions, also coupled in with that court martial, and I hope you will excuse me for butting in on your own private affairs, but I just want to throw this hint out to you." They got the message. Both found reasons to cancel their plans to meet her in London. Whenever they saw her subsequently at the hotel dances, they could not without appearing ungentlemanly pass up dancing with her, but all courtship ceased. "She intrigued us about as much as a case of smallpox," said Vorys.

They had no doubt that she might have been another Mata Hari. Vorys could laugh about it after the war. "She could certainly find out anything you knew," he said, "and with a little persuasion you would tell her a lot of things you did not know."[6]

The charms and pitfalls of their life onshore made it "a funny sort of war we had there," said Vorys.[7] While learning to avoid the terrestrial snares, most days they faced more directly life-threatening challenges in the air. The Felixstowe flyers flew the "Spider Web" patrols, a systematic search over the North Sea's southern reaches for the sinister, prowling grey steel U-boats. The Germans were known to steam for a rusty, red-painted lightship on the North Hinder shoals—anchored there by the neutral Dutch so it went unmolested—midway between Felixstowe and the Hook of Holland. There the U-boats took their bearings before sailing south or for the journey home after a typical twenty-five-day hunt at sea.

Running on diesel engines while on the surface, submariners switched to battery-powered electric motors when submerged. They could swim about only for two hours at eight knots before exhausting their batteries and ran blind underwater except for the periscope's blinkered eye. Therefore, most of the time they stayed on the surface, making them easy prey if found. No better sleuth existed than the patrolling flying boats that could sweep miles of sea at a time in clear weather. With the lightship as hub, the Spider Web patrol ranged sixty miles in diameter and swept inward over an area of four thousand square miles, through which the U-boat had to pass. The patrols formed an octagonal web with eight radial arms thirty sea miles-long, crossed by flight paths at ten, twenty, and thirty miles out from the center. Two of the Spider Web's eight radial sectors could be covered in a five-hour flight. With all eight of the station's flying boats out in pairs, the entire Spider Web could be completed in a single day.

"The tables were turned on Fritz, the hunter," wrote squadron leader Hallam, "for here he was the hunted, the quarry, the fly that had to pass through one or more sectors of the web. The flying-boat was the spider." Patrols were carried out at the height of one thousand feet because at this height silhouettes of the submarines and surface craft could best be seen and bombed. Although sub sightings were rare and the long flights over empty water could be exhaustingly tedious, by the end of the war, Felixstowe flights were credited with sinking twenty-five U-boats. The patrols sent many more too deep to cause any harm. Just knowing the aircraft might pass overhead kept the terrorized submariners submerged for much of the day. They resurfaced at night, but were far less destructive in the dark.[8]

German prospects for victory depended on the U-boats' success. The Admiralty invested heavily in the shipyards at Weser, Danzig, Hamburg, Vagesack, Kiel, and Bremen that worked day and night turning out new U-boats, from 90 to 225 feet in length. While the number of ships lost had started to decline, when the two Americans began flying out of Felixstowe in December, 400,000 tons of shipping had been sunk just that month, and more than one thousand men having drowned in one particularly harrowing week. It would be another four months before total shipping losses would decline to 300,000 tons. With large convoys of American doughboys beginning to make their way over, keeping the subs at bay so the transports and cargo could make their way through would determine the outcome of the war.[9]

Before dawn each day, the duty officer roused Sturtevant, Vorys, and the other men, then they mustered to bagpipes on the quarterdeck, and from there marched to the mess. When they were on flight patrol, they made their way from there to the three huge sheds, 300 feet long by 200 wide, that sat beside the harbor. Beyond them was a concrete apron on the waterfront. Wooden slipways ran out from there into the harbor. Within each hangar lay the sleeping shapes of the monstrous Curtiss H–12 aircraft. Bulbous, 42 feet from prow to stern—wood below the waterline, canvas above—with a 98-foot wingspan and two big tractor engines, each sat perched on wooden trolleys, trim, clean, gray, like an enormous biwinged whale. A panoply of machine guns, barrels askew, bristled top, aft, and through hatches on the sides like harpoons stuck in the whale's flanks.

Yawning and stretching, a working party of twenty men trudged in and rolled back the sixty-foot doors. If the usual winter storms had abated, they pushed out each five-and-a-half-ton boat and loaded her up out on the apron with enough fuel for up to seven hours on patrol. Armorers hauled trays for the machine guns on board and tucked the depth charges into place under the wing roots. The bombs were outfitted with delay-action fuses that detonated them about two seconds after they hit the water or a submarine, up to eighty feet below the surface.

While the pilots and crews received their instructions, the two 350-horsepower motors were run slowly for 15 minutes to warm the oil. Then they were opened up with a thunder audible for miles. The engines shook the whole structure of the boats so badly that they could fly only a few missions before they needed complete overhauls.[10]

Climbing aboard via wooden ladders, the typical flight crew consisted of a first pilot, second pilot who also navigated, wireless operator, and engineer. After a month's practice together on smaller flying boats, Sturtevant and Vorys started out as extra observers, but soon flew as second pilots. Flying the big boats required acute attention to detail. The captain of his ship, the first pilot, had to be very experienced getting up and down in the busy harbor. He sat in a little padded arm chair on the right-hand side of the control cockpit that ran across the full width of the boat ten feet back from the nose. The cockpit was covered by a transparent wheel house so he did not have to wear goggles. Before him on the instrument board was the compass, air-speed indicator, the altimeter, a bubble cross-level for balancing the boat, inclinometer that gave the fore-and-aft angle, oil pressure gauges, and tachometer. Close to his hand were the engine switches and throttle control levers. Directly in front of him was an eighteen-inch wooden wheel like that of an automobile, but carried vertically upright on a wood yoke. He worked the steering rudder with his feet. Sitting forward of the engines, he had sweeping views below and ahead, but partial vision at best when looking back.

The second pilot stood to his side. His jobs were vital to the success of any mission, above all keeping the ship on course. Navigation over the blank sea surface in wartime, where there were often none or only shifting marks, required careful calculation. Frequent clouds, heavy fogs, and strong winds added to the complexity. As the engines roared overhead, he had to work out the compass correction for drift and the time correction for the air-speed indicator. With his mathematical mind and mechanical engineering training, Sturtevant proved especially adept at keeping a ship on course. On the relatively rare occasions a sub was sighted, he had another essential task. The second pilot ducked forward into the exposed cockpit in the very prow of the boat. There he had his bomb sight and bomb-release levers and a machine gun to defend the fore in an attack.

The wireless operator sat facing forward on the right-hand side of the boat, just behind the first pilot. The primitive radios could send and receive telegraphed signals up to a maximum range of one hundred miles through a thirty-foot antenna spooled out from under the fuselage. The engineer squatted in an open cockpit in the middle of the boat, surrounded by the fuel tanks, a maze of piping and innumerable gadgets. From there he could climb out on a wing if he needed to work on the engine. Both crew men also had to be ready to jump down into the hull to slide open the side hatches through which they fired Lewis guns to ward off attackers from the aft end. All communicated through tubes and hand signals.

Once the flying boat was readied for takeoff, the heavy trolley was rolled out on the slipway into the water. Six men in waders guided the boat. The remaining work crew played out a line until she floated free.

On ship-escort duty, the flying boats circled in advance of the vessel or convoy. When attacking single ships, U-boats closed to a range of 300 to 600 yards before firing a torpedo. But when firing on a convoy they sent off their torpedoes at ranges of 500 to 1,000 yards and sometimes longer, in which case they did not pick out an individual ship but merely fired into the flock. They waited in front of a convoy until the ships were sighted and then submerged. To pick them up, pilots flew in great loops from five to ten miles ahead of the convoys.[11]

The flight crew did not only watch the surface. They had to scour the skies for sudden swarms of attackers flying in from bases along the coast of Belgium. The Germans never bothered to develop their own flying boats. They had no need. Their pilots wanted to stop the Allied reconnaissance and bombing operations. Therefore the Germans depended upon speedy two-man monoplane seaplanes—essentially land machines not much bigger than the tail section of the flying boats with big boots on to keep dry in water landings—for darting assaults on the flying boats and bombers.

Their speed and agility gave them important advantages in a fight. They would sit on the water waiting for the flying boats, which were audible miles before becoming visible on the horizon. They would then fly up high to dash down on the big boats. The seaplanes could easily outrace the heavy, slow-maneuvering flying boats. Still, an enemy had to be experienced and gutsy to charge in against the gunship's machine guns. To improve their chances, the Germans usually attacked in successive pairs. They hoped to catch the big "hotels," as the lumbering ships were called, at their most vulnerable moment: banking into a turn. In turning, the ship's guns' limited arc of fire left its broadside unprotected. With its flanks exposed and nearly indefensible like a boxer caught turned sideways to his opponent, an aggressive enemy would drive home his attack.

Sturtevant and Vorys roomed together in an old seaside manor house off base and flew out on regular patrols through the winter months. For a few weeks, Bob Lovett joined them, training on the big boats and poking his nose into every corner of the station. "By jingo it was fun," he wrote Trubee Davison.[12] However, he had hoped to fly scouts. According to Kenney MacLeish, with the "very high-strung" Lovett's "nerves . . . going back on him," aviation chief Cone had decided his brilliant, tightly wound staff officer should instead prepare to become C.O. of one of America's own flight stations.[13] Lovett admitted to Trubee that he had "been pretty cut up at missing single-seater work," but becoming C.O. of his own air station would be nothing to sniff at.[14] His extraordinary mind would be better applied behind a desk than in the cockpit. Lovett, Vorys, and Sturtevant spent Christmas 1917 in London with Crock Ingalls, Kenney MacLeish, and Shorty Smith, the younger brother of Ken from the Second Yale Unit.

Throughout the long, dark winter in Felixstowe, flights were washed out frequently by storms. After spending so many months together on the ground and in the air, Sturtevant and Vorys had grown close. Both were homesick, but long conversations about their families and girls in the States helped ease the pain. They joked about their rivalry for Mrs. Dowson and laughed at the dramatic turn of events when her identity as a spy was revealed to them. "As I look back on it," Vorys recalled later, "these times we had together were the best of my life, just because we had such talks."[15]

In February, Vorys lucked into a string of clear days for flying while storms hit several straight days when Sturtevant was scheduled to fly, keeping him beached. Frustrated and bored, on Valentine's Day, February 14, he went to see Felixstowe commander Colonel John Porte about getting more work. "I wish I had a few more like him," Porte remarked.[16]

That night, Al looked over the sea from his house. The air was crisp, stars out. Good flying in the morning. He turned to his roommate. "What do you say we trade the flight tomorrow?" No, John replied, unwilling to give up his patrol. Al pointed out that John had several more flights in. Moreover, the Canadian first pilot for his morning patrol, Claude Purdy, was considered a lousy pilot, and it would be deadly dull in any case, a beef ship escort from Holland back to England.

John finally relented. "All right, we will trade," he said.

Later on they lay in their bunks in the darkness talking and smoking the Fatimas popular with American servicemen lucky enough to get their hands on them. Al had just received a cablegram from his girlfriend at home. He handed it to John. "What do you suppose that means?"

"Received your letter," John read. "Don't understand. Am writing you." He was puzzled. "If you will tell me just generally what was in your letter," he said, "I will be able to tell you the meaning of that cablegram."

"I will not."

"Well, you are going out with Purdy in the morning, and he is a rotten flyer and you will never get back and I will read all your mail, so you don't need to tell me how your letter went."

Al smoked his cigarette in silence. Finally he said with a sense of the ridiculousness of it all, "Say, it just occurred to me we are in this war anyhow. We might even get killed."

John did not like that sort of talk. "You are pretty gloomy for a nice February evening," he said. "Go on to sleep."

"Well," he said more to himself than John, "that is right."[17]

Sturtevant left early in the morning before Vorys awoke. Two big H–12B boats flew off the water before dawn. A South African named Faux captained the second escort. They met the beef ships shortly after daylight near Holland and began the long slow convoy back. They circled about one thousand feet up with clouds scudding a couple hundred feet overhead.[18]

The flight continued uneventfully with nothing in sight except choppy seas. About twenty-five miles from the North Hinder lightship and nearly half way home, the two machines roared along about eight hundred yards apart. Suddenly dropping out of the low clouds, right between the two flying boats, ten German seaplanes dove and, in a carefully orchestrated ambush, separated into two wolfpacks. Each went after a flying boat.

Faux, on the western, homebound side of the attackers, immediately turned toward England. He dropped his depth charges to lighten his load and then plunged down within a few dozen feet of the sea. Not having had time to retract his radio antenna in the sudden evasive dive, its end struck the surface and tore away. Unable to call for help, he could only flee for home.

Three German machines chased Faux for several miles before turning back to join the attack on Purdy's lone aircraft. With the German fighters between him and home, Purdy threw his flying boat full throttle on a due south course. He had no hope of outrunning his attackers. The buzzing German seaplanes darted in, two by two, guns blazing. Sturtevant at the nosegun and the engineer and navigator to the rear fired off burst after burst at their attackers who came sweeping in from below and above, bow and stern. The running gunfight continued southward. Purdy kept trying desperately to turn toward the safety of England. Each time he banked, the seaplanes darted in like ravenous mosquitoes stinging the soft underbelly. The flying boat was being drawn ever closer to the enemy strongholds along the Belgian coast.

Whether by radio signals or sheer misfortune for the British flying boat, another German squadron flew out from the shore. Although the men on Purdy's ship could not know it, the leader of the German squadron, Oberleutnant Friedrich Christiansen, was one of Germany's most feared airfighters. Famed throughout his homeland, he had already become the first naval man and only seaplane pilot to be awarded his nation's highest military honor, the *Pour le Mérite*, the famed Blue Max. He was credited with downing twenty-one Allied aircraft during the war. (In the Second World War, he would serve as governor of occupied Holland.) With his arrival, the game was over. The flock of German aircraft raked the lumbering British hotel until the oil and gas tanks burst. Her canvas and wood hull caught fire, and she rolled over and fell into the sea. The triumphant Germans circled over the wreckage several times and then left it burning on the water.

Later that afternoon, Christiansen returned and found the wreckage still afloat. Three men clinging to the debris waved to him. He circled overhead, but the seas were running dangerously high and on the horizon he could see British destroyers patrolling. He did not dare land. Christiansen, like many pilots of the war, came from aristocratic origins and was steeped in the chivalrous tradition of respecting his foes. His opponents, once downed, were victims in need of aid. Seeing the helpless survivors, he would, he later reported, have landed to ferry them to safety, had he not feared for his own safety. He expected that their comrades would come to their rescue. The next day, though, when he came out to the site of the wreckage again, all signs of it along with any survivors had vanished.[19]

After Faux returned home in the other British flying boat, questions began to be raised about his conduct. Vorys was furious. Faux "ran away and left Al" to fight alone, he grumbled.[20] Faux claimed he had had no alternative. He had opened his engines intending to turn back toward Purdy's aircraft to create a defensible formation, but his port engine failed and the flying boat swung away to the left, opening an unbridgeable gap between himself and the southbound Purdy.

In the court of inquiry that followed, Faux said he had shortly discovered that, in pushing his throttle forward, his air-fuel mixture control lever had moved as well, shutting down the engine. By the time he had started the engine and throttled back up, three Germans were firing at him. Caught up in his own life-and-death gunfight, he could not return to Purdy's aid. After a thirty-minute chase, Faux had finally slipped inside a thick bank of mist and shaken his pursuers.[21]

The need for the Allied navies to remain on good terms forced Vorys to protest in silence, but he never forgave Faux.

After the war, Sturtevant's long-grieving father, a Washington, D.C., lawyer, reached out to the German pilot Christensen, who told him the story of his son's final flight. The senior Sturtevant also contacted Admiral Sims about Faux's conduct. The head of naval forces refused to press the matter further with his English counterparts. Finally, Sturtevant went from town to town along the coasts of Holland and Belgium, inquiring among local residents whether any remains from the crash may have washed up on their shores and been buried. His search proved fruitless.

The first American sailor and the first aviator in U.S. service to die in action, Al Sturtevant received the Navy Cross posthumously. Newspapers around the country reported the Yale crew captain's death. The death of the famed athlete was seen as an "early warning" of the likely costs of the war.[22] The university held a memorial day in his honor a few weeks after his downing. In July 1920, the navy added the torpedo boat USS *Sturtevant* to its fleet. Twenty-two years later, again at war with Germany, the navy launched a second *Sturtevant*, a destroyer escort to protect the big convoy transports sailing, once again, for Europe.

News of Al's death knifed through the unit. It made brutally real the nature of the fight they were in and the risks at stake. "War seemed suddenly to creep right up on us," Alphie Ames observed to Trubee Davison after they learned of their unit mate's death.[23] In the days ahead, war would come diving at them again and again, at the speed of a streaking airplane firing both barrels—with death peering through the sights.

CHAPTER 18

England and Scotland, Winter 1917–1918

Getting the Wind Up

K ENNEY M AC L EISH HAD BARELY ABSORBED THE NEWS OF A L S TURTEVANT'S
death when two weeks later he "got the most awful shock . . . that I ever received."[1] The two friends had explored London together earlier in February.
While there they had made plans for what they were going to do after the
war.[2] The day before going out on what proved to be his last flight, Al had
written to Kenney. He suggested they meet up again for "a small soiree in London" before Kenney headed to the front. As if a voice had called out to him
from the grave, the letter arrived just as he was winding down his training and
awaiting his final orders. Al wrote that if they could not find a time to meet in
London, he wished his friend success in his first war posting. Rumors had
spread that the Germans were gearing up for a massive spring offensive before
large numbers of American forces, expected to begin arriving in the summer,
poured into the lines. Kenney would be stepping right into the brunt of it.
"Don't get yourself 'crocked' if you can help it," Al joked, "because a wooden
kimono would not be becoming to your style of beauty."[3]

Kenney was shattered. He spent a sleepless night thinking about what "must
have been a frightful death!" After a night's grieving, he gained a hard-won
truth that would help carry him in the even harder days to come. "I [had]
thought that the greatest things in life were the visible, tangible realities," but
the experience of the suddenness with which a dear friend could be torn away
had forced him to reconsider. "I must be wrong," he realized. "The best things
about Al, the friendship, the influence, and all that, are still realities to me—but

they're unseen. I must be wrong, the truly great realities must be the unseen realities."[4] His time for growing up had finally come. The unshakable horror of war was making a man of him, not just physically but spiritually.

His will for battle had also grown. Al's death was an inspiration to him. He knew now what he was fighting for: "Well," he told Priscilla, "the game is started. . . . I'm out for blood."[5]

The way he had acted in his first days overseas, though, had been anything but mature. Sent to Moutchic for his first round of training, he put in for posting to Dunkirk, but feared he would instead be sent to do convoy duty, work he considered necessary but menial. He longed to join Di Gates in active combat service in the most fearsome corner of the Western Front. He jumped into the sky in a French flying boat like a man possessed, stunting in an airplane not designed for stomach- and strut-wrenching maneuvers. On the notion that one had to be nuts to want to see active service at the front, Kenney thought flying like a fool would help his cause. His "dope" proved wrong. He was beached for a week and told that, instead of being sent to the front where "they didn't want any damned fools," he would probably be given a patrol on the Irish coast, the least desirable spot of all.[6] It would not be the last time his superiors would fault him for being so headstrong.

Once permitted to return to the air, he flew more cautiously. Watching others fall convinced him that it might be wise if he tried to keep his neck unbroken long enough to be posted to the front. "Everything is at stake," he realized after witnessing several deaths in flying accidents. "One foolish move usually ends up in a slow procession with soft music."[7] When he finally received his orders, the news was both better and worse than he had hoped. He, Crock Ingalls, and Bob Lovett were to travel to England for final training in scouts—high-performance single-seater fighter airplanes—before shipping over to Dunkirk. Alone among all the naval aviators streaming into France, they were chosen for the English "Top Gun" School of Special Flying at Gosport, in recognition of their exceptional piloting abilities and as a diplomatic gesture to American forces. Kenney's "very cheerful" C.O. told them that if they were lucky enough to survive training they would be "shot down like birds" once they got to Dunkirk.[8] Still, he was thrilled at the prospect of finally getting the chance to test himself. The chosen three were the envy of the unit. Harry Davison, still at Hampton Roads, remarked that the trio had "drawn the high cards in our outfit."[9]

They had a week's stopover in Paris before heading to England. They were soon joined by unit mates Curt Read, the football team manager, and his younger brother Bart, who had freshly arrived from the United States and was bound for training at Moutchic. Kenney guided the gang on nightly stops at Ciro's, a fashionable nightclub and restaurant. For Kenney, said Crock Ingalls, "Nothing would do but the best," and the dollar went far in wartime Europe.[10] Kenney introduced the eighteen-year-old to the joys of Pol Roger champagne, favoring the 1904 or 1906 vintage. They made "a point," Crock observed, of sharing a bottle of the costly champagne at every dinner after that.[11] At the famously elegant Crillon Hotel next to the American embassy on Place de la Concorde, they saw nearly the entire Allied leadership conferring, including Generals John Pershing and Tasker Bliss; Admirals William Sims and William Benson; the President of the Supreme War Council Marshall Joseph Joffre; British Prime Minister Lloyd George; and President of France Raymond Poincaré.

As the three Yale boys made the rounds of fashionable clubs and bars, they went in for good-natured ribbing of each other. Much of their joking was about the women vying for their attention and money. The sexual opportunities and temptations seemed limitless. The young Ingalls, with "a girl in every port," came in for the heaviest kidding because of his riotous pursuit of his Parisian education.[12] He barked out his high-pitched laugh over and over. Eventually, the excitable Crock began "getting touchy," MacLeish observed, "because we've kidded him too much."[13]

Despite the numerous temptations, Kenney kept his distance, fighting off the painted ladies grabbing hold of his arms in the Paris streets and approaching him in Ciro's. Still, "just lately," he admitted, "some ideas have entered my head that scared me." His duty to his family and his fiancée Priscilla, his own pride and religious beliefs had held him back so far. But he now understood how strong the odds were that he might never again see his family or Priscilla. He had to ask himself, "Why should I refrain?" Ultimately he could repress that thought. His love for Priscilla would carry him through, because "I have decided to live, while I live, in a way which would make you happy," he wrote her, "and, if I must die, in a way which would make you proud."[14]

Although he steeled himself against temptation, he could not help being infected by the corrosive psychology of war all around him. Without yet facing a bullet, he began to sense the great cosmic joke all fighting men lived with when perched continuously on the precipice of sudden, violent death. He was readying himself for the game ahead in which his life might be lost at any moment with a single well-placed bullet or, far worse, after a long fiery plunge to earth. It all came to seem terrifyingly funny. "After you pass the stage where you care a darn what happens to you," he wrote his sister Ishbel, "you take things easy and laugh—laugh at anything, laugh at nothing. The main thing is—you laugh. I've never felt so darn free and easy in my life."[15] He refused to abandon the sturdy foundations of his growing sense of self, but he would find his own way through a dark world gone mad.

When London navy headquarters assigned Lovett to administrative duties, Ken Smith's pint-size younger brother Shorty replaced him for scout training. He, MacLeish, and Ingalls reported to Gosport where the acrobatic flying school spread across the Hampshire peninsula between Southampton and Portsmouth Harbor southwest of London. Crock Ingalls immediately declared it "a paradise for a flyer." The famed Royal Flying Corps (RFC) aviation instruction reformer, Major Robert Smith-Barry, had established what he thought would be ideal conditions for perfecting a fighter pilot's skills and teaching instructors who could spread his methods to other flight schools around the country. His basic notion was that there would be no rules at all. The only thing expected of a pupil was that he fly as many hours as he wanted, push his abilities to their limits, "and do it well."[16] If a pilot did not want to spend hours each day aloft learning just what those limits were, he quickly washed out. Most Gosport students were already veterans, some were decorated war pilots. The Americans were both the youngest and least experienced of the pupils in their class.

Each student got his own dual-control, rotary-engine A. V. Roe (Avro) aircraft—"the greatest bus for playing around in that I've ever seen," Kenney proclaimed after his first few flights.[17] The student took up the two-seat land machine along with an experienced, one-on-one instructor who sat behind him and communicated through specially designed headphones called the "Gosport tube." The instructor would demonstrate the flying first, taking his student up, and perform an acrobatic maneuver such as a climbing turn or virage, barrel roll, or cartwheel, or side-slip into a landing by crabbing the plane to the ground in a crosswind. Then he talked the student through the same trick. They practiced over and over until the student could complete the stunt solo.

An important part of the Gosport experience was simply learning to pay constant attention while flying through crowded, entirely unregulated airspace. Crowded barely describes the chaotic skies. Overhead, taxiing, high up and low down, fast machines darted about constantly in all directions, taking off and landing without regard to wind direction, some looping, others chasing over the field a few feet off the ground, carving sharp turns around hangars, stunting at every altitude, while scores of pilots huffed—engaged in mock dogfights—above. There was plenty of showing off of all kinds by the competitive flyers.

With a toss of their scarves, the cocky Americans put their goggles on and flew straight into the furball. A surprised Ingalls learned "how quickly you come together" when two aircraft flying at one hundred miles per hour converge on a point after his first, narrowly averted collision.

Accidents were an inevitable, almost daily experience. But conditions were far better than in the first two years of the war when sink-or-swim methods had prevailed and many new flyers fell fast to the ground. Pilots at Gosport were experienced, handpicked men, and Smith-Barry's craft-apprenticeship instruction methods, only recently given support by the RFC, had already led to significant declines in the notoriously high training accident rates. Still, flying school remained an especially hazardous period in a pilot's always dangerous career. The RFC had calculated "wastage" for 1917 approaching a third of the pilots-in-training at flight schools, ten percent lost for lack of aptitude or "flyer's temperament," the remainder due to death or serious injury in crashes. Of the 14,000 British pilots killed in the war, 8,000 died in training.[18]

Some thought that more conservative training methods would reduce the wastage. Smith-Barry looked at the grim statistics and thought just the opposite. Instead, he convinced the RFC that pilots should prepare to deal with the aerial dangers they would face by working through the dangerous maneuvers many times in practice situations. "The object," explained Smith-Barry, "has been not to prevent flyers from getting into difficulties or dangers, but to show them how to get out of them satisfactorily, and having done so, to make them go and repeat the process alone. If the pupil considers this dangerous, let him find some other employment, as whatever the risks he is asked to run here, he will have to run a hundred times as many when he gets to France."[19]

The death rate in training fell by fifty percent with the institution of Smith-Barry's instructional methods.[20] Although this resulted in far better prepared war fighters, the costs were staggering. The British estimated each pilot's training ran $25,000 at a time when a single-seater scout typically cost $4,000. No matter how much better trained the pilots were, that investment was most often quickly lost. Squadrons typically ran casualty rates over one hundred percent at the front.[21]

Smith-Barry's methods were the costly ideal—available most often only to the experienced pilot who had survived long enough to win a relief from combat to instruct or in a break from patrol duty. The high casualty rate at the front and increasing demand for aircraft support placed steep demands on flight schools to send out pilots to fight as fast as possible. Most flyers were in fact barely trained. Many went into battle with as few as fifteen total hours of flying under their belts and, of that, often only a couple hours had been spent learning to fly the hard-to-handle types of single-seaters carrying them into combat. Not surprisingly, they fluttered about briefly and then got swatted down, usually before their new squadron mates had the chance to learn their names.

Running risks never seemed to disturb Crock Ingalls. Just the opposite: a risk that he survived prepared him better for the next challenge. He tried rolling his Avro solo for the first time and ended up toppling out-of-control in a tailspin, watching the earth turn dizzily on an axis toward him for seven hundred feet before pulling out. On another flight his thumb, frozen stiff in the cold, would not respond. Unable to cut the switch, he landed with his motor full on before he finally smashed the gas cock just before plowing into a hangar. Practicing a forced landing in a small farm field in the nearby countryside, he was suddenly knocked inexplicably nose down while still about twenty feet off the ground, but managed to pull up to land, bouncing to a stop at the brink of a ditch. He looked back to see a long trail of telephone wires behind him. He had not seen them strung across the field. His ailerons damaged, he waited until his South African instructor, who had been monitoring him, flew in. The South African took one look at the situation and "nearly split laughing" at the young American's fix.[22] Crock got a kick out of his predicament, too.

Not yet nineteen, he had fallen in love for the first time. The ultra-responsive, high-powered land machines that could do such stunts and live on to fly again had opened his eyes. "Never again," he declared, "will I embark in a water machine. I like something that is touchy, that is in aeroplanes."[23] Returning to base after the near-disastrous tangle with the telephone wires, he remembered his father's words each time he had smashed up an automobile at home: "It is a good thing so long as nobody is hurt, as you have the experience."[24] He was gaining the experience that would soon enable him to confront far greater violence than any auto wreck on the roadways at home.

The others had plenty of their own incidents to share with their American mates. Flying solo upside down at the top of a loop, Shorty Smith was at about three thousand feet when he did not notice the loosely fastened front-seat strap swinging back over his joy stick and holding it back as far as it would go as he came out the other side of the loop. With his elevators stuck fully up, he started to loop back up again. Not knowing what was causing his stick to freeze, he realized he could not continue looping until his fuel ran out. He cut his engine and the machine, pointed straight up, stalled, then it tail-slipped backward before diving down several hundred feet; at which point, picking up enough speed, it started back up again. The cycle of diving, climbing, stalling, tail-slipping, and diving again continued all the way down until, just one hundred feet from the ground, he started to climb again. He knew the next dive would be his last.

Throughout the length of this terrifying roller-coaster ride down through the sky, Smith had plenty of time to think things over. He thought about his girlfriend back home to whom he had gotten engaged by wire just the day before, and it occurred to him he would probably never think about her again, much less marry her. He also considered what, if anything, he might do to avert a final head-on dive into the ground. Then, as he started up on that last climb, an idea finally hit him. He swung the rudder and ailerons together hard to the right, sending the aircraft skidding sideways through the air and not up for a few seconds, which also slowed his descent as he mushed downward. He straightened out just before hitting the ground. The biplane pancaked on top of a fence, smashing a wing, and ripping apart the undercarriage, but he landed without hitting its nose or flipping.

Smith sat in his wrecked Avro's cockpit, red-faced, air sick, but in one piece. He started laughing. His instructor flew in and found him still sitting there laughing. He put Smith into his airplane and brought him home. All that night Shorty could not stop laughing. Eventually he was taken to the infirmary and given sedatives. He returned to the air a few days later, but afterward could never fly again without getting sick all over the cockpit.[25]

"I'm afraid for him," worried Crock.[26] But he took heart. Shorty's misadventure "proves that one has wonderful control in pretty adverse conditions."[27] Bad things could happen in mid-air, yet a good pilot could walk away from a wreck in one piece, all except his nerves intact.

Pushing their machines beyond their mechanical limits invariably caused problems. Out flying, Kenney MacLeish forgot his Avro could sustain only one roll at a time without the engine conking out. He spun from one roll into the next, but his motor sputtered out at 2,500 feet. With a long glide to the aerodrome and "a stiff breeze in my face," he held on nervously. He managed to skim in over some telephone wires before he "fell into the field." He stepped onto the ground and declared, "Gee, it was fun for a while!"[28] After touching down in a field during another solo, Kenney headed right back up. Turning as he climbed, his engine began to fail, sending him sideslipping toward a large brick house at the edge of the field. He pulled out just in time to avoid the chimneys.

Another time, as he climbed out of a field over some telegraph wires and treetops, his instructor yelled through the tube, "Do you like flying Mac?"

"Yea, Bo!" he shouted back at the top of his lungs. The enthusiastic American accentuated the "Yea" with a violent push forward on the controls, and the "Bo" with a yank back, sending the Avro gamboling into the treetops. Snagging its undercarriage on the branches, the plane cartwheeled straight into the ground. Kenney stepped out to inspect the damage. The undercarriage was smashed apart, the propeller snapped. He had left a deep dent in the aluminum cowling inside the cockpit and "a crump on my jaw to fit it."[29]

Back home Priscilla had told her friends how much she loved Kenney and was passionately happy about the prospect of a life together with him. However, she had a gnawing fear that they might never have the chance. His letters described one brush with death after another, and he blithely declared afterward, "Lord, there's no game like this in all the world. You're always taking such wonderful chances, and it's a grand feeling to get away with them, because you gain such self-confidence."[30] She had no desire to be a widow before she ever married.

Uncertain that she would ever see her beloved again, she also could not ignore the stories about the "education" the Yale boys were gaining overseas. Evelyn Preston, a close friend of Adele Brown's living in Paris, wrote Adele complaining, "The boys come to Paris on leave and have a hell of a gay time (excuse my language, but you know what I mean). . . . Of course I've given up trying to understand it, how nice, respectable boys can suddenly break loose and find their fun in that way."[31] The word had spread among the Radio Girls that their Yale boys had left their courtly manners at home. Despite Kenney's protestations that he avoided the more sordid side of life in a world at war, Priscilla began to have her doubts.

Other men started to call on her. Chief among them was Harry Davison, Jr., the younger brother of unit leader Trubee. As head of a test-pilot squadron based at Hampton Roads, Harry moved regularly between bases and had frequent chances to visit the family's Park Avenue mansion in New York City, where Priscilla and the other Radio Girls were staying. Priscilla enjoyed being squired around town by the dashing navy pilot. Those outings turned into a minor romance. Word soon got back to Kenney in England that he had a rival for her affections whose attention she seemed to be enjoying.

Noting the number of men he knew who had lost girlfriends back home while they were fighting overseas, he reminded her, "This staying-at-home business, instead of fighting . . . it's h___ on the men over here." Half humorously, he admitted, "Oh, I loathe the thought of him." He tried to make light of her reports about their time together, but the images of the two tore at him. "You ought not to tell me when he kisses you," he grumbled about one of her letters, "it spoils the rest of the month for me and, if carried too far, may spoil an otherwise promising career."

He understood, or tried to, her need to get out and to enjoy her lifelong friend and neighbor's company. He even pretended that he did not mind their kissing, "but what drives me nearly crazy is the fact that he can and I can't."[32] His inability to keep unit mate Harry away from her drove him "mad" with jealousy and inevitably revived the sting he had felt at his rejection by the senior societies back home. Everything he thought he was leaving behind had raced three thousand miles over the ocean to haunt him.[33]

Stuck a continent and a war away from his fiancée, he did his best to hold onto her heart, writing to her, professing his love, nearly every day. With their engagement as-yet unannounced, the teenage woman's sense of insecurity was understandable. Kenney promised her he would soon tell the whole world, but feared his parents' negative reaction.

Continuing to pursue a girl in every port, Crock Ingalls looked upon his friend's mooning over his girl back home as so much wasted effort. Besides, he wanted Kenney's company on his educational forays with the local girls. At the same time, he was more than a little envious of the mail flowing to Kenney and other unit members from their girlfriends back home. "I think I'll advertise for a girl," he snickered, "one who will write a lot. That's all a girl is good for if she's in the old U.S.A., at least so far as I'm concerned. Me, I like them closer to hand."[34]

Unhappy on the ground, the love-torn MacLeish now more than ever felt truly at home only in the air. He spent every minute he could flying. He celebrated New Year's Day, 1918, by flying out alone "like a perfect, brainless nut." Giddy with the dawning of a new year and the feeling that he and his airplane were moving as one, he went out dancing on a cloud—literally. After taking off into a loop at two hundred feet, barely high enough to keep from plowing straight back into the earth, he skated right back up into the gray clouds and then dropped back out in a tailspin. With the icy wind rushing into his face, he "was singing to myself and just having a wonderful time." He went chasing after what the experienced pilots called "Huns," the new men who were just learning to fly and who had a propensity to kill themselves and their instructors. MacLeish probably did not add to their longevity when he snuck up and then buzzed over them within yards of their heads, leaving them startled and terrified.[35]

How long any of them would last seemed a toss of the dice in any case. The first day of the year brought Kenney "the worst news yet" about his likely fate. A U.S. naval aviator who had been stationed with Di Gates at Dunkirk had arrived at Gosport earlier in the day. Dunkirk pilots, he told the other Americans, had a ninety-nine percent casualty rate. About eighty-five percent of those were killed "and the rest lost their nerve." The gloomy prospects just made him "wish we could get started and have it over with." The anxiety of waiting was worse. "This lingering death," he found, "is awful."[36] Then the English decided it was time to give their American guests their first Camel rides.

Two days later, MacLeish's instructor, an English officer named Williams, walked over from the hangar as MacLeish stepped down from his Avro. "Well," Williams said, "you're ready to go up in a Sopwith Camel." MacLeish almost fell over backward. "He was either doing his damndest to kill me," he thought, "or he had an exalted opinion of my flying ability."[37]

They walked into the hangar. There she was. MacLeish examined his gleaming khaki-color wood and doped canvas Camel biplane with the RFC's red, white, and blue cockade painted on the gossamer wings and fuselage. At a few inches under nineteen feet long—not much more than one of Henry Ford's Model Ts—and a twenty-eight-foot wingspan, he could have tucked her easily inside the library of his family's rambling house on the shores of Lake Michigan. Her twin forward-firing Vickers machine guns were mounted atop the fuselage directly in front of the cockpit. Their breeches were enclosed in a faired metal cowling, the "hump" that gave the Camel her name. The Camel crammed a powerful rotary engine, armament, instrumentation, gas tank, and cockpit into a space the length of a bicycle and barely big enough for MacLeish to fit inside. He climbed aboard and twisted about in glee. "You can touch the tail planes from the pilot's seat," he exclaimed, "and the motor is practically in your lap."

His instructor warned him he would be flying a petite but potentially deadly bird. A machine gun-packing ballet dancer on a three-dimensional stage, the Camel could pounce and leap away with terrifyingly lethal swiftness. Significantly over-engined, the Camel's nine-cylinder, 130-horsepower Clerget rotary motor—the crankshaft remained stationary while the cylinders and propeller spun together—could deliver plenty of power. In little more than the blink of an eye a Camel could leap thousands of feet—up to a maximum 19,000-foot ceiling—and shoot along at around 112 miles per hour at three miles high, 125 miles per hour near the ground.

Many flyers were scared to death by the Camel. MacLeish's instructor advised him to take her up carefully and practice flying about gingerly for several flights before beginning to stunt. With nearly all the weight packed forward, the Camel danced about beneath a pilot at the slightest movement of the stick. She took a careful, experienced pilot to fly. The skittishly agile airplane could snap off a sudden, unexpected turn on an unwary pilot. During takeoff and landing, the engine's tremendous torque, the gyroscopic spin imparted by the twirling rotors and prop, could easily send the aircraft corkscrewing to earth. Until a pilot reached sufficient speed during takeoff, he had to push hard on the right rudder to counteract the engine's torque-effect. Failing to do so, scores of pilots had spun straight down into the ground on their very first take off. Even at cruising speed, a right-hand turn could easily become a dizzying pirouette before a pilot knew what was happening.

Its deliberate instability made the Camel the perfect dogfighter, unsurpassed in the tight corners of an aerial melee. With ailerons on both wings, a pilot could perform aerial gymnastics with ease, turning corners so sharp that, with heart-stopping quickness, a German pursuer could suddenly find he was the pursued. Since reaching the Western Front the previous July, the Camel had gone a long way toward leveling the technological battlefield above the trenches. Already the most famous Allied dogfighters of the war, Camel pilots would eventually rack up 1,300 victories.[38]

With all that power and twitchiness, the Camel had to be flown all the time. When MacLeish finally took her up, he found it was impossible not to do acrobatics—even when he had no intention to stunt. Like driving a finely tuned race car, he thought his Camel was cruising at sixty and was shocked to discover she was making ninety-five. The Camel leaped upward and then pitched down at speeds incomprehensible to him. With little more than a thought of pushing on the stick or rudder, he turned sharply and, unprepared for the turn, fell into a tailspin. She would, he realized, "do a thing so quickly that you barely have time to decide upon it."

Finally, he gave in to the Camel's natural longing to dance and began experimenting. He shot up into the clouds and then dropped her nose down at high revs. The earth swept toward him faster than he thought possible. The guy-wires screamed, the skin on his face pushed back against his bones. His airspeed indicator read a phenomenal 205 miles per hour. In his very first Camel flight, he had exceeded the aircraft's maximum speed by better than 80 miles per hour and may have flown as fast as any human to date in a production aircraft. More in awe and fear than pride, he was stunned by the Camel's performance. "I never went so fast in my life," he wrote shakily afterward. That his bird did not break up was testimony to its durability. He tried a climbing turn and found himself immediately "next door to a spin, with my motor full out. That put the wind up. . . . I was scared pea green."[39] She was a thoroughbred with a mind of her own, a machine he would have to respect.

When, a week later, Crock Ingalls took his Camel out for the first time, he, too, was stunned. "It's so touchy," he found, "it just seems to jump if you shiver, and goes into a spin every time you make a turn unless you do it perfectly." After landing, he proclaimed himself "full of pride that I got back in the same World as when I started."[40]

If not quite love at first sight, the unit's lead pilots soon found nothing they had ever flown the equal of their new "magic carpets." With practice, the Camel became an aerial extension of the pilot's body, translating his thoughts into instant action. "One forgets about simply flying," Ingalls found, "and does so instinctively, keeping one's eye always on the other fellow, and also a general lookout for other machines." With practice, he soon felt "perfectly at home."[41]

The three Americans spent hours huffing with each other in their Camels. While Smith could not shake Ingalls off his tail—and usually vomited during the chase—MacLeish, Crock reported, "puts it all over me." Kenney was winning a reputation as an exceptional flyer, "one of the best pupils the school has had," Crock admitted with some jealousy.[42]

Besides its prowess in a dogfight, the Camel was being used regularly for trench-strafing. To prepare, they headed out on contour-chasing runs, also called bush-bouncing or hedge-hopping. The object of contour-chasing was to shoot along at high speeds as close to the surface of the earth as possible. Skimming along at about 120 miles per hour and five feet above the ground, they would head straight for a hangar, fence, or tree. At the last moment they would "get the wind up" and jump the object. They went racing through the countryside, across fields, and down roads, startling people and animals. The line of Camels zoomed past at eye level in a blur of brown, shower of castor oil, and storm of noise, leaving behind a tattered silver contrail and tree-bending wash of wind. "It's great fun," Ingalls noted of the escapades, "unless the motor stops, when you are up the creek."[43]

To finish up the last link in the chain of preparation, they traveled to the southwest coast of Scotland for a final two weeks of machine gunnery and aerial combat training before heading off for the front. In approaching the gunnery course, MacLeish thought how anyone could hit anything while flying was "an unsolved mystery. . . . Let's hope the mystery isn't solved at my expense."[44] Their program was based at Turnberry, a famous and handsome seaside golf resort, home of the British Open, where the hotel had been turned into a barracks and the links into a field for shooting practice. While there, they attended lectures on gunnery, synchronization gearing for firing machine guns through the propeller arc without shredding it, deflection sighting, and fixing guns that jammed frequently in mid-air. Usually a slam with the hammer pilots always kept on board for just such purposes did the job. And, of course, they practiced shooting targets. Ingalls found the guns "darn hard to shoot," not at all like spraying a hose, which he had expected.[45]

Out his window at the Turnberry base, Kenney suddenly realized he could spy Goatfell, the treeless mountain on the Isle of Arran that he had raced up in defiance of his parents' wishes eight years earlier. He recalled the feeling—as if called to the heights—upon reaching the summit of being "carried off my feet with ecstasy." His life had come full circle now that he was flying thousands of feet over the top of the very same mountain that he once thought "so high."[46] Soaring up into the clouds and higher now gave him that same sense of elation flight after flight. He had surpassed the summit.

Each evening after supper at Turnberry, the Yale boys ran out with the other student pilots to see the newly posted overseas list. The British were so hard pressed for pilots that they called up at least half a dozen new pilots each day, dispensing with the final week at the School of Aerial Fighting in Ayr. A somber crowd would gather around the bulletin board to learn who would be leaving on the next morning's train. With so few qualified for what lay ahead, Ingalls saw condemned men all around him. Seeing the faces of the chosen go ashen made him "appreciate the feelings of those in the Bastille, or wherever they kept the poor French devils en route to the guillotine, when the jailer came in with the list of those to be honored."[47]

With his usual introspection and search for a life lesson, MacLeish observed how the selection suddenly changed the chosen. "They are smiling, care-free, happy-go-luckies, one minute," he wrote his mother, "and, the next, they're so serious, determined men." Life that went from easy and fun practice the one day to deadly serious the next caused "the most violent metamorphoses." He wondered what would happen to him when his number was called. One thing he knew was that anything could happen and his fate was not solely his own to determine. The flyer's life was carrying him to places unknown. "You never clearly know what is what," he realized, "or what you may develop into tomorrow."[48]

From Turnberry, the Yale flyers moved on to nearby Ayr where, when the rains and fogs of the Scottish winter would lift, they huffed with the other apprentice scout pilots—the air "black" with dogfighters—and practiced formation flying and contour-chasing, and continued learning to master the Camel. Many of the less-experienced men could not handle the tricky machines. In four days of flying, MacLeish counted twenty-three crashes at the school, killing four Americans and several British pilots.[49] He knew a number of the dead men and each new casualty reminded him of the loss of Al Sturtevant and several other close friends as well. "I try not to let this sort of thing affect me," MacLeish reflected, "but it's not natural. . . . I guess I take [their] deaths a bit too badly, but I simply can't be coldhearted enough to make it otherwise."[50]

Finally, in late January 1918, their orders came through. The three left Great Britain behind and went to Paris on their way to join Di Gates in Dunkirk.

While in Paris, they saw Bob Lovett, who was sharing an apartment with the unit's former C.O. Eddie McDonnell in the Latin Quarter. Living "among the long-haired men and short-haired women" in the artist's colony, Lovett humorously proposed that McDonnell was "going to take up painting," and for him, "well, sculpture it will have to be."[51] Both men were putting their creative skills to work elsewhere as aids to Hutch Cone, chief of naval aviation. Cone's trust for Lovett had grown nearly boundless. He was constantly in motion. When Lovett was not off "getting the stations ready for operations, and back down to this station to set things right, then hurrying back to the front to see a bombing stunt and back again," he was dashing off memos on establishing America's own coastal patrol program to Admiral Sims.[52]

In early February, Cone went off on an inspection tour, leaving the twenty-two-year-old reserve lieutenant in charge of all naval aviation operations in Europe. He marveled at the "mystery" of how he had landed so much authority over many older, career navy men. He smirked at the military pomp that went with being a headquarters staff officer, but admitted that he could "look quite ferocious" in his dress uniform on state occasions.[53] He took it all in stride. Although MacLeish had never been entirely comfortable with Lovett's mordant wit and distant reserve, his admiration for his brilliant classmate grew and grew. "That boy," he observed, "has a better head and more ability than any two men in this branch of the service, and I'm glad they're beginning to appreciate the fact."[54]

Kenney's brother, Archie, a shavetail in the field artillery, also happened to be on leave in Paris. He would soon see action for the first time in the Second Battle of the Marne. In a poem the older brother wrote after the war, he described directing fire from the big French 155 millimeter guns: "The Marne side. Raining. I am cold with fear./ My bowels tremble . . . I am very brave:/ Magnificent. I vomit in my mask."[55] The brothers got "dizzy" together hopping from café to café along the Champs Elysées before joining up with the senior Henry Davison. He was on his way to the front on Red Cross business and had stopped over in Paris to meet with General Pershing. The MacLeish brothers, Ingalls, and Smith enjoyed a string of spectacular meals in Davison's company. "What a full day," declared MacLeish with satisfaction as his Paris layover drew to a close.[56]

On his last night in the French capital, Kenney packed his kit for the train to Dunkirk. In his final hours before leaving for the front, he sat down in his hotel room and wrote numerous letters. He tried to sum up for himself the meaning he had found in his months of training and in the unknown but surely hazardous and difficult business that lay ahead. The cumulative shock of so many sudden deaths and his own frequent brushes with the hereafter had reaffirmed and deepened his youthful ideals. The experience had also taught him how different life could be than expected.

Above all, he understood that he had been given a gift, a harsh but precious opportunity. The war had brought him the possibility to serve a greater cause, to strive for honor, to achieve what he could for the sake of his friends and his ideals, and, should death be his fate, to overcome the inevitable regrets of a lifetime and, instead, live eternally in glory. "To me," he reflected, "the finest miracle in life is to be able in the last few moments on this earth to revolution-ize one's entire existence, to forget a life of failure and weakness, and to die a hero. The Gates of Honor are opened to us, those lucky ones of us who are over here."

His resolve firm, he had concluded that this crusade for honor, his own and that of his nation, was worth whatever price he was called upon to pay. "I'm going to the front tomorrow," he wrote a young family friend. "I don't think anything will happen to me. If it should be my lot to make the supreme sacri-fice, you'll know that I did it gladly, and that I bought life's most marvelous re-ward, Honor, at a dirt-cheap price."[57]

CHAPTER 19

Dunkirk, Winter–Spring, 1918
On the Edge

Hunkered down in the late winter gales and fogs of Dunkirk, Di Gates awaited his friends' arrival anxiously. And not only because he missed them. As Al Sturtevant had warned Kenney MacLeish in his last letter, and most Allied soldiers dug in along the Western Front had expected for several weeks, the Germans were preparing to launch a massive offensive. Planning the attack, General Erich Ludendorff decided to strike early in the spring, using troops newly freed from the Eastern Front by the collapse of the Russian army. He wanted to move fast, he said, "before America can throw strong forces into the scale."[1] Both sides rushed all available men forward in preparation for the largest battle in world history. On March 21, the very day MacLeish, Ingalls, and Shorty Smith finally arrived at the Dunkirk Naval Air Station, Germany launched its initial thrust, "Operation Michael" along the old Somme battle-field of 1916. Ludendorff aimed to split the French and British armies where their trench lines met in the wasteland of shell holes and abandoned emplace-ments between Arras and Laon. Breaking through there, he planned to close on Paris while also wheeling forces west, "rolling up" the flanks of the British Expe-ditionary Force against the Channel barrier forcing a precipitous end to the war. By that evening, the battered forward positions of the BEF were falling back along nineteen miles of front in its first true defeat since trench warfare had begun three and a half years earlier. More than 7,000 Allied infantrymen had been killed and another 21,000 captured. Two days later, overwhelmed British troops had retreated a further eleven miles. German long-range guns were firing on Paris. The jubilant Kaiser Wilhelm II gave German schoolchild-ren a "victory" holiday.[2]

With Ingalls moaning over his hangover from "too damn much party in Paris," he, MacLeish, and Smith stepped onto the platform in Dunkirk after "a long, long" train ride.[3] Their ears perked up. A low, incessant thunder rumbled in the distance, the artillery percussion at the front. They could see the effects of war in the buildings around the station reduced to scorched timbers and rubble. War was unmistakably near. They could smell it for the first time.

They stowed their gear in their new quarters, an old French mansion facing a beach a mile from their base where most of the American officers slept. Like all structures still standing in Dunkirk, the house was sandbagged around the foundation and lower floor, and all the windows were covered with iron-plated shutters. Any remaining pinhole through which a glimmer of interior light might escape after dark had been painted shut. Inside they found good and mostly plentiful food and wine, stoves for heating, and even some coal to keep them warm against the bone-chilling sleet and winds slanting off the stormy North Sea. In the parlor, they could tinkle the keys of a piano and found a few not very good French records to play on a phonograph they had picked up in Paris. The French family living in the house had descended like mice into the relative safety of the cellar after the Americans had moved in upstairs.

The new men shared supper with the other base officers and its Commanding Officer Godfrey Chevalier. They were also joined by Bob Lovett, who had arrived in Dunkirk that same day from Paris by motorcycle. Along with Eddie McDonnell, their First Yale Unit C.O., Lovett had been detached by naval headquarters to the Royal Navy Air Service 5th Wing, No. 7 Squadron at an aerodrome in nearby Couderkerque, where he would soon begin flying heavy land bombers. McDonnell and Lovett would be the first U.S. Navy aviators to fly on regular combat missions against the Germans in France. Lovett hinted that they had not come there just to lend a hand. He had big things in the works, "a wonderful stunt upon the success of which hangs our future profession."[4] But he refused to let the others in on what he was doing for the navy because "everything depends upon unostentatious work." It would have to remain "a deep secret."[5]

Di Gates scoffed at his classmate's puffery and resented the unnecessary secrecy between Bonesmen. If he could not keep Bob's plans in confidence, who could? "The same old Bob," he grumbled, "very secretive and chasing all over the country with the wildest stories that never seem to match up."[6]

The former football star did have an item of his own to share. He passed around a press clipping. In New Haven and around the country, the Yale boys in the service had not been forgotten. News of Gates's posting to Dunkirk had reached America. Damon Runyon, a reporter famed for his cynical, hardnosed demeanor, now a war correspondent for the Hearst newspaper syndicate, could not contain himself in a gushingly patriotic ballad he had penned, inspired in part by Gates and other Yale football heroes turned war heroes. "Hold 'Em, Yale" had appeared in the *Los Angeles Examiner*:

> *There's a Bowl in old New Haven.*
> *(There's seventy thousand paid.)*
> *The sun looks down on a pop-eyed town*
> *On the day that The Game is played.*
> *"Hip!"*
> *The signal passes!*
> *"Hip! Hip!"*
> *The ball flips true!*
> *There's a whirl, and a swirl,*
> *And the lean-flanked backs*
> *In the jerseys blue plunge through!*
> *Hark! There's a song from the bleachers!*
> *Hark! It's the old, old hail—*
> *"Bulldog! Bulldog!*
> *Bow-wow-wow!*
> *Eli Yale!"*
> *There's a storm-ripped stretch of ocean,*
> *Where the Dutchman's U-boats trade.*
> *There's a young patrol from the big, round Bowl*
> *On the day that The Game is played.*
> *"Aim!"*
> *The signal passes!*
> *"Fire!"*
> *The shot goes true!*
> *There's a swish, and a swash,*
> *And a gurgling squash*
> *As the lean-flanked backs drive through!*
> *Hark! There's a song on the water*
> *That floats from the victor's rail—*
> *"Bulldog! Bulldog!*
> *Bow-wow-wow*
> *Eli Yale!". . . .*
> *There's a street in old New Haven*
> *That the sighing elm trees shade.*

And they sigh, perhaps, for the lean-flanked chaps
Of the day when The Game was played.
"Come!"
The signal carried!
"Come! Come!
The Flag needs you!"
Oh, a nation stirred at the magic word,
And the backs came plunging through.
Hark! That's a song from the nation!
Hark! That's a proud, proud hail—
"Bulldog! Bulldog!
Bow-wow-wow!
Eli Yale!"[7]

As the six Dunkirk-based members of the Millionaires' Unit were taking the first bites of their supper, a siren blew. Shortly after, they heard the unmistakable droning of the big German Gotha night bombers approaching down the coast. Fiery iron lightning exploded directly overhead, sending thunderous echoes through the streets. Lovett and MacLeish rushed out, nervously, to watch the tremendous antiaircraft barrage fountain up from all corners of the city, bursting into a spray of fireworks overhead.[8] Wheezing out his notorious laugh to hide his jitters, Ingalls strolled out beneath the starbursts. Collecting himself, he scanned the sparking night sky and denoted it an entertainment "better than a movie."[9]

Lovett glanced back inside and asked if they should not join the French family in the safety of the cellar. Di Gates indicated the door and stayed seated. After four months in Dunkirk, he now ignored the almost nightly air raids and frequent pounding by long-range artillery. He found "no use hiding." After seeing the arbitrary fall of the bombs over the previous four months, he felt, "If one's name is on one of the shells it is impossible to get away from it."[10] The staccato explosions subsided as the Gothas flew further south. Lovett and MacLeish returned to the table. Kenney looked with concern at the scowl on Di's face. His closest friend was "just so sick of bombs." After witnessing so much war, Kenney worried that Di had "lost some of his old, true interest in life."[11] As far as Di was concerned, it was just a question of whose number came up next. The war, he acknowledged, had made "an awful fatalist" of him.[12]

Although he sometimes lost himself in "dreaming about the good times at Peacock Point," Gates had no regrets. He was the chief pilot at the hottest spot a navy pilot could find.[13] He had much to share about his experiences since arriving. Having dropped their payload somewhere around Calais, the German raiders turned away. The newly arrived Americans settled in at the table to hear Gates's report about life in Dunkirk.

His stories were coldly sobering—with one tragic loss felt especially keenly by all. Although hardened by his months under fire, losing Curt Read, he admitted, "just about knocked the bottom out of everything for me."[14] Falling just a couple weeks after Al Sturtevant, Read was the second member of the unit to "go West," and the first navy aviator to die in France. Had the war not intervened, the sweet-natured Read would have been manager of the Yale football team that Gates was to have captained. Gates believed they would have come together to lead one of the best Yale teams of all times.

After completing his training in Moutchic, Curt had arrived in Dunkirk in late February. At Moutchic, his trainers had warned him that he was not meant to be a flyer. He never "got the hang of it," according to his friend from the unit, John Farwell, but insisted on going forward anyway.[15] He had hidden his nervousness from Di, but confessed to his brothers he was scared from the start. Before shipping out from New York, he had spent a day with his twin brother, William, who along with their two other brothers also flew for the navy. Already having walked away once from a crash, Curt believed he had used up his luck. He left, said William, with a "premonition that he would not survive."[16] Shortly after his arrival in France, Curt had written to Trubee about the "discouraging" state of affairs he had encountered. Some of that discouragement came from within himself. Although he had recognized that he would one day face danger, at home he had been carried along by what he remembered as "the romance of war which you feel so much in the U.S." Overseas, the reality startled him. He saw the young amputees staring blankly as they sat drinking in the cafés of Paris and listened to the downcast men tell their tales of enduring artillery attacks in the mud of the trenches or watching as aircraft flown by friends fell flaming down through the sky. Now, he felt "the horrid actuality of it all" in the pit of his stomach.[17]

His "feeling of fatalism" grew when he learned his orders for the front were imminent. At twenty-two years old, he readied himself for "the privilege of making the greatest sacrifice." He did not believe he would make it home. "There is absolutely no other way out."[18] As it did for many flyers fresh to the front, the end came quickly.

On his first morning at the base, Gates took Read up for a practice hop in one of the base's Donnet-Denhaut flying boats, showing him the lay of the land around Dunkirk and how to operate through the heavy traffic of the basin where the base was located. The Donnet-Denhaut was "flying all right" according to Gates, who then turned the machine over to Read for more practice with his observer, an enlisted quartermaster, Edward Eichelberger, who had flown with him at Moutchic. They took off and circled over the city and then swung back out to sea. Returning into the basin, the flying boat glided down toward a landing when she struck a patch of rough air. A strong puff knocked the unstable machine about. Di watched as it pitched over into a sudden, low-altitude nose dive. Curt, Di told his friends, was "practically gone" by the time the rescue party reached the wreckage. Eichelberger disappeared with the sunken engine.[19]

A long line of French, American, and British officers, soldiers, and sailors marched to the cemetery behind Curt Read's American flag-draped coffin, pulled on a gun carriage drawn by six horses. Thousands of people lined the streets of Dunkirk to honor the first American to die there.

He had carried a letter in his pocket addressed to his widowed mother that he never had time to send. In it, he urged her not to "worry about us [him or his brother Bart, also from the unit and now heading for his posting in Italy], for we are both as safe as can be." Although he was not much of a pilot, having "come all the way over here" he preferred flying rather than "keep a desk chair in Paris warm or some job like that."[20] He was buried in his naval aviator's uniform with his Yale letter sweater underneath and a picture of his mother tucked in his coat pocket.[21]

The loss of "dear Curt," remembered Alphie Ames, "with his beautiful character so rich with love," sent another shock wave of chill realism through the scattered men of the unit. They shared their feelings only among themselves, but Ames acknowledged, "Behind the smile and carry on everyone is tightening his jaws."[22] Curt's closest friend and Yale roommate, Erl Gould, hid his tears from his staff at the Key West Naval Air Station when he learned of his death. He told Trubee, though, "I feel as though a knife were sticking in my heart."[23]

Di Gates claimed he never allowed himself "to think about or consider for an instant" what losing first Al and now Curt meant to him. At quieter moments, he could not refrain from lamenting the war's tragedy. "This whole performance that has happened in the last couple of weeks," he wrote Trubee, "seems like a dream, doesn't it?" He wondered if perhaps, "Someday we will wake up and find everything all right and things going along perfectly normally."[24]

After telling his mates about Curt's final moments, he had mostly more disturbing news to share about the precarious and largely futile situation they, too, were stepping into. The Germans were doing everything in their power to push Dunkirk's remaining inhabitants into the North Sea, erase the city from the map. The Allies kept their fragile grip on the region, but if the Germans succeeded in pushing south and west just a few miles they would quickly drive the defenders out. Trying to avert that, British bombers, scouts, and escort seaplanes took off night and day from the many bases in and around the city for raids against the German ports forty miles north of the lines along the Belgian coast, and over the German lines just a few miles distant.

Artillery shelling and nighttime air raids had turned Dunkirk's streets into a curious mix of brave French citizens carrying on near-normal life by day, after sweeping up the rubble and shattered glass and putting out fires from the previous night's attacks. Once the sun fell, a breathless stillness and utter darkness coffined the city's streets. When the siren the Americans called "Mournful Mary" moaned out from the cathedral tower, sleeping families and soldiers would start up in bed and pile together into airless, often muddy dugout shelters and dank cellars of buildings where they waited out the attack and quietly prayed while sleep-starved children whimpered and cried.

When the shelling started up, Gates refused to flee underground. He would "duck under the covers with great dignity" and "stuff fists, pillow, mattress, and everything else" into his ears and try to sleep through it.[25] He could still hear the shells go whizzing past, falling through the night sky on their course to ground followed by the earth-shaking, window-shattering concussions. Stepping out the next day, he would see crushed and torn bodies of men, women, and children being removed from the rubble. "Believe me," Di growled, "one can have no sane opinion left for the Germans after seeing the great amount of destruction and damage they do to the poor innocent civilians."[26]

The battering, though, did its job. The Royal Navy Air Service had already had enough. The preceding September they had abandoned their own coastal installation and moved inland to fly land machines after German air raids had largely obliterated their seaplane facilities. The Americans moved in to replace them. Gates and the rest of the first American contingent had arrived in late November to set up a base on a site adjacent to the one abandoned by the British. With Lieutenant Chevalier in command and Gates as his chief pilot, the Americans set to work at a triangular point along a stone quay fifteen feet above the sea at the confluence of the main basin leading into the port and a smaller basin. Gates soon realized the Americans were not likely to remain there long either. With no room for hardened hangars on the seawalls, the location was particularly exposed to German air attack. Even if the site could have been defended, the location proved impractical for the base's anti-submarine mission. There was not enough room for a runway off the quay, so aircraft had to be lowered into the water one by one using a single crane atop the seawall. By the time a patrol was in the air after a German submarine had been spotted, the U-boat was usually long gone.

Once aloft, other problems frequently developed. As chief pilot, Gates was responsible for training the aircrews and for assuring that their aircraft remained airworthy. He took each machine up regularly for test flights. He quickly recognized that the equipment the French had handed off to the Americans was "far inadequate" to the task his crews had been assigned. The French had again given the Americans aircraft that should have been junked or used as trainers. Badly underpowered, the flying boats' engines had to run continuously at full throttle in order to carry a sufficient payload and crew for combat missions. That put such a strain on the motors that they broke down after just a few flights. Much of Gates's time was spent looking for missing aircraft gone down at sea.

The French aircraft also flew agonizingly slowly, barely fifty miles an hour. That left them vulnerable to the much faster and more powerful German seaplane scouts that protected the Belgian coastal installations. The American crews were under orders not to engage German patrols they encountered. The aircraft were also often too slow to catch up with a U-boat before it submerged. If they did manage to arrive before the sub disappeared, the two 100-pound bombs they carried may as well have been made of rubber. The small explosive payload was not powerful enough to sink a submarine without a direct hit on a vulnerable spot.[27]

With the others increasingly wearied by his description, Gates perked up. For all that, he was proud of Dunkirk. They had landed in a "wonderful district." Despite the headaches, dangers and futility, the action was nearly nonstop. This was what they had come for. He smiled. "You couldn't ask for a more exciting spot for a naval flyer, could you?"[28]

Lying in bed that first night in Dunkirk, Ingalls listened to the steady bass drum of the guns at the front. Like the waves pounding the shore outside his doors, the rumble was "just at the right distance to lull one to sleep."[29] He slept like a baby except when aroused by the sirens warning of the next of the night's five Gotha raids. The following morning he flew one of the base's Hanriot single-seater pontoon machines for the first time. He found it "too clumsy to loop." Flying land machines had "spoiled" any joy he had previously taken in a water machine. However, he was pleased finally to have joined the fight. "The war," he declared, "is on."[30]

MacLeish went up for the first time as well. He was more sanguine about the water scouts they would fly. However, while up in the air, he looked overhead. A few hundred feet up he saw the Iron Crosses beneath the wings of a German Albatross from which he could clearly make out a reconnaissance photographer leaning over the side to snap pictures of the city below. An anti-aircraft barrage burst overhead. What goes up must come down and he "happened to be just where it was coming down." Before the shrapnel hit him, he dove away. After landing, the other men peppered him with questions. Although most had been there four months already, on his first flight Kenney enjoyed the distinction of having flown closer to an enemy aircraft than anyone else to date.[31] That passing encounter with the enemy would soon seem like a comparative stroll in the park.

Less than a week later, the British and French were beating a hasty retreat all along the old Somme front, evacuating bases, abandoning heavy ordnance and ammunition, and flying away from established aerodromes. Operation Michael, however, badly stretched Ludendorff's supply lines and exhausted his army, which suffered even heavier casualties than the Allies. He halted the advance at the banks of the Marne River. On April 9, his forces launched a second phase of the offensive, Operation George, with the aim of crossing the river Lys in western Flanders, overrunning the southern sector of the Ypres Salient, and concluding with a drive to split and crush the BEF forces against the coast between Calais and Dunkirk. For six days, the Germans pushed back the lines. The British lost the Passchendaele Ridge that they had taken at such terrible cost in the Battle of Third Ypres the summer before. Plans were made to abandon the air station at Dunkirk.

On April 11, the BEF seemed on the verge of collapse. Field Marshall Haig issued a Special Order of the Day, his famous "Backs to the Wall" order: "There is no course open to us but to fight it out. Every position must be held to the last man: there must be no retirement. With our backs to the wall and believing in the justice of our cause, each one of us must fight to the end."[32] The battle was bitter, violent, unrelenting. MacLeish could hear the guns "roaring up and down the line."[33]

The war looked pretty interesting from where Ingalls sat. He viewed the British collapse as a personal opportunity. "What's our loss," Crock remarked insouciantly, "is another's gain."[34] In the all-hands pushback against the German army's onslaught, to his delight, he, MacLeish, and Smith were reassigned to fly Camels with the RNAS No. 13 Squadron. Gates also finally received permission to leave the station to fly day bombers with the RNAS No. 17 Squadron. Both squadrons flew out of the nearby Bergues Aerodrome. MacLeish was ecstatic. Flying against the Germans "in the middle of the greatest battle the world has ever known" was "the most wonderful thing that ever happened to me." His chance had finally arrived, "doubly worth" all the wearying months of training.[35]

He took off on scout patrols carrying small bombs and searching for enemy aircraft targets. Looking down from three miles up through "big fluffy bunches [of clouds] that make one want to climb out of his bus and jump into them and roll around," he could see the nearly parallel trenches of the warring sides stretching off like jagged white lightning bolts to the south through the brown and gray patchwork quilt of the bombed out Flanders landscape. The nickel reflection of the Lys snaked through the countryside. Gray observation balloons floated like gigantic plump sausages over both sides of the line. Cottony puffs of white smoke from the intense artillery exchanges flowered and drifted off far beneath them like dust motes.[36] The violent land below seemed far distant and even beautiful from his formation's perch amid the golden light-tipped cloud canyons. Proceeding on over the lines into German-controlled Belgium where they were to drop their bombs, he was at first reluctant "to destroy those cities lying apparently so peacefully." He changed his mind when he saw the first black burst of the German antiaircraft fire and heard the drum crack and flick of hot shrapnel screeching past and ripping through his bird.[37]

Barring pea-soup fog, driving rain, or blinding snow, they flew on three and even four missions a day over the line. No combatant before had experienced battle conditions comparable to the Great War flyer. MacLeish, Ingalls, and Smith and their fellow scout pilots rose up to elevations and encountered atmospheric conditions known before only to Edwardian mountain climbers in the Himalayas. Unlike men scaling peaks, they went from base camp to summit and returned in a little more than two hours in an open, unpressurized cockpit, vastly compressing and increasing the physical forces at work on them. Encased in layers of rubber, silk, and fur and squeezed inside the cockpit, they had no room to stamp out the icy needles building in their feet and little time to pound their hands together to circulate the antifreeze of blood to their fingers.

The castor oil-freezing cold and relentless razory wind, oxygen-deprivation, and extreme gravity forces could leave a pilot frozen, sick, and senseless in midair. To keep his hands from freezing up on a high altitude patrol, Ingalls pounded them against his knees. Just that little effort at 15,000 feet, though, was enough to leave him gasping for breath and dizzy. "You sit still and freeze and recover," he recorded, "until you have strength enough to pound your hands again."[38] MacLeish was unfortunate enough to freeze two fingers solid and get frostbite on two others in his first few flights.

Today's aircraft use pressurized cabins and pump in oxygen when flying in the thinning air above 12,500 feet. Allied flyers leaped up to fly hours daily far higher than that with no oxygen assistance. (German high-altitude airmen did often carry oxygen on board, an important advantage in combat.) Only the rare climber who fell from a high mountain cliff and sprang upward at the suddenly clenched end of his rope could understand the bodily compression scout pilots experienced diving and zooming in lightning bursts of speed through the frigid air. And airmen did this day after day. The reduced atmospheric pressure and lowered oxygen concentrations took a toll on their nervous systems, lungs, muscles, and hearts. Hearts pounding, flyers gulped for air like sprinters dashing for the line. Fluid accumulated in their swollen lungs making them gasp as they breathed, further depleting their oxygen supplies. Hypoxic pilots regularly blacked out at high altitudes. Long exposure to the noise of the engine and guns blasting directly in front of their faces and the continuous vibrations that drummed through their heads resulted in an unceasing high-pitched ringing in their ears. Many pilots incurred permanent physical debility—if they survived.

All of the Yale flyers suffered "worse torture than any I have ever read about," MacLeish reported, as they flew through the upper ceiling of their Camels. He recounted one high altitude patrol that at first "was nauseating." Then he felt "weak and dizzy." After about half an hour, he "got used to" the splitting headache and funny noise in his ears. Soon he was in a dogfight, his senses so stunted that victory or death became primarily a matter of luck. The veins around MacLeish's ears expanded enormously at every heartbeat, cutting off his hearing entirely, "so that when my heart throbbed I couldn't even hear the terrific roar of my motor or the tat-tat-tat of my machine guns which were firing about eight or ten inches in front of my face."[39]

His woes were not only physical. Once aloft, the strains of war the pilot had to face were far more than that. Dulled by the lack of oxygen and numbed by the cold, flyers could faint outright, more often falling into a vacuous state of inattention, losing their good judgment, a deadly curse at the wrong moment. In the thin frozen air at nearly twenty thousand feet, Ingalls noted the temptation he felt "to murmur gently: 'To Hell with the Huns, I don't care if there are some around.'"[40] But once over the lines, there often were.

As their flight approached the lines, they had to scan the air constantly for lurking enemies, twisting completely around, peering down and over the wings. All the while they had to ignore the cold and shortness of breath and maintain formation amid the turbulence and buffeting winds. "I actually winced all over with the pain every time my heart beat," MacLeish noted after one flight. "I don't see yet why my head didn't pop open."[41] He, like nearly all pilots flying with the British, flew with no parachute—considered too weighty and bulky for the scouts and, according to some nonflying staff officers, an encouragement to abandon a fight—so the only way down was a safe landing or crash.

As MacLeish flew, from time to time he fired off a few of the 300 to 400 rounds of ammunition he carried. His air-cooled guns froze up and jammed so often that he frequently had to slam them with his hammer, sometimes in mid-battle. If that failed, he had to pull out and race for safety behind the lines.

When the time to fight came, often a pilot never realized it. He was dead, blown apart by the sudden impact of a machine gun burst from below or above which could completely obliterate his body within his machine's fragile canvas skin. Even more terrible, a bullet could rupture the gas tank and set the machine on fire, turning it into a toppling funeral pyre, burning him alive. Or he might get hit in a vulnerable spot in the airframe or controls, sending him toppling down in a slow, inexorable spin to the final crunch. For those who saw their friends fall in this way the return home meant nightlong battles with images of terror.

Once in battle, though, the adrenaline flowed and flying instincts took over. "One even forgets one's name in a scrap," Kenney exalted. "Oh, it's a wonderful, wonderful game. . . . A man can use his skill and his brain, and once in a while his nerve, if he has any. It's glorious."[42] After combat, some pilots boasted of their exploits, others never mentioned them. All knew they had experienced something few others ever had faced.

By the end of each day's flying, though, the glorious moments were over. Kenney and the other pilots were exhausted, their intact bodies battered, nerves frayed, their minds at war with searing memories, always fighting an unwinnable battle against fear. If they survived, most men lasted no more than a few months at the front before cracking up or losing their nerve and will to fight. Shorty Smith, who froze his nose into a bulbous red knob and already sickened easily in flight, finally washed out. In early May he was declared unfit for flying and reassigned as a ground officer in charge of repairs at the Dunkirk station.[43]

For all its violence and physical and emotional stress, though, a pilot's war had a peculiar irony. He was a breed apart. Like the knights of old, he entered the lists, witnessed the unbearable, his friends falling in horrid, terror-filled plunges to their deaths, and inflicted the same on his enemy if he proved lucky and skillful enough. Then he was back on the ground and the only danger came from enemy raids. The rain, fog, and sleet sweeping in from the North Sea also frequently kept him grounded. Frostbitten hands, minor wounds, and the need to recover from the strain of battle brought him occasional leave and usually the opportunity for a quick flight away from the war zone. As a result, MacLeish and his mates fought intense, deadly air battles that were followed by stretches of leisure and fun.

Unlike the men in the trenches, once a pilot stepped to the ground, life offered plenty of ways to escape the war. The proud flyers thought this was as it should be. "Aviators," insisted the former Whiffenpoof Chip McIlwaine, who had recently arrived in France and would soon begin flying land bombers, "were not infantry men; they could not be treated the same. Flying was a test of nerves, a sport for which you had to be kept fit. Shave in the evening, take a hot bath, get your shoes shined whenever you pleased—a perfect snap."[44]

Night and day, the batsman brewed "his" flying officer's tea, woke him in the morning, laid out his flying uniform, and saw to his personal needs. Back on the ground, MacLeish and his friends played baseball on the beach and bridge in the mess, where they gathered at night to sing and drink and sneak off on prankish raids against other squadrons' messes that often collapsed into drunken brawls, or found a friend among the local women. Anything to relax and forget.

With his hands rendered useless for flying in combat by frostbite, MacLeish and a group of squadron mates flew down to Calais, which while subjected to aerial bombardment, lay far enough below the lines for its citizens to carry on a more normal life. There he found a jeweler who could make up a small pair of gold souvenir aviator wings with his name engraved on them to send to Priscilla back home. He also ate an elegant meal—"china plates, plenty of knives, forks, spoons, even napkins"—and laughed at a Charlie Chaplin short before flying back.[45]

Back in the hunt a few days later, MacLeish, with Ingalls and Smith in his flight, took part in a series of daylight, low-altitude bombing runs against the Zeebrugge Mole, a massively fortified seawall that spooled nearly a mile out in a curving dragon's tail. The Mole protected moored ships and the canal entrance through which U-boats, along with destroyers and torpedo boats, entered and exited their inland port in Bruges. A rail line ran its length and numerous machine gun nests and heavier batteries protected it. Kenney believed attempting raids against it was "suicidal."[46] The Royal Navy brought destroyers up the coast frequently to shell the Mole and tried to coordinate those attacks with air support.

As of April 1, the RNAS and RFC combined into the renamed Royal Air Force, an independent fighting branch. Now part of the RAF, on their first mission against the Mole, the Americans were to fly in low from the sea then, sighting the Mole, rise up fast to take advantage of the low-lying cloud cover. With their compasses to guide them, they were then to dive back down through the clouds directly over the Mole to three hundred feet and let go of their bombs while also strafing the fortifications.

As Ingalls leaped up into the clouds in his approach to the Mole, his compass spun about wildly, sending him far off target. Again he tried, with the same off-course result. Finally on a third attempt, he saw the Mole through the clouds and dove on it. Streams of tracers and bursts of flak swept past him before he dropped his "pills" and raced for home. Piloting the sixth Camel in the flight, MacLeish dove on the target, but by then the anti-aircraft batteries had him in their sights. He could laugh at it afterward, but found in his "wildest dreams of all hell turned loose," nothing like what he had faced. "The tracer bullets were doing loops and split turns around my neck," he wrote home. "I got dizzy watching them." Diving into the bursts of rapid-fire pom-poms, he lost track of the target and zoomed back into the clouds. By the time he dropped back down, he was completely lost. He flew right into a heavy anti-aircraft barrage and dove for it—"you should have seen them drop their work" and run for cover. "Their ankles were smoking." He leveled off, dropped his payload somewhere near Ostend and made his way home.[47]

Arriving back at Bergues, Crock Ingalls "figured everybody else must have been killed, for how could more than one be lucky enough to get near and away from that Mole."[48] However, luck was with the squadron as all the aircraft returned. Afterward Kenney did have to report to Priscilla that the sweater she had knitted was "beginning to show signs of wear." Those signs included a bullet hole through it that had somehow left the wearer unscathed.[49]

Whenever weather permitted in the weeks leading up to April 23, they continued to fly against the Zeebrugge Mole and a second canal entrance at Ostend that formed a triangle of waterways leading to the Bruges sub base. Those missions were intended to soften up the defenses along the two canal entrances in preparation for one of the most famous raids of the war. Hoping to close the mouths to the U-boat lairs, that day the Royal Navy brought 70 vessels, most famously the HMS *Vindictive*, carrying 1,700 men to storm the Mole and sent cement-filled blockships into the canal entrance to be scuttled. Simultaneously subs were sent to be scuttled to close off the canal entrance at Ostend. In hand-to-hand combat on the Mole, the raid destroyed many of its facilities and the railroad viaduct leading to it and partially plugged the mouth of the Zeebrugge canal. Carried off course by wind and tides, the attackers at Ostend failed to reach their target at all. The daring raid on the Mole gave a badly needed morale boost at home, but U-boats were going in and out again within days and destroyers within weeks. More than 240 men were killed and 400 wounded in the day's action.[50]

The occasional assaults on the German submarine pens seemed to do little to impede the U-boats in their campaign against Allied shipping. The Allies needed to find some other solution if they hoped to drown the German's most effective weapon.

A few days after the Zeebrugge Mole raid, Ingalls lamented, "My joy is over." His army battered and overstretched, Ludendorff finally halted its onslaught. The Americans were recalled to their Dunkirk base, "So goodbye to the Camels."[51] Gates was still concerned that they might have to evacuate the base, but soon things settled back into a stable but steadily active front.[52] As the most intense fighting eased, Seth Low and Cord Meyer from the Yale crew and the Aero Club, Lafayette Escadrille cofounder William Thaw, and the former Princeton hockey great Hobey Baker—all flying with the army's 103rd Aero Squadron under Thaw's command in the fight to stem Operation Michael—stopped in together at the Dunkirk base for a visit. What they saw did not impress them. A day earlier a sharpshooting Gotha bomber had landed a direct hit in front of one of the hangars, destroying six of the station's eighteen aircraft.

Enemy attacks were not the only cause of trouble. Several accidents also put the station's patrol craft out of commission. In early May, two big Donnet-Denhaut flying boats went out on morning patrol. One spun into a watery crash, killing the front observer, seriously wounding the pilot, and breaking the rear observer's leg. The other machine came in to rescue the survivors. However, with five men on board, the flying boat started to ship water and sink. Meanwhile five more aircraft from the station had flown out to help in the rescue and to provide cover against any approaching German aircraft. The injured and stranded men were put onboard passing torpedo boats. When the other seaplane scouts and flying boats headed back to the base, only one managed to return all the way without a mechanical failure. "The machines are simply antiquated," groaned Ingalls. "Anyway it's no place for slow water machines; if we met any Huns we'd be meat for them."[53]

Even without enemy encounters, between mechanical failures and pilot error, several other pilots and observers died or suffered serious injuries. One took off too close to the docks and hit a smokestack, sending him diving down into a street, killing him. Another flyer disappeared at sea and was never heard from again. Still another spun into the water in front of the station, leaving two pontoons floating on the surface as the only remains for the recovery boat to pick up.[54]

The station did have its occasional victories. A patrol managed to put a couple bombs directly on U-boat U–71, forcing it to submerge and limp home for repairs. Other patrols spotted enemy minefields for destroyers to eliminate. While under frequent attack, the station played its part as the frontline in the increasingly comprehensive naval strategy to suppress U-boat activity.[55]

That strategy had become more effective in recent months. Allied shipping losses from U-boat torpedoes were declining. By late spring the tonnage sunk had slipped below 300,000 per month, according to British statistics. (The German Admiralty reported a much higher success rate for its U-boats, claiming Allied shipping losses were still well over 500,000 tons.)[56] Despite the improving fortunes, appalling Allied losses continued. In April, German submarines sank more than 100 merchant ships, taking the lives of 488 men.

Troop transports faced constant threat. However, Britain no longer risked imminent starvation. Too open to detection and constrained by minefields, netting, and air and sea patrols, U-boats now generally avoided attacks on convoy ships, and surfaced only at night or in stormy seas, or preyed on lone, unescorted ships. Admiral Holtzendorf's promise to the kaiser "that not one American will land on the Continent" was proving far from prophetic. Not a single American troop transport brought over in convoy was ever sunk. By the end of May, 650,000 Americans were in Europe. More than one million American soldiers would be in the field by the beginning of July.

The Kaiser relieved Holtzendorf of his command. In early August, Field Marshall Hindenburg and General Ludendorff told his replacement as chief of the naval staff, Admiral Reinhard Scheer, that any German hope for victory lay in the U-boat campaign. Although facing severe shortages of steel, oil, and men, Germany continued to invest heavily in submarine warfare, their most promising asset.[57] The American navy hoped to have an answer to that. Moving back and forth between Paris and British and American air stations, Bob Lovett set himself the task of formulating that response.

The American base at Dunkirk was not likely to figure into any action plan. "Poor old Di hasn't smiled for . . . days," reported MacLeish.[58] Gates had become increasingly sullen about the station's inadequate equipment and its personnel's lack of sleep. The long day's work as the daylight lengthened, nightly multiple air raids and intermittent artillery shelling exhausted him and his men. "It is awfully hard on everyone," Di admitted to Trubee.[59] The futility of the work left him nearly as wearied as the nightly wake-up calls by German bombers. He wanted to transfer back to a fighting squadron, but his requests kept getting rejected. He blamed Lovett for blocking the transfers he put in for.

After a visit by Lovett to Dunkirk with several "brass hats" in tow, Gates exploded. He declared himself "fed up on his general attitude" and his "very secretive ways." Even more, he hated what he perceived as his classmate's arrogance, particularly when, in the company of more senior officers, "he almost refuses to associate with us." Bob, Di complained to Trubee, had become "about ten times worse than he ever was at college."[60]

Lovett was not alone in rubbing shoulders with the upper echelons, though. In early August, King George V visited Dunkirk and received Gates and other American officers aboard the HMS *Terror*, a monitor moored in the harbor, a significant honor for a junior officer.[61] A few days later, the young officer gave the British reason to honor him again.

A radio alert came in to the base that a British Handley-Page land bomber had been shot down off Ostend and the survivors were floating aboard the wreckage in range of German shore guns. Gates bounded out of his office and raced over to a fueled flying boat moored off the quay. An escort of Camels out of a nearby aerodrome was sent to accompany Gates. The Camels nowhere in sight, Di took off alone. "Trust him to wait for no escort," recorded Ingalls.

Defenseless, he flew the forty miles to the downed aircraft and landed. Two survivors clung to the wings at either end to keep it afloat. The Germans continued to shell the bomber from shore and were sending their own aircraft out. The Camels finally arrived in time to see Gates splash down and motor around to pick up the first man. He cut his engine, always risky because of the difficulty cranking it at sea. The first man climbed aboard. He cranked his motor. It would not catch. He tried again and it started up. He taxied over to the second man and cut his engine once more. Di pulled him in. The pilots overhead watched and worried as the flying boat now drifted while Di cranked the motor. Finally the propeller began spinning. Back at the base, the Camel pilots who had witnessed the rescue shared their admiration, reported Ingalls, for "the guts of old Di."[62]

The British Admiralty awarded him the Distinguished Flying Cross for his heroism. "A very gallant officer," declared Royal Navy Admiral Sir Roger Keyes. When he learned of the rescue, U.S. Navy Chief Admiral Sims recommended Gates for the Medal of Honor—one of only three men in the navy recommended for the highest award for heroism during the war. Gates received the Distinguished Service Medal.[63] Back at home, Americans across the nation read about the Yale football captain's heroics in the popular weekly *The Saturday Evening Post.*[64]

Biding his time and hoping for a chance to return to Camel patrols, Ingalls found much to enjoy each day in the "picturesque and interesting" life on the ground at Dunkirk where he could savor the spectacle of the war. After a day at the station, he would sit out on the porch of his house overlooking the beach, awed by the phantasmagoric panorama and violent sensual beauty surrounding him. The sun would set over the sea, spreading a blood-red hue across the tossing green waves and white sand beach. "In the channels just off the coast," he recorded one particularly splendid evening, "loom majestically the British destroyers. While continually, planes of every sort and description soar overhead, either steadily climbing towards the front or, throttled down, half gliding back to rest, their dangerous tasks completed. Now, when the evening quiet has fallen, the low rumble of the guns on the lines becomes more audible, and often at the explosion of one of the heavier guns, the house shakes, and the whole earth seems to tremble, as if in response to some mighty Satanic blow."

As the night's true natural darkness enclosed the lampless modern world, the engines of war painted a dizzying kaleidoscopic tableau of sight and sound in every direction. "With a beautiful new moon shining down upon the smooth sea, with countless Archie [antiaircraft] batteries barking along the coast for miles on each side, with shrapnel bursting high in the heavens, whence comes (during the lulls between salvos) the distinct and never to be mistaken hum of the Bosche-flown motors, with the many far-reaching searchlights, star shells, flaming onions and the occasional rattle of machine guns—the last defense against some daring Hun who has slipped through the barrage and, coming in low over the city to drop his load of bombs, has become plainly visible to those on the ground—with all this, I say Dunkirk at night is a wonderful sight."[65] For Crock, war still had the capacity to put on a great show.

With seventeen hours of daylight during the summer days, weather permitting, MacLeish flew as many as five two-hour patrols out of Dunkirk each day. Still he found plenty of time to fret about Priscilla's fidelity. Priscilla wrote him daily letters reaffirming her commitment to him, but his lack of confidence would color her actions in his eyes and leave him blue. Even as he had the name "Priceless Priscilla" painted on his Hanriot seaplane scout and declared her "the best-looking" machine at the station, he went to Di Gates "with a long tale of woe." He now worried that John Vorys, who had been sent home to instruct, would make good on his boast that he would steal Priscilla away.[66] His worries about Harry Davison's dalliance with Priscilla also continued to gnaw at him. He wrote Trubee asking him to "tell that dude brother of yours that I'll absolutely kill him. . . . The low down snake—when I'm 3000 miles away, and 'Priscy' is so chubby and kittenish!"[67]

That was especially true after he picked up the engraved gold aviator wings he had had made for Priscilla in Calais, only to learn that, "as usual," Harry Davison had beaten him to the punch. He had already given her the prized romantic token. Kenney sent the wings off to his sister Ishbel instead.[68] With his old friend in misery, Di reported to Trubee that "poor" Kenney's "daily prayers seem to be that 'Harry be sent soon to France.'"[69] Priscilla assured him that Harry meant nothing to her and that she remained Kenney's alone. Urged by Priscilla, Harry wrote to his closest friend, Dave Ingalls, asking him to "tell Ken for me that he need have no worries at all, he is in as strong as anyone could be."[70]

Reassured, Kenney continued to put aside his extra pay, saving the five thousand francs he would need to buy her an engagement ring. He wanted to be able to say, "I earned every cent of the money I paid for it."[71] Once he knew that ring was on her finger, they could declare their engagement publicly and he could fly off in "Priceless Priscilla" certain about the good days that lay ahead for the couple.

Then "Priceless Priscilla" exploded into flames while being cleaned and refueled, badly injuring a mechanic. Kenney was grounded. No matter, for that meant he could sleep in. Two days later, word arrived from Bob Lovett that he, Crock, and a few others from the old Yale Unit had been selected to train to fly land bombers. Bob had a plan in the works that might bring the original unit back together. More important, it might be key to winning the war.

CHAPTER 20

Dunkirk, March–April 1918

Flaming Onions

A LIGHT MIST HUNG IN THE NIGHT AIR OVER THE COUDERKERQUE aerodrome. In the total-blackout darkness, the four RNAS Handley-Page O/400 bombers were barely visible. As the pilots warmed the biplanes' twin Rolls-Royce engines, armorers lugged in 100-pound ammunition trays for the Lewis machine guns and hung nearly 1,800 pounds of bombs in the racks inside the belly of each aircraft. They ignored the continuous thunder and flashes from the frontlines in Flanders. They did not take time to notice the young American officer climbing the ladder up to the cockpit of one of the Handley-Pages.

Bob Lovett saluted the pilot, Canadian captain John Roy Allen, whom he had met in the mess earlier that day, and the bomb aimer/forward gunner who stood on a round parapet extending forward from the open cockpit. He walked to the rear ladder and hauled himself awkwardly into the exposed upper-rear cockpit, taking care not to put his foot through the taut canvas skin covering the wooden airframe. Though he was swathed in so many layers of silk, wool, leather, raccoon skin, and rubber that he could only lumber about like a circus bear on its hind legs, he already shivered in the cold wind blown back by the propellers. The stench from the burning oil and exhaust filled his nose.

The Royal Navy crew was happy to have the Yank on board. Two days earlier—at dawn on March 21—Ludendorff had launched Operation Michael. Rumors were flying through the aerodrome that the German army was approaching Paris. The Allies were desperate for more men to throw into the fight that raged all along the Western Front. Lovett knew how to handle a machine gun and was trained to pilot big flying boats. In a pinch, he could fly the bomber should the first pilot get hit by bullet or shrapnel. He would do.

When the twenty-two-year-old learned a month earlier that he would be joining the British bombing crews flying out of Dunkirk, he could "hardly breath" he was "so blamed excited." The "scary" prospect of flying over German-controlled territory for the first time, though, left him "all cold at night thinking about it."[1] Those missions were considered so hazardous that any flyer who survived just seven missions was automatically awarded the Distinguished Service Cross (DSC), one of Britain's highest honors for valor. With its dense rings of antiaircraft batteries, stabbing searchlights, and cordon of scout aerodromes, the submarine pens at Bruges and in the interconnected canal outlets at Zeebrugge and Ostend were considered the most dangerous objectives in the entire European theater.[2] Lovett stowed away his fears because, as he wrote in his now openly loving letters to Adele Brown, "the more one has to live for the more readily one is willing to die for it."[3]

Checks complete, each pilot signaled to clear the chocks, the starting light flashed, the exhaust glowed red, the dust swirled up in the wash and one by one the seven-ton bombers rolled out onto the runway. The planes, among the largest land machines yet built, were about the length of one of today's tractor-trailer trucks. But when fully loaded, they could cruise at no more than about 75 miles per hour and climb to just 8,000 feet, well within antiaircraft artillery range. However, by flying at night, they could generally elude detection and needed less armament to fight off enemy scouts, allowing them to carry larger payloads. The smooth night air also made the ride less bumpy—until the clump-clump of antiaircraft fire started. The vast one hundred-foot upper wingspan flopped about as the slow-moving, graceless aircraft bounced over the rutted hardpack and cinder runway, built up speed, and finally struggled into the air. They flew out over the North Sea to gain altitude. Watching for the flash of the Véry flares in the night sky, the pilots gathered in formation and then turned up the coast.

Lovett shivered while he squinted into the darkness, scanning for German scouts who might be out searching for them in the black night. The ground fog lifted as they crossed over the shoreline into German-controlled Belgium. The antiaircraft batteries immediately sprang to life. From his perch, Lovett could look down to see the flashes of scores of guns firing at once, in a hellish mirror image of the starry sky overhead. Searchlights darted about, seeking out the bombers the Germans could hear buzzing overhead. Lovett had expected a scary ride, but "the defenses far exceed anything one could imagine."[4] He held tight to his gun when, a few seconds later, the plane dropped sharply beneath him and then began to jerk and bounce in the concussions from the Archies, the airman's name for antiaircraft fire, bursting around them.

Terrified and suffering from chronic stomach pain, Lovett still wanted to be on the mission. In fact, he was living his "wildest dreams."[5] For the young advisor to the head of the U.S. Navy's air force operations in Europe, it was a chance to fight, but it was far more than that. He planned to spend the next six weeks on bombing runs against the U-boat docks, amassing experience in aerial bombing. If he survived, he would use this experience to convince the navy that it needed to move in a bold, new, and untried direction. He could not know that he was on the first flight into the future of American military power and the eventual development of its unrivaled air might.

During his stint at the RNAS aerodrome in Felixstowe in January, Lovett had learned to fly the Spider Web patrols. He also scrutinized base operations. His objective had been to help organize the new American coastal air stations and prepare himself to become the C.O. of one of those stations on the Brittany coast. While at Felixstowe, though, he became curious about the effectiveness of the antisubmarine strategy of scouring vast tracts of open water for prowling enemy vessels. The station's commander John Porte gave him a free hand to look into the intelligence on the base's work and its impact on enemy operations. What he learned dismayed him. Over the life of the base, a seaplane needed, on average, to cover 22,000 square miles before ever sighting an enemy submarine—several weeks of largely fruitless crisscrossing of an empty sea nearly half as large as all of England. Even when a patrol finally spotted a U-boat, odds appeared about even whether pilots could fly within bombing range before the enemy vessel disappeared. And when depth charges were dropped on the enemy, only one time in four did they actually hit the target. Spotting and knocking out a submarine via the Spider Web patrol was long, laborious, costly, and rarely successful. The Spider Web patrols did reduce the aggressiveness of the U-boats, but Germany could build new submarines faster than the flying boats could destroy them. At this rate, the combined Allied navies would lose the war against the enemy's submarines. With American troop transports starting to load up along U.S. coasts, many new targets were fast approaching Europe.

Lovett dug deeper into intelligence records on enemy operations. Then twenty-one years old, the son of the chief of the Union Pacific knew more than most much older navy men about logistics. In his inspection tours of the railroad's lines with his father, he had seen that maintaining a large fleet of locomotives required extensive down time for refueling, repairs, rest, and change of crew. He figured that the diesel-driven submarines could not be any different. What he learned did not surprise him. Up to that point, Germany had built some 350 submarines of which only fifty or fewer were known to be cruising in British or European waters in the course of most months. Given that some of those U-boats had already been sunk or badly damaged, at any one time about eighty-five percent of the German fleet would be berthed in port being readied for their next cruise.

Many subs operated out of the Baltic Sea ports, too far to reach by air, but a significant number of those U-boats were based in Zeebrugge, Ostend, and Bruges, home to the enemy's largest pens, all accessible by air. "Instead of chasing these Huns separately," Lovett figured, a better strategy was "to get them when they were together."[6] The commonsense notion seemed obvious enough, but finding the will and the means to carry through such a strategy had proven impossible so far.

Britain had tried to knock out the U-boat nests with intermittent bombing raids from its bases in Dunkirk. The effort had proven largely ineffective. The British *Vindictive* raid on the Zeebrugge Mole had inconvenienced German submarine warfare for just a few days. Moreover, however valuable destroying the U-boats while in port may have been, Britain was hard pressed to come up with the men, matériel, and leadership to apply the kind of unremittingly destructive force needed to flatten the hardened U-boat facilities.[7] Other more pressing tactical needs of the military in the field frequently diverted the bombers away from the docks. And as the courageous but futile *Vindictive* raid demonstrated, a frontal assault gained little and cost much. At this stage in the war, only the United States, with its vast, still untapped resources, could muster a degree of power capable of wiping out the U-boats in their port. However, getting the navy, amid the welter of conflicting schemes and Allied demands for help pouring into its headquarters, to consider such a major investment in a wholesale bombing program would require firsthand knowledge and the weight of a significant, convincing strategic plan. Ships of the air stilled seemed exotic, sometimes out of science fiction, to many navy men who had spent their entire careers on surface vessels.

But Lovett's personal success over the years had helped give him the confidence to take on a hidebound military branch and to come up with an innovative bombing strategy and implementation plan. He had a young man's brash disdain for tradition and a mind trained to absorb vast quantities of information and deliver practical conclusions. He already had won the trust of his boss, Captain Hutch "Eye" Cone, who was willing to consider his young aide's revolutionary proposal for the navy.

Once back in Paris, Lovett spent his days preparing for the formation and coordination of the new American seaplane patrol stations on the coast. During the evenings, he worked together with his apartment mate and former C.O., Eddie McDonnell, to develop a plan for the creation of America's first strategic bomber force. The aircraft would focus on attacking enemy concentration points, submarine and naval ports, depots, and factories. At first he figured the navy would use flying boats, like the lumbering H–12 ships he had flown out of Felixstowe, and the American aircraft that would soon begin coming off the lines from the new navy factory in Philadelphia. But then he met Wing Commander Colonel Spencer Gray of the Allied Air Council, a leading British authority on bombing. Gray convinced him that the slow-flying boats would be no match against defending German aircraft. The painful loss of Al Sturtevant confirmed that. Moreover, flying boats would have to travel by daylight, which would require high-altitude bombing to avoid enemy ground fire. Given the primitive sighting instruments for bomb aimers, many, if not most, bombs were likely to go astray. Gray urged him to consider faster land machines, especially night bombers, as an alternative. He introduced Lovett to Wing Commander Captain C. L. Lambe, head of the British night-bombing squadrons operating at Couderkerque and the leading Admiralty proponent of concentrated bombing on the submarine docks. Lambe let Lovett review his wing's records and advised him in the formulation of his plan.

At the end of January, Lovett submitted a memorandum to the navy summarizing his findings to date. The surface navy, which had long resisted the value of aviation and was institutionally opposed to land machines, would need to be convinced of a radical reorientation to base naval aircraft on land. After examining the merits of the "one-duty [flying] boat" for submarine patrol work and its inadequacy as an offensive bomber, Lovett urged consideration of "a many motored land machine of the Handley-Page or Caproni [a large Italian bomber] type" for offensive purposes. "The effectiveness of these machines," he contended, "cannot be overestimated." He did not let the little-known facts about the bombers' true effectiveness constrain him when he declared the night-bombing squadron at Couderkerque "by far the most deadly weapon any of the Allies have yet discovered."

His memorandum carried conviction and logic, but no American officer had ever flown a heavy land bomber in combat. The reality of what a bomber could do was as well known to American naval aviation officials as the color of the kaiser's nightshirt. That is, not at all except by conjecture and secondhand accounts. In his Paris desk job, Lovett was "in the pink" and so well fed that his slender frame was "almost getting a bay widow."[8] The offer to take charge of his own air station stood, but he asked that instead he be detached to one of Lambe's squadrons at Couderkerque to "gather all possible firsthand information" about its operations.[9] Above all, he needed to learn how bombers operated effectively against the Germans. There was only one way to find out.

By the end of February, he and Eddie McDonnell had permission to join the RNAS 5th Wing, No. 7 Squadron of Handley-Page night bombers and de Havilland day bombers. Arriving in Couderkerque three weeks later, Lovett found his British squadron mates "a fine lot—the most fearless, clean-cut, happy men imaginable—and awfully good fun."[10] Given his Felixstowe training, Lovett immediately joined the crew of the bomber the *Evening Star* under Captain Allen. He and Allen shared a similarly dry sense of humor about their precarious existence. The plucky young American and the decorated Canadian veteran took an immediate liking to each other. Soon, Lovett, who maintained a wall of reserve with all but his oldest and closest friends, had found an "intimate" friend in "good old Roy Allen." He declared to Adele, "I'd go anywhere with him."[11]

For six weeks, Lovett flew and fought as Allen's rear gunlayer, "sailing over a German base and dropping eggs on it while shrapnel bounces the machine about, and the searchlights stab at you."[12] On that first mission over Bruges, Lovett tried not to show his fright to the other crewmen as the plane bucked wildly as high explosives burst around them and hot shrapnel fragments zinged past their heads and pocked the skin of their airplane. Lovett's jaw dropped when he saw a barrage of "flaming onions" for the first time. These devices burst open into a luminous net of green flame that swayed about like the petals of a deadly jade flower spread across the sky. The flaming onions were designed to set fire to the aircrafts' oil- and gas-spattered wooden frames and fabric skins by flinging fiery phosphorous jelly over the wings, struts, and tailplanes. Allen never deviated, flying straight through the tightening gauntlet of lethal iron, explosives, and liquid fire that spiraled about them in the flashing darkness.

When the formation approached the docks, the four bombers moved into a line. Allen throttled down his engines, the propellers windmilling in the breeze. With the bomb aimers in the forward parapet guiding the pilots, the Handley-Pages began their nearly silent, throat-tightening glide down to five thousand feet—the minimum height from which bombs might be accurately dropped. When Allen reached that altitude, searchlights lit up his airplane against the clouds like an escaping fugitive. All Lovett heard was the whistle of the wind in the wires, the snap of high-caliber bullets, and the crump of Archies exploding and knocking the big "bus" about. "Frequently hit by shrapnel and high-explosive fragments," Lovett was happy to be able to report afterward, "never, however, in a vital spot."

He watched the flash of the first bombs lighting up the port a mile below through the gun port in the floor of his cockpit. He could not believe his eyes as "the earth seemed to split, the sky was alive with green onions and high explosive and Archie made a wall through which we dove for our objective." After their 1,750 pounds of bombs fell, Lovett "had the distinct satisfaction of seeing our bombs lift some ammunition stores sky high." The motors came back to life and the bombers turned for the safety of home with sixteen searchlights darting about looking for them. Lovett fired tracers down the beams until the tip of his machine gun glowed red and the glow crept up the barrel. Twice lights flashed out. Two hours after setting out, they landed, the *Evening Star* shot up "but none the worse for wear." Shaking and barely able to control his nerves even once he was back on the ground, the mission was, he told Adele, "the greatest experience of my life."[13]

After that, raids took place "every possible night," rain and hail driving the bombers back several times.[14] Over the course of one five-day period, the bombers returned to Bruges four times. Each time they flew into what appeared to be an impenetrable box barrage, with "walls, ceilings and floors" composed of high explosive, shrapnel, and flaming onions. Lovett was startled by the accuracy of the enemy fire. "They seem to have little difficulty finding the correct height almost immediately upon warning of our approach."[15] He could smell the burning gunpowder. Shrapnel shattered a propeller blade and knocked a tail plane out of commission.

With each successive mission, though, the antiaircraft response faded until on the fourth raid, only high explosive shells and flaming onions were being fired at them. The absence of shrapnel led Lovett to conclude that the batteries' supply had been exhausted.

He saw with his own eyes that steady, concentrated bombing raids could work. Day after day, the British bombers sapped the enemy's capacity to make war. "Due to the enormous expenditure of [German] anti-aircraft ammunition," he reported back to headquarters, "the continuous use of their guns, and the effect on the morale of the gun crews, their defenses became weaker each succeeding night." As the German defenses weakened, continuing offensive missions could operate ever more safely at lower elevations, enabling more accurate bombing of objectives. They would quickly pulverize the docks. Here was the proof he needed that "a submarine stronghold . . . could be made untenable if not stamped off the map."[16]

As the German spring offensive continued, the pressing needs of the beleaguered troops in the lines forced No. 7 squadron to turn away from the Bruges docks to other objectives inland. Lovett flew on raids against railway junctions and ammunition dumps. Although the new targets took him off his intended course, Lovett was pleased with the "wonderful opportunity to do invaluable work."[17] Before each mission, though, he would still get what he called that "gone" feeling in his stomach.[18]

On one of the raids against a railway junction behind German lines, Lovett in the rear gunner's cockpit could see inside the fuselage that a 250-pound bomb had hung up in the rack after the initial run over the target. Lovett alerted Allen in the cockpit to the problem, and then climbed into the racks suspended above the open bomb bay door. His prep school gymnastics came in handy as he looked down thousands of feet of open air. The beams of more than a dozen white searchlights coned the aircraft and poured through the open hatch. The sucking wind tried to pull Lovett out while the concussions from antiaircraft fire knocked him back and forth against the fuselage and rack. Peering through a gaping tear in the fabric left by a shell that had pierced the side of the airplane, he could see multiple holes where shrapnel had punched through the wings.

Rather than just dump the bomb, Allen turned back and dove on the junction again. The antiaircraft fire intensified—"if possible." Lovett expected at any moment they would be blown out of the air. When the bomb aimer finally flashed a signal to him that they were again over the target, Lovett shoved the reluctant bomb free. He climbed back and took up his gun again. As he fired away down the light beams, he started singing like a maniac, "Have you seen the ducks go by for their morning walk? Quack quack quack, quack, quack, quack," much to the grinning Allen's enjoyment.

Once back on the ground, he and Allen did a "hopscotch dance" to celebrate their survival. Lovett admitted, "I could have cried I felt so lucky to have been through it and come out safely." Just then he noticed a shrapnel fragment embedded in his side and plucked it out.[19]

The raids left him exhausted, nervous, and terrified. Kenney MacLeish saw his Yale classmate the day after a raid and found he still "had the wind up so badly that he can't stand still."[20] Lovett now popped malted milk pills throughout the day to calm his roily stomach.

But he was alive. He had seen what the bombers faced and that they could survive the worst the enemy could give.

McDonnell also flew day and night missions to prepare a separate report about his own experiences and make recommendations for the bomber force as well. On a daylight raid as part of a formation of six British De Haviland D. H. two-seat light bombers carrying eight twenty-pound bombs, antiaircraft fire put a large hole through a wing near the fuselage. Then five German scouts attacked. One enemy airplane was quickly shot down. Another flew in on Mc-Donnell who, firing his Lewis gun, got his "sights right on the front of the machine," which appeared to be hit before it dove off in a steep turn and dropped away. After that, the remaining enemy aircraft shadowed the British formation at a safe distance until it crossed back over the lines. Nearly all the aircraft were badly shot up. Part of one airplane's rudder was torn away; a gaping hole in the side and top showed where a shell had passed through another. But all made it home safely.

Not every mission was so lucky. In a night raid, McDonnell saw two of the ten bombers hit by antiaircraft fire and could only watch as the flaming aircraft and crew, who carried no parachutes, toppled and spun to earth.[21]

Despite the inevitable losses, in his report to U.S. Navy officials, McDonnell contended that "great damage has been done" by the raids he flew. The enormous antiaircraft defense built up around the ports "shows that the Germans dread these bombardments." He recommended establishing a U.S. force of 100 night bombers and 200 day bombers as "a beginning." From that start, concentrated bombing of the submarine pens would, he asserted, soon put the U-boats "*hors de combat.*"[22]

Captain Cone accepted all of Lovett's and McDonnell's recommendations. On April 17, he sent a long cable to Admiral Sims outlining the requirements of America's first strategic bomber force. The Northern Bombing Group—he planned for a southern group to follow in Italy—would consist of two wings, night and day, six squadrons each, comprising nearly 300 airplanes. Some 460 officers and nearly 3,100 enlisted men would be needed to staff the two wings. The squadrons were to be based at existing Allied aerodromes around Dunkirk, but shadow bases would have to be built deep in the countryside in case the Germans overran or concentrated their attacks on the existing aerodromes. To support the enterprise, a huge new receiving, assembly, and repair depot—with more than a thousand men of its own—would have to be established elsewhere in England or France.

The on-the-ground requirements for such an undertaking were enormous and the complex logistics mind-boggling, but in the American rush to build up a new modern air force, nothing seemed beyond the realm of possibility. The plans called for construction of camps for the bomber force's 5,600 men and their support services, along with hangars, mechanical, and ordnance facilities, plus purchase of 94 trucks, dozens of Cadillacs, ambulances, motorcycles, and other vehicles, as well as odds and ends such as 7,000 fifty-gallon gasoline drums, miles of telephone wire, cranes, handtrucks, and more. Most of that would need to be brought over on ships from America. Back home, flight schools had to prepare men to fly, navigate, and bomb at night. Cone even requested a meteorological school be established to train forecasters to make all-important flying-weather predictions.

The Northern Bombing Group was to be a monumental step for the early days of American aviation. However, Lovett, McDonnell, and Cone were looking well ahead, not expecting major operations to commence until 1919. They wanted to put the frustrations of fighting with borrowed and obsolete equipment behind them and make America second to none in the skies. Even then, they had their eyes set well beyond the ports in Belgium. Current heavy bombers could already fly for nearly ten hours with a full payload. Future aircraft would likely be able to penetrate far deeper into enemy territory with larger and larger payloads. With its burgeoning bomber force, Lovett expected to prepare the navy to "take part in the warfare ahead of anything at present contemplated."[23] Strategic bombers would become the decisive weapon. In a strategy for total victory, the Allies would eventually have to blacken the heart of Germany. Cone cabled Sims: "Strongly recommend . . . program be undertaken immediately."[24]

A few days later Sims cabled back advising Cone to begin immediately organizing the Northern Bombing Group.

Lovett's "wildest dreams" seemed destined to become a reality. The navy had committed itself to the nation's first strategic bombing program, the largest aerial undertaking in history. Much of that future program hung on his bony shoulders. "So proud and happy I can hardly see," Lovett packed his bags on April 11 and prepared to leave his squadron in Couderkerque to attend a planning conference with Cone and the head of the RAF. Preparing to fly a mission against the Zeebrugge Mole that night, Roy Allen asked him to come along on one last flight. Increasingly superstitious after having survived so many harrowing missions together with the resourceful Yank aboard the *Evening Star*, the Canadian pilot had begun to regard Lovett as a good luck charm. Cone refused to let his valuable young assistant go. "Orders are orders," said Lovett about "the first and only trip" he missed while serving with the now renamed RAF No. 217.

The mission was a fiasco from the start. Orders canceling the attack on the treacherous Mole due to bad weather in the low-lying clouds came too late to reach the bombers. Within minutes of take off, hail began drumming against their wings and striking the crew like grape shot fired by the cannon of the gale-force winds. The fifty-knot winds from the south blew them about through the darkness like canvas sacks. The squadron's instructions called for each aircraft to drop its bombs one at a time, making fourteen passes over the target. That,

Lovett felt, "meant almost certain death." By the end of their second run, the German antiaircraft barrage had the bombers squarely boxed in. Hit by antiaircraft fire, Allen's Handley-Page caught fire. As he veered away to the south, an engine failed. The *Evening Star* fell into the sea off Ostend. The other crew members swam free, but the pilot Lovett considered "the bravest man in the world" drowned before a rescue ship could reach the wreckage. Out of six airplanes sent out on the raid, only two made it back.[25]

Grief-stricken, convinced somehow he might have saved his friend, Lovett told Adele, "I wish to God I had been along." Friends were dying in a war that had barely begun for America. Much more grief lay ahead. But that was the price that had to be paid. "Any victory they get means only an additional incentive to us. We must win in the end if it takes us all. We must win and will win."[26]

CHAPTER 21

Paris, St. Inglevert, May–June 1918

The Northern Bombing Group

Captain Cone named Captain David Hanrahan overall commander of the Northern Bombing Group, the NBG. Hanrahan had previously been senior officer of a destroyer division convoying transports. Like most of the rest of the navy's leadership, he had no aviation experience at all. However, he ceded nearly unlimited authority to Lovett and McDonnell to carry out their program. To succeed, though, they would have to face off against more than the Germans. When the navy moved to establish the NBG, interservice rivalries broke out all across the aviation front. First Hanrahan encountered political infighting with the marine corps, which objected to the navy's sole command of such an epochal, land-based operation. Eventually, the marines agreed to share the project by staffing and operating the day wing, leaving the night wing to the navy.

An even more tenacious opponent then emerged: Major General Benjamin Foulois, head of the Army Air Service overseas. When he heard about the NBG project, he was livid and rushed to Pershing at headquarters. The leader of the 1st Aero Squadron during Pershing's Punitive Expedition to Mexico demanded that the navy be kept out of land machines and leave attacking land bases to his forces. Lovett was outraged at the army's shortsighted view of the navy's efforts. "What difference does the means make as long as the objectives are ours?" he asked. "If you could sink a battleship with a rowboat more easily than with a submarine you'd use it, wouldn't you?"[1]

Fortunately, Pershing took a broader view of winning the war than Foulois and accepted the navy's role. Foulois complained to Washington. Eventually the secretaries of the navy and of war were forced to weigh in, reaching an agreement "that the extension of operations against submarines in their bases . . . is purely naval work."[2] Faced with conflicting demands for precious aircraft, the army forced the navy to reduce the NBG to four squadrons for the night and day wings, not the six each Sims had put in for. Still, the NBG remained "the most ambitious and the most enterprising" aviation undertaking of the war, according to a post-war report.[3]

Pershing's support mattered little. Given America's continued lag in production, procuring aircraft remained a fundamental obstacle to putting any bombing program into action.[4] Hanrahan sent McDonnell sailing back to the United States to oversee the process of assembling the first American-made equipment for the NBG. McDonnell acquired two-man, American-made De Havilland DH–4 bombers for the Day Wing. Foulois still fought to keep the navy from getting any of the limited DH–4 production. Finally, McDonnell succeeded in winning a promised delivery of seventy-five day bombers for the NBG.[5]

Even then, only seven of the machines ever reached Europe. Those proved barely airworthy. The DH–4 program was just one more mistake that the United States made in its rush to manufacture an air force where none had previously existed. When Congress appropriated the huge funds for air force needs, it established the Bolling Commission, a civilian-military committee headed by Colonel Raynal Bolling, whose National Guard aviation squadron Henry Davison had supported long before the United States entered the war. Bolling took his study group to Europe to learn the best manner for gearing up U.S. aircraft production. The Commission reviewed available aircraft and chose to produce the DH–4 because of its apparent adaptability to mass production methods and to installation of both American and European engines. However, the change in engine required extensive redesign of the aircraft, slowing its arrival at the front. In any case, airmen came to fear the bomber. Its gas tanks sat in the convenient gap between the pilot's and the observer's seat. That placement required pressurizing the gas. A well-placed bullet or piece of shrapnel that pierced the tank or fuel line sent gas spraying out onto the engine exhaust pipes, easily igniting. Many of the bombers went down in flames. The reviled airplane soon won the "flaming coffin" label. On one mission, the famous racecar driver-turned-army pilot Eddie Rickenbacker saw three American DH–4s shot down in flames, their crews dying what he called "this frightful and needless death."[6]

McDonnell took what he could get. After spending $40 million stateside on the first aircraft and weaponry orders, he sailed back to France, leaving Trubee Davison's brother Harry in charge of shipping over the expected equipment. A few months later, he, too, sailed over to France to join the NBG.

Procuring night bombers proved even more challenging. Hanrahan made Lovett commander of the night-bomber wing and eventually of the first squadron in the wing as well. As the assembling of equipment, establishment of bases, and assignment of men began, he shuttled back and forth between Paris headquarters and the Western Front, where he continued to fly day- and night-bombing missions to learn more about the bombers in use by the Allies. Impatient to get operations underway, Lovett did not want to wait for American manufacturers to begin delivering aircraft. "To hell with the cheese," he told his staff. "Let's just get out of this trap."[7] He set out to acquire any bomber he could.

McDonnell traveled to Italy where he flew the Caproni bomber in missions. The Caproni looked like something out of a Jules Verne science fiction version of armed flight. The enormous flying tank flew with one gunner standing in a rounded prow that hung forward of the cockpit like a balcony and another man defending the rear from an open birdcage. It had double boom tails, triple vertical stabilizers, and double tractor engines working in tandem with a single pusher engine. However ungainly it appeared to be on the ground, once in the air it was one of the most effective heavy bombers. McDonnell tested a Caproni, looping the loop, a significant feat in any heavy airplane, and strongly endorsed purchasing as many as possible. In exchange for American aircraft motors, which had been coming out of the factories much faster than airplanes, the British agreed to supply Handley-Page O/400's, while the Italians would provide Capronis in return for raw materials until the United States could begin to produce enough aircraft on its own.[8]

With Lovett's first bombers on their way, he established headquarters for the Night Wing at a chateau in St. Inglevert outside of Calais, to the south of Dunkirk. Working with Captain Lambe, he selected three RAF fields in the region to serve as sites for the first NBG aerodromes. The NBG also took over a massive British base being constructed in Eastleigh, England, near Southampton, to serve as its assembly and supply base for new aircraft and repair for those damaged at the front. In July, Lieutenant Chevalier left Dunkirk, where he had been commanding officer, to take over the Eastleigh base. Di Gates took command of Dunkirk, still the navy's most active air station.

Lovett began to select officers to command his own squadrons. He had long harbored a personal dream to bring his First Unit mates back together under a single command. Now was his chance. He knew "the Unit offered a backbone . . . on which to build the muscles" of the NBG.[9] He set about drawing his old friends into his plans for the bombing campaign. Soon he had more than half the surviving members of the squadron working with him in varying capacities, "in it up to their neck."[10] He wrote gleefully to Adele Brown, "I have gotten all the old [Yale] crowd together."[11] Others in the navy wanted the Yale men for their own developing aviation programs as well. When the first head of aviation, Lieutenant Whiting, now C.O. of the Killingholm Naval Air Station in England where several other unit members flew, heard accusations that he was being allowed to "hog all of the Davison Unit," he shot back that "the only place he knew of in the air service that was getting the pork was the Northern Bombing Group."[12] Gradually coming together again, the original Millionaires' Unit composed a formidable team at war, with Lovett now at its head.

Lovett handled most of the logistics of forming the new bomber force. On a visit to the Navy Air Service headquarters in Paris, Kenney MacLeish watched in awe as Lovett went about his work. On his desk, MacLeish saw a stack of reports about navy operations "about two feet high" that had previously been reviewed by other staff members. Lovett spent the next two-and-a-half hours working through them and then wrote up his analysis of the situation. MacLeish wrote: "It took men who in civil life were getting about $40,000 a year two days to come to any conclusions on the reports." After Lovett's speedy review and report, "Every one of the older men agreed with him on every single conclusion but one." Lovett was not just an analyst, though, he was a doer. When bombing operations finally began in the late summer, he had nearly 1,500 men under his direct command. "Without him," MacLeish believed, "we would never get anywhere. They don't give men ability like that more than once in a million times."[13]

MacLeish had not always marveled so at his classmate's abilities. The war, though, had lent a new maturity to both young men. To the earnest Midwesterner, his classmate had long seemed snobbish and distant. Even their senses of humor—Lovett's bone dry and marked by witticisms, MacLeish's full of pranks and jokes—differed. The high society New Yorker had not lost his delight in entertaining a company of fellow wits, but the Chief of the Wags, the leader of the haughty club within the already clubby unit, had now become more approachable. MacLeish observed that his Yale classmate was "easier to know than he used to be."[14]

For Lovett the days were long. He had "seen so much misery and unhappiness." Skirting death so often and witnessing the abrupt end of many good men's lives had deepened his outlook on life. He commanded a growing air force that would soon number 135 officers in his night wing, including 88 pilots, and 1,336 enlisted men. Once his squadron's operations got underway—often in conjunction with the British—his leadership skills were put to the test night after night. As the sun set, he walked from his headquarters to the runways, where he urged the crews to hurry their airplanes aloft before the nightly German bombers struck. When the raids began, he made his way through the dank, tightly packed dugouts where the exhausted men stirred uneasily as the bombs fell and the antiaircraft batteries barked. In the noisy, stinking darkness amid so many men trusting in him for courage and reassurance, he donned the mask of leadership, taking the stage again as he had not so long ago at Yale.

Once back in his room, away from this stomach-knotting theater, he fell into despair at being "absolutely alone with one's self in a strange place and knowing no one and nothing except war." As "the cynosure of all eyes," the twenty-two-year-old had few men to whom he could turn to share the emotional burdens of his responsibilities. The gravity of his life at war made him appreciate all the more the men with whom he had once shared a lustrous, pleasure-filled world at home.[15]

As he and MacLeish related stories about their Yale Unit mates and the war, MacLeish found, "I have really been able to understand him." As a result, he developed a newfound loyalty for his friend. "I'll stick up for him through anything now," he proclaimed.[16]

The previous gap between MacLeish, the striving son of an immigrant, deeply religious, merchant father and a socially committed mother, and his gifted, New York high society classmate had closed for good. Lovett, too, had discovered a new appreciation for MacLeish's sincerity, search for honor, and dogged work ethic, especially after a string of highly favorable reports came in about MacLeish's performance in the English flight and gunnery schools. Lovett applauded his friend for his "sheer singleness of purpose, for real idealism and for rare spirit," and knew he would "give up everything for his ideal of service and honor." Ever frugal with his displays of friendship, he wrote Archie MacLeish that his brother was considered the "best" pilot in the navy, and confided, "I don't want a finer pal."[17]

He had big plans for MacLeish within the NBG. He sent him, Ingalls, and Freddie Beach from the unit, along with several men from the Second Unit and a group who flew as observers, to an army bomber training program in Clermont-Ferrand. After their training, the Yale men were to become commanders of the navy's first day-bomber squadrons. MacLeish, excited to be "in on the ground floor" with his Yale mates, thought the opportunity to head up a squadron of his own would be "perfectly tremendous and worth working like a slave for."[18]

Through his discovery of his real "home" in the air, he was finally gaining the respect and admiration of the Yale mates that he had missed out on while on campus. He had won that personal battle, but the real war was still in the balance. Although the carnage swept onward, his ideals of service and honor never waned, while the siren call of becoming a true war hero remained irresistible. "Full up to the eyebrows with high purpose," he proclaimed himself more ready than ever to go "through trials and deprivations of every sort, with the hope that at the end honor would be given where honor is due."[19]

Not all men of their privileged world were so prepared to face the miseries and hazards of the war for the sake of honor. Roland "Bunny" Harriman, the childhood and Yale friend with whom Lovett had gone joyriding through Switzerland two years earlier, had used his wife's family connections to gain release from army duties at the front. He had been dispatched back stateside to a desk job with the Army Ordnance Department. Lovett was livid and depressed when he heard. "Great God," he exclaimed, "doesn't he know that his friends are being slaughtered over here by the thousands." Mutual Yale friends had openly accused the heir to the Union Pacific fortune of being "a slacker." Bunny's brother Averell had also opted out of the military, instead starting up a company building merchant ships under government contract. In later years, he admitted he "long regretted" the decision not to serve.[20] Perhaps out of shame, Bunny had stopped answering Lovett's letters. Lovett refused to believe the worse about his oldest friend. "That boy's not a quitter," he insisted to Adele. "He wouldn't 'lay down.'" He offered to bring him over to become part of his night wing—to no avail.

The flight from service he saw in his old friends and the self-defeating turf battles among military branches showed him an uglier side of life than the selfless idealism his unit mates had demonstrated. "I must fight certain phases of life and institutions and attitudes that this war has shown to be imbedded in the American nation," he realized. Those who put self-interest in the way of the greater purposes of the nation would not prevail. He would not turn his back on one of his oldest and closest friends, but "such things," he knew in his heart, "are squared sooner or later."[21]

Dunkirk, May–July 1918

Mournful Mary

As PART OF A COMPANY OF SEVENTEEN NAVY MEN SENT BY THE NBG, Kenney MacLeish, Crock Ingalls, and Freddie Beach arrived in Paris in late May on their way to the day bomber school at the American army air base two hundred miles south in Clermont-Ferrand. Just as they reached Paris, on May 27, the desperate Germans renewed their spring offensive. Despite having badly depleted their forces in the previous assaults, they mounted yet another massive attack, firing off 2 million shells from 6,000 guns along a 24-mile front—a cannon or howitzer every 20 feet—in a few hours before their troops annihilated exhausted French forces and drove to the Aisne River in Champagne. By the next day, the Germans had slammed a wedge 40 miles wide and 15 miles deep through the Allied lines. On May 30, General Ludendorff's forces were at the Marne River near Chateau-Thierry, within 40 miles and striking distance of the great prize, Paris. The French government made preparations to leave Paris as did hundreds of thousands of civilians. That night General Pershing dined with his French counterpart, Marshall Foch, and his senior staff officers. "It would be difficult," Pershing later recalled, "to imagine a more depressed group of officers. They sat through the meal scarcely speaking a word as they contemplated what was probably the most serious situation of the war."[1]

While the front appeared to be on the verge of collapse, the Third Battle of the Aisne also marked the first entry of American troops in large numbers into the lines. An aide to General Pétain at the front reported seeing the doughboys marching toward the lines, "bare headed and bare chested, singing American airs at the top of their voices. . . ." For the demoralized and nearly defeated

French, "Life was coming in floods to reanimate the dying body of France."[2] The tide of war would soon turn.

Making his way through Paris, Kenney MacLeish did not notice the panic around him. He was in a funk of his own. Away from the battle zone he felt adrift, moving toward an unknown future, facing more training when the only things he wanted were either the chance to fly and fight or to find his way home to his beloved Priscilla. "Talk about homesick!" he muttered.[3]

What could be better than to find a bit of home in Paris? American troops were now arriving in France at the rate of a quarter million men a month. While walking through the mobs of Americans jostling against each other, bargaining with whores, and gawking along the crowded walkways of Paris, there, right in front of him, was his big brother, Archie. "I've never come so near to fainting!" he wrote Priscilla. He had been certain that Archie was in the lines. Even a German victory could not have darkened his spirits at the moment.

The two of them spent the rest of the day wandering through Paris. Both now knew the city well and each made a point of showing off his favorite cafés and hotel bars. Archie was heading to an artillery school near Clermont-Ferrand. They made plans to meet up while there. In company with the other Yale flyers, they went drinking with army pilot Quentin Roosevelt. Champagne flowed as they shared stories of family and friends in the war.[4]

It was to be one of the final days of revelry for some of those on hand. A little more than a month later, on Bastille Day, July 14, 1918, a year after the charity baseball game at Peacock Point, the chubby, myopic Quentin, "the brightest of the children," according to his father, charged into a dogfight and fell to his death over France. Just three days before Quentin's death, the *New York Sun* saluted him for "attacking three enemy airplanes single-handed and shooting one of them down." Quentin was "running true to Roosevelt form."[5]

For his father, the blow of losing his favorite son was crushing. Shortly after learning that Quentin had been shot down and likely killed, a stoic Roosevelt traveled to Saratoga to deliver an already scheduled speech. At one point he broke away from his text and reflected, "The finest, the bravest, the best of our young men have sprung eagerly forward to face death for the sake of a high ideal; and thereby they have brought home to us the great truth that life consists of more than easygoing pleasures, and more than hard, conscienceless, brutal striving after purely material success."[6] The heartbroken former president died less than six months later.

Two days after their happy day in Paris, the navy contingent arrived in Clermont-Ferrand, a small industrial city in the rugged upland region of the Massif

Central, some two hundred miles south of Paris, near Vichy. The ancient city sat in a valley surrounded by low, green mountains, deeply cut river gorges, and wildflower meadows where sheep and goats grazed. Fascinated by the hectic streets and racy nightlife of Paris, MacLeish loved the rustic Gallic villages and rugged countryside where he wandered beyond the American base at a former Michelin factory airfield. The warming weather and spring rains brought a green glow to the blossoming landscape. In the peaceful, hopeful setting, he observed, "You'd never guess there was a war on."[7]

He enjoyed the picturesque qualities of the region and visits with his brother, but longed to get back to the front. The navy bomber trainees flew two-man French Breguet bombers, learning to pilot the slow aircraft and practicing team work and bombing with their observers. MacLeish found it "a let-down" after flying in combat, where he had been in command of two hangars, their crews, and five other pilots, now to be sent off for "a little teamwork with our observers, and a lot of abuse" from the army instructors. Most of the instructors had never been to the front and had little to teach. However, MacLeish and the observer he had handpicked while at Dunkirk, Ensign Irving Sheely, a rough-hewn Upstate New Yorker with a knack for engineering bomb sights, formed an impressive bombing team. Using a harness contraption, the observer in the rear cockpit would guide the pilot over the target and then let go of the bombs. Setting school records in target practice, the flight teammates were soon on a first-name basis, unusual for an officer and his observer. Even rarer, from time to time, MacLeish let Sheely take the controls, teaching him how to fly so he might have a chance to save himself should MacLeish get hit.[8]

After months as respected navy officers, the Yale men found themselves snubbed and, worse, by the army men, who refused to recognize their naval rank and housed them in enlisted men's tents with wooden slabs for beds. One night a group of drunken army men raided their bunk. The resulting fight put one of the army men in the hospital.[9]

MacLeish's simmering resentments soon got him into trouble. He was assigned to fly as a target machine for camera gunnery practice. During the training sessions, a student in an instructor's plane would practice "shooting" an "enemy" aircraft using a camera mounted on his machine gun. In theory, review of the resulting film would help him improve his aim. Shortly after a rough takeoff, MacLeish's motor sputtered and then what sounded like a shot whizzed past his head. The aircraft banked vertically and then dropped out of control before he pulled out and landed. "I figured we were cooked," he told the mechanic. The engine had blown a spark plug out of a cylinder. The explosive force had probably damaged the motor. One of MacLeish's closest Yale friends, Leslie MacNaughton, had recently been killed while instructing in a training program. He had no intention of dying that way. With no other plane available, he stepped out of the cockpit. His day was over. The ranking army instructor thought otherwise. He ordered the plug replaced and the navy officer to head back up, without overhauling the engine. MacLeish insisted that a mechanic inspect it for damage. The army officer refused. Rolling back out from the hangar, MacLeish fumed. "I didn't care after that."

He took to the air. His assignment was to fly over the airfield while the trailing army gunnery instructor attacked him in mock battle. MacLeish flew away from the field and then roared back across it. He put on a flying display that made it impossible for the instructor, whose flying skills were no match for his, to close on him even though he flew a slower machine. With hundreds of men watching on the ground, MacLeish turned the tables, locking himself on the army instructor's tail and not letting go. He crowed afterward, "I had him cold every single minute that we were up there."[10]

If possible, the cocky Crock Ingalls hated returning for further training even more than MacLeish. He showed little interest in the coursework and spent most of his time seeing to the "Americanized repopulation of France" among the local women and otherwise doing what he could "to get fired out of this dump." His "damned fat baby of an instructor" finally gave up on him, declaring he "would never be able to fly decently." Ingalls coughed with laughter and explained to the instructor that he found flying in the school especially tough because he was so used to having something to distract him from the actual flying "like Archies." The instructor who had never been under fire just looked at him "popeyed."[11]

One incident, though, reminded Ingalls that even training flights could be dangerous. On a sunny early June afternoon, practicing formation flying, he and four other two-man bombers flew together in a V at about two thousand feet over the countryside. Suddenly instructors in scouts darted into the formation, pretending they were attacking enemies. In the rear cockpit of the bomber flying next to Ingalls, the excited observer spun about wildly firing at an attacking scout flying overhead. Swinging the gun around on its mount to track the machine as it passed, the man leaned out of the cockpit just as the bomber bounced sharply in rough air. The gun and the camera, followed by the observer, pitched up and out of the cockpit. He flew over the fuselage until his foot caught in a tail wire. Dangling off the back of the airplane, he flopped about like a rag in the slipstream while staring down at the formation's shadow undulating at nearly one hundred miles per hour over the green meadows, valleys, and hills below.

Ingalls saw the whole incident and watched in shock and fear, certain the man would fall the rest of the way to his death at any instant. The pilot of the aircraft, "pale and nerveless," turned back to watch the ejected man, unsure what to do. Briefly stunned, the observer finally roused himself and fought his way back against the hurricane-wind. He climbed onto the tail. Hugging it with all his terrified might, he drove his knees into the fuselage until he had bored two holes into it. Then he jammed his fists through the stiff fabric to make handholds and slowly grappled his way back to the cockpit. Once inside he dropped limply to the floor.

When they landed, Crock saw the man "raving gently" as they took him away to the hospital. "The devil," he remarked, shaking his head, "was certainly cheated that time."[12]

Amid his griping about the training, MacLeish also fretted over the prospect of becoming the commanding officer of the first of Bob Lovett's day-bomber squadrons. A debate raged within him as he flew. A C.O.'s responsibilities were immense. Although a great honor to initiate and take charge of the first squadron, he confronted a major drawback: C.O.'s were no longer allowed to fly. The navy did not want to risk losing its leaders. He did not know what to do. Nothing compared to the intensity of flying into battle. He was torn at the prospect of giving up the thrill. Even a few days away from the front had left him feeling restless and gloomy. "I've just had a large enough mouthful of the real stuff," he observed, "to make me perfectly miserable without it."

The prospect of giving up his one great opportunity in the war of winning real honor also disturbed him. A C.O. enjoyed a large measure of prestige and freedom to operate, but taking on his own squadron would prevent him from achieving his personal goal for the war. There was, in his mind, nothing heroic about sending other men to fight. He wanted to fly, to test himself in combat, and to have a chance for real honor that only courage in battle could bring. "That's what I came over here for."[13]

The debate was soon decided. He could not give up flying. "I'd never do it," he concluded, "it really couldn't be done."[14] The dilemma proved moot in any case. His fate was not in his own hands. "The whole thing . . . is crumbling away under our very eyes," he discovered.[15] The marines insisted on taking charge of the NBG Day Wing operations. The dream of "a crack naval squadron," lamented Freddy Beach, was "vanishing into thin air."[16]

MacLeish wondered what would come next. He had spent many more months training for war than fighting it. Practicing dummy bombing runs over a peaceful landscape far from the lines was dulling his edge. Knocked about from job to job and base to base, he feared, "If I can't fight pretty soon,

I'll lose all my nerve." Flying was a game of nerves. He had seen it before: Once a pilot lost his confidence and aggressiveness, they were hard to win back. His old lack of self-confidence came flooding back. "I never had enough [nerve] to make a dog chase a cat anyway," he recorded. "What will happen if I lose what little I have?"[17]

Happily the news from the homefront was good. His blooming long-distance love distracted him from his daily woes. As part of the Yale men's transfer to bombing operations, the navy had promoted them to full lieutenants. For MacLeish the increase in rank held far more significance than mere military advancement; the boost in pay meant he could finally afford an engagement ring for Priscilla. With his ring on her finger, he could shout out to the entire world—most importantly to any other men at home who sought her heart—that she belonged to him. Getting a ring to Priscilla, though, was no simple matter. Heavy wartime export duties and luxury taxes were prohibitive and mail routinely searched. Valuables disappeared. Fortunately, Bob Lovett was now MacLeish's covert collaborator. He had special access to couriers.

After several false starts, "having the devils own job" getting the ring off to her, Lovett managed to smuggle it out in the pocket of a cooperating officer returning to the States.[18] Even then, with German U-boats still sinking ships every day, there was no guarantee that it would not end up at the bottom of the sea. Before the summer's end, though, Priscilla placed the engagement ring on her finger.[19]

Her husband-to-be cabled his parents the eventful news. His parents cabled back swiftly with their objections. They were both young and long-separated, his parents protested. How could they know what changes in their hearts the war would bring once they were reunited? Why not wait until the war ended? Cables flew back and forth over the ocean. His parents were strong willed, but on this point, their son refused to budge. "They think I'm kidding when I tell them there's a war on," he groused, "but they will wake up to the fact that there is a war in their own front yard!" He threatened to "arrange matters without the announcement," by bringing Priscilla over to France for a swift ceremony.[20] His parents finally conceded and grudgingly accepted the situation. He and Priscilla made their engagement announcement officially public on August 22, 1918.

The long months of uncertainty, his sleepless nights of worrying over losing her to Harry Davison or some other stateside suitor, were finally over. He no longer cared if he were given "a desk job that may last from now till the end of the war. . . . Never have I been so happy." All of his fears had been swept aside. "I can't seem to worry," he proclaimed to his future wife, "as for once in my life there isn't anything to worry about!"[21] Taking note of the "look of inane simplicity and joy" on MacLeish's face as he went about his business, Lovett concluded his friend was "dreaming of his wife."[22]

For now, all he could do was dream. Their training complete, MacLeish and the other navy flyers returned north for temporary duty on bombers with British RAF squadron No. 218, at a muddy field in Fretnum near Calais. The Yale mates bunked for a few days with Di Gates in Dunkirk. The city and the naval air station were, if anything, worse off than when they had left for training. During the spring offensives, the German raids and shelling had reduced most structures in the landscape to piles of rubble. The exposed base was defenseless against them. During one night, German bombers dropped 320 bombs on the station.[23] MacLeish walked into the ruins of his former office, "with broken glass, plaster, and bricks heaped a foot high on the desk, and the blue sky over my head instead of a roof!"[24]

Most of the men spent nights in the scattered dugouts, fifty in each, fifteen feet underground. MacLeish stayed in bed. Lying there his first night back he listened to "Mournful Mary," the gut-piercing, two-note baritone wail that announced each cannon flash of the long-range guns behind German lines. He did not budge. There was little to be done in any case except wait out the "terrifying" seconds. He lay there for nearly a minute of "agony that seem like ninety years" until he was bounced out of bed by the nearby explosion. Nobody, not even those firing the gun, knew where the shell was going to land at such a range. "All one hears is the screech through the air," he recorded, "that is, if he's lucky; if he doesn't hear it he never hears anything else. . . ."[25]

The navy offered little in answer for the misery of Dunkirk. Gates, once a carefree, hard-charging boy, still never bothered to go underground during bombing raids. With his promotion to C.O., his sense of discouragement had grown. He had come to Dunkirk expecting that would be the fastest way into the stiffest part of the action. Now, he was no longer even permitted to fly. He would have to sit and wait out the war while his unit mates got into the fight, and he was responsible for a badly equipped base that was steadily being chopped to pieces by the enemy. He did not have the tools to respond or even defend his base and its hundreds of men. He repeatedly applied for transfer to fighting squadrons, but his requests were denied. He appealed personally to Lovett, but got nowhere. He complained often about the inadequate aircraft and poorly situated base, even requesting that the base be moved inland to a more defensible location and given more effective land machines for its antisubmarine and ship escort missions.

Finally, risking his own command, he sent off a blunt official memo to the NBG chief, Captain Hanrahan, and Lovett, describing the foundering state of affairs. Demanding that something be done, he openly declared, "Our anti-submarine patrols are highly ineffective and it is recommended that a change be made as soon as possible."[26]

The NBG leaders did not budge and insisted that he remain at the station helm and that it continue its work. Gates found Lovett's attitude "absolutely incomprehensible." He knew his fellow Bonesman was "doing his best to win this old war," but Gates, blowing off steam in a letter to Trubee Davison, declared himself "fed up on his general attitude."[27]

MacLeish listened to his old friend's increasingly bitter complaints. With Gates convinced that Lovett was "keeping him from flying land machines," MacLeish worried that the two friends he trusted most in the navy were on the verge of breaking off relations with each other.[28]

Like his friend, MacLeish felt his own enthusiasm for the war escaping. He feared, "My best days are over until I get a few months' rest."[29] He was not only suffering from war-weariness. While in Clermont-Ferrand, he had been laid up with a body-pounding flu that had sapped his strength and left him with a wracking cough. He was one of the lucky ones.

His case in mid-summer marked one of the first of what would, by September, become a global pandemic of the so-called "Spanish flu." The devastatingly virulent virus killed, by some estimates, anywhere from 50 to 100 million people worldwide, including 650,000 Americans, making it the worst epidemic in world history. Unlike most influenza outbreaks that tend to strike the elderly and the very young, the Spanish flu proved deadliest for the strongest, those between their teens and middle age. The men at war faced their most lethal foe. The bug flashed through battle-weary soldiers crowded together by the tens of thousands in muddy trenches, ships, and camps. All the warring armies suffered enormous losses. Some 62,000 American troops died during the few months of the epidemic, half again as many as all those killed in battle.

The flu seemed to hit airmen particularly hard. The physical and emotional exhaustion and the damage to their lungs from the grueling, stress-filled hours of combat and patrols at high elevation had weakened their resistance. Some squadrons lost so many men they ceased to fly.[30]

Weak and still emaciated, MacLeish returned to the front in July in a "'don't care' mood, so blue and hopeless" over his long stint in Europe with only two "glorious months when I was really doing something."[31] Even his latest assignment would only be temporary, a few raids piloting day bombers. He also feared that his nerve had gone. "Not the least bit keen for going out," on the morning of July 16 he flew again over the lines.[32] There he discovered a deep reserve of idealism that would keep him in the fight.

In a flight of thirteen British D.H. 9 bombers, he and Sheely were sent once again to attack the infamous Mole at Zeebrugge. The Mole's defenses were even stronger than the last time MacLeish had flown over the lip of the mouth leading to the German U-boat pens. The underpowered bombers could generate no more than 75 miles per hour despite carrying a payload of just two 130-pound bombs. The Germans were there to greet them. MacLeish could see the silhouettes of nine enemy scouts approaching far off on the eastern horizon. As the Anglo-American formation flew in at 13,000 feet toward the target, the sky suddenly went "black" with exploding antiaircraft fire. MacLeish leaned over the side to watch as he let go his bombs and shouted down at the ground as they fell, "Now you run for a change!"[33] He smiled in satisfaction when he saw them explode. That feeling did not last. The airplane jerked and flopped about in the concussions from the antiaircraft barrage. Suddenly, as if a great hand had slapped her tail, his D.H. 9 spun sharply sideways. Stunned, MacLeish looked back. Shrapnel had shattered the rudder.

The bomber went out of control, going "into all kinds of dives and gizzy-wiggles." Using the throttle and tail planes, MacLeish finally stabilized the wounded bird. Just when he thought that he and Sheely could breathe again, the engine died. Headed into a strong wind, the gliding airplane would soon stall and plummet to earth. The barrage continued to knock them about as they began to lose altitude. He briefly touched the handkerchief from Priscilla he kept in his flying suit pocket and told her "goodbye forever by mental telepathy." He looked back at the ashen-faced Sheely, but could not speak. "My mouth," he found, "was so full of my heart that I would naturally have died if I'd opened it." Working the choke, he heard a backfire. The engine sputtered and then caught on five of its nine cylinders. Barely above a stall and still exposed to enemy fire, the aircraft began to recapture some altitude.

During MacLeish's struggle to regain control, the bomber had continued to drift north while the rest of the formation had turned for home. MacLeish and Sheely now passed over the border of neutral Holland. To make it home, they would have to return across a long swath of German-controlled territory in a barely operable machine limping through the antiaircraft fire. MacLeish considered ditching. He and Sheely would face internment in Holland for the remainder of the war. Out of the battle, they could spend their days in relative safety on the ground. He looked down at Holland "so peaceful and green." He considered his wheezing engine and his shredded rudder. "It's my duty to go back," he muttered, and then turned his face up to the endless blue of the morning sky overhead, "but it's up to You to get me there—this bloody engine won't—Amen. . . ." He "never meant any words more in my life." Babying the D.H. 9 through a slow, wide U-turn, he banked around and headed back. With an engine barely powerful enough to keep them aloft, he cruised and turned without the aid of the rudder through the German barrage. After a little over an hour, they dropped back over the lines and a few minutes later bounced down in Fretnum.[34]

He was "absolutely sick of having engine trouble when everything is against me," but after grabbing his lunch, he took out another aircraft and headed back up.[35]

A week later, MacLeish was again on a train heading across France. This time he was destined four hundred miles south for Paulliac, the fast-growing American navy base on the Bay of Biscay near Spain. All that training and his wide knowledge of engines and ordnance were now his enemy. Captain Hanrahan respected MacLeish's "all-round ability" and assigned him special responsibilities away from the battlefields.[36] He designated him chief pilot at the station, in charge of testing and inspection of the growing volume of aviation matériel arriving at the port. That did not last long. After just two weeks, he packed again, this time for Paris for a few days of desk duty. While there, he had lunch with Eddie Rickenbacker and his old Hotchkiss schoolmate Douglas Campbell, "men who are really doing something," he remarked enviously.[37] Both Americans had begun to rack up kills and renown as Aces, flying scouts in the army air service's already famed 94th "Hat in the Ring" squadron under Rickenbacker's command.

Hanrahan knew that MacLeish was "thoroughly unhappy" with his behind-the-lines duties, but needed his skills in the long run up to the start of the American bombing campaign. Finally in early September, he sent MacLeish to Eastleigh, England, the NBG's fast-growing assembly and repair base. He would now be responsible for all planes destined for the front. He slumped back on a wooden banquette as the airless, overheated, jampacked train out of London rattled slowly through the dark countryside. He counted: It was his twenty-fourth all-night trip since coming to Europe. "The sight of a train makes me ill," he spat.[38] He kept falling "out of one job and into another," with, he felt, "no qualification whatsoever." Now he even envied those being sent home as instructors. "All that is keeping me from wanting to go back too is my sense of duty."[39]

Above all he resented that he was not getting back to the front. "If I have to sit through the rest of this war without ever doing any more fighting," he wrote his father, "it will simply break my heart."[40]

CHAPTER 23

The Alps, July–August 1918
O, Mia Nosediva

THE NAVY WAS DOING WHAT IT COULD TO GET INTO THE FIGHT. WITH the day wing now in the hands of the marines, Bob Lovett focused on getting his night bombing operations underway. Despite the lack of equipment, he began to mobilize his Yale Unit mates for the new squadrons he was forming. He was able to get the release of several First Unit members from their stateside duties and bring them over, and also plucked others from their stations in Europe. He had "never been so gloriously happy and scared in one moment of my life" as he was in seeing his plans begin to take shape.[1] With "almost all the old crowd" from the unit together, he crowed to Adele, "you can imagine the full out lot they are."[2] The first thing was to get men trained to fly bombers and, until America could deliver its own aircraft, to acquire machines from the Italians and the British. Under Eddie McDonnell, he sent Harry Davison, Henry Landon, Kenneth Smith, Reginald Coombe, and Samuel Walker from the First Unit and A. A. McCormick from the Second Unit to Italy along with some thirty other navy pilots and crewmen to train on the Capronis the NBG had ordered. Once comfortable in the machines they were to ferry them back to St. Inglevert so rudiments of a night-bombing campaign could finally begin.

Arriving in Milan, the Americans received a rude welcome from Army Major Fiorella LaGuardia, a U.S. representative from New York City—and future mayor—on leave for war duty. He was in charge of army training at the Caproni School and oversaw delivery of land machines to the navy under the agreement brokered by the two departmental secretaries. To the impatience of the navy flyers, LaGuardia kept his attention on his army trainees and did his best to reserve most of the Capronis for his forces. Otherwise he shared his Italian hosts' relaxed pace. "*Domani*, tomorrow, was the word," said Coombe. Struggling to get time aloft at the training academy at the Malpensa aerodrome—today the major international airport in northern Italy—the Americans grumbled, "The Italians were in no hurry about anything." The Italians for their part did not know what to make of their American guests. "They seemed to think us a bit crazy for being in such a blazing hurry to get through with it," recalled Coombe.[3]

The Italians generally preferred not to fly at all. "Perhaps," snorted Walker, "this was because so many of them were killed in practice." When they did fly, they often came down hard. During their month at Malpensa, the Americans saw forty men killed in crashes. "A record!" declared Walker.[4] On one practice flight, Coombe was in the second seat when the Italian pilot tried to land with a tail wind. He blew onto the field, smashed off the landing gear, and threw the airplane onto its nose. With Coombe's face pinned to the ground, the dazed and bleeding pilot and the Caproni's leaking gasoline tanks piled on top of him, he feared the wreckage would blaze up and roast them, but they were pulled free. Badly cut up, he spent two weeks recuperating.

The trouble in Italy was only beginning. The Caproni Ca–44s the Americans received flew on different Fiat-built engines than the reliable Isotta-Fraschini motors on the Capronis McDonnell had looped in months earlier. The Fiat motors were underpowered for the heavy bombers and, the Fiat factory stumbling badly in trying to introduce American mass-production methods, broke down frequently. The Americans struggled to explain the problems to the Italian mechanics. Delays mounted, keeping the men grounded, "almost long enough to take our naturalization papers," Walker said.[5]

Finally, their few hours of flight training having taken several weeks to complete, the American crews flew their new NBG aircraft to Turin, jumping-off point for the leap over the Alps to France. But their engine troubles were just beginning. While continuing the shakeout of the Capronis prior to their big hop over the mountains, almost all the motors broke down. Several caught fire. "The machines given us," spat Walker, "were a very inferior lot."[6] The Americans were in serious trouble.

They spent their nights together worrying about their Italian aircraft and their days gesturing to their uncomprehending Italian mechanics about ways to salvage the engines. They were not the Americans' sole worry. What lay immediately ahead would test not only the Capronis' airworthiness but the flyers' skills. Fewer than twenty pilots had ever flown over the high Alps, and only a couple heavy bombers. They would be crossing three mountain ranges over 11,000 feet, with several peaks topping 13,000, skirting the aircrafts' upper ceiling of 15,000 feet, that is, if the engines were working properly. Only experienced pilots should test such conditions, but Smith had never even been up in a land machine before flying the Caproni and "knew nothing about cross country flying."[7] On top of that, the Fiat engines, with their frequent breakdowns, "were liable to make a fellow feel a bit uncomfortable," muttered Coombe.[8] While awaiting his turn to fly out, Smith looked at the piles of wreckage scattered about the aerodrome and dryly noted that the Americans found it "unpleasant to see so many machines crashing and burning while we were waiting."[9]

Walker flew in the first flight of four Capronis out of Turin on August 7. He got up into the Alps, but became hopelessly lost amid the peaks and sinuous valleys. He flew about looking for a safe site to land and could find no landing place that looked like "anything easier than sudden death." On the verge of running out of gas, he finally put down on a slope. The Caproni, he said, "tried to knock the top off a small mountain," turning a complete somersault, before smashing "into kindling wood." His second pilot required hospitalization. Walker escaped unharmed.[10] The other airplanes eventually arrived in St. Inglevert but in barely operable condition.

Back in Turin, the Capronis were now universally reviled and feared. Landon noted how "even the Italians hated to fly them." The Americans had no choice. They installed new radiators, magnetos, carburetors, anything to increase horsepower and reliability. Ten days later the next American crew scheduled to attempt the Alps crossing took off. Coombe looked on from the ground as the first Caproni, with Ensign Alan Nichols as pilot and a two-member crew, taxied down the runway. The slow machine climbed to 150 feet off the ground when the port engine quit. Nichols made a wide righthand turn to go back to the field when the starboard engine also failed. The big bomber veered over into a steep banking turn and then, falling off its wing, dropped nose-first to the ground. Coombe leaped on a truck and raced to the wreckage.

He arrived at an airplane broken into "little pieces, utterly demolished." The crushed bodies within the wreckage were barely recognizable as human. The Italians threw a fine funeral for the dead Americans. After marching somberly behind the three caskets to the Turin Cathedral, Coombe noted with great restraint how the fatal accident made them "feel even more uncomfortable about flying the Capronis."[11]

His turn to cross the Alps came next, two days later. The flight of four bombers took off without incident, but then flew straight into an impenetrable cloud cover. The mountains were impossible to see and the ill-starred aviators turned back.

The combination of weather, mountains, and cranky motors seemed a toxic brew for the Americans. The Italian ground crews were now prepared for the worst. As Coombe waited in the cockpit for the engines to warm for his next try on August 23, his stomach clenched. He saw several ambulances at the ready alongside the aerodrome. "They expected some of us to repeat poor Nichols's disaster," he said. He feared they might be right. Finally, he taxied out on what all on board feared might be their last flight. Coombe said his prayers and checked his instruments. All seemed to check out. As he picked up speed, he sensed a hesitation in the aircraft. The engines refused to power up to higher than eight hundred revolutions per minute. Too late to abort the takeoff, he raced toward the brick factory walls that faced the end of the runway. He pulled the stick back as hard as he could and clenched his body in anticipation of the impact. The machine lifted from the ground, its wheels barely clearing the factory roofs.[12]

His aircraft and one piloted by McDonnell, along with two others, were away. Even before they reached the first mountain, balky engines forced the other two Capronis to turn back to Turin. Coombe and McDonnell flew on into the looming gray rock and gleaming white snow walls of the mountains. As the two bombers penetrated the first high Alps, they split around a peak, heading into separate narrow valleys and expecting to meet up on the other side of the mountain. They never found each other. With one engine still refusing to generate full power, Coombe could not gain enough altitude to cross over a ridgeline as planned. Instead he plotted a lower elevation route. His aircraft could barely handle the buffeting from the swirling mountain air currents. A tremendous gust of wind would strike one wing and send the machine lurching toward the mountain on one side. Then an equally hard bump would hit it on the other, turning the aircraft in the opposite direction. "I never had to work so hard in my life to keep the machine steady," Coombe reported.[13]

The reluctant engine at last started to respond, allowing Coombe to push the Caproni to higher elevations where "the air was clear as crystal" and the wind currents steadier. Less worried about impending disaster, he had time to look around him. Few men had previously beheld such a sight. Despite the exposure to freezing temperatures and high winds in the open cockpit, Coombe was enraptured by the view. As far as his eyes could see all around were snow-capped peaks, glaciers, and narrow green winding valleys. To his right the majestic Mont Blanc towered above the other peaks. Passing over ridges, he looked down a couple hundred feet at "nothing but desolate ice and snow," and then suddenly a steep escarpment dropped away and a lush green valley yawned open many thousands of feet below.[14]

Keeping his bearings by mountaineering charts, he soon made his way out of the Alps near Grenoble, the country gradually flattening out into a wide plain of farms and vineyards as he passed over Chambéry. He finished the first leg of his trip by following a long white ribbon of highway to an aerodrome outside of Lyons. Three hours and ten minutes after setting out he landed. McDonnell in his Caproni was waiting for him on the runway. He had arrived a few minutes earlier.

It took several more days to complete the final hops, passing through Paris and on to the field at St. Inglevert, but by the following week the pilots were happy to turn over the Capronis to the NBG. The Capronis that reached the navy quickly made a terrible impression. One arriving from Italy stuck in the mud after landing. The pilot ran the motors to shake her free, but the wheels held firm. He tried again, throttling up higher. The results were tragic. The tail came up and the airplane teetered over onto her nose. Gas poured out from the tanks and spilled over the aircraft. The three-man crew fell forward in the cockpit as the propellers struck the ground and shattered. The screaming engines raced until they overheated and caught fire. In a few seconds, the fire spread and engulfed the machine in flames. Two of the three men were burnt alive; their horrible cries could be heard above the engines' screeching.[15]

Soon all the Americans at St. Inglevert feared the machines. It proved virtually "impossible to use these pieces of junk," fumed Coombe. On the night of August 15, a single Caproni carrying 1,250 pounds of bombs attacked the U-boat pens at Ostend. On its return, the first-ever flight of a U.S. bombing raid ended with a crash on the beach off Dunkirk. The next two raids attempted had to be aborted after motor trouble developed. All further Caproni missions were scrubbed until new engines could be secured.[16] Bob Lovett's first squadron gave up on its own aircraft and began flying regularly with the British squadrons based at the airfield.

The long delays and the mishaps in bringing America's potential air might to bear on the battlefield soon inspired the British to refer to the NBG as "No Bloody Good."[17] Of the eighteen original Capronis handed over to the Americans in Italy, only eight ever made it to the NBG, at the cost of five men's lives, along with numerous other injuries. By the time replacement engines finally arrived at the assembly station in Eastleigh, the Armistice put an end to any further need for the bombers.[18]

The Yale men never forgot or forgave the Capronis. An unnamed Wag Crew member of the Yale Unit penned a song about the hated machines. It was titled "O, Mia Nosediva." A verse went:

Aviatóre he fly th'Caproni;
Maladito! Machina is phony!
He go up for a hop,
Por Baccho! She flop!
An' il bimbo he breaka da boni.[19]

Pilots generally spoke of their aircraft with passionate affection, but Walker recalled with glee his last detail before shipping home after the Armistice. He flew the "infernal" Capronis to the U.S. Army airbase at Issoudun, where they were to be "kissed good-bye." He felt the "aerial caskets" received a fitting end when "they were finally burned as junk."[20]

Later on, Lovett had to agree that the NBG had proved "a dismal fiasco." He observed, "We had the men ready, the unit was on hand," but the night wing "did not have a ruddy thing to fly except these Capronis which could fly once in a while, then that was all."[21] A quarter century later when he had a chance to make a difference in wartime production of bombers, he made sure U.S. forces had the airplanes they needed.

The NBG's day wing fared somewhat better. Starting on August 9, under RAF command, marine pilots began attacking German positions. Slowly, the first day wing squadron accumulated its own equipment, until, on October 14, U.S. crews carried out the nation's first air raid under sole American command, in part on American-built aircraft. The mission flew eight American DH–4's and British D.H. 9's that dropped a large payload and tore up the German railway yards at Thielt. Seven further raids followed.

Even if this did not remotely equal Lovett's "wildest air castles of ambition," he did not care.[22] The "consummation of all our effort," America was in the fight and the bombs were falling.[23]

His enthusiasm for the NBG's prospects remained high. Expecting the war to continue into the following year, sooner or later he knew his crew would play a crucial role in defeating Germany. "In spite of lack of essentials," he declared, "in spite of the failure of machines, the whole crowd are magnificent in their energy and spirit. We have not reached our strength yet, but the goal is within sight. . . . Even now the Hun is getting to know us—we 'drop in on him' quite often."[24] Lovett was looking ahead. Once the new motors for the Capronis and the first Handley-Page bombers reached his squadron, the NBG would quickly ramp up its attacks on the U-boat ports.

He had no intention of stopping there. A bomber force could serve as aerial artillery against any important target within flying range. As German forces started their pullback from Belgium, he looked beyond the coastal bases to the next stage in the bombing campaign, "when every blow counts towards shortening the war." Despite the previous army resistance to a land-based navy force attacking even shoreline targets, he called for the NBG to fly against targets in the landlocked German heartland, "for the sooner Germany is hit in the arteries of her military power, and on her own soil, the sooner will peace be made, unconditionally." The navy may have historically confined its mission to sea and shore objectives, but he urged military leaders to consider giving the bomber force he was assembling a leading role in "the work of carrying the war into the [German] manufacturing centers." He knew that many men in the military bureaucracy objected to the navy attacking inland targets, but he pointed to the Royal Navy Air Service's success as the great innovator in British aviation. "No one questioned whether the pilots had anchors on their caps or not," he explained in a report to headquarters, "so long as Huns were shot down and important objectives were bombed."

Risking charges of heresy, he went further to suggest that an independent air force should be created and given a free hand in the concentrated push against Germany. "Whether one organization or another flies the machines makes little difference," he contended, "as long as 550 and 1660 pound bombs alight on munition factories and do so at once."[25] He would have to wait twenty-five years to see his strategic bombing plan put into action and still longer before an independent American air force would come into being, but his outlines for an Allied aerial strategy in World War II and American airpower in the years to come had already been drawn.

While the air services struggled to weigh in on the war, news from other sectors was much better. Americans were finally reaching the battlefields in force. The doughboys turned the tide, helping to drive back the Germans along the Somme front and leading the way in a stunning victory at the St. Mihiel Salient on the Meuse River in mid-September. Lovett and McDonnell had a more famous and controversial counterpart in the army, similarly advocating and organizing American aviation forces. The pugnacious, outspoken Colonel Billy Mitchell assembled the largest and most coordinated use of aircraft in a single operation in history: 1,481 airplanes for the St. Mihiel campaign. The aircraft flew observation, bombing, combat, and strafing missions. The flying weather for much of the battle was atrocious, but by the end of the campaign, Mitchell's forces had flown 3,300 sorties, guided artillery and troop deployment, shot down at least fifty enemy aircraft and blasted German trenches, supply trains and retreating columns as their lines gave way.[26]

The frontlines began to quake, and the trench stalemate to fracture. The Germans fell back from the positions they had taken all along the Western Front. Austria and Bulgaria were tottering, and more and more fresh American troops and munitions were pouring into the lines. Crown Prince Rupprecht of Bavaria, a senior army commander, acknowledged the Central Powers' worst unspoken fears had been realized: "The Americans are multiplying in a way we never dreamed of."[27]

As the battle of St. Mihiel raged, Kenney MacLeish was in charge of receiving aircraft in England. He saw the extraordinary spectacle of seemingly endless lines of tanned and healthy American boys stepping down the gangways off the transports, mustering for war. "There are doughboys of every possible kind," he proclaimed in his proudest "the-Yanks-are-coming" spirit. "Bunches of splendid young men, many of them college men, crowds of men who were 'boys' in every city and town at home. Big, awkward, gawky, yet powerful farmers from the backwoods. And here and there a 'weak sister' with watery blue eyes, glasses a foot thick, but with an expression that never passed over his face before." As he had already experienced in himself, the war was turning a nation of boys into fighting men. "If the old kaiser could see some of the sights I've seen," he declared, "he'd pull in his neck and ask who got America sore at him."[28]

Even away from the action, MacLeish sensed the change in fate for the Allies. "I can't help feeling," he observed as Americans began to enter the battlefield in force, "that it is the beginning of the end."[29]

While the United States still did not have its own aerial equipment, every available pilot was being poured into the offensive to drive the Germans out of Belgium and France and to prepare to attack Germany itself. Until sufficient aircraft could be found for his men, Lovett billeted those he could spare as reinforcements with the French and British squadrons in the Flanders area. Most of the Yale Unit men he had assembled flew bombers. For now, harassment of the fleeing Germans to keep them from regrouping was the order of the day. Strafing and low-altitude bombing were tearing apart the already fraying German forces and sapping their supply lines.

Hemming in the German U-boats no longer presented as important an objective. At long last, Di Gates got his wish. Hanrahan agreed to transfer him to fly scouts with a French naval escadrille at St. Pol, south of Dunkirk. Crock Ingalls was also reassigned from bomber duty to RAF No. 213 Aerosquadron at Couderkerque, the former RNAS No. 13 where he, Shorty Smith, and Kenney MacLeish had first flown Sopwith Camels into German-held territory.

Across the Channel, MacLeish steadily labored on preparing the first American DH–4 aircraft in Eastleigh for the NBG. When he heard about Ingalls's return to a Camel squadron at the front, he seethed with jealousy. "Isn't he the luckiest stiff who ever lived," he wrote Priscilla. "How does he rate all that flying when his old sidekick has to sit here and do nothing?"[30] All he could do was carry out his assigned duties and wait for the call that might never come. Meanwhile, Ingalls embarked on the greatest string of aerial combat successes of the war by an American navy pilot.

CHAPTER 24

Couderkerque,
August–September 1918
The Ace

ACCORDING TO BRITISH ACE CECIL LEWIS, FIGHTING IN THE AIR DIFFERED
in one essential way from war on the ground: "Its absolute coldbloodedness."
Nothing could cloud a pilot's judgment. He did not fire at the enemy in anger.
"You cannot 'see red,' as a man in a bayonet fight," explained Lewis. Airmen
fought man against man. Circling, bobbing, and weaving about one another
in their green, red, gray, camouflage, or black mono-, bi-, or triplanes like box-
ers in a three-dimensional ring, each waited for an opportunity to end the
bout, avoiding at all costs giving his opponent the same. "So," Lewis observed,
"like dueling, air fighting required a set steely courage, drained of all emotion,
fined down to a tense and deadly effort of will. The Angel of Death is less cal-
lous, aloof and implacable than a fighting pilot when he dives."[1] Ingalls returned to No. 213 ready to deliver death from on high.

Pilots resuming combat after long periods away were expected to hang back
for a few flights to readjust to battle conditions. The morning of his return, on
August 9, Ingalls clung tight to his formation on a high-altitude offensive patrol searching for enemy aircraft. He was pleased the Camel they gave him was
"a peach" that would "do anything." The day's two patrols were uneventful.
"There wasn't any excitement," he complained afterward, "but Hell," he assured, "there will be now."[2] His English flight leader, Captain Colin Brown, a
decorated Ace, recognized the aggressive American's readiness for action. The
next day, the two took off by themselves, coasting along the lines at 17,000
feet, "watching for meat." The sharp-eyed Brown waggled his wings. Two

miles below them, Ingalls saw what Brown had spotted: a camouflaged German observation airplane flying behind its lines. The two birds of prey dove. They closed quickly on the slow, two-man Albatross. Brown opened fire first. The German observer fired back. Ingalls pulled his trigger and watched his tracers strike home. A cloud of smoke enveloped the German machine. It broke into flames and crumpled, dropping almost straight down. In his second day at the front, he had his first kill. With antiaircraft fire bursting all around them, he feared it might be his last. The two Allied fighters swooped down toward the lines and the safety of home.[3]

Three days later, Ingalls joined in on what may have been the largest aerial raid of the war to date. Some seventy-five machines from three squadrons joined together for a dawn raid on the massive German aerodrome at Varssenaere, five miles outside Bruges. At the mission briefing, Major Rondal Graham, No. 213's C.O., assigned each member of the formation a target along the parallel lanes of hangars. Ingalls was to hit the western hangars with his four 25-pound Cooper bombs. Others carried incendiary explosives. After a first pass, each man was to return to strafe the field with bursts from his 650 rounds. At 4:30 in the morning darkness, Ingalls could see the sparks flying out from the line of engines as they waited for the order to depart. One pilot after another then opened his throttle and took to the air. Nearly invisible, the swarm circled upward into the black sky, spiraling in the same direction to avoid collisions. At 10,000 feet over Dunkirk, each flight leader fired a Véry light of different color to gather his Camels. Soon the many flights merged to form an enormous flock arrayed in a vast, staggered V. The formation migrated out to sea and then turned up the coast.

As Ingalls flew through the dawn, he savored "a bloody red sunrise befitting the occasion." The clouds billowing high above him glowed with the crimson light. He looked about to see a string of buzzing biplanes, wingtip-to-wingtip, stretching back more than a mile, ahead and to his side. As they dove in over the land, no antiaircraft fire rose up to greet them. To the pleasant surprise of the flyers, the Germans were sleeping. Tightly bunched, the Camel circus parade dropped down to 150 feet and raced at 125 miles an hour over the blasted treetops, bombed-out farmhouses, ruined villages, and shellpocked fields until they spied the German aerodrome ahead, the shadows of the humped hangars and warming aircraft stretching out in the slant morning light. The long rows of hangars, shop buildings, ammunition dumps, and messes looked exactly like the photographs they had reviewed in their evening briefing. They dropped down lower, though staying above one hundred feet to avoid getting caught in the explosions of their bombs. Ingalls roared in toward a row of warming

Fokkers. He could see their propellers spinning. He watched mechanics flee in panic as his double line of tracers streaked into the parked airplanes. He pulled his bomb levers over the hangars. Like tossing a rock at a stationary object from a streaking car, they kept trailing him until they landed two hundred yards past his intended target.

Others were more accurate with their "eggs." He swung back around and roared back over the field. As he passed, he leaned over to watch the firestorm two tons of bombs had unleashed. "My God," he thought, "what an inferno!" All around him, hangars, aircraft, ammo, and fields lit up with fireballs. Clouds of black smoke eddied over the field and soon hid much of it from view. Their bombs away, the pilots strafed the aerodrome. They returned for circuit after circuit, pouring thousands of rounds into airplanes, trucks, hangars, shops, and men. Ingalls saw men dive into a shop building for cover and followed them inside with his bullets. Camels dived past him on all sides, machine guns shuddering. With what seemed like "a million Camels" stunting about like ravenous flies over a carcass, he was amazed that none collided.

Finally the leaders broke off the attack, and one after another the Allied fighters hightailed back toward the lines. The enemy below was now wide awake. "Covered with fleeing Camels," the countryside lit up with machine guns and rapid-fire pom-pom batteries. Whenever a German battery started firing on one of the airplanes, though, the pilot dove on the gun until it grew silent. Ingalls enjoyed the "great fun" watching "the Huns run from my stream of bullets."

The scattered Camels soon chased back over the lines for home. Not a single plane failed to return. Inspecting his machine, Ingalls barked out his high-pitched laugh as he poked his finger through the four bullet holes in his fuselage. That was nothing. Observers reported the Germans lost twenty Gotha bombers and eighteen Fokker biplanes, along with the destruction of numerous hangars and ammunition dumps and some sixty men killed.[4] Ingalls then shared "a joyous breakfast," washed down with "good likker," with the rest of the squadron.[5]

Ingalls wanted to be aloft as much as possible after that, flying as many as eight hours when the weather was clear. He and the other scout pilots went out on regular morning and late afternoon patrols, the times when enemy aircraft were most likely to be flying. Two flights of five or six Camels flew together, one formation above the other for protection. When they encountered Germans, with so many planes in the air, Ingalls found distinguishing friend from foe in the melee "the most confusing affair imaginable." Twice he saw German airplanes collide "with the most gratifying result."[6] The patrols he flew varied among flying high-altitude offensive searches for enemy aircraft, escorting the fleet at sea to guard against marauding seaplanes during coastal bombardments, and protecting bomber formations heading over German-held territory. Nearly all action took place over enemy territory. German aircraft defended their lines, but, seeking to preserve Germany's limited aerial resources, rarely ventured out on daylight offensive patrols of their own—although their night bombers flew most nights. Between the regular patrols, the more aggressive Allied pilots often took off by themselves in search of spotter planes or reconnaissance aircraft photographing the lines. Ingalls jumped at the chance.

On his fifth day back at the front, done with his regular patrols, he headed up by himself at seven in the evening. He flew along the lines at 18,000 feet watching on all sides for prowling enemy. Seeing nothing, he came down to 12,000 feet. Spotting other aircraft was an acquired skill that took excellent eyesight and an ability to scan the horizon for tiny, often-camouflaged objects that might or might not appear to move, depending on their speed relative to the observer and the multidimensional, many-hued background of patchy earth, grey and white mottled clouds, harsh sunlight, and shifting horizon. Ingalls failed to realize that he was being watched. Suddenly, three fast German monoplanes were diving on him from behind. He had wandered four miles over the lines "and never regretted anything more sincerely." As their guns began to pop, he swerved, climbed, dove, turned. He could see their tracers streak past him, zipping between his wings on both sides.

Finally one of the speedy enemy machines closed to within a few feet before zooming up to the right. Ingalls spun about, firing on him until the German dropped away. Ingalls could not see the other aircraft, but could hear shooting he assumed came from his unprotected lower rear. Unsure which way lay escape, he feared flying directly into the enemy fire. "It was," he observed, "a rotten feeling." He turned and dove. Two German fighters chased him. He turned back again, got an enemy fighter in his sight and fired off a burst. Suddenly the Fokkers broke off the attack and headed away from the lines. Ingalls turned back and chased them, firing continuously, until they were out of range.

Now realizing he was several miles behind enemy lines, he turned toward home. To his surprise, as he raced along nobody shot at him and no enemies were visible. The sudden peacefulness was "the worse part." He did not believe it and kept fearing another attack was coming, but did not know from where. Stunned and scared, Ingalls turned and twisted nervously in his seat, "jumping about almost, waiting for the expected rat-tat-tat."

Finally reaching Couderkerque, he landed and climbed out, "giggling" with giddiness at having survived. As he described the scrap he had been in to some other pilots, his mechanic came up to report that his machine had been shot up so badly it might have to be junked. Major Graham took a look at the Camel and yelled at him for going out so far over the lines alone. "Believe me," he recorded, "I didn't need any fatherly advice then or ever again."[7] He realized he "had been a perfect fool." He did learn by surviving, though, never to let enemy fighters attack him from above or the rear. After that he climbed anytime he needed to feel more secure.[8]

He took more precautions, but continued to go out on frequent wolfpack and single patrols. The planes would go tearing along in formation so close they "nearly touched," searching for targets of opportunity. Those patrols bore fruit. He began to rack up kills. On his way home after another large raid on a German aerodrome, at Uytkerke, he flew back toward the lines off Ostend. He spied a two-seat Rumpler trying to attack another member of the patrol. Together with another Camel, he ignored the ground fire and chased it down to five hundred feet just off the Ostend piers before they sent the Germans crashing in flames in shallow water off the beach.[9]

On his patrols he noticed an observation balloon up regularly in good weather near Ostend. Tethered kite balloons floated their observers in baskets, where they relayed information to help aim long-range artillery against enemy targets. Although they "looked like such easy meat," the hangar-size, sausage-shape balloons rose up around a mile at most and, with the height marked by large numbers of batteries below, any enemy brazen enough to attack flew immediately into a hail of shrapnel and high explosives. Few dared venture within range of balloons; only volunteers ever flew missions against the gas bags. Ingalls was game. Now a flight leader, he drew together two other volunteers to "go get the beggar." They started out late on the morning of September 18. With a high-altitude, three-aircraft escort, the three balloon busters, guns loaded with incendiary tracer bullets, flew up the coast at seven thousand feet and curved in screaming toward the gray canvas balloon. Antiaircraft fire opened up as they crossed over land. The beginning of the raid proved unnerving for Ingalls. The first burst from the barrage exploded just under his right wing. Shrapnel crashed through the fuselage in front of his knees and smashed into the cowling. A chunk broke through the cockpit and struck his leg, giving him "quite a start." He ignored the flash of pain and continued diving on the "big, fat target."

Hearing the approaching aircraft, the German ground crew scurried to winch down the kite balloon as fast as they could. When it reached 3,500 feet, the diving Camels, guy-wires singing, began firing at it from different angles. Their incendiary bullets zipped into it, but without effect. Ingalls came about and dove again. This time his guns did the trick. Just five hundred feet in the air, the gray sack of hydrogen blazed up. The two observers leaped from the gondola. Their white parachutes bagged out as the balloon crumpled in a mass of flames over them. The attackers' luck proved supreme as the torched hydrogen sack floated down onto the wooden balloon shed below, which burst into flame. The shed exploded in a great fireball that set fire to two neighboring sheds housing more balloons. The entire station went up in flame. "It was a lovely sight," thought Ingalls as he flew past. He dropped down and emptied his remaining incendiary bullets on a row of wooden huts that quickly caught fire. They must have been full of straw or ammunition, he guessed, "to touch 'em off in such elegant fashion."[10] The flames and black smoke from the fires were visible to Allied observers fifteen miles away in Nieuport. The balloon busters touched down and counted the holes in their planes. Ingalls's Camel was again shot up so badly he needed another replacement.

He was still not satisfied. What he wanted was to down an opponent by himself. On a visit to Dunkirk, he stomped about complaining to Gates about having to share credit for all his kills to date. Gates wrote to Trubee Davison that the Baby Daredevil was "crazy to get one all alone and will be much happier after he has thus succeeded."[11] Finally, he got his wish.

In an escort flight accompanying bombers on a mission over Bruges, he spied four Fokkers coming straight at the formation from the right as they passed over the Belgian coast. His flight turned toward the approaching enemy. He flew straight at the lead Fokker, firing as he went. He turned and zoomed up just before they collided. The Fokkers broke away and flew off, but continued to shadow the bombers at a distance. Ingalls returned to escorting the bombers. After they let their payloads fall and turned toward home, one of the bombers developed engine trouble and fell beind the others. Two of the Fokkers started for him. So did Crock. One of the Germans pulled directly behind the lagging bomber and began firing from 150 yards while the other overran the Allied machine. Ingalls dove on the one firing from behind, cutting across the German's fuselage. He immediately fell, smoke trailing out of his machine as he arced gracelessly toward the ground.

Ingalls then turned on the other German. He got within fifteen yards and had "a perfect shot," almost running into him. The enemy aircraft turned turtle and went spinning down. Ingalls watched him until he was near the ground when three Fokkers started shooting at him from below. He dove on them and they split off. He turned back toward the bomber that was hurrying toward the coast. The Germans pulled back together and began shooting at him, but soon fell off. He returned home. He had his confirmed kill. The fate of the other plane could not be confirmed, but Crock was certain he had a second.[12]

His next victim, four days later, almost proved his last flight of all. He flew out with a fellow Ace, English pilot George Hodson, "for one last look in the growing dusk for a low two-seater." He saw one, an old Rumpler. He signaled to Hodson who had turned back toward the lines. Ingalls dove alone, but flew too fast and, in his first pass, overshot the German machine. He circled back widely, trying to stay below the Rumpler, away from the observer's arc of fire. Ingalls zoomed back up, ignoring the tracers flickering between the struts on his left side. Just ten yards away, he could "see the two Huns perfectly in their black helmets." He dropped back behind them, took aim. The enemy aircraft exploded.

He dropped down to contour-chase home to avoid antiaircraft fire. Although he flew faster closer to the ground, that put him within range of "the spiteful sharp crackle of ground machine guns with their tracers flashing by first on one side, then the other."[13] A sharp or lucky marksman could down a scout with a single, well-placed bullet. As Crock flew along, he heard a burst of fire from below. His motor stopped and gas poured out of the tank beneath the seat. A cloud of white vapor rose from the tank. His machine fell. Pulling back on the stick, the elevators did not respond. A clump of trees loomed ahead. He switched to the gravity tank and the motor started back up. The tail-heavy Camel rose up and missed the top branches by inches. His troubles were not over. The motor was hitting on only six of the nine cylinders. He also found only his downward elevator control worked, and his ailerons responded weakly to the stick. His rudder still answered. Ground fire continued incessantly as he flew over, but afraid to use the controls, he "sat still," using the rudder and his one working aileron to make little turns toward home. He felt like he was holding his breath the entire time until he crossed the lines. As he approached the aerodrome, though, he had to figure out how to land. He could go down but could not stop going down once he started unless he turned on the motor. But if he revved up the motor he would zoom right back up again. Finally, after rising up and falling down time after time, he sailed across the field at treetop level until he toppled down for good, mashing his landing gear in the process.

His inspection of the aircraft showed the ground fire had perforated his gas tank and knocked out the wires he needed to go up, as well as some of those to go down. One aileron had been hit in a hinge. The wings were peppered with holes. His luck was holding and his reputation for destroying aircraft, including his own, was growing. He told his mechanic to prepare him a new Camel for the following day. He had no time to waste and rushed to his barracks. A dance was about to begin and Di Gates was bringing some of the American nurses from the hospital in Durkirk. The dance would be, he recorded, "a good ending to my day. Nothing like relaxation from this business."[14]

With the Allies beginning to take the offensive, the No. 213 Camel squadron was dispatched more and more to attack enemy supply lines and trenches in support of attacking troops. In one day, Ingalls flew four separate low-altitude missions. He carried small bombs on each and "beaucoup ammunition." His flight came upon a long line of horse-drawn gun caissons racing up a road to the front. The Camels dropped their bombs and then returned back over the artillery train, strafing the road and sending masses of men and teams of horses harnessed to their burdens bounding off in confusion and terror, crashing and dying in heaps. Crock watched as the battery captain riding a white horse galloped off back down the road, his coat tails and sword flying out, with a single Camel in hot pursuit. The bullets followed the German for nearly a mile until the horse fell and the captain flew headfirst into a ditch. The Camel swiveled tightly around a tree and came back up the road. Just as the airplane passed a few feet over his head, the German officer tossed a rock at his attacker. The stone struck the end of the Camel's wing and tore an enormous hole through it. Watching the deadly comic theater, Ingalls coughed out an ironic laugh. The Stone Age men on the ground were reduced to throwing rocks at the wingéd gods of all future wars.

He flew back over the remains of the artillery train. Smoke and dust wafted over the road, which was a scene of chaotic devastation. The German column was almost totally annihilated. Ingalls noticed "one plucky devil who had guts" as he unhitched a terrified horse team from its crashed caisson. He led them off the road into the neighboring field where he now stood at their heads quieting them. He was an easy target, but none of the buzzing war birds shot at him. "That fellow," Ingalls commented, "was on the wrong side in this war."

The price of No. 213's low-altitude patrols was high. When it came time to fly off on the last air raid of that day, only seven out of the eighteen Camels that had started in the morning remained. Flying so close to the ground made the airplanes vulnerable to more than stones. The Germans kept machine-gun emplacements scattered throughout the countryside to knock down low-flying aircraft. The loud motors alerted the gun crews long before the plane flew by, giving them plenty of time to prepare. Still, the surviving men had grown proficient at their deadly business, aiming their bombs with precision and spreading devastation with their streaming machine-gun bullets. That evening, the remaining handful of machines went out and demolished a troop transport train. Returning to the base mess afterward, Ingalls looked around at the empty chairs that had been filled that morning. "My God, how long will this last?" he asked. "About one day more and our squadron will be a thing of the past."[15]

The low-altitude attacks continued to whittle away at No. 213. In one stretch of six days, nine of the fifteen current pilots, along with twenty machines, were lost. An apparently unending stream of new men flowed in from the flight schools to fill the emptied cockpits.[16] Although Ingalls and others took to the air time after time as ordered, "everybody," he noticed, "expects each trip to be the final one for him." The more hopeful carried extra clothing, money, and toiletries up with them thinking they might be taken prisoner. Ingalls, though, did not want to go quietly. "To hell with the stuff," he remarked. He only carried extra ammunition for a .32 caliber automatic he kept in his pocket. If he forgot to stick what he called his "rabbit's foot"in his pocket before taking off, he returned to the ground to grab it.

As the Allies became more and more aggressive in their drive to break the heart of the tottering German army and chop away at the supply arteries and communication lines that kept it fighting, strafing runs became more and more a part of the pilots' day. For Ingalls, the hockey star turned Air Ace, the fair chance chivalric men gave one another facing off in airplanes disappeared in what he called the "really dirty work" of strafing trenches, railways, ammunition dumps, ground transports, and supply convoys. Anonymous, desperate men fired up at his Camel as he streaked past at 120 miles per hour spraying bullets indiscriminately into the exposed masses of troops, munitions, horses, and railway carriages. He found the brutal, dangerous work increasingly wearying. With "no competition," this type of fight, he admitted, was "not my idea of sport."

Hardened and businesslike in pursuing the enemy to the end, he still found the product of his work repulsive. On one mission, he came upon a long horse transport moving up to the front and raked its length with pan after pan of ammunition, passing back and forth several times. His ammunition exhausted, he flew slowly over the roadway. He looked down at the steaming, bloody tangle of human and horse entrails, waiting for someone to stand up and fire back at him. He buzzed over low enough for anyone to reach up and grab his landing gear, "but none were moving." He recorded the scene afterward and concluded his hellish handiwork was "necessary perhaps but nauseating."17

In his six weeks with No. 213, Ingalls had flown nearly 110 hours, an average of close to three hours every single day, but because of weather that kept him grounded for many of those days, on the days he flew, he was generally in the air for six to eight hours or more, while flying an astounding sixty-three missions over the lines. The Northern Bombing Group's C.O. Hanrahan decided the navy's first Air Ace needed a rest. In early October, over Crock's curses, he ordered him to be relieved and sent to the base at Eastleigh where he would trade places with Kenney MacLeish.

CHAPTER 25

Couderkerque, October 1918
The Lone Wolf

ON OCTOBER 3, KENNEY MACLEISH FLEW AN AMERICAN DH–4 HE HAD assembled and tested over the Channel from Eastleigh for delivery to the Northern Bombing Group's Marine Day Wing base near Calais. He took Crock Ingalls up for his first time in an American-made bomber. The aircraft's notoriety as a flaming coffin was already spreading, but Crock liked the ride. "From what I'd heard," he noted after they landed, "I was in doubt whether or not an American ship would actually fly." He was, however, "agreeably surpised." It flew, "and beautifully."[1]

With MacLeish's delivery of the bomber, the marines could now fly their own machines in the day-bombing raids they were already carrying out with the RAF. After turning the DH–4 over, early the next morning MacLeish drove up to visit with Ingalls and his other old flying mates at No. 213 at Couderkerque. He found his friend looking greener than his khakis. Crock tried to recall the previous night's events. No. 213 had held a blowout to cele-brate his impending departure and the end of his extraordinary six-week stint over the lines. "He is," proclaimed C.O. Graham, "one of the finest men this squadron ever had."[2] After Ingalls stumbled through a "bum" speech in the crowded mess, the drinking commenced. In the morning he found himself in bed with no clue how he got there. "About all I remember," he recorded about the night's events, "is that Di came out and brought some American girl from the hospital."[3]

After he had sobered up, they drove over the cobbled, shellhole-pocked roads to nearby St. Pol to catch up with Di Gates. He had just transferred to the French scout squadron.

Gates had had plenty to celebrate as well. Flying a single-seater over the lines was the one opportunity he had been clamoring for since he first stepped foot on French soil more than a year ago. On October 1, with the Central Powers ready to collapse, German Admiral Scheer had abandoned the much-feared Belgian coastal bases. Navy aviation headquarters closed down the "bum" Dunkirk Naval Air Station and merged its personnel into the NBG. "'Them Huns,'" Bob Lovett wrote Adele, "seem to be pretty well fed up with the U.S. and the war."[4] His planes and men moved to forward bases, their attentions focused on blasting the Germans completely out of Belgium and France, and plans were in the works to carry the fight to Berlin.

As soon as enough equipment arrived, Gates would take command of a new NBG squadron. Until then, he wanted to fight. Although he was a C.O. and thus not normally permitted to fly over the lines, he had petitioned Captain Cone to be detached to a fighting post. The head of naval aviation in Europe consulted with Lovett, who believed that the disbanding of the Dunkirk station had "hit [Gates] very hard." Gates did not want to wait around with nothing to do while others carried on the fight. Idle waiting when there was work to be done, agreed Bob, "breaks one's spirit more than anything I know." Recognizing his long-enduring service, heroism, and pent-up frustrations with his Dunkirk command, Cone decided to make an exception to the no-fly rule for C.O.-level officers "to cheer him up." Unlike other pilots, given his long experience, they did not bother to send him back to flight or gunnery school for further training.[5]

Gates could not wait to get started. He immediately joined a new Franco-American squadron at St. Pol near Dunkirk. He took a few practice flights in a SPAD, the fast-diving but largely outmoded French scouts his squadron would fly over the lines. Before Ingalls and MacLeish arrived that morning he had taken off on his first raid into German-held territory.

The two leaned against their car beside the hangars at the St. Pol field, joking about what their big friend was up to over the lines. MacLeish smoked the American Fatimas his parents had sent him and Ingalls clenched his pipe between his teeth while they waited for the SPADs to return from their patrol. They knew how jealous Gates had been of their time in scouts. They planned to razz him mightily when he landed. They laughed, but they also scanned the sky nervously from time to time.

The flight of seven SPADs had gone out an hour earlier, heading over the lines at about twelve thousand feet. The big-shouldered American could barely squeeze into the small cockpit. However, he felt right at home in the formation. Flying ahead of him, he could see the helmeted head of George Moseley scanning the sky in his SPAD. "Mose" was a man he would follow anywhere. Two years before, he and Moseley, an All-American end, had lined up together on the Yale football team. Gates's old teammate had plenty of experience over the lines, having come over even before the declaration of war to fly with the French. Turning toward the other tail of the V, Gates gave the thumbs up to a smiling Freddy Beach, his Yale Unit mate. Another American, William Van Fleet, who had also flown with the French before U.S. entry into the war, two French pilots, and the French squadron captain completed the flight. Gates enjoyed sharing his first mission with men he knew well, but the flight like many squadrons in the heavy push of recent weeks was sending inadequately trained men into aerial combat. Of the four Americans only Moseley and Van Fleet had ever flown scouts before over the lines—and Moseley alone had received any formal gunnery training. The two French pilots were enlisted men also new to the game. More than half the flight had never encountered enemy aircraft before. There was no predicting how inexperienced pilots might react in a fight. It was, MacLeish thought, "a foolish move to put them all in the same flight."[6]

In what felt like an ill omen, the two green French pilots flew back into St. Pol with engine trouble shortly after Ingalls and MacLeish drove up. A little over an hour later they could hear the buzzing engines of the first SPADs returning and then make out their insect-like silhouettes in the distance. As the string of aircraft spooled out onto the field, they counted only four airplanes. One was missing. The SPADs rolled up to the hangar. One was badly shot up. The grim faced pilots climbed out. Di Gates was not among them.

Ingalls and MacLeish ran over to where Beach, Moseley, and Van Fleet had gathered. They spoke quietly among themselves. Clearly shaken, their faces looked ashen behind the whale grease. Di, mumbled Moseley, "was with us when the attack began, and after that no one saw him."[7] A jumpy Beach said, he "must have gone down."

The flight had started out uneventfully. They had been flying through clouds about fifteen miles behind the lines over Courtrai, a small city in Flanders, with no enemy in sight. Beach and Gates were at the back of the formation when Beach saw the three forward machines, the French flight captain, Moseley, and Van Fleet, drop away without warning. He looked up and there right over his head was an airplane. Never having even seen an enemy aircraft before, he was "astounded" at first by the sudden appearance of the Iron Cross emblazoned on the black wings of one of Germany's new and fast Fokker D-VII. The enemy bird was close enough, it seemed, to reach up and touch. "It was several seconds before I came to," Beach said. That hesitation nearly cost him his life. He looked back. At least a dozen more red-and-black enemy bi- and triplanes burst out of the clouds directly behind him. Gates was still flying with him but "the rest of the squadron had disappeared in front of us," diving into the billowy clouds below. Beach thought of everybody who had been dying. "I never had been so scared in my life," he admitted. Fortunately, the SPAD was justly famed for its ability to drop like a stone, falling faster than almost any machine in the air. As the Germans began to shoot, he jammed the stick forward and went into a screaming dive. Just as he started to spin, he looked back to see Gates swing around in a virage onto the tail of one of the attacking Germans. That, said Beach, was the last he had seen of the "poor fellow." He shook his head about the chances he had facing such odds. "Rotten luck."[8]

Ingalls and MacLeish refused to accept that Gates had "gone West." Both had escaped from plenty of bad scrapes before. "If any man can get out of a tight fix," declared MacLeish, "Di can."[9] The aviators scoured the horizon, expecting to see him come flying home at any moment ready to tell a tale about a razor-close brush with death they could all laugh over. They waited until all hope for his airborne return faded. He was not coming back. "Bad leadership, damn it!" cursed Ingalls. All of the Americans were distraught. "To lose old Di," he said, expressing their shared realization, "is the biggest loss there could be." They concurred with him that "he's the best fellow I ever saw or heard about."[10]

Stricken MacLeish wandered away from the airfield. He did not want to cry in front of the others. "Of all the men on earth that it's hard to lose!" he moaned. To lose Di was to lose a brother. They had been through more together than almost any two boys—venturing East, overcoming the loneliness of prep school, growing up in the Connecticut countryside, and then making their way through the thorny social thicket of Yale. Di had brought him into the Yale Unit where he had discovered the incomparable joy of flight. They had gone to war together, sharing the adventure, terror, and thrills, the searing longing for home and the immeasurable cost of losing friends. He had always been able to turn to Di throughout the ups-and-downs of his long courtship with Priscilla. They were truly brothers. "I surely love him like one," he confessed freely to his sister after he got back to Eastleigh.[11] And now Di was gone.

As always, he shared his deepest feelings with Priscilla Murdock. The pain of losing his closest friend, he wrote, was unbearable. "Oh pal," he cried to her, "I'm just crushed—I've never, never taken anything so badly."[12]

Gates's Yale Unit mates waited for confirmation of his fate. When Lovett received word of Gates's disappearance, he could not "believe that the jackals crashed him." How was it possible "that one so full of life as Di could have lost it?" He now kicked himself for supporting the decision to permit him to fly. "The cost to us has been irreplaceable."[13]

He scoured the other Flanders squadrons for any sightings. Belgian pilots reported seeing two aircraft go down in the sector where Gates had last been seen, but nobody knew if they were Allied or German, or if there were any survivors. Lovett tried to hold onto the hope that Di was still alive. "We are stretching every effort to get word of him in the prison camps," he wrote an anguished Trubee Davison, still recuperating at home. Trubee and his sister, Alice, with whom Di had corresponded about a possible future together after the war, were desperate for word. Through his father who was traveling in Europe, Trubee mobilized an all-out search for the missing aviator at the highest levels. Finally, no longer able to bear hearing about the war through cables and letters that arrived sometimes weeks after events, he booked passage to England.

While no news of Gates's fate turned up after more than a week, Lovett refused to accept his death. "We must regard him as a prisoner," he insisted.[14] The *New York Times* reported him as "captured."[15] The *Saturday Evening Post* was less sure. "With the same spirit he had shown on the gridiron," the popular magazine wrote of his last flight, "Gates flew at them. They got him."[16]

As the days passed, MacLeish, too, clung to the possibility that Di had somehow beaten the odds. "It seems almost hopeless, doesn't it?" he wrote Trubee. He tried to buck up his own spirits. "I can't picture him in a position that he couldn't get out of."

Grieving over his friend, he prepared to return to Eastleigh. Before leaving St. Inglevert, he ran into Captain Hanrahan, the NBG commander. Hanrahan asked him where he was going. MacLeish told him. "No, you're not going back," said Hanrahan. "You're going out to 213 squadron again!"

Stunned, MacLeish "nearly fell on his neck and kissed him."[17]

He returned to Eastleigh one last time to get things ready for Ingalls, who would take his place, and to pack his bags. Despite a deep exhaustion from another bout of pneumonia that had whittled nearly fifteen pounds off his already slender frame and feeling more than "pretty low" about Gates's disappearance, he was about to return to single-seater flying for the first time over the lines in six months. His mission was now hauntingly clear. He intended to even the score. "Some of those dirty ___ will pay me!" he vowed.[18]

As devastating as losing Gates was, MacLeish had needed a jolt to renew his sense of purpose. Less than a month earlier, he had visited Di, who had written to Trubee afterward that their old classmate seemed "to have lost all interest in his work and to be thoroughly tired of flying." That was shocking because nobody, not even Crock Ingalls, loved to fly more or flew with such exuberance. But MacLeish was burnt out, disappointed time and again by his behind-the-lines assignments that changed so often he no longer even knew where he had last checked his baggage, and exhausted by illness. He missed Priscilla badly and complained often about feeling homesick. "A nice trip to the States for a rest would be about the best thing in the world for him," suggested Gates.[19]

For the first time since coming to Europe, Kenney agreed. "I would rather loaf at home where I can have you," he told Priscilla, "than loaf over here."[20]

Bob Lovett had big ambitions for MacLeish, though. Bob wanted him to take charge of a second night bombing squadron the NBG would soon begin to assemble. As C.O., MacLeish would have absolute say over 386 men, 42 flying officers, and their ten hulking British-built Handley-Page bombers. In mid-September Lovett wrote MacLeish a note requesting that he consider becoming the new C.O. But sensing a hesitation on MacLeish's part, he asked him to come in "whole-heartedly or not at all."

Kenney wrote back quickly. He was "tickled stiff" at the display of trust in him and "appreciated the honor." But "honest, Bob, it won't fit me." What he really wanted to do was to get back into the fight. He "couldn't stand not being in it every minute." He concluded with a cry from the heart, "For the love of Pete get me out of this hole and back to 213."

Lovett made one further appeal, but to the same end. Kenney wrote back that he was simply not interested in being a C.O. "if I can't fight and fly all I want and when I want." It had taken a lifetime, but he had finally come to know himself and to know his destiny. There was only one place he felt completely at peace with himself. "Some people," he explained, "were born to paint, some to write, some to lead and some to just plain go out and do-it-all-by-yourself." All he wanted until the war ended was "a good Camel, beaucoup ammunition, plenty of gas," and a chance to battle the enemy.

Lovett finally understood about his friend that there was only one "job he was made for." Deeply impressed by MacLeish's "utter disregard of his own advancement in contrast to so many," here, Bob thought, was "an honest-to-goodness man." He let the matter of the squadron command drop.[21]

In reflecting on Gates's disappearance, though, he advised Hanrahan against letting MacLeish fly back over the lines. Over his chief deputy's better judgment, Hanrahan agreed to MacLeish's return to the RAF's No. 213.

Kenney was "crazy to get started." He proclaimed his intention to "to make one last try at really doing something." Crock had made his mark in the air. Di needed to be avenged. With Germany on the run, it might be his final weeks of flying. "If the luck is with me," he wrote Priscilla, "all well and good, if it isn't. . . ." His words trailed off. The rumor mill brought him word of Bob's efforts to keep him away from the front. "It's just my luck," he grumbled, "not to get a chance to go out at all."[22] Finally, he got his way.

After an initial packing his few things together on the night of October 10, he was unable to sleep and passed "the queerest night" lying in his room smoking and thinking about the many twists and turns his life had taken over the past year and a half. It was "a perfect night," chilly enough to require adding coal to the fire in the stove, the crisp fall air electric beneath a swollen harvest moon. The moon's reflected light washed over the still base and illuminated the few contents of his small room with a spectral glow. He could hear the tide sighing in the distance and thought of Priscilla just beyond the far shore. His heart ached to think of the same moonlight shining down on her. "Wasn't it gorgeous?" he asked her in his thoughts.

As the sun came up and the base came to life, he realized the ghosts of the night had spoken to him. They delivered a hard-to-discern message about love and war, the dawning love he and Priscilla had won through the long trials of the grinding months of war. The young pair had earned their great love. "The whole thing seemed to foretell the future," MacLeish felt. "It seemed to give me an insight into the perfect, the beautiful Love that was to be mine, yet it was stern—it seemed to indicate that the price of such a marvelous Love was very dear." He wrote her, "It has turned out that way, hasn't it, little pal?" Their love, "such a wonderful love," was worth everything to him, "yet the price is this long separation." The war seemed endless, its physical and emotional demands relentless, the pain at times beyond bearing, but he felt their time apart "must cease soon. It can't go on this way much longer!"

He walked over to the hangars where a warming DH–4 was waiting for him. He posted his letter and assured Priscilla that the long separation would soon be over. "I feel sure that it will stop soon."[23]

He flew a new DH–4 over to St. Inglevert with Frank Lynch, a unit member set to join the NBG. They delivered the bomber and met up with Ingalls and Lovett for dinner. Lovett noted afterward that Kenney was "the most nervously elated person I'd ever seen."[24] Ingalls wished they would be flying together again. He was certain "he'll have a wonderful time." He urged Kenney to hold back on his first few missions. "It's the first scraps that are a bit dangerous," he warned.[25] If he took care in those times when survival was "entirely a matter of luck," he would have a genuine chance of "really accomplishing something in the end."[26]

For his part, MacLeish had no interest in delaying. After so much time away from the front, he was ready to test his luck. A large offensive was planned for the next day. After dinner, he called Major Graham at No. 213 and asked if he could come to the aerodrome that very night. He drove the four miles over to Couderkerque and found the survivors among his old mates at the mess. At dawn he was back in the air.[27]

After a low-level bombing run destroyed a German column along a road near Ardoye, the morning patrol flew back up until it came upon a German aerial circus. In the massive dogfight, together with his old friend from No. 213, Canadian Ace John Edmund Greene, MacLeish knocked down his first German. He came down and punched the air in excitement. It was one for Di. He wanted more. After lunch, he rushed back up for the afternoon patrol.

The formation of fifteen Camels flew up the Belgian coast, but then MacLeish's flight, with Greene and a third pilot, an English lieutenant named Allen, lost the larger formation in the clouds. They continued inland until they spied two slow-moving German observation aircraft flying beneath them a couple miles north of the village of Dixmude. MacLeish saw nothing to fear. The three Camels dove toward the enemy machines. They had just begun firing when a large force of Fokkers unleashed its surprise attack. With no chance to defend themselves, Greene and Allen went spinning quickly down in their flaming Camels. MacLeish was luckier; their first shots missed. Desperate to shake the remaining Fokkers from his tail, he stunted and dove for the safety of the lines. Finally, unable to outrun the faster German aircraft, he damned the odds and turned to face the Fokkers swarming about him. Before he could get an enemy in his sights, German bullets found their mark. His engine sputtered. He began spinning toward the ground.

Out of control, he dropped helplessly, the earth's gray quilt spinning closer and closer. Just before crashing he brought the nose of the dying Camel up, and the biplane flopped down onto the spongy earth. It plowed into the mud, shattering the propeller and sending up a spray of green muck. His head slammed forward into the cowling, knocking him out.

Regaining consciousness, he extracted himself painfully from the rags, wooden bones, and tangled cables of his bullet-riddled Camel. He dropped to the ground and sank into two feet of water and mud. Four years earlier the Belgian army had sought to slow the German advance by flooding the low-lying eastern Flemish lands. After they breached the canal walls in the valley of the nearby Yser River, the spilling waters had turned a huge region of farmland into a vast swamp. Standing in the cold water, MacLeish surveyed a bleak scene of total desolation. He had fallen in the midst of miles of marshy No-Man's Land neither side had been able to retake since the flood. Tall grasses gone straw for the winter coated the featureless flats that spread out to the gray horizon. Except for the wreckage of farmhouses and barns, no signs of human life were visible. Dug in for years now, the two warring sides remained more than two miles apart and fired off long-range cannons against each other. Explosions shivered the viscous mud as shells lofted back and forth. Uncountable numbers of graywater-filled craters dotted the fields around MacLeish. Bloated, rat-eaten corpses floated here and there in the muck that belched out the stench of death and rot. Gunsmoke and the lung-burning remnants of poison gas wafted through the air. Miles away, he could see a dogfight in progress. As the airplanes looped and chased about like a cloud of insects, their roaring engines and the rat-tat-tat of their guns were too far off for him to hear. He crawled and stumbled across the straw stubble of what had once been fields of Belgian wheat.

After struggling through hundreds of yards of boot-sucking muck, he sat down to rest on a pile of debris beside a group of bombed-out farm buildings. His dreams of glory had carried him high into the sky, but now he was alone. His battered body hurt worse than any pain he had known before. His head pounded and the gray horizon wobbled and grew fuzzy. He struggled to remain conscious. He could not contain himself. He had to laugh at the swift end to his fighting career. He thought back to his dreams of glory. This was not the heroic finish he had expected, stranded on the blasted freezing mud. All his desire for honor in the air had brought him down in No Man's Land. His heart ached for Priscilla's embrace. He wondered where she was at that very instant. Working perhaps. Hopefully thinking of him. He reached into his flight suit pocket for the handkerchief she had given him. He clutched the cool worn silk to his bloodied face and tried to inhale the faded perfume she had left for him.[28]

Back at Couderkerque, the squadron waited for MacLeish to return. For No. 213, it had been one of the bloodier days of the war: six pilots missing or killed. Other pilots flying over the lines reported seeing the German circus dive into MacLeish's flight and, after the two other aircraft fell, his Camel turn on his German attackers. Major Graham noted in the squadron log: "Lieutenant MacLeish was last seen attacking about seven Fokkers single-handed."[29]

Two days later, Frank Lynch went looking for him. The battle was thought to have taken place over the Belgian town of Leffinge, a few miles southeast of Ostend. The Germans were falling back so rapidly that the day after MacLeish disappeared they fled the coastal zone that he had flown against so often. While the bombers and scouts continued to hammer the retreating Germans, Allied ground forces had to push their trucks and wagons through axle-deep mud and over nearly impassable roads to reach the abandoned German positions. Lynch flew back and forth for three full days over the gray patchwork landscape looking for MacLeish. Major Graham and his close friends in No. 213 were doing all they could to locate their popular American mate as well. But they could find no trace of him.

As with Di Gates, Bob Lovett "refused to believe that anything more serious than capture had befallen him." The evidence was hopeful. A search party he sent out to Leffinge had encountered an old Belgian woman who said she had seen two "English" pilots come down and then get taken prisoner by the Germans. The Germans had told her one of them was an American, and she remembered he was wearing an airmen's uniform similar to that worn by the navy men at her door. Both captured men walked out without aid, she reported, one "slightly wounded in the nose." Heartened by the news, Lovett wrote Priscilla Murdock and urged her "to wait patiently for Ken to come home." He assured her he was bending every effort to locate him in prison and, as soon as he did, would send him whatever assistance he could. His words meant a great deal when he wrote, "There are few friends that I have ever cared for as much."[30]

Foster Rockwell, who had helped manage the Yale Unit during its training days, now served under Henry Davison with the Red Cross in London. He cabled Trubee that both Gates and MacLeish were almost certainly being held by the Germans. "Red Cross Prisoner Bureau has the matter in hand," he wrote, "and will see that both have every care when located."[31]

CHAPTER 26

Villingen, November 1918
Flight

WHILE THE FRANTIC SEARCH EXPANDED TO INCLUDE KENNEY MACLEISH, a closely watched Di Gates sat alone in a tiny, dank German prison cell in Ghent. During the melee over Courtrai, the attacking Fokkers' machine gun fire had shot his motor out. Three enemy fighters continued to shoot at him as he dove toward the ground while dodging the bullets as best he could without power. Trying to level off, he snagged telephone wires and turned turtle into a field. He crawled out uninjured from the wreckage. Oil and gas spilled out over it through the bullet holes that had pierced the engine and fuel tank. The three Fokkers flew back and forth over the downed American to attract the attention of nearby German troops, who went running toward the crash site. Pilots were told in training to try to destroy their aircraft if they were brought down in enemy territory. As the Germans approached, Gates calmly struck a match and flicked it onto the SPAD, which burst into flame. A crowd of soldiers rushed him before two officers took him away.

He traveled under armed guard for two days, passing through long columns of bedraggled German soldiers before he was brought to Ghent. The guards took him to a comfortable private house where he was free to move about inside. During the next three days, English-speaking German officers offered him plenty of good food to eat and wine to drink. Attractive young German nurses and female office workers came by several times. They invited Gates to dance with them while the Victrola played jaunty tunes. They asked him to teach them a new American dance called the Fox Trot. In the festive atmosphere, the friendly German officers inquired about his flying experiences and about Allied aerial strategy. Their knowledge of Allied troop movements, locations of aerodromes and squadrons, even the names of their officers, came as "a great surprise" to him. He quickly surmised that he was in the savvy hands of German intelligence officers. "The Indian" knew how to keep silent. Deciding he was useless to them, they soon moved him out of his comfortable surroundings. The burly American was placed in solitary confinement in the old Ghent penitentiary, allowed into a small yard to walk for a few minutes each day under armed guard and fed a daily ration of just two pieces of bread, a tepid cup of coffee, and a bowl of soup made from a "mystery" substance.

As he sat alone and famished in his cell, the sounds of Allied bombers pounding Ghent again and again, night and day, cheered him. When he first arrived, the frontlines were too far off to hear the sound of fighting. Each day, though, the drumming of artillery and gunfire drew nearer until, by his fifth day in the prison, "the roar became almost deafening" as the lines moved to within six miles of the city. With the city about to fall, on October 22, armed guards put him on a train for Karlsruhe, in Germany. At station stops, numerous soldiers traveling toward the front broke strict rules against fraternizing with enemy prisoners and came up to ask him about the war. Their morale low, their army in obvious disarray, they told him they expected to be back home by Christmas.

A few days after arriving in the German city, he was put on another train for transfer to an American aviation officers' camp in Villingen. Eluding his guards' notice, he tore a rail map off the carriage wall and stuffed it in his pocket. He pretended to fall asleep, and his guard left the compartment to chat with other soldiers. In the noisy darkness of a long tunnel, Gates opened a window and squeezed out. He dropped from the slow-moving train onto the rail bed and rolled to the side of the tunnel. After letting the train pass on, he raced back out of the tunnel and into the surrounding woods where he hid out until dark. When night fell, he consulted his map. If he followed the tracks south as shown on his map, he would eventually reach neutral Switzerland.

For four days he hid by day and walked at night, diving into the bushes each time a train rumbled past. Finally, he reached Konstanz, a lakefront city on the Swiss frontier. Unaware in the darkness just how close he was to the border, he blundered straight into a German patrol. They leveled their arms at the American. He was three yards short of freedom when he was retaken. Shackled and closely guarded, he was loaded onto a train and taken to the prison camp in Villingen.[1]

Soon after learning of Gates's disappearance, Trubee Davison sailed for London intent on doing what he could to help in the search for his missing squadron mate. While onboard, word came that MacLeish, too, had gone down. Davison arrived in late October and, in uniform, went straight to navy headquarters. The head of the navy in Europe, Admiral Sims, recalled him "limping into my office in London, badly crippled but determined to locate" his missing unit members.[2]

Davison's arrival in London coincided with the first real news about Gates's fate. Advancing Allied forces had stumbled onto the remains of his charred SPAD on October 23. A week later, Henry Davison cabled his son in London that he and his other son, Harry, had driven into Belgium to inspect the crash site. They found the burnt wreckage lying in a field. Judging from the furrow the airplane had left in the soft ground, they were sure he had not crashed badly. They found no evidence of burned clothing, dried blood, or any other indication that Gates might have been killed or even seriously injured in the crash. Henry Davison was "bringing souvenirs home" from the crash, including a bent machine gun and broken propeller.[3]

That was not the only good news to reach headquarters. On every front, the Allies were advancing against a collapsing enemy. One by one the nations allied in the Central Powers, their battered armies in retreat, their governments on the brink of dissolution, began to negotiate a separate peace with the Allies. On the Western Front, French, American, and British forces had broken decisively through German defenses for the first time. A quarter of Germany's soldiers had been taken prisoner and half its army's guns captured since the Allied offensive began in August. More and more, entire squadrons refused orders to advance. Rumors of the possible abdication by the kaiser were spreading. At sea, his fleet's ability to wage war was also at an end. On October 19, Admiral Scheer ordered all German submarines home. The kaiser's grand strategy to strangle British sea traffic and keep America out of the war had failed. Two days later, in a final deadly gesture, a German submarine fired the last torpedo of the war, sinking a small British merchantman in the Irish Sea, drowning eight crewmen. No matter: Germany's navy was defeated. Shortly before that final brutal gesture, Lovett crowed to Adele, "We've got the beggars on the run now and we'll break their ruddy necks before the month's gone. Then with them in the open we can take an eye for an eye."[4]

To the south, though, the war was essentially already ended and two of Europe's oldest royal lines had reached their final moments as well. By the last days of October, the armies fighting on behalf of Austria-Hungary had disintegrated and returned home. The many small lands composing the Austro-Hungarian Empire broke free of the Hapsburg throne, and, on October 30, it ceased to exist. That same day, representatives of the Ottoman Empire signed an armistice with the British, ending the war in Mesopotamia. After six centuries of Ottoman rule, Turkish military leaders declared a republic. The Austrian armistice was signed on November 3 and, the following day at three in the afternoon, fighting stopped on the Italian Front.

The remaining German forces on the Western Front, fighting from their heavily reinforced defensive positions, continued to resist. The kaiser's generals urged him to seek armistice terms, but he refused. The Allied Supreme War Council went ahead with planning for an invasion of Germany in the spring. The attack into Bavaria would combine aerial bombardment, long-range artillery, and the greatest massing of troops in history. It would not prove necessary. Wilhelm's support was collapsing. Admiralty sailors, now mostly in port, mutinied. Many cities fell into the hands of revolutionary factions. Ignoring Wilhelm's demands for military support of his rule, a German military delegation traveled into France on November 9 to negotiate terms to halt the fighting. While they met in Marshall Foch's railway carriage in the forest of Compiègne, much of the German army at home deserted. His monarchy doomed, the kaiser fled to asylum in neutral Holland. The Allied demands were onerous, but the German officials had no choice but to accept the terms—surrendering most of their nation's heavy armaments, including its entire submarine fleet as well as scores of naval and merchant ships, 1,700 airplanes, thousands of locomotives, railway cars, and trucks; withdrawing its army from all occupied territories all the way back to the far banks of the Rhine; returning the Alsace-Lorraine region won from the French in 1871; and agreeing to make heavy reparation payments.

The deadly fighting continued until the very last moment agreed upon under the terms of the Armistice. On the eleventh hour of the eleventh day of the eleventh month, at 11:00 A.M., November 11, 1918, the war ended. A rippling of cheers came out of the lines for hundreds of miles from the Swiss border to Belgium. The surviving combatants dropped their weapons, climbed out of the mud, and returned home. In cities across the globe, bells tolled and jubilant people flooded the streets, singing and cheering. For those who had lost loved ones among the fourteen million dead, tears mingled with the rejoicing. For the first time in more than four years, not a shot was fired in anger on the Western Front.[5]

Two months before the conclusion of the final armistice, rumors began spreading that a negotiated settlement might soon bring a cessation to the war. That worried Bob Lovett. Writing from his St. Inglevert headquarters, he told his future wife that "should there be peace without complete and determined extermination [of the Hun], we would merely be handing a war over to our children and we would have to start them in military training at the age of five or thereabouts."[6] He believed that Germany, with fighting forces still holding captured ground in Belgium and France, did not understand it had been defeated. His prediction would prove almost exactly correct. But victory was declared. He and the rest of the boys would be going home.

Since being imprisoned, Di Gates had heard no news at all about the war. Four days after the Armistice, he and the other men in the camp were released from captivity. While he waited to be handed over to neutral diplomats from Switzerland for passage out of the chaotic land, in his excitement at getting out his first word to his friends since being captured, he dashed off a jovial postcard to Trubee from the prison camp. "This," he blithely declared, "is a great life." The war that had consumed his life and that of the other members of the Millionaires' Unit for two-and-a-half years was finally over. He was ready to move on. Before Di had been taken prisoner, Trubee had written to him suggesting that they return together to Yale after the war ended. With his duty in Europe now concluded, Di's first words to his friend were that he was "seriously considering your proposition of returning to college." They might be able to make it back to campus in time for the spring term.

"How about rooming together?" he asked.[7]

CHAPTER 27

Schoore, December 1918
This Long Separation

THE DAY AFTER THE ARMISTICE WAS SIGNED, AN ELATED CROCK INGALLS flew a DH–4 from Eastleigh over to France. After refueling, he took off and passed back and forth over large portions of Belgium. He flew across a landscape devastated almost beyond imagining. The warring armies that had swarmed over Europe in a series of vast destructive waves and then collided repeatedly along the Western Front during the past four years had left behind a blighted landscape littered with ruins and human remains, bereft of the rudiments of civilized life. Once-grand cities with their great Gothic cathedrals and markethouses were reduced to piles of rubble, entire villages had simply disappeared, and thousands of square miles of former farm fields and once-vast forests had become moonscapes of mud and shellholes, the unmarked cemeteries of millions of men. Just a few weeks earlier, Crock's life would have been in danger every instant that he flew over this same land. Death could have struck him from any angle, and he would have delivered death to all who dared challenge him. As he flew over the land freed of enemy fighters, he still felt jumpy and could not help scanning the sky for possible attack. "I couldn't get used to it," he wrote his father, "and seemed to imagine I heard a machine gun every now and then." He made a tourist flight over the same German aerodromes he had raided and the roads he had strafed. Abandoned and blackened German weapons and structures of war dotted the countryside. He felt like a conquerer. "Gosh, it was great."[1]

Word of Di Gates's whereabouts had finally arrived, to the profound relief of his unit mates. Still no word came from Kenney MacLeish. In London, Trubee Davison continued to direct the search for him. At his instigation, the Red Cross ran ads in newspapers throughout Great Britain seeking information about an "American Naval officer taken prisoner" in the vicinity of Leffinge. As the days and then weeks following the Armistice passed, hope that Kenney would return began to wane. The unit members in Europe helped to decommission bases and to fly their airplanes to depots for salvage, sale, or transport home. Then they followed, along with more than one million other American military personnel.

On the day after Christmas, 1918, a Belgian landowner, Alfred Rouse, returned to his devastated fields in Schoore, not far from the village of Dixmude. He walked about the ruins of the farm buildings and looked out over the frozen snow-dusted swamps that had formerly been his wheat fields. Walking behind the stables, he discovered the remains of a dead airman. It was Kenneth MacLeish.

His face, partially eaten by rats, was turned to the side. His flying helmet was still strapped to his head and his coat buttoned. Although badly decomposed, his body showed no signs of having been shot. He held a bloody handkerchief to his face.[2]

Rouse took a picture of the dead man and then collected MacLeish's few possessions. He purchased a plain casket and then buried MacLeish beneath a simple wooden cross on the spot where he found his body. He boxed up the effects and sent them off with a letter describing the conditions in which he discovered him to MacLeish's parents in Illinois, care of the American ambassador in Brussels.

Navy representatives who later spoke to Rouse and examined the body believed that MacLeish had walked away from his crash landing, but stopping to rest, may have died from internal injuries suffered in his crash or a gas attack from advancing British forces. In his weakened state, he also may have died from exposure in the frigid early winter weather. With the roads through the region badly damaged and the fields virtually impassible, his body had gone unnoticed except by rats. No trace could be found of his wrecked Camel, which may have sunk into the flooded land or been taken away by German troops withdrawing from the area.

In the post-war confusion, Rouse's package went astray. Not until late January 1919, two and a half months after the Armistice, did word of MacLeish's fate reach American military headquarters and, from there, his unit mates. A representative of No. 213 went to the site, as did Foster Rockwell. A more permanent marker was placed over MacLeish's grave.

As she had feared for so long, Priscilla Murdock lost the man she loved. On January 30, ironically the day she got definitive word of her fiancé's death, she also received a cable from Di Gates whose supposed loss Kenney had sought to avenge. "My own grief," the laconic Gates wrote her, "helps me to appreciate yours to some extent."[3]

Later that year, Kenneth MacLeish's sister, Ishbel, traveled to Philadelphia to christen a new navy destroyer, the *MacLeish*, in his memory. When news of Kenney's death reached his beloved older brother Archie, he renamed his newly born son Kenneth. The grief-stricken Priscilla Murdock would not marry for another six years. She kept Kenney's letters from the war for the rest of her life and passed them on to her children.

SECTION IV

Home

CHAPTER 28

1919 and After

The Decisive Power

DEMOBILIZED, THE SURVIVING MEMBERS OF THE MILLIONAIRES' UNIT back in the United States resumed their long-disrupted lives. Many went straight to work or graduate school, but several returned to New Haven and Yale. Among the hundreds of veterans who made their way back to campus— nearly a thousand undergraduates had departed for the war—Di Gates and Trubee Davison roomed together, as did Crock Ingalls and Harry Davison. They brought several souvenirs of war back with them. Along with the uniforms they wore in victory parades through downtown New Haven and the medals they had won, they carried home the broken propeller and bent machine gun recovered from Gates's downed SPAD. Gates had a clock made out of the propeller and installed his old gun on the wall of the Skull & Bones tomb where it remains today.[1]

They came back to a campus—an entire country—dramatically altered from the one they had left behind in spring 1917. The formerly largely rural nation had become far more industrialized, urbanized, and mobile. The Jazz Age world of fast music, cars, and women was dawning, and the young men, many now experienced in ways their predecessors never dreamed, wanted their place in it all. Those changes left their mark on Yale College as well. Yale had maintained a skeletal academic program and served as a military training center for the duration of the war. Attempts to resume the intellectually stultifying, socially stratified, and tradition-weighted pre-war campus life proved futile. Students complained about the tiresome droning of their professors, useless recitations, and hidebound social constraints they had docilely accepted in the past. "Restless, rowdy and dissatisfied," according to George Wilson Pierson, a student of the period and Yale historian, far more worldly and impatient to get on with life, the post-war students rebelled. As a result, "change was in everything."[2]

The university faced pressure from within and without to transform itself into a modern educational and scholarly institution, dynamic enough to ready its students for the competitive demands of modern economic life and a rapidly changing society. Echoing pre-war warnings about military weakness, alumni and student critics condemned Yale's "educational unpreparedness," and demanded reform.[3] There were even calls to drop the more than two-century-old requirements of mandatory Morning Prayer and proficiency in Latin for admission.

The cautious and conservative President Hadley admitted the time had come "for Yale to choose between its character as a national institution and its position as an upholder of the old classical traditions."[4] The choice was clear. Tradition-soaked Yale would have to modernize or become irrelevant. So, too, would its students and their expectations about campus life. Within three years, Dean of Freshmen Roswell P. Angier could write a previously inconceivable, peevish letter to the parents of prospective freshmen, insisting that, contrary to what they might expect, "the main purpose of a college is intellectual. . . . All else is secondary. . . . Other things than study have a great value. . . . But the chief job is study."[5] Nobody could have written that of the Yale of old.

When President Hadley announced his plans to retire in 1921, the university acknowledged that great changes were afoot. It cast its net wide for his successor and even considered such nontraditional candidates as Henry P. Davison. (Indicating just how much things had changed and how much more change Yale would undergo, the university trustees selected James Rowland Angell, a noted psychologist and educational reformer, to become the first Yale president without a Yale degree since the Reverend Thomas Clapp left the office in 1766.)[6] While the intimate cousinhood of the old Yale, drawn almost exclusively from the prep school-educated sons of Yale alumni, still retained its front seat at the college, the modern university—academically centered, priding itself on its advanced research, scholarly faculty, able teachers, and carefully selected and nurtured student body—was born. Planning and construction began for an entirely new campus consisting of the neo-Gothic and Georgian quadrangles that form the architectural identity of today's Yale. The modern Yale University would require many decades of change before it would come to resemble America more closely, but the inexorable transformation had begun.

Reformed or not, returning to Yale held no interest at all for Bob Lovett. Not bothering to complete his undergraduate degree program, in April 1919 he married his neighbor and confidante Adele Brown and went directly to Harvard Law School in the fall. When he found the arcane rules of legal reasoning unsuited to his more analytical temperament, he soon transferred to the business school. A year later, Trubee Davison wed Dorothy Peabody, daughter of the headmaster of Groton School, the prep school he had attended. Two years after that, when his father was suffering from a brain tumor and unable to attend the ceremony, Trubee gave away his sister Alice in marriage to Di Gates. Most members of the unit attended all three weddings. Soon after, unit patriarch Henry P. Davison died. The *New York Times* declared in a prominent, page one obituary that his "life story reads like fiction."[7] With Mrs. Davison living in the big brick Georgian main house at Peacock Point, Trubee and Dorothy built a large white clapboard house next to hers overlooking the Sound, while Di and his wife moved into a house of their own in the woods on the property.[8]

In the triumphant exultation of the immediate post-war years, the Millionaires' Unit fame did not die. In his 1920 Pulitzer Prize-winning history of the navy at war, *The Victory at Sea*, Navy Commander Rear Admiral Sims described the "romantic beginning" of American naval aviation, developing from "almost nothing" to a force of forty thousand men. He wrote, "The great aircraft force which was ultimately assembled in Europe had its beginnings in a small group of undergraduates at Yale University." He recalled his aide for aviation, Lieutenant-Commander W. Atlee Edwards, saying, "'I knew that whenever we had a member of that Yale Unit, everything was all right. Whenever the French and English asked us to send a couple of our crack men to reinforce a squadron, I would say, 'Let's get some of the Yale gang.' We never made a mistake when we did this.'"[9] Similarly, Hutch I. Cone, who headed naval aviation forces in Europe, credited the unit as the "nucleus" from which his air corps grew.[10]

Each year, Trubee Davison brought together his unit for a lavish reunion celebration in New York City. Sometimes they were joined by other aviation pioneers. The ill-fated encounters with the erratic Italian Capronis seemed to have been forgiven as army aviator Fiorello LaGuardia, now a popular New York mayor, attended as well. In 1925, with funds from the Davison family, a privately printed two-volume history and document compendium, *The First Yale Unit*, was distributed to libraries around the country. The unit worked in other ways to keep public awareness of its name. It helped that Henry Luce, a member of Skull & Bones and friend of classmates Harry Davison and David Ingalls, launched *Time* magazine a couple years after graduating Yale and found his friends' activities newsworthy.

Several unit members were not done flying and pioneering in aviation. The Roaring '20s loved speed, and the nation's infatuation with aviation blossomed.

Many once-insurmountable time and geographical barriers fell away, but nothing equaled the Western world's fascination with the ultimate dream of flying over the Atlantic. In 1919, the unit's first instructor, the ungovernable David McCulloch, now a career navy man, finally fulfilled his war-disrupted ambition to attempt the crossing. Trans-Oceanic's big Curtiss-built *America* flying yachts paved the way for the NC (Navy-Curtiss) flying boats. With John Towers, the officer who got the unit into the navy in the first seat, McCulloch won the coveted assignment to copilot the NC-3, the lead aircraft in a three-flying boat fleet. (A fourth machine started out but failed to reach the jumping-off point for the transatlantic flight.) Taking off from Newfoundland, the three Nancies, as they were called, set off on the 1,300-mile nonstop flight to the Azore Islands.

Only one aircraft, the NC-4, under the command of Lieutenant Commander Albert Cushing Read, the same man who had tested and awarded the unit members their navy wings in the summer of 1917, managed to complete the grueling all-air crossing to the Azores before continuing on to Lisbon—arriving on May 27, 1919, eight years before Charles Lindbergh's historic solo flight. Brought down by mechanical troubles two hundred miles short of their goal, Towers, McCulloch, and crew sailed the crippled NC-3 *backwards* the rest of the way over the open ocean to the Azores, arriving with one wing destroyed.[11] First in London and then at home, the Nancies' crews received a hero's welcome.

Military aviation was not the unit members' only aerial pursuit. Several worked in various guises in the rise of commercial aviation in the country. Juan Trippe, a member of a third Yale Unit that was eventually absorbed into regular navy training programs, worked closely with various other unit members as he built Pan American Airways into the world's largest passenger airline. Among his Yale colleagues, Di Gates served on the board of his company, and he served on the board of aircraft manufacturer Boeing as well. Trippe also employed David "Crock" Ingalls as a Pan Am vice president. Ingalls kept many aviation-related business interests and occasionally test-piloted aircraft for a high-performance airplane manufacturing company in which he invested.

Through his multimillion-dollar inheritance, Trubee Davison could afford to devote himself to public service. Not yet thirty, he was appointed by President Calvin Coolidge in 1925 to chair the prominent National Crime Commission formed to deal with the spreading wave of organized crime set off by Prohibition (for which Luce's *Time* magazine put him on its cover).[12] The next year he joined the Harding administration as the nation's first Assistant Secretary of War for Air. Despite his injury, he could still pilot an aircraft, and in his first act after being sworn in, he flew over Washington, D.C.[13] He returned frequently to Peacock Point to escape the pressures of Washington. Under the watchful eye of his mother, the estate continued to be the scene of numerous public events, with many notables passing through its gates, including the grateful King of Belgium and General Pershing. Charles Lindbergh came there to escape the crowds following his 1927 solo transatlantic flight, and he and his wife Anne Morrow Lindbergh visited Peacock Point regularly after that.

The MacLeish family understood that Kenneth had flown to a death they had dreaded but knew he was prepared to face. They collected the letters he had written to his family during the war into a privately printed edition titled simply *Kenneth*. His older brother, Archibald, felt the loss most keenly. He wrote several poems about Kenney during a distinguished career that won him three Pulitzer Prizes for poetry, a stint as Librarian of Congress, and a prestigious professorship at Harvard. In the years immediately following the war, his brother's death seemed to him a leap toward greatness and something to be celebrated as well as mourned. In a poem written soon after he learned of Kenney's death, he invoked religious symbolism and declaimed,

> *. . . in the rose that dies*
> *Something there is . . .*
> *Something that lives, that lives, that does endure.*[14]

The passing of time forced him to revisit what would endure of his beloved younger brother. Two days before the second anniversary of Kenney's death, he wrote to his mother about how "the current of time & change is bearing me away from the things he & I knew together, & gradually wearing out my memory of the tone of his voice & the way he had of laughing as though he were really glad & the carriage of his head & his smile." With the eventual complete loss of memory of these singular characteristics that had made his brother an individual, he wondered, "What will Kenney be to me then?"

With America's triumph in the war still filling the nation, and him, with pride, he believed with their disappearance his dead brother's existence would then become "truer" by becoming a symbol of an idea. "He belongs now & will belong more & more as time passes to the immortality of great ideas." Kenney, the funny, freewheeling-yet-earnest brother he had grown up with, was dead and would soon fade into memory's oblivion, but "the symbol of brave youth content to die for the battle's sake" had already won Kenney the "immortality" and the honor he had longed for. His brother would not "die so long as men believe in youth and the beauty of youth and the perfect generosity of youth's sacrifice."[15]

Within a few years, though, his view of his brother's sacrifice had changed. In pursuit of his literary ambitions, MacLeish moved to Paris. While there, he—like many writers of the age and others reflecting on the causes, costs, and accomplishments of the war—reached the bitter conclusion that the entire war had been "an awful, awful, failure. A hideous joke."[16] He visited Kenney's grave for the first time on May 31, 1924, to attend the dedication of the Flanders Fields American Military Cemetery at Waregem, Belgium, where his body had been reinterred. After placing a wreath at the simple white marble cross among a sea of crosses, he knelt and touched the sandy earth over the grave. He burst into tears. "I suddenly knew—it seemed for the first time—that he was dead," he wrote his sister, Ishbel. "I cried so that I could not stop."[17]

One of his most famous poems, the disquieting "Memorial Rain," dedicated to Kenneth, recounts that day at the cemetery. Its final lines read:

> *The earth relaxes, loosens; he is sleeping,*
> *He rests, he is quiet, he sleeps in a strange land.*

America, too, slowly began to rethink its romantic infatuation with the war, with aviation, and, as the dire effects of the Great Depression began to unfold, the exploits of the wealthy. Even some of the formerly well-to-do men from the Millionaires' Unit—many with families to support in the wake of the stock market collapse—struggled. Several complained to Davison about the lavish cost he asked them to pay for their annual reunions. Several stopped attending. As if to signal the changing fate of aviation and their own lives, Bart Read, younger brother of Curt who had died during the war, also fell to his death while flying outside New York City in 1931. Davison, who continued to serve as the civilian head of the army's air wing into President Herbert Hoover's administration, tried to maintain the nation's air strength, but as the country slipped deeper into economic crisis, many condemned aviation as a peacetime luxury. He was forced time and again to defend his already steeply slimmed air force budget against even deeper cuts.[18]

Living on an estate outside Cleveland, David Ingalls was spotted frequently overhead doing acrobatics in his latest airplane. He had bulked up his already considerable wealth by marrying Louise Harkness, heir to the Standard Oil fortune. He also tried to stave off federal cuts to military aviation after he went to work in Washington with Davison when President Herbert Hoover appointed him the nation's first Assistant Secretary of the Navy for Air. Upon his appointment, the buoyant assistant secretary told the *New York Times*, "The roaring of an airplane motor is jazz music to my ears. I believe that I would rather hold an aviation post than be President of the United States."[19] His ambitions, though, did include elective office. He and Davison, fiscally conservative Republicans, ran for political office, each winning seats in his state legislature. As unemployment rose and poverty spread, though, a blacklash ensued against the business-first policies of the Republicans. In 1932, Davison failed in a bid for governor of New York. In the same election cycle, Ingalls ran for the Ohio governorship. Gaining the nickname "Flying Ingalls" for piloting his own airplane to campaign stops around the state, he, too, lost.[20]

Davison withdrew from active politics and became president of the American Museum of Natural History in New York City. (In that post, he oversaw the museum's growth into the world's largest institution of its kind during a tenure that lasted until 1951. He then served as the first director of personnel for the Central Intelligence Agency and was also named a trustee of Yale University. He became a conduit for many Yale men joining the CIA.) Hoover offered Davison's old position in the War Department to his unit mate, the voluble debator John Vorys, but he declined. Espousing the isolationist spirit of the 1930s, he was more successful in his political aspirations and, toward the end of the decade, won election to the House of Representatives, where he served for twenty years.[21] The national love affair with aviation was largely over. After Ingalls and Davison left Washington, their military aviation posts remained vacant for the rest of the decade.

Di Gates and Bob Lovett managed to put their youthful conflicts behind them. They transferred their organizational and leadership skills and their many Yale and unit relationships to the business world. The two shared a room in New York City during the week as they worked their way into Wall Street. Both soared to swift success. Lovett became a partner at the venerable Brown Brothers, his wife's father's bank. In 1931, working alongside several Yale friends and fellow Bonesmen, including Prescott Bush and Roland and Averell Harriman, he helped oversee the merger of his father-in-law's bank into Brown Brothers Harriman & Company, the nation's largest private banking firm.[22] Among the numerous corporate and charitable boards Lovett sat on, he followed his father to become chairman of the Union Pacific Railroad. Gates quickly climbed the heights of the investment banking world, becoming president of New York Trust, at age thirty-three one of the youngest men to head a Wall Street bank since Henry P. Davison. He saw the bank through various mergers leading to its emergence as one of the nation's largest financial institutions, a predecessor to today's J. P. Morgan Chase & Company. He called on his old friends to help direct his bank. Prior to banking reform laws passed in

1935 that forbade interlocking corporate boards of directors, Harry Davison, a partner at J. P. Morgan & Company, and Lovett served on the board of Gates's New York Trust Bank. Gates in turn sat on the board of Union Pacific.

Wall Street, though, would soon give way to larger national needs. As Lovett had predicted in the closing months of the Great War, Germany had struggled for a period but was once again emerging as a threat to world peace. But in the economically trying times of the Depression, an inward-turned America had largely abandoned all but skeletal efforts at maintaining a war-capable air force. In May 1940, with war declared in Europe and Hitler on the brink of invading Holland, Belgium, and France, Lovett traveled on Brown Brothers Harriman business to the Continent. In Milan, he encountered a group of German airmen in a hotel bar. The drunken Luftwaffe officers boasted of the vast scope of Germany's air force and their country's plan "to give England a taste of frightfulness which will make what has gone before look like a light workout." War, Lovett realized, would soon sweep the world, and, like it or not, the United States would have its part to play again. And once again, he feared America was not prepared. Returning home, he set out on one of his regular national inspection tours of the Union Pacific rail lines. This time, with the Germans airmens' words ringing in his ears, he combined stops on the tour with visits to airplane contractors.[23]

As he suspected, America did not have the infrastructure it would need for a global confict, and the government was showing little leadership in the face of technologically advanced adversaries with many years' headstart in industrial build-up. He knew what it was like to try to win a war without the necessary equipment. With the same logic he used to convince the military to embark on its first strategic bombing campaign, he drafted a confidential report summarizing his findings about the capabilities of American aircraft manufacturers, and circulated it among friends in Washington. "The government," he warned, "will not get the plane production being talked about from present or planned plants." He found that American airplane manufacturers were custom builders. Gearing up small-scale craft shops to produce the enormous numbers of modern fighters and heavy bombers needed in an air war would not be feasible. "This is a quantitative war," he concluded. "The airplane industry has, so far, been qualitative."[24] He urged an alternative course: development of assembly line processes brought over from the automotive industry.

His report eventually found its way into the hands of Secretary of War Henry Lewis Stimson. The aging former Wall Street lawyer, fellow Yale graduate, and Bonesman had served in the cabinets of Democratic and Republican administrations stretching back to William Howard Taft. He convinced Lovett to become his Assistant Secretary of War for Air. Writing a report was one thing. Now he would have responsibility for building the air force, tackling America's production lag, and carrying out the plans he had outlined in his report. Lovett would need plenty of help. He soon drew Di Gates to Washington, where he became Lovett's counterpart as Undersecretary of the Navy for Air. The old unit mates took command of the skies. They began to build a modern airpower.

If America was to fight, it would need trained men to fly those airplanes. Now President Franklin Delano Roosevelt, the same former assistant secretary of the navy who had helped the eager young Yale students pursue their flying ambitions, had begun to arouse an isolationist nation for the likely possibility of war. That campaign was carried out on many fronts, not just weapons production but propaganda. Almost a year before the attack on Pearl Harbor, the army sponsored "Wings Over America," a popular series of stirring NBC radio network programs dramatizing the rise of aviation. In three consecutive weekly half-hour episodes targeted largely at young men, the radio program retold the now dimly remembered story of the First Yale Unit to huge national radio audiences. Several unit members spoke on the live broadcasts, while actors took the parts of others in the unit to dramatize its most decisive and heroic moments.[25]

Large numbers of young men who listened in were inspired to join the air forces. Among those who knew the story of the unit best was a young future U.S. president, George H. W. Bush. Fresh out of Andover Academy, the eighteen-year-old son of Prescott Bush knew about the unit in the First World War through his father's close friends, particularly Robert Lovett and Trubee Davison. "The Yale Unit," he said, "was a sort of inspiration to me and to other aspiring naval aviators." Roused by their "courage and determination," the young Bush graduated prep school and immediately signed up to become a naval aviator.[26]

Many other unit members also worked in support of the military or returned to active duty. Among them, Ingalls at first ran Pan Am's military ferrying operations and then rejoined the navy. A rear-admiral, he risked his life surveying the Pacific Islands as possible bases for the Naval Air Transport supply routes and then designed the logistical plans for the system. He later took command of the vital Pearl Harbor Naval Air Station. Erl Gould also went on active duty, eventually becoming a rear admiral. As he had at Key West, he headed a training unit and then served as island commander of the important Tarawa Atoll in the Pacific.

Trubee Davison also rejoined the military, this time the army. Eventually made a brigadier general, he served as assistant chief of staff of the Army Air Corps in charge of personnel. His office was right down the hall from Lovett's in Washington. In the Navy Department, Gates kept a telephone on his desk that was, he said, "almost a private wire" among the three men.[27] Their shared experiences in building a fighting force in the previous war taught them much that they now applied to knocking down the Axis foes. In a 1942 interview, Lovett described his frustrations as a young air crewman on the Spider Web patrols over the North Sea, "I got tired of chasing submarines all over hell." At the time, he said "that the way to get 'em was to pound their bases from the air until reduced." His experiences on missions over the U-boat pens had taught him that, "The success of the use of this weapon depends on its employment en masse, continuously and aggressively."[28] Nothing had changed. "That's what we've got to do now."[29]

Lovett and his inexperienced colleagues at the Northern Bombing Group had struggled to build America's first bomber force and never attained the means to carry through his strategy. Although America failed to deliver the deathblow from the air in World War I, Gates, Davison, Ingalls, and Lovett would not let that recur. American pilots in World War II would fly superb machines and have more than enough of them to win decisively. "Air power alone will not win the war, but," Lovett insisted, "the war cannot be won without it."[30]

As part of that victorious effort, he made his First War dream a reality by establishing an independent Army Air Corps, leading to the post-war creation of the Air Force. By 1942, the bombers were flying in overwhelming numbers into the ports and manufacturing and munition centers of the Axis forces, just as he had planned in the previous war. Before the war was won, every Air Corps commander knew his mantra by heart: "Keep it incessant!"

He gave them the tools they needed. In 1938, the Army Air Corps possessed 1,773 airplanes and trained 500 pilots. Qualitatively and quantitatively, when the attack came at Pearl Harbor at the end of 1941, the United States possessed the weakest air force of any warring power. Two years later, the opposite was true. The United States dominated the skies. Its factories turned out 8,000 airplanes each month. In less than four years after Pearl Harbor, the United States produced nearly 300,000 aircraft—a number far beyond its enemies' totals and of a quality that stood up to every test.[31] The navy, too, had the aerial firepower it needed. Gates directed the build up of the navy's air corps from a fleet of seven aircraft carriers and 5,200 airplanes at the start of the war to more than 100 carriers for 70,000 airplanes.

In awarding Lovett the Distinguished Service Medal in September 1945, President Truman called him "the eyes, ears, and hands of the Secretary of War in respect to the growth of that enormous American air power which has astonished the world and played such a large part in bringing the war to a speedy and successful conclusion." Truman also cited Gates for building the "air-sea power which ultimately eliminated the submarine menace in the Atlantic, and which, spearheading the Allied Offensive across the Pacific, blasted and destroyed the enemy coastal defenses in advance of every amphibious landing and provided decisive support during major naval engagements with the Japanese fleet."[32] Applying what they had learned as young flyers on Long Island and Palm Beach, and in England and France in 1917 and 1918, these men made the greatness of the "Greatest Generation" possible.

By 1948, Lovett had moved to the State Department where, as undersecretary under General George C. Marshall, he was dubbed one of the so-called "Wise Men" of the foreign policy "Establishment," formulating Cold War strategy along with his old Yale friends Dean Acheson and Averell Harriman and a group of other well-to-do Ivy Leaguers. When Stalin's Soviet Union forces blockaded Berlin in April, many voices in the Truman Administration called for abandonment of the encircled city; others prepared for open warfare. The world again stood at the brink of war in Europe, this time with use of atomic bombs likely. Lovett, acting Secretary of State during the crisis while Marshall was traveling, sought a third route. The airman among the federal government leaders knew about supply logistics and suspected that the Air Force could feed the starving city by air. He explored the practicality of an airlift and convinced a reluctant Air Force to take on the task. Within days, supply-filled American transports began landing at Berlin's Templehof Airport. The flights were soon arriving at the rate of more than one every four minutes over the course of the next several months, enough to keep the city from starving or freezing.[33] The Soviet Union and the United States stepped back from open war.

Soon after that Lovett returned to Wall Street, but two years later General Marshall, now Secretary of Defense, called him back as his deputy. The United States was again at war, this time in Korea. Lovett continued to pursue dominance of the skies as the spearhead of the world's most powerful military. When Marshall retired in 1951, he succeeded him as Secretary of Defense.[34] With the threat of nuclear warfare now a constant, Lovett developed numerous programs to ensure continued American dominance of the world's skies. "We tried weakness," he explained wryly. "It didn't work. As a result of aircraft, electronics and other forms of communication which annihilate distance, the oceans which once protected us no longer provide defense. Our task is to get ourselves geared to these realities." He had concluded: "There is no other way but strength."[35]

The consummate Washington and Wall Street insider, at the end of the Truman Administration, in 1953, he returned to Brown Brothers Harriman for good. In 1960, newly elected President John F. Kennedy so coveted the elder statesman's advice—despite his having voted for his opponent—that he purportedly asked him to join his Cabinet as Secretary of State, Defense, or Treasury, whichever he preferred. However, his lifelong stomach ailments tormenting him, Lovett declined the offer. "My bearings are burnt out," he told the young president.[36] He did return to the White House in response to Kennedy's urgent request two years later after the United States discovered the Soviet Union had installed missiles with nuclear warheads in Cuba. Several military advisors urged immediate airstrikes on the missile sites and preparation for full-scale war. The old airman again sought a third way. He advised Kennedy to avoid so-called "surgical" attacks against small concealed targets. He believed airpower could only be effective in sustained bombing operations and taking such a "bloodthirsty step first" would increase the level of violence swiftly without a predictable outcome. Instead, he suggested a U.S. blockade of Cuba. Kennedy accepted the advice, and within less than two weeks the Soviets agreed to remove the missiles.[37]

Back home in New York, Lovett remained deeply proud of his naval aviation service. Still given to driving at speeds he had once flown, he had a special license tag made for his car, number "66," his Naval Aviator number.[38]

On July 1, 1966, the navy marked the fiftieth anniversary of the founding of the Navy Air Reserve with a celebration that included a gathering of the surviving members of the Millionaires' Unit and the Second Yale Unit at Peacock Point. Half a century had passed since the men, now elder grandfathers in their seventies, had come together as boys to learn how to fly. Beneath a clear sky with no ceiling and unlimited visibility, they sat out on the same breezy bluff overlooking the Long Island Sound where they had started out on their flying adventure. Like the men, Peacock Point had changed. Trubee Davison's mother had died four years earlier at age ninety, and the big brick Georgian mansion where the unit had spent its first idyllic summer had been torn down. Several members of the group had also died over the years, including Trubee's younger brother Harry. And the long years of pain since the crash that broke his back in 1917 had not been easy for Trubee. He was now wheelchair-bound. But with his protruding lower lip and crease over the thick bridge of his nose, he still had the pugnacious demeanor of a young fighter.

Out on the lawn, the men gathered and spoke of the days long ago. A gray-haired David Ingalls, still slender and dapper, still clenching his pipe in his teeth, had flown in for the event in his own seaplane. He stood with the tiny Shorty Smith and recounted for their wives the day Shorty had been flying at Gosport when a loose strap had caught his stick while he was looping the loop, and, unable to control the aircraft, he had nearly crashed at the end of a slow progression of climbs and stalls. Ingalls coughed in laughter at the memory of how Shorty had laughed so uncontrollably afterward and could never fly again without getting sick and how nobody wanted to fly with him anymore after that.

Di Gates, heavyset and wearing thick glasses, sat quietly next to Trubee. He called out the roll from memory. "Ames, Beach, Brown, Brush, Coombe. . . ." Without hesitation or stumble, he named all twenty-eight men on the unit roster, just as he had done each morning in Palm Beach and Huntington. "Yes," he remembered of their first notions about taking to the air, "we all wanted to fly and that we did."

A reporter asked Bob Lovett what motivated the young men to undertake such a dangerous adventure. Puffy-eyed, bald, and skeletally thin as ever within his custom tailored suit, Lovett responded in his quiet patrician's drawl. "You could have," he recalled, "the satisfaction of loyalty, of service, of doing something you believed in with a group of friends that you loved and respected. That's what kept us going. No question."

The men and their families sat out on the lawn while Vice Admiral Paul Ramsey, then Deputy Chief of Naval Operations for Air, recalled for them that Trubee Davison had been denied his navy aviator's Wings half a century ago. He then pinned wings to Davison's lapels while those on hand stood to applaud. As they admired the Wings of Gold, the festive group looked up to see six fighter jets of the Navy Blue Angels flying team releasing red, white, and blue contrails roar by in tight formation overhead. Davison remarked in wonder, "If anyone had told me or my classmates that aircraft would fly faster than the speed of sound, we would have locked them up."

As they watched the jets fly down the Sound, more than a few of the elderly men on hand would have liked to have been in the cockpit flying one of those birds.[39]

That was to be the last full-scale reunion of the flyers. The aging men who had once strayed so far stayed, for the most part, close to home after that. Although Trubee Davison could not travel much, he kept close track of his remaining friends from the unit until he died at his Peacock Point home in 1974, at age seventy-eight. Two years later, his friend for life, Di Gates, died nearby at his Peacock Point house. David Ingalls, the "Baby Daredevil," never lost his love of flying. He continued to fly into his last years. He and his family gave Yale University the money to build a hockey rink named for him and his son. He was eighty-six in 1985 when he died at his home outside Cleveland. Despite his lifelong medical complaints, Bob Lovett remained sharp and active into his tenth decade. He died at his home a short drive from Peacock Point on Long Island in 1986. He was ninety years old. A few years later, Yale University created a professorship in military history in his honor. John Farwell III, the myopic flyer who nearly knocked over a petty officer while landing his flying boat, was the oldest surviving member of the Millionaires' Unit. He worked in his Chicago real estate development business into his nineties. He was ninety-seven years old when he died in 1992.

At Yale there is a circular rotunda between Woolsey Hall and the Commons where the young men had danced the night away in 1917 during their gala Junior Prom under the watchful eye of floor manager Bob Lovett. Covering nearly every inch of wall space in a large curving foyer to that rotunda are the inscribed names of Yale students, faculty, and alumni who have died in American wars. Among the names are Albert Sturtevant, Curtis Read, Kenneth MacLeish, and the 221 others who fell in World War I.

New Haven, 2006

About a decade ago, I wrote an article about Yale Aviation, the heir to the 1916–1917 Yale Aero Club, the campus organization that became the First Yale Unit. It was through the members of the modern incarnation of the group that I learned about their illustrious predecessors. The current club was founded by Frederick W. Smith, a member of Skull & Bones, Class of 1966, who, after Yale, flew as a marine pilot in the Vietnam War and then went on to found FedEx. His classmate and fellow Bonesman, John F. Kerry, a future U.S. senator and presidential candidate, learned to fly with the club. They were both close friends with another Bonesman in their class, Richard W. Pershing, grandson of John J. Pershing, the general in command of all U.S. forces in Europe during World War I. Pershing followed his grandfather into the army and was killed in combat. For the article, I spoke with an Israeli student in the flying club who planned to return home after Yale to enter his nation's air force. I did not meet any Americans who envisioned a similar path after graduation. Even today, in a time of war, a Yale student who would contemplate entering the military is rare indeed.

Yale, along with every other elite institution of higher education, has changed dramatically since the days of the Yale Aero Club. A walk through the Yale campus reveals many differences. Although the buildings that form the Old Campus quadrangle remain much the same, many other buildings where past students lived and studied are long gone. The former hodgepodge of heavy Victorian buildings has been largely replaced by an artfully planned, graceful, and handsomely detailed neo-Gothic, Georgian, and modern campus. The national spotlight on sports has shifted off Yale. Harvard and Yale still meet at the Yale Bowl for their most important football game of the year, but anyone who wants a ticket can walk up on game day and get a good seat. As they have since 1852,

Yale and Harvard crew teams face off each June, racing the same four-mile course in New London covered by the teams in 1916, but no horn-tooting and cannon-firing yachts line the course, nor do observation trains filled with thousands of cheering spectators chug alongside the eights as they row. Parents and alumni, numbering a few hundred, wait at the finish to applaud the exhausted oarsmen. Morning Chapel is long a thing of the past, but President Hadley got his wish: those who achieve in the classroom today enjoy a respect every bit the equal of those who lead on the athletic field and in campus organizations.

Most dramatic of all changes are the students themselves. The cousinhood of pre-World War I Yale would not recognize the faces on today's campus that welcomes women, people of different religions, colors, and nationalities. Extracurricular activities continue to be important in their lives, but the striving for social rewards has moved into a completely different orbit. The secret society tombs still dot the New Haven streetscape, but a tap carries little prestige. Tap Day attracts scant interest, even on campus. The most esteemed rewards for "sand" at Yale today, instead, are measured by post-graduate scholarships, admission to elite graduate schools, or employment offers from leading financial firms.

One important aspect of Yale and other elite colleges that has not changed is their preparation of students for leadership in nearly all fields. Although the family background of many students has changed, today's students still share the striving for success, prestige, and power that marked the lives of Yale students of the past. From the board rooms to the foundations, from the U.S. Congress to the movie studios, much of America's—and increasingly other nations'—leadership still emerges from many of the same schools as it has for the past century. In the last two races for the U.S. presidency, five of the six competing major party running mates attended either Yale or Harvard—four of the five went to Yale. In the 2000 presidential race, both the Democratic and the Republican candidates had graduated from Yale within two years of each other, and both were members of Skull & Bones. Only in one major area do the nation's most prestigious and competitive academic centers no longer lead—the military. Both presidential candidates served during the Vietnam War, one in active combat duty, one in the Air National Guard. John F. Kerry and George W. Bush each sent a child to Yale, neither of whom served in the military. They are in no way atypical.

Few students or recent alumni at Yale, or most other elite colleges, serve in the military any longer. In 1960, a peacetime era with a low-level military conscription, twenty percent of Yale graduates planned to enter the military after graduation. Since the end of the draft and the forced departure of the Reserved

Officers Training Corps from the Yale campus following protests against the Vietnam War in the early 1970s, most years one percent or less of each graduating class has gone into the military.[1] Most of America's privileged families no longer expect their children to serve in the world's only superpower's military. The rare wealthy family's child who chooses military service after attending Yale or Harvard provokes bewildered headshaking no different than would a married man who opted to enter the priesthood. While many of these young people will one day become national and international leaders and some may emerge as decision-makers responsible for the military, very few will have experienced training or battle. In this, perhaps above all other changes to campus life, the members of the Yale First Unit would not recognize today's students as their successors.

In 1927, outside Commons, Yale erected a classical stone colonnade over which are listed the locations of the major U.S. combat engagements of World War I; a memorial cenotaph completes the monument to the war dead. Few students stop to read the inscription reminding them of "the men of Yale who true to her traditions gave their lives that freedom might not perish from the earth." If you walk from there through the large doors leading into the curving rotunda foyer to Commons and Woolsey Hall, you can read the 1,020 inscribed names of the Yale dead who have fallen in every U.S. war since the Revolution.

No more names have been added since the Vietnam War. Not for lack of wars.

Notes

Unless otherwise indicated, all documentary materials cited come from the F. Trubee Davison Papers, Manuscripts, and Archives, Yale University Library, quoted by permission of Daniel Davison and the Davison family. Robert A. Lovett letters to Adele Q. Brown come from the Estate of Adele Brown Lovett and Robert A. Lovett, and are quoted by permission of their families. David S. Ingalls's diary and letters are from his archives and are quoted by permission of Barbara Brown. Kenneth MacLeish and other MacLeish family letters are quoted by permission of William MacLeish. Many of the documents cited are typescripts, handwritten notes, or newspaper clippings and do not have source information, dates, or page numbers.

Introduction

1. Thucydides, *The History of the Peloponnesian War*, 2.43.6, trans. Richard Livingstone, (London: Oxford University Press, 1943), 116.

Prologue

1. Description of typical takeoff from Denis Winter, *The First of the Few: Fighter Pilots of the First World War* (Athens, GA: The University of Georgia Press, 1983), 91–92; and interview with Chad Willey, at Old Rhinebeck Aerodrome, September 22, 2004.

2. Kenneth MacLeish letter to Priscilla Murdock, October 11, 1918, quoted in Geoffrey L. Rossano ed., *The Price of Honor: The World War One Letters of Naval Aviator Kenneth MacLeish* (Annapolis: Naval Institute Press, 1991), 226; hereafter referred to as Rossano.

3. Ibid., Letter to Bruce, Elizabeth, Jean, and Hugh MacLeish, April 5, 1918, 133.

4. Ibid., Letter to Murdock, October 8, 1918, 223.

Chapter 1

1. On Morning Chapel during the period, see Wilmarth Sheldon Lewis, *One Man's Education* (New York, Alfred A. Knopf, 1968), 97.

2. Quoted in Brooks Mather Kelley, *Yale: A History* (New Haven, CT: Yale University Press, 1974), 308.

3. Quoted in "Crime Chairman," *Time* magazine, August 24, 1925, 5–6.

4. Quoted in Thomas C. Mendenhall, *The Harvard-Yale Boat Race, 1852–1924, and the Coming of Sport to the American College* (Mystic, CT: Mystic Seaport Museum, 1993), 183.

5. Ralph D. Paine, *Sons of Eli* (New York: Charles Scribner's Sons, 1917), 10.

6. Lewis, *One Man's Education*, 100.

7. *Buildings and Grounds of Yale University* (New Haven: Yale University Printing Service: 1979), 12.

8. Interview with Daniel Davison, November 8, 2004.

9. William H. MacLeish, *Uphill with Archie: A Son's Journey* (New York: Simon & Schuster, 2001), 39; Rossano, 93.

10. *Harvard Alumni Bulletin*, April 1, 1919, 55.

11. Ralph D. Paine, *The First Yale Unit: A Story of Naval Aviation, 1916–1919*, vol. 2 (Cambridge: Riverside Press, 1925), 86.

CHAPTER 2

1. *SPS Record 1915–1916*, 111, 118; *Horae Scholasticae*, Jan. 29, 1916, 109–110.

2. *Time* magazine, March 2, 1931, cover, 15–16.

3. Henry Seidel Canby, *Alma Mater: the Gothic Age of the American College* (New York: Farrar & Rinehart, 1936), 37–38.

4. Ibid., 34.

5. Quoted in Kelley, 313.

6. Lewis, *One Man's Education*, 102.

7. *New York Times*, June 23, 1915, 6.

8. Sheffield students like Al Sturtevant had their own senior societies, such as St. Anthony's Hall and Berzelius, his society.

9. Walter Isaacson and Evan Thomas, *The Wise Men: Six Friends and the World They Made* (New York: Simon & Schuster, Touchtone Edition, 1988), 82.

10. Lewis, *One Man's Education*, 112.

11. Quoted in *Yale Alumni Magazine*, March 2001, 53.

12. E. Roland Harriman, *I Reminisce* (Garden City, NY: Doubleday & Company, 1975), 42–43.

13. *New York Herald*, April 13, 1890.

14. From an unidentified newspaper in 1916 section of a crew scrapbook, Yale Athletics Archives.

15. Undated article in 1916 crew scrapbook, Yale Athletics Archives.

16. The *Utah* was sunk in the Pearl Harbor attack, December 7, 1941.

17. Ralph D. Paine, *The Twisted Skein* (New York: Charles Scribner's Sons, 1915), 288.

18. Typescript of dinner remarks at annual reunion dinner, Brook Club, June 14, 1924; hereafter referred to as Reunion Dinner typescript.

19. Unidentified source, *Crew Scapbook*, 1916–1921, microfilm.

CHAPTER 3

1. Friedrich Katz, *The Life and Times of Pancho Villa* (Palo Alto: Stanford University Press, 1998).

2. Theodore Roosevelt, *America and the World War* (New York: Charles Scribner's Sons, 1915), 25–26.

3. *Yale Daily News*, June 3, 1916, 2.

4. Stephen Vincent Benét, *The Beginning of Wisdom* (New York: Henry Holt and Company, 1921) 97.

5. John. G. W. Husted, "Freshman Year History of the Class," in *History of the Class of 1920* (New Haven), 7.

6. Benét, *The Beginning of Wisdom*, 97.

7. *Class History, 1916*, Sheffield Scientific School, vol. 1, 419.

8. *New York Times*, May 23, 1915, 3.

9. Ibid., March 14, 1915, 12.

10. *New Haven Journal-Courier*, June 20, 1916, 1.

11. *Yale Daily News*, June 2, 1916, vol. 34, no. 191; *New Haven Evening Register*, June 2, 1916.

12. *New York Tribune*, June 21, 1916, 11.

13. Ibid., June 22, 1916, 7.

14. Paul Jayson, "The First Yale Unit," from Adrian O. Van Wyen, *Naval Aviation in World War I* (Washington, DC: Chief of Naval Operations, 1969), 22.

15. Reunion Dinner typescript, 14.

16. Letter to Trubee Davison, January 24, 1916.

17. *New York Times*, July 29, 1917, 1.

18. On the Lafayette Escadrille, Philip M. Flanner, *The Vivid Air: The Lafayette Escadrille* (Athens: University of Georgia Press, 1981).

19. "50 Years After," *CBS News*, video, 1966.

20. Reunion Dinner typescript, 14; Paine, *The First Yale Unit*, Vol. 1, 10.

21. Jonathan Fanton, *Robert A. Lovett: The War Years* (Dissertation: Yale University, Department of History, 1978), 4; Mrs. Robert S. (Dorothy) Lovett II, interview by Marc Wortman, December 27, 2005; Letter to "My Dear Son," circa 1917.

22. Isaacson and Thomas, *The Wise Men*, 63–64, 90; Lewis, *One Man's Education*, 100; Fanton, *Robert A. Lovett*, 6.

23. Harriman, *I Reminisce*, 45.

24. Reunion Dinner typescript, 14.

25. Ames Report on World War I Experiences, typescript.

26. John M. Vorys testimonial, typescript.

27. Reunion Dinner typescript, 15.

28. *New York Times*, August 24, 1916, 1.

29. Ibid.; "Wings Over America: The Yale Unit," January 5, 1941, NBC radio broadcast.

30. *New Haven Journal-Courier*, June 20, 1916, 20.

31. Ibid., June 21, 1916, 6.

32. Ibid., June 23, 1916, 6.

33. *New York Tribune*, June 23, 1916, 7.

34. *New York Times*, June 23, 1916, 12.

35. *New Haven Journal-Courier*, June 23, 1916, 6.

36. Ibid.

37. Ibid.

38. *Harvard Alumni Bulletin*, July 1, 1916, 740–741.

39. *New Haven Journal-Courier*, June 24, 1916, 1.

40. *New York Times*, June 23, 1916, 12.

41. Martin Gilbert, *The First World War: A Complete History* (New York: Henry Holt and Company, 1994), 258–260.

42. Stephen Budiansky, *Air Power: The Men, Machines, and Ideas that Revolutionized War, from Kitty Hawk to Gulf War II* (New York: Viking Penguin, 2004), 68.

CHAPTER 4

1. Budiansky, *Air Power*, 3–54.
2. W. Atlee Edwards, "The U.S. Naval Air Force in Action 1917–18," *United States Naval Institute Proceedings*, vol. 48, no. 11, November 1922, 1882.
3. Quoted in A. A. Hoehling, *The Fierce Lambs* (Boston: Little, Brown & Company, 1960), 37.
4. "Story of F. Trubee Davison Taken at Interview by John Farrar, November 5, 1919," typescript.
5. Quoted in Achibald D. Turnbull and Clifford L. Lord, *History of United States Naval Aviation* (New Haven: Yale University Press, 1949), 93.
6. Noel C. Shirley, *United States Naval Aviation, 1910–1918* (Atglen, PA: Schiffer Military History, 2000), 21.
7. Ibid., 20.
8. *New York Times*, December 26, 1916, 13.
9. Ibid., and undated article, *Leslie's Weekly*.
10. Reunion Dinner typescript, 22.
11. "Story of F. Trubee Davison Taken at Interview by John Farrar, November 5, 1919," typescript.
12. *New York Times*, August 24, 1916, 1.
13. "Wings Over America: The Yale Unit," January 5, 1941, NBC radio broadcast.
14. Ibid.
15. *New York Times*, August 24, 1916, 1.
16. Details of Davison's life from Thomas W. Lamont, *Henry P. Davison: The Record of a Useful Life* (New York: Harper & Brothers Publishers, 1933), 44; B. C. Forbes, *The Men Who Are Making America* (New York: B. C. Forbes Publishing Company, 1917), 44–52; Henry Davison's obituary in the *New York Times*, May 7, 1922, 22.
17. On the panic of 1907 and Davison's role, see Jean Strouse, *Morgan: American Financier* (New York: Random House, 1999), 573–596.
18. Lamont, *Henry P. Davison*, 232.
19. Forbes, *The Men Who Are Making America*, 50.
20. Quoted in Ron Chernow, *The House of Morgan: An American Banking Dynasty and the Rise of Modern Finance* (New York: Atlantic Monthly Press, 1990), 217.
21. On Harry Davison's safari, see Lamont, *Henry P. Davison*, Appendix A.
22. Forbes, *The Men Who Are Making America*, 44–52.
23. Daniel P. Davison, "The First Yale Unit," *Over the Front*, vol. 12, no. 3, fall 1997, 265–266.
24. Chernow, *The House of Morgan*, 188.
25. *New York Times*, May 7, 1922, 22.
26. Davison interview with Farrar.
27. *New York Times*, August 24, 1916, 1.
28. Paine, *The First Yale Unit*, vol. 1, 23.

CHAPTER 5

1. Paine, *The First Yale Unit*, vol. 1, 28.
2. Henry Woodhouse letter to Josephus Daniels, July 6, 1916.
3. Josephus Daniels letter to F. Trubee Davison, July 14, 1916.
4. "Wings Over America: The Yale Unit," January 12, 1941, NBC radio broadcast.
5. Paine, *The First Yale Unit*, vol. 1, 26.

6. Undated letter, Robert E. Peary to Henry Woodhouse.

7. Brown Interview typescript, undated.

8. Ames Interview, undated.

9. Davison interview with Farrar.

10. *Curtiss* catalogue (Buffalo: Curtiss Aeroplane Company, 1917), 6.

11. Lee Kennett, *The First Air War: 1914–1918* (New York: The Free Press, 1991), 115.

12. Brown Interview typescript, undated.

13. On learning to fly, see Wolfgang Langewiesche, *Stick and Rudder: An Explanation of the Art of Flying* (New York: McGraw-Hill Book Company, 1972).

14. Chad Willey, interview by Marc Wortman, at the Old Rhinebeck Aerodrome, September 22, 2004.

15. John Farwell Interview typescript, undated.

16. Allan Ames Interview typescript, undated.

17. *New York Times*, August 24, 1916, 1.

18. "Twelve Men with Wings," *Time* magazine, vol. 38, no. 10, September 8, 1941, 28.

19. Allan Ames interview, undated.

20. Davison interview with Farrar.

21. Newsprint article. Source not identified.

22. *New York Times*, August 24, 1916.

23. "Wings Over America: The Yale Unit," January 5, 1941, NBC radio broadcast.

24. Paine, *The First Yale Unit*, vol. 1, 42.

25. *New York World*, undated article.

26. Reunion Dinner typescript, 25.

27. Davison interview with Farrar.

28. Reunion Dinner typescript, 20.

29. Paine, *The First Yale Unit*, vol. 1, 48.

30. *Chicago Sun-Times*, April 17, 1966, 7.

31. Undated and unidentified newspaper article, "Davison Plane in 1,000-Foot Drop," Adele Q. Brown scrapbook; Davison interview with John Farrar.

32. Alan R. Hawley letter to Trubee Davison, September 22, 1916.

33. *Flying* magazine, October 1916, 378.

34. *Aerial Age Weekly*, September 18, 1916, 9.

35. Yates Stirling, Jr., letter to Eugene S. Willard, Aero Club, October 7, 1916.

CHAPTER 6

1. F. S. Blackall, Jr., *The Yale Courant*, October 1916, vol. 53, no. 1, 38.

2. *Yale Daily News*, "A Notable Record," October 16, 1916, 1.

3. *Yale Daily News*, November 14, 1916, 1.

4. Reunion Dinner typescript, 32.

5. Davison interview with Farrar.

6. Gilbert, *The First World War*, 291–292.

7. Davison interview with Farrar.

8. *Yale Daily News*, January 13, 1917, 1.

9. F. T. Davison, "A Proposal to Memorialize the First Yale Unit," July 24, 1974, 1–4.

10. Transcript, "Oral History Interview with David S. Ingalls by Raymond Henle, November 5, 1969" (Stanford, California, and West Branch, Iowa: Herbert Hoover Presidential Library and the Hoover Institution on War, Revolution and Peace, 1971), 8.

11. Paine, *The First Yale Unit*, vol. 1, 71.

12. Alistair Horne, *The Price of Glory: Verdun 1916* (London: Penguin Books, 1993), 210.

13. *Yale Daily News*, November 29, 1916, 1.

14. Noel Shirley, ed., "Wartime Memoirs of John Jay Schieffelin," *Over the Front*, vol. 9, no. 2, Summer 1994, 99.

15. See John Jay Schieffelin, "The Second Yale Naval Aviation Unit," *Yale in the World War* (New Haven, CT: Yale University Press, 1925), 449–453; Schieffelin, "The Second Yale Unit," *Naval Aviation News*, January 1968, 14–17.

16. *New Haven Evening Register*, November 25, 1916, 1.

17. *New York Times*, November 25, 1916, 10.

18. *New Haven Register*, November 23, 1916, 1.

19. Quoted in Thomas G. Bergin, *The Game: The Harvard-Yale Football Rivalry, 1875–1983* (New Haven: Yale University Press, 1984), 122.

20. *New York Times*, November 25, 1916, 10.

21. Bergin, 122–123.

22. *New York Times*, November 25, 1916, 10.

23. Quoted in *Yale Daily News*, November 27, 1916, 1.

24. *Yale Daily News*, December 7, 1916, 1.

25. Paine, *The First Yale Unit*, vol. 1, 64.

26. Davison interview with Farrar.

27. Archibald MacLeish, ed., *Martha Hillard MacLeish* (Chicago: Privately Printed, 1949), 56.

28. William H. MacLeish, *Uphill with Archie*, 28–32.

29. Rossano, *The Price of Honor*. Kenneth MacLeish letter to his mother and father, March 1917, 9; on this letter, see Linda R. Robertson, *The Dream of Civilized Warfare: World War I Flying Aces and the American Imagination* (Minneapolis: University of Minnesota Press, 2003), 154–155.

CHAPTER 7

1. Quoted in Hoehling, *Fierce Lambs*, 20.

2. Gilbert, *The First World War*, 306.

3. *Yale Daily News*, January 19, 1917, 1.

4. *Class History 1916*, Sheffield Scientific School, vol. 1, New Haven, 31–32.

5. Lewis, *One Man's Education*, 115.

6. On Porter's Yale years, see William McBrien, *Cole Porter: A Biography* (New York: Random House, 1998), 34–52.

7. *Yale Alumni Weekly*, January 21, 1916, 537, and February 11, 1916, 619.

8. *New York Times*, February 7, 1917, 13; undated newspaper article, Adele Q. Brown scrapbook.

9. Walter Camp, "A Junior Promenade," *Outing for February*, undated, 400.

10. Davison interview with Farrar.

11. *Yale Daily News*, March 3, 1917, 2.

12. Davison interview with Farrar.

13. Letter, March 10, 1917, in Paine, *The First Yale Unit*, vol. 1, 73–76.

14. Noel C. Shirley, *United States Naval Aviation: 1910–1918* (Atglen, PA: Schiffer Military History, 2000), 27.

15. Davison interview with Farrar.

16. Paine, *The First Yale Unit*, vol. 1, 82.

17. Ibid., 83–84.

18. Ibid., 83.
19. *New York Tribune*, March 25, 1917, 2; *Yale Daily News*, March 24, 1917, 1.
20. *Yale Daily News*, March 24, 1917, 2.
21. Reunion Dinner typescript, 36–37.
22. *New York Tribune*, March 25, 1917, 2.
23. Alton Rufus Hyatt, "Junior Year," *History of the Class of Nineteen Hundred and Eighteen Yale College*, vol. 1 (New Haven: Class Secretaries Bureau, 1918), 37.

CHAPTER 8

1. Davison interview with Farrar..
2. John M. Vorys Interview, typescript.
3. "Wings Over America," January 5, 1941, NBC radio broadcast.
4. "Story of F. Trubee Davison Taken at Interview by John Farrar, November 5, 1919."
5. Paine, *The First Yale Unit*, vol. 1, 87.
6. Ibid., 93.
7. "Wings Over America," January 5, 1941, NBC radio broadcast.
8. Allan Ames report on his World War I experience, typescript.
9. Davison interview with Farrar.
10. Lewis Thompson letter to Harry Payne Whitney, April 2, 1917.
11. Lewis Thompson letter to Henry Davison, April 1, 1917.
12. Paine, *The First Yale Unit*, vol. 1, 106–107.
13. "Wings Over America," January 5, 1941, NBC radio broadcast.
14. Byron Farwell,*Over There: The United States in the Great War, 1917–1918* (NY: W. W. Norton & Comkpany, 1999), 35.
15. Lewis Thompson letter to Henry Davison, May 8, 1917.
16. John M. Vorys interview notes.
17. Reunion Dinner typescript, 43.
18. Paine, *The First Yale Unit*, Vol. 1, 110.
19. Rossano, letter to mother and father, May 1917, 13.
20. Ibid., letter to Ishbel MacLeish, April 1917, 11.
21. Archibald MacLeish, ed., *Kenneth: A Collection of Letters* (Chicago: Privately Printed, 1919), 2.
22. Ibid., letter to mother and father, 11–13.
23. *Martha Hillard MacLeish*, 73.
24. *Kenneth*, letter to his family, Feb. 12, 1918, 47.
25. Ibid., letter to mother and father, 14.

CHAPTER 9

1. Hyatt, "Junior Year," *History of the Class of Nineteen Hundred and Eighteen*, 37.
2. Kelley, *Yale: A History*, 353.
3. John G. W. Husted, "Freshman Year History of the Class," *History of the Class of Nineteen Hundred and Twenty* (New Haven, CT: Class Secretaries Bureau, 1920), 10.
4. *New York Times*, October 16, 1917, 10.
5. Quoted in the *New York Times*, November 1, 1917, 12.
6. *New York Times*, May 4, 1919, 25.
7. Lewis Sheldon Welch and Walter Camp, *Yale: Her Campus, Class-rooms, and Athletics* (Boston: L. C. Page and Company, 1899), 99.

8. Quoted in Alexandra Robbins, *Secrets of the Tomb: Skull and Bones, the Ivy League, and the Hidden Paths of Power* (Boston: Little, Brown and Company, 2002), 111.

9. *New York Times*, May 21, 1915, 8.

10. Morris Hadley, *Arthur Twining Hadley* (New Haven, CT: Yale University Press, 1948), 83.

11. *The Yale Courant*, vol. 52, no. 8, 315.

12. On Yale's role in the intelligence agencies, see Robin Winks, *Cloak and Gown: Scholars in the Secret War, 1939–1961* (New Haven, CT: Yale University Press, 1996).

13. Donald Lamm, interview by the author, May 4, 2002.

14. On the tap at West Palm Beach, see Robbins, *Secrets of the Tomb*, 108–109.

15. *New York Times*, April 20, 1917, 13.

16. Rossano, letter to Priscilla Murdock, September 30, 1917, 27.

CHAPTER 10

1. April 9, 1917 telegram.

2. Lewis Thompson letter to Josephus Daniels, June 25, 1917.

3. Reunion Dinner typescript, 44.

4. Reunion Dinner typescript, 45.

5. Letter from Wilson to Davison, May 10, 1917, quoted in *The Red Cross Magazine*, vol. 12, no. 6, July, 1917.

6. *New York Times*, September 9, 1917, 56.

7. Ibid.

8. Reunion Dinner typescript, 49.

9. *Chicago Sun-Times*, April 17, 1966, 7.

10. Reunion Dinner typescript, 54.

11. Burt M. McConnell, *Saturday Evening Post*, September 1, 1917, 20 and 47.

12. *Washington Post*, "Rotogravure Section," October 21, 1917, no page number.

13. David Ingalls letter to his father, January 3, 1918, in Paine, *The First Yale Unit*, vol. 2, 122–123.

14. Interview typescript, no date.

15. Archibald MacLeish, *Kenneth*, letter to his mother, July 10, 1917, 17.

16. Ibid.

17. Reunion Dinner typescript, 51.

18. *New York Tribune*, August 12, 1917, 7.

19. Davison family, *Sketches of Mother at Peacock Point* (Locust Valley, NY: privately printed, 1964), 27; *Flying* magazine, August 1917, vol. 6, no. 7, 580; *New York Times*, July 15, 1917, 12.

20. Reunion Dinner typescript, 137.

CHAPTER 11

1. Account of the day based on Foster Rockwell letter to David McCulloch, July 31, 1917; Lovett memo to Paine, October 31, 1924; and "Record of Proceedings of a Board of Investigation Convened at Huntington, Long Island, New York, by Order of Commanding Officer, U.S. Naval Aviation Detachment to Inquire into the Causes of the Accident of Seaplane No. 2 on July 28, 1917," August 1, 1917.

2. Reunion Dinner typescript, 138.

3. Letter from Caroline Read to Trubee Davison, undated.

CHAPTER 12

1. W. H. Sitz, *A History of U.S. Naval Aviation, Technical Note No. 18, Series of 1930* (Washington: Government Printing Office, 1930), 9.
2. See Reginald Wright Arthur, *Contact!* (Washington: Naval Aviator Register, 1967).
3. Daniel P. Davison, "The First Yale Unit," *Over the Front*, vol. 12, no. 3, fall 1997, 268.
4. The Marine Corps also had a small aerial contingent, including ten pilots.
5. John H. Morrow, Jr., *The Great War in the Air* (Washington: Smithsonian Institution Press, 1993), 216 and 227.
6. Ibid., 268.
7. Budiansky, *Air Power*, 112.
8. Byron Farwell, *Over There*, 197.
9. Morrow, *The Great War in the Air*, 266–68; Budiansky, *Air Power*, 112.
10. Farwell, *Over There*, 190.
11. Ibid., 200.
12. Hiram Bingham, *An Explorer in the Air Service* (New Haven: Yale University Press, 1920), xii.
13. W. Atlee Edwards, "The U.S. Naval Air Force in Action, 1917–18," Reprinted from the *United States Naval Institute Proceedings*, vol. 48, no. 11, November 1922, p. 1866.
14. Archibald D. Turnbull and Clifford L. Lord, *A History of United States Naval Aviation* (New Haven: Yale University Press, 1949), 119.
15. Edwards, *United States Naval Institute Proceedings*, 1873–1874.
16. Ibid., 1882.
17. Farwell, *Over There*, 71.
18. Paine, *The First Yale Unit*, vol. 1, 190–191.
19. Letter to Trubee Davison, August 15, 1917.
20. Letter to Trubee Davison, August 23, 1917.
21. Letter to Trubee Davison, September 8, 1917.
22. Letter to Trubee Davison, September 24, 1917.
23. Letter to Trubee Davison, October 1, 1917.
24. Morrow, *The Great War in the Air*, 367.
25. Letter to Trubee Davison, September 9, 1917.
26. Letter to Trubee Davison, October 1, 1917.
27. Letter to Trubee Davison, October 15, 1917.
28. Letter to Trubee Davison, November 11, 1917.
29. Letter to Trubee Davison, September 24, 1917.
30. Shirley, *United States Naval Aviation*, 314.

CHAPTER 13

1. Rossano, letter to Priscilla Murdock, September 11, 1917, 20.
2. Paine, *The First Yale Unit*, vol. 1, 215.
3. R. Livingston Ireland, *Naval Aviation News*, March 1979, 39.
4. *Chicago Sun-Times*, April 17, 1966, 7.
5. Rossano, letter to Priscilla Murdock, October 1, 1917, 28.
6. Unsourced article, Adele Q. Brown scrapbook.
7. Rossano, letter to Priscilla Murdock, September 1917, 19.
8. Paine, *The First Yale Unit*, vol. 1, 194.

9. Reunion Dinner typescript, 56.

10. Paine, *The First Yale Unit*, vol. 1, 267.

11. Ibid., 266–267.

12. Letter to Trubee Davison, December 25, 1917.

13. Paine, *The First Yale Unit*, vol. 1, 245.

14. Erl Gould, letter to Trubee Davison, July 12, 1918.

15. Reunion Dinner typescript, 56.

CHAPTER 14

1. George L. Upshur, "To F. Trubee Davison—An American Hero."

2. Letter to Trubee Davison, August 22, 1917.

3. Letter from Robert Lovett to Trubee Davison, September 24, 1917.

4. Ibid.

5. See Lee Pearson, "Developing the Flying Bomb," *Naval Aviation News*, undated article.

6. Reunion Dinner typescript, 138.

7. Isaacson and Thomas, *Wise Men: Six Friends and the World They Made* (New York: Simon & Schuster, Touchtone Edition, 1988), 93.

8. Letter to Trubee Davison, June 7, 1918; on the Geronimo Skull & Bones controversy, see Robbins, *Secrets of the Tomb*, 144–146.

CHAPTER 15

1. Paine, *The First Yale Unit*, vol. 2, 2.

2. Letter to Trubee Davison, September 25, 1917.

3. Paine, *The First Yale Unit*, vol. 2, 22.

4. David S. Ingalls, unpublished diary, September 23, 1917, 1.

5. Rossano, letter to Priscilla Murdock, Oct. 4, 1917, 29.

6. McIlwaine, undated narrative addressed to John [Farrar], 2.

7. Letter from Reginald Coombe to Trubee Davison, October 17, 1917.

8. Ingalls diary, undated entry, 4.

9. Letter to Trubee Davison, October 17, 1917.

10. Ingalls diary, undated entry, 5.

11. Paine, *The First Yale Unit*, vol. 2, 10.

12. Ingalls diary, October 19, 1917, 8.

13. Ibid., November 13, 1917, 9–10.

14. Letter to Trubee Davison, November 25, 1917.

15. MacLeish, *Kenneth*, 22.

16. Ibid., 23.

17. Rossano, letter to family, November 10, 1917, 40.

18. MacLeish, *Kenneth*, 25.

19. Rossano, letter to Priscilla Murdock, November 22, 1917, 44.

20. Quoted in Gilbert, *The First World War*, 372.

21. John Keegan, *The First World War* (New York: Alfred A. Knopf, 1999), 354.

22. Rossano, letter to Priscilla Murdock, November 22, 1917, 44.

CHAPTER 16

1. Reunion Dinner typescript, 84.

2. H. Wickliffe Rose, *Brittany Patrol: The Story of the Suicide Fleet* (New York: W. W. Norton & Company, Inc., 1937).

3. Description of incident based on Paine, *The First Yale Unit,* vol. 2, 31–49; Shirley, *United States Naval Aviation,* 238–9; and Terry C. Treadwell, *America's First Air War: The United States Army, Naval and Marine Air Services in the First World War* (Osceola, WI: MBI Publishing, 2000), 88–91.

4. Paine, *The First Yale Unit,* vol. 2, 62–67; Shirley, *United States Naval Aviation,* 245; H. Wickliffe Rose, *Brittany Patrol,* 230–232.

5. "Preface by Franklin D. Roosevelt" in Joseph Husband, *On the Coast of France: The Story of the United States Naval Forces in French Waters* (Chicago: A.C. McClurg & Company, 1919), xvii.

CHAPTER 17

1. Keegan, *The First World War,* 16.

2. Reunion dinner typescript, 67.

3. Reunion dinner typescript, 67–68.

4. Ralph D. Paine, *The Fighting Fleets: Five Months of Active Service with the American Destroyers and Their Allies in the War Zone* (Boston and New York: Houghton Mifflin Company, 1918), 153.

5. T. D. Hallam, *The Spider Web: The Romance of a Flying-Boat Flight in the First World War* (London: Arms and Armour Press, 1979, reprint of 1919 edition), 186.

6. Reunion dinner typescript, 71–73.

7. Ibid., 67–68.

8. Hallam, *The Spider Web,* quotations, 33; description of Spider Web patrol, 32–34.

9. Keegan, *The First World War,* 354.

10. Hallam, *The Spider Web,* 39–40.

11. Hallam, *The Spider Web,* 42–47.

12. Letter to Trubee Davison, February 4, 1918.

13. Rossano, letter to Priscilla Murdock, December 1, 1917, 51.

14. Letter to Trubee Davison, February 4, 1918.

15. Reunion Dinner typescript, 75.

16. George Henry Nettleton, ed., *Yale in the World War,* vol. 1 (New Haven: Yale University Press, 1925), 226.

17. Reunion Dinner typescript, 76.

18. See Chris Hobson, *Airmen Who Died in the Great War 1914–1918: The Roll of Honour of the British and Commonwealth Air Services of the First World War* (London: J. B. Hayward & Son, UK, 1995).

19. Reunion Dinner typescript, 75–78.

20. Ibid., 78.

21. Hallam, *The Spider Web,* 196–197.

22. Nettleton, *Yale in the World War,* 225.

23. Letter to Trubee Davison, March 20, 1918.

CHAPTER 18

1. Rossano, letter to Murdock, March 1, 1918, 108–109.

2. MacLeish, *Kenneth,* letter to his mother, Feb. 24, 1918, 53.

3. Rossano, letter to Murdock, March 1, 1918, 108–109.

4. Ibid., letter to Murdock, February 24, 1918, 107.

5. Ibid., letter to Murdock, February 23, 1918, 106.
6. Ibid., letter to Henry, November 23, 1917, 47.
7. MacLeish, *Kenneth*, letter to his family, November 25, 1917, 31–32.
8. Rossano, letter to Murdock, November 29, 1917, 50.
9. Letter to David Ingalls, March 22, 1918.
10. Reunion Dinner typescript, 109–113.
11. Ingalls diary, March 21, 1918, 25.
12. Rossano, letter to Murdock, December 29, 1917, 72.
13. Ibid., letter to Murdock, December 13, 1917, 64.
14. Ibid., letter to Murdock, December 4, 1917, 54.
15. MacLeish, *Kenneth*, letter to Ishbel MacLeish, December 9, 1917, 37–38.
16. Ingalls diary, December 19, 1917, 13.
17. Rossano, letter to Bruce MacLeish, Feb. 16, 1918, 99.
18. Lee Kennett, *The First Air War: 1914–1918* (New York: The Free Press, 1991), 129; Denis Winter, *The First of the Few*, 36.
19. Quoted in Nigel Steel and Peter Hart, *Tumult in the Clouds: The British Experience of the War in the Air 1914–1918* (London: Hodder and Stoughton, 1997), 89–90.
20. Winter, *The First of the Few*, 38.
21. Budiansky, *Air Power*, 78.
22. Ingalls diary, January 3, 1918, 15.
23. Ibid., December 21, 1917, 14.
24. Paine, *The First Yale Unit*, letter to his father, January 3, 1918, vol. 2, 122–123.
25. Rossano, letter to Murdock, January 3, 1918, 78; "50 Years After," *CBS News*, video 1966.
26. Ingalls diary, February 1, 20 (date apparently misidentified).
27. Paine, *The First Yale Unit*, letter to his father, January 3, 1918, vol. 2, 123.
28. Rossano, letter to Murdock, December 25, 1917, 70.
29. Ibid., letter to Murdock, January 19, 1918, 84.
30. Ibid., letter to Murdock, December 29, 1917, 73.
31. Ibid., 67.
32. Ibid., letter to Murdock, February 1, 1918, 90–91.
33. Artemus Gates letter to Trubee Davison, April 19, 1918.
34. Ingalls diary, January 10, 1918, 16.
35. Rossano, letter to Murdock, January, 1, 1918, 75.
36. Ibid.
37. Ibid., letter to Priscilla Murdock, January 3, 1918, 76.
38. On the Sopwith Camel, see Thomas R. Funderburk, *The Fighters: The Men and Machines of the First Air War* (New York: Gross & Dunlap, 1965), 121.
39. Rossano, letter to Murdock, January 3, 1918, 76–78.
40. Ingalls diary, January 10, 1918, 15.
41. Paine, *The First Yale Unit*, letter to his father, January 17, 1918, vol. 2, 125.
42. Ingalls diary, January 21, 1918, 16.
43. Ibid., Jan. 22, 1918, 17.
44. Rossano, letter to Ishbel MacLeish, December 9, 1917, 58.
45. Ingalls diary, February 5, 1918, 21.
46. MacLeish, *Kenneth*, letter to his family, February 12, 1918, 47.
47. Ingalls diary, February 5, 1918, 22.
48. MacLeish, *Kenneth*, letter to his mother, February 24, 1918, 53.
49. Rossano, letter to Murdock, February 20, 1918, 101.

50. Letter to Murdock, March 12, 1918, 113.
51. Letter to Adele Brown, February 2, 1918.
52. Letter to Adele Brown, February 24, 1918.
53. Letter to Adele Brown, February 2, 1918.
54. Rossano, letter to Murdock, February 22, 1918, 103.
55. Quoted in William MacLeish, *Uphill with Archie*, 38–39.
56. Rossano, letters to Murdock, March 20 and March 22, 1918, 115 and 121.
57. Letter to unidentified friend Henry, March 19, 1918, 115.

CHAPTER 19

1. Keegan, *The First World War*, 393–394.
2. Ibid., 403.
3. Ingalls diary, March 21, 1918, 25.
4. Letter to Adele Brown, March 7, 1918.
5. Letter to Adele Brown, February 24, 1918.
6. Letter to F. T. Davison, April 15, 1918.
7. Reprinted in *The Yale Courant*, December 1917, vol. 54, no. 2, 53.
8. Rossano, letter to Murdock, March 22, 1918, 122.
9. Ingalls diary, March 28, 1918, 27.
10. Letter to Davison, March 24, 1918.
11. Rossano, letter to Murdock, March 22, 1918, 122.
12. Letter to Davison, March 3, 1918.
13. Letter to Mrs. Kate Davison, March 10, 1918.
14. Ibid.
15. Letter to F. T. Davison, May 17, 1918.
16. Quoted in Arthur, *Contact!*, 48.
17. Letter to Davison, December 8, 1917.
18. Diary entries quoted in Arthur, *Contact!*, 48.
19. Letter to Davison, March 3, 1918; Richard T. Whistler, "The Making of a Dunkirk Aviator: The Experiences of Ensign James Henry O'Brien, USNRF (Part II)," *Over the Front*, vol. 17, no. 1, Spring 2002, 11.
20. Letter to Mrs. William Read, his mother, February 25, 1918.
21. Funeral description from article in an unidentified American newspaper in Paris.
22. Letter to Davison, March 20, 1918.
23. Letter to Davison, March 13, 1918.
24. Letter to Davison, March 3, 1918.
25. Letter to Davison, January 27, 1918.
26. Letter to Davison, December 9, 1917.
27. On the problems with the Dunkirk NAS, see Gates's Letter to Commander Naval Bombing Squadrons, August 5, 1918, quoted in Whistler, "The Making of a Dunkirk Aviator," *Over the Front*, 5.
28. Letter to Davison, Dec. 2, 1917.
29. Paine, *The First Yale Unit*, Letter to his father, March 22, 1918, vol. 2, 151.
30. Ingalls diary, March 22, 1918, 26.
31. Rossano, letter to Murdock, March 22, 1918, 122.
32. Quoted in Gilbert, *The First World War*, 414.
33. Rossano, letter to Murdock, April 16, 1918, 142.
34. Ingalls diary, March 28, 1918, 27.

35. Rossano, letter to Murdock, March 28, 1918.

36. Ibid., letter to Murdock, April 2, 1918, 132.

37. Ibid., letter to Bruce, Elizabeth, Jean, and Hugh MacLeish, April 5, 1918, 134.

38. Ingalls diary, September 26, 1918, 72.

39. Rossano, letter to his family, April 7, 1918, 134.

40. Ingalls diary, September 26, 1918, 72.

41. Paine, *The First Yale Unit*, letter to Mary Hillard, April 11, 1918, vol. 2, 159.

42. Ibid., 160.

43. Rossano, 136.

44. Reunion Dinner transcript, 138.

45. Rossano, letter to Murdock, April 9, 1918, 136.

46. Ibid., letter to Murdock, April 18, 1918, 144.

47. Ibid., letter to Bruce, Elizabeth, Jean, and Hugh MacLeish, April 11, 1918, 137–138; letter to Davison, April 11, 1918.

48. Ingalls diary, April 11, 1918, 30.

49. Rossano, letter to Murdock, April 13, 1918, 140.

50. Gilbert, *The First World War*, 417–418.

51. Ingalls diary, April 26, 1918, 32.

52. Letter to Davison, April 30, 1918.

53. Ingalls diary, May 19, 1918, 37.

54. Rossano, letter to Murdock, May 21, 1918, 161.

55. Whistler, "The Making of a Dunkirk Aviator," 16–17.

56. See Reinhard Scheer, *Germany's High Sea Fleet in the World War*, Chapter 14a, in translation online at http://www.richthofen.com/scheer/scheer14a.htm.

57. Gilbert, *The First World War*, 451.

58. Rossano, letter to Murdock, May 21, 1918, 161.

59. Letter to Davison, May 24, 1918.

60. Ibid.

61. Whistler, 22.

62. Ingalls diary, August 22, 1918, 55–56.

63. Shirley, *United States Naval Aviation 1910–1918*, 289.

64. Samuel G. Blythe, "The Flying Sailors," *The Saturday Evening Post*, December 21, 1918, 12.

65. Ingalls diary, May 14, 1918, 35–36.

66. Artemus Gates letter to Davison, April 19, 1918.

67. Letter to Davison, April 11, 1918.

68. Rossano, letter to Murdock, May 21, 1918, 161.

69. Letter to Davison, May 24, 1918.

70. Letter to Ingalls, June 7, 1918.

71. Rossano, letter to Murdock, May 21, 1918, 161.

CHAPTER 20

1. Letter to Adele Brown, February 24, 1918.

2. Paine, *The First Yale Unit*, vol. 2, 176.

3. Letter to Brown, March 19, 1918.

4. Paine, *The First Yale Unit*, vol. 2, 176.

5. Letter to Brown, March 7, 1918.

6. Reunion Dinner typescript, 140.

7. On British bombing strategy along the Belgian coast, see Neville Jones, *The Origins of Strategic Bombing: A Study of the Development of British Air Strategic Thought and Practice up to 1918* (London: William Kimber, 1973), 126–129.

8. Letter to Brown, March 19, 1918.

9. Paine, *The First Yale Unit*, vol. 2, 172–174.

10. Letter to Brown, March 19, 1918.

11. Letter to Brown, April 14, 1918; for a vivid first-person account of an RNAS bombing squadron pilot's experiences at Couderkerque, elsewhere in the Dunkirk region, and over the Western Front, see C. P. O. Bartlett, *In the Teeth of the Wind: The Story of a Naval Pilot on the Western Front, 1916–1918* (Annapolis: Naval Institute Press, 1994).

12. Letter to Brown, March 19, 1918.

13. Letter to Brown, March 26, 1918.

14. Paine, *The First Yale Unit*, vol. 2, 176.

15. Ibid., 177.

16. Ibid., 179.

17. Letter to Brown, March 26, 1918.

18. Letter to Brown, April 14, 1918.

19. Letter to Brown, April 14, 1918.

20. Rossano, letter to Murdock, April 1, 1918, 130.

21. Paine, *The First Yale Unit*, vol. 2, 181–183.

22. Ibid., 184.

23. Ibid., 174.

24. Ibid., 185–186.

25. Trevor Henshaw, *The Sky Their Battlefield: Air Fighting and the Complete List of Allied Air Casualties from Enemy Action in the First War. British Commonwealth, and United States Air Services, 1914 To 1918* (London: Grub Street, 1995), 309.

26. Letter to Brown, April 19, 1918.

CHAPTER 21

1. Lovett to F. T. Davison, June 28, 1918.

2. Edwards, "The U.S. Naval Air Force in Action 1917–18," (reprinted from the *United States Naval Institute Proceedings*), 1876.

3. Ibid., 1875.

4. Ibid., 1876.

5. Turnbull and Lord, *History of United States Naval Aviation*, 137–138.

6. Farwell, *Over There*, 197.

7. Quoted in *Time* magazine, September 24, 1951, vol. 58, no. 13.

8. "The Northern Bombing Group," undated, unidentified article drawing on the report of the Northern Bombing Group by Captain David C. Hanrahan, December 3, 1918.

9. Reunion Dinner typescript, 141.

10. Ibid.

11. Letter to Brown, June 15, 1918.

12. Paine, *The First Yale Unit*, vol. 2, 189.

13. Rossano, letter to Murdock, July 28, 1918, 193.

14. Ibid.

15. Letter to Brown, June 15, 1918.

16. Rossano, letter to Murdock, July 28, 1918, 193.

17. Robert Lovett letter to Archibald MacLeish, October 26, 1918.
18. Rossano, letter to Murdock, June 2 and 7, 1918, 168 and 171.
19. Ibid., 167–168, 171.
20. Isaacson and Thomas, *The Wise Men*, 84.
21. Letter to Brown, June 15, 1918.

CHAPTER 22

1. Gilbert, *The First World War*, 427.
2. Farwell, *Over There*, 168.
3. Rossano, letter to Murdock, May 30, 1918, 165.
4. Ibid., letter to Murdock, June 9, 1918, 172; Roosevelt would soon join the 95th "Kicking Mule" Squadron, which was sister unit to Eddie Rickenbacker's famed 94th "Hat in the Ring" Squadron.
5. Quoted in Farwell, 192.
6. Quoted in Warren Zimmermann, *First Great Triumph* (New York: Farrar Strauss & Giroux, 2002), 484–485.
7. Rossano, letter to his family, June 2, 1918, 170.
8. Irving Sheeley letter to Andrew MacLeish, January 5, 1919.
9. Ingalls diary, July 1, 1918, 40.
10. Rossano, letter to Murdock, June 9, 1918, 172.
11. Ingalls diary, June 5, 1918, 39.
12. Ibid., June 9, 1918, 39–40.
13. Rossano, letter to Murdock, June 2, 1918, 168.
14. Ibid., letter to Murdock, June 7, 1918, 171.
15. Ibid., letter to Murdock, June 18, 1918, 176.
16. Quoted in Rossano, 176.
17. Ibid., letter to Murdock, June 19, 1918, 177.
18. Lovett to Brown, July 12, 1918.
19. Rossano, letter to Murdock, July 11, 1918, 184.
20. Ibid., letter to Murdock, July 24, 1918, 191.
21. Ibid., letter to Murdock, August 23, 1918, 202.
22. Letter to Davison, July 23, 1918.
23. John R. Cox, "U.S. Naval Aviation in the War," in *Flying Officers of the USN* (At-glen, PA: Schiffer Military History, 1997, reprint of 1919), 19.
24. Rossano, letter to Murdock, July 8, 1918, 182.
25. Ibid., letter to Murdock, July 10, 1918, 184.
26. "Memo from Commanding Officer NAS Dunkirk, to Commander, Northern Bombing Squadrons, Subject: Policy of U.S. Naval Air Station, Dunkirk," August 5, 1918, quoted in Whistler, "The Making of a Dunkirk Aviator," *Over the Front*, 9.
27. Gates letter to Davison, May 24, 1918.
28. Rossano, letter to Murdock, July 7, 1918, 181.
29. Ibid., letter to Murdock, July 16, 1918, 186.
30. Richard P. Hallion, *Rise of the Fighter Aircraft, 1914–1918* (Baltimore: The Nautical & Aviation Publishing Company of America, 1984), 156.
31. Paine, *The First Yale Unit*, letter to "Old Henry," July 10, 1918, vol. 2, 353.
32. Rossano, letter to Murdock, July 5, 1918, 179.
33. MacLeish, *Kenneth*, letter to his family, July 18, 1918, 96.
34. Rossano, letter to Murdock, July 16, 1918, 187–188.
35. Ibid., letter to Murdock, July 19, 1918, 189.

36. Ibid., David Hanrahan letter to Bruce MacLeish, January 31, 1919, 233.
37. Ibid., letter to Murdock, July 28, 1918, 194.
38. Ibid., letter to Murdock, September 13, 1918, 213.
39. Ibid., letter to Murdock, Aug. 17, 1918, 200.
40. Ibid., letter to his father, Aug. 28, 1918, 208.

CHAPTER 23

1. Letter to Brown, July 12, 1918.
2. Letter to Brown, August 29, 1918.
3. Paine, *The First Yale Unit*, vol. 2, 220.
4. Ibid., 221.
5. Ibid., 224.
6. Ibid., 223.
7. Ibid., 231.
8. Ibid., 234.
9. Ibid., 231.
10. Ibid., 224.
11. Ibid., 234.
12. Ibid., 235.
13. Ibid.
14. Ibid., 236.
15. Ibid., 239.
16. Turnbull and Lord, *History of United States Naval Aviation*, 139.
17. Lawrence D. Sheely, ed., *Sailor of the Air: The 1917–1919 Letters and Diary of USN CMM/A Irving Edward Sheely* (Tuscaloosa: The University of Alabama Press, 1993), 155.
18. "The Northern Bombing Group," *Naval Aviation News*, October 1968, 84–87.
19. Paine, *The First Yale Unit*, vol. 2, 213.
20. Ibid., 225.
21. Reunion Dinner typescript, 142.
22. Letter to Brown, July 12, 1918.
23. Letter to Brown, August 29, 1918.
24. Letter to Brown, October 14, 1918.
25. Paine, *The First Yale Unit*, "Report on Future Operations of the Northern Bombing Group," vol. 2, 325–327.
26. Farwell, *Over There*, 213–214.
27. Quoted in Gilbert, *The First World War*, 452.
28. Rossano, letter to Murdock, September 15, 1918, 215.
29. Ibid., letter to Murdock, August 24, 1918, 203–204.
30. Ibid., letter to Murdock, September 27, 1918, 218.

CHAPTER 24

1. Cecil Lewis, *Sagittarius Rising* (Harrisburg, PA: The Stackpole Company, 1963), 169–170.
2. Ingalls diary, August 9, 1918, 43.
3. Ibid., August 10, 1918, 43–44.
4. Frank J. Olynyk, "David Ingalls, United States Naval Reserve Flying Corps," *Cross & Cockade Journal*, no volume or date, 102.

5. Ingalls diary, August 13, 1918, 44–48.
6. Ibid., dated August 15, 1918, but likely written later, 53.
7. Ibid., August 14, 1918, 48–49, and August 21, 1918, 54.
8. Reunion Dinner typescript, 127.
9. Ingalls diary, September 15, 1918, 63–64.
10. Ibid., September 18, 1918, 65–67; D. S. Ingalls letter to "Dad," September 18, 1918.
11. Letter to Davison, Sept. 9, 1918.
12. Ingalls diary, September 20, 1918, 67–69.
13. Ibid., September 29, 1918, 77.
14. Ibid., September 24, 1918, 69–72; Reunion Dinner typescript, 132.
15. Ibid., September 28, 1918, 73–77.
16. Ibid., October 2, 1918, 81.
17. Ibid., October 1, 1918, 78.

CHAPTER 25

1. Ingalls diary, October 10, 1918, 83.
2. Frank J. Olynyk, "David Ingalls, United States Naval Reserve Flying Corps," *Cross and Cockade*, no volume or date, 97.
3. Ingalls diary, October 2, 1918, 82.
4. Letter to Brown, September 14, 1918.
5. Lovett letter to Davison, October 11, 1918.
6. Kenneth MacLeish letter to Davison, October 9, 1918.
7. Quoted in Rossano, 221.
8. Reunion Dinner typescript, 96.
9. Rossano, letter to Murdock, October 8, 1918, 223.
10. Ingalls diary, October 4, 1918, 82.
11. Rossano, letter to Ishbel MacLeish, October 8, 1918, 222.
12. Ibid., letter to Murdock, October 8, 1918, 223.
13. Lovett to Davison, October 11, 1918.
14. Ibid.
15. *New York Times*, October 24, 1918, 10.
16. *Saturday Evening Post*, December 21, 1918, 12.
17. Rossano, letter to "Aunt" Emma Guthrie, October 10, 1918, 226.
18. Letter to Davison, October 9, 1918.
19. Ibid., Gates to Davison, September 9, 1918.
20. Rossano, letter to Murdock, September 18, 1918, 216.
21. Paine, *The First Yale Unit*, Lovett to Archibald MacLeish, October 26, 1919, vol. 2, 358–359.
22. Rossano, letter to Murdock, October 10, 1918, 225.
23. Ibid., letter to Murdock, October 11, 1918, 226.
24. Paine, *The First Yale Unit*, vol. 2, 360.
25. Ingalls diary, October 13, 1918, 84.
26. Reunion Dinner typescript, 119.
27. Francis (Frank) R. Lynch, "Account of Military Service," ca. 1920.
28. Description based on Foster Rockwell's letter to Davison, February 13, 1919, and Robert E. Rackwood's letter to Davison, May 5, 1919.
29. Quoted in Rossano, 227.

30. Rossano, Lovett to Chub (Murdock), October 29, 1918, 228–229.
31. Ibid., Rockwell cable to Davison, October 23, 1918, 227.

CHAPTER 26

1. Typescript, Artemus Gates's account on his imprisonment, no date or other identification.
2. Paine, *The First Yale Unit*, "Foreword by Rear Admiral Wm. S. Sims, United States Navy (Retired)," vol. 1, vi.
3. Henry Davison cable to Trubee Davison, November 1, 1918.
4. Lovett to Brown, October 14, 1918.
5. Gilbert, *The First World War*, 488–502.
6. Letter to Brown, September 14, 1918.
7. Gates to Davison, November 15, 1918.

CHAPTER 27

1. David Ingalls to Albert Ingalls ("Dad"), November 12, 1918.
2. MacLeish's body's condition is based on Lieutenant John C. Menzies letter to Captain David Hanrahan, February 2, 1919, in Rossano, 230–231; Rockwell letter to Davison, February 13, 1919; Rackwood letter to Davison, May 5, 1919; and interview with William MacLeish, December 3, 2005.
3. Rossano, Gates to Murdock, January 30, 1919, 234.

CHAPTER 28

1. Interview with Daniel Davison, November 8, 2004.
2. George Wilson Pierson, *Yale College: An Educational History* (New Haven: Yale University Press, 1952), 539 and 535.
3. Ibid., 483–484.
4. Ibid., 493.
5. Ibid., 532.
6. Kelley, *Yale: A History*, 370.
7. *New York Times*, May 8, 1922, 1.
8. Interview with Daniel Davison.
9. William Snowden Sims, *The Victory at Sea* (Garden City, NY: Doubleday, Page & Company, 1920), 327–329.
10. Quoted in Nettleton, *Yale in the World War*, 447.
11. W. H. Sitz, *A History of U.S. Naval Aviation* (Washington: United States Government Printing Office, 1930), 36–38. The restored NC–4 can now be seen at the National Museum of Naval Aviation in Pensacola, Florida.
12. *Time* magazine, vol. 4, no. 8, August 24, 1925.
13. *New York Times*, July 17, 1926, 13.
14. "To K. MacL. (Brought down above Schoore, Belgium, October 14, 1918)," in Paine, *The First Yale Unit*, vol. 2, 372–373.
15. R. H. Winnick, ed., *Letters of Archibald MacLeish 1907–1982* (Boston: Houghton Mifflin Company, 1983), Archibald MacLeish letter to Martha Hillard MacLeish (mother), October 12, 1920, 75–76.
16. Ibid., Archibald MacLeish letter to Ishbel MacLeish (sister), May 31, 1924, 137.

17. Ibid., 135.

18. See "Air Armada Poised to Repulse 'Enemy' off New England," *New York Times*, May 25, 1931, 1.

19. *New York Times*, March 17, 1929.

20. *New York Times*, September 4, 1932, 13.

21. On Vorys's tenure in Congress, see Jeffrey C. Livingston, *Swallowed by Globalism: John M. Vorys and American Foreign Policy* (Lanham, MD: University Press of America, 2001).

22. For the history of their involvement in the bank, see John A. Kouwenhoven, *Partners in Banking: an Historical Portrait of a Great Private Bank, Brown Brothers Harriman & Co., 1818–1968* (Garden City, NY: Doubleday, 1968).

23. Isaacson and Thomas, *The Wise Men*, 184.

24. Ibid.

25. "Wings Over America, The Yale Unit," NBC radio broadcast, January 5, 12, and 19, 1941.

26. Letter to the author, September 17, 2005.

27. Fletcher Knebel, "Boy Flyers of 1917–18 Now Busy Again, Helping Uncle Sam Fight Another World War," *Cleveland Plain Dealer*, May 31, 1942, 1.

28. Quoted in Isaacson and Thomas, *The Wise Men*, 206.

29. Knebel, "Boy Flyers," 1.

30. *The New Yorker*, "The Thirteenth Labor of Hercules," November 6, 1943, 32.

31. On Lovett's wartime service, see Fanton, *Robert A. Lovett*, and Isaacson and Thomas, *The Wise Men*, 203–209.

32. Quoted in Lewis, *History of the Class of 1918 Yale College Forty Years On*, 84.

33. On the Berlin airlift, see Isaacson and Thomas, *The Wise Men*, 458–461.

34. On Lovett's service in the Department of Defense, see Isaacson and Thomas, *The Wise Men*, 525–526, 555–556.

35. Edward B. Lockett, "'There Is No Other Way But Strength,'" *New York Times Sunday Magazine*, 179.

36. On Lovett's relationship to John F. Kennedy, see David Halberstam, *The Best and the Brightest* (New York: Random House, 1972), Chapter 1; and Isaacson and Thomas, *The Wise Men*, 593–594.

37. Isaacson and Thomas, *The Wise Men*, 624–625.

38. Interview with David Brown, Jr., September 5, 2005.

39. The television program, "50 Years After," produced by CBS News in 1966 depicts the day's events.

EPILOGUE

1. Yale University Office of Institutional Research, "Post-Graduation Activities, Classes of 1960 to 2004."

Acknowledgments

Books happen through will, circumstance, talent, and chance. All converged when Talia Rosenblatt Cohen saw an article I had written about the Millionaires' Unit and inquired whether I was interested in doing a book on the subject. For many years, yes! She became my agent and, together with her partner Laura Dail of Laura Dail Literary Agency, shepherded the project forward. Peter Osnos and Clive Priddle at PublicAffairs recognized the poignancy and power of this story and its significance for today. Clive was simply a superb editor, responsive, responsible, demanding, caring. Lori Hobkirk's careful copyediting prevented numerous errors from reaching print. Along with Susan Weinberg and Whitney Peeling, they helped make this book take flight. (No more aviation metaphors after this, except one.)

Before then, I was helped by many people. I am thankful that more than a decade ago Carter Wiseman assigned me an article for the *Yale Alumni Magazine* about Yale aviation that brought me an awareness of the original Yale Aero Club. Conversations with John Ryden, Donald Lamm, Nathaniel Philbrick, Larry Eisner, Robert Harris, and Zach Morowitz proved invaluable in clarifying my thoughts on many subjects relevant to the book. Zach read and made incisive comments on large portions of the manuscript. The resulting book is much improved for his help. I trusted Jeff Fuller, terrific pilot, outside shooter, and jazz musician, with my life when he took me flying several times and clarified many mysteries of flight in midair. He also read relevant sections and helped me avoid some errors about aviation. Any errors that did get through in any aspect of this book are, of course, my fault.

As my exploration of the individuals in the group deepened, their descendents proved wonderfully cooperative. They are to a person deeply proud and highly private, yet they opened up to me, giving me access to personal papers, their homes, and their memories. Nobody has been more helpful in writing this book than Daniel Davison. A memorable visit to Peacock Point and talks with him and his son, Harry, brought F. Trubee Davison, his friends, and their world to life. Several members of the Lovett family have been gracious and helpful. In particular Adele Q. Brown gave me access to Robert A. Lovett's loving and vivid personal correspondence with his future wife, Adele, and their extraordinary scrapbooks from the 1916–1919 period. Her brother, David Brown, Jr., also shared insight and knowledge. Mrs. Robert S. (Dorothy) Lovett, Jr., required of me a historical precision to match her own sharp memories of her father-in-law. Barbara Brown and family gave me privileged access to David S. Ingalls's archives that proved indispensable. Polly Hitchcock was the reliably helpful hand who organized those archives and made access to them a pleasure.

Geoffrey Rossano's superbly researched edition of the letters of Kenneth MacLeish to Priscilla Murdock gave me a significant leg up in writing my book. I thank the Naval Institute Press for publishing such a valuable work. William H. MacLeish, a wonderful writer himself, guided me to useful materials about his family. President George H. W. Bush shared his memories of his father's friends and humored me by allowing me to pester him more than once about his and their past.

David Levesque and Pamela Susi at the Saint Paul School provided information about the schoolboy years of David S. Ingalls. The staff of the Emil Buehler Naval Aviation Library sought out helpful documents in their holdings. The staff of the Old Rhinebeck Aerodrome, the place where the early years of flight continue to live, opened their grounds and hangars to me. I spent three invaluable hours there smelling the castor oil and hearing the roar of the rotary engines and grilling Chad Willey about the experience of early flying, which was so different from today. I also flew in a biplane to feel that extraordinary sensation of the open cockpit.

I came to know the pre-Great War Yale University through many sources, but the countless hours I spent exploring the extraordinary holdings of the Yale Library and especially its Manuscripts and Archives Department opened up that world to me. The entire library staff made me feel welcome and helped me in innumerable ways. In particular, my guides included the superbly knowledgeable archivists William Massa and Judith Schiff. Richard Warren, curator of historical sound recordings at the Yale Library, played for me the rare recordings of the "Wings Over America" NBC Radio broadcasts from 1941. Beverly Waters in the Yale Office of Institutional Research provided me with useful statistical information.

The staff of the Yale Alumni Magazine, in particular Kathrin Day Lassila, Bruce Fellman, Mark Branch, and Barbara Durland, gave me generous access to their own valuable archives. In addition, the magazine published the article that led to the book. Michael Fitzsousa, Cheryl Violante, Claire Bessinger, and the staff of Yale Medicine Magazine provided me with administrative assistance and a home away from home. Geoffrey Zonder opened the Yale Athletics Department archives to me. Jamie Snider took me on a memorable tour of Gales Ferry and helped bring the world of the Harvard-Yale Boat Race to life. The reference staff at the Mystic Seaport's G. W. Blunt White Library helped me track down information about the yachts at the Harvard-Yale Boat Race in 1916.

Numerous times I called upon the authoritative knowledge and libraries of Noel Shirley and Colin Owers, leading experts on Great War naval aviation. Both advised me on important points about the technology and history of the war, and Noel read an early version of the entire manuscript and helped prevent some significant errors. I am deeply in his debt. Other members of the League of World War I Aviation Historians also generously shared their rich knowledge of the early years of flight.

My father, Bernard, researched some questions for me, and my brother, Paul, took helpful photographs. My entire family has been there when I needed them and by their love I have grown.

Now, to a last and final flight metaphor: When a pilot takes off, he wants to know the air and weather conditions he may expect to encounter, his course, the state of his equipment, and all he needs to ensure a safe journey. My wife, Jodi P. Cohen, my daughter, Rebecca, and my son, Charles, were my runway, the check on my emotional weather, the dependable equipment, and everything I needed to get me through the long journey, even in the most unpredictable moments of the flight. I knew everyday that I would land safe and loved. Nobody can ask for more.

Marc Wortman, New Haven, January 2006

Index

PublicAffairs is a publishing house founded in 1997. It is a tribute to the standards, values, and flair of three persons who have served as mentors to countless reporters, writers, editors, and book people of all kinds, including me.

I.F. STONE, proprietor of *I. F. Stone's Weekly*, combined a commitment to the First Amendment with entrepreneurial zeal and reporting skill and became one of the great independent journalists in American history. At the age of eighty, Izzy published *The Trial of Socrates*, which was a national bestseller. He wrote the book after he taught himself ancient Greek.

BENJAMIN C. BRADLEE was for nearly thirty years the charismatic editorial leader of *The Washington Post*. It was Ben who gave the *Post* the range and courage to pursue such historic issues as Watergate. He supported his reporters with a tenacity that made them fearless and it is no accident that so many became authors of influential, best-selling books.

ROBERT L. BERNSTEIN, the chief executive of Random House for more than a quarter century, guided one of the nation's premier publishing houses. Bob was personally responsible for many books of political dissent and argument that challenged tyranny around the globe. He is also the founder and longtime chair of Human Rights Watch, one of the most respected human rights organizations in the world.

For fifty years, the banner of Public Affairs Press was carried by its owner Morris B. Schnapper, who published Gandhi, Nasser, Toynbee, Truman, and about 1,500 other authors. In 1983, Schnapper was described by *The Washington Post* as "a redoubtable gadfly." His legacy will endure in the books to come.

Peter Osnos, *Founder and Editor-at-Large*